Adversarial Legalism

Adversarial Legalism

The American Way of Law

Robert A. Kagan

Harvard University Press

Cambridge, Massachusetts, and London, England

First Harvard University Press paperback edition, 2003

Second printing, 2003

Library of Congress Cataloging-in-Publication Data

Kagan, Robert A.
    Adversarial legalism : the American way of law / Robert A. Kagan.
        p. cm.
    Includes bibliographical references and index.
    ISBN 0-674-00621-6 (cloth)
    ISBN 0-674-01241-0 (paper)
        1. Adversary system (Law)—United States.   2. Justice, Administration of—
United States.   3. Law and politics.   I. Title.
    KF384 .K34 2001
    347.73—dc21   2001024227

Contents

Preface

On the evening of December 12, 2000, Americans by the millions—and for all I know, millions of people around the world—watched their television sets for the announcement of a decision by the Supreme Court of the United States. After weeks of postelection litigation concerning the proper counting of ballots in the state of Florida, the Court's ruling could determine whether the Democratic Party's candidate for president, Vice President Albert Gore, or the Republican Party's candidate, Texas Governor George W. Bush, would be declared the victor. A few days earlier, on December 8, a decision by the Supreme Court of Florida left Bush ahead, or so it appeared, by fewer than 200 votes (out of some 4.8 million in the state). The Florida court, however, had ordered a manual review of thousands of ballots to determine whether votes for president had not been recorded by Florida's voting machines. The Bush campaign organization, fearing that the recount would propel Gore into the presidency, had appealed to the U.S. Supreme Court. On December 9, a bitterly divided Supreme Court accepted the case and ordered a temporary stop to the manual recount, dashing spirits in the Gore camp. On December 11, the Court heard oral arguments. But there was no consensus among legal experts about how the Court, which traditionally had deferred to state courts in the interpretation of state electoral law, would actually decide.

Finally, late in the evening of December 12, the Court's ruling was distributed to waiting journalists, who struggled to decode a cryptic per curiam opinion, four dissenting opinions, and one concurrence. The Court, it was clear, had vacated the Florida Supreme Court's ruling by a seven-to-two margin, employing an unprecedented "equal protection clause" argument. But it also held that the recount could proceed if the Florida courts would issue uniform statewide standards for counting disputed ballots. Then it gradually dawned on the television reporters, and hence on the waiting viewers, that by a five-to-four vote, the Supreme Court had interpreted Florida law to impose an inalterable December 12 deadline for the certification of Florida's electoral votes. That deadline made the belatedly permitted recount impossible. The next day, Gore conceded. By a one-vote majority, the five most politically conservative justices had enabled Bush to gain the presidency.

To many foreign observers, it may have seemed simultaneously remarkable and typical that the political contest for the American presidency had triggered an explosion of litigation—fourteen separate lawsuits, numerous appeals, and two U.S. Supreme Court reviews, the second of which, by blocking the counting of the disputed ballots, had determined the winner. As an earlier foreign observer, Alexis de Tocqueville (1835: 290), had written, "Scarcely any political question arises in the United States that is not resolved, sooner or later, into a judicial question." Yet even de Tocqueville would have been astonished by the nature of the postelection litigation in 2000—so sprawling, so resistant to legal finality, so legally unpredictable, so combative in its intensity. A complex set of legal rules and institutions designed to contain the passions and opportunism of politics became a partisan battleground itself.

In the weeks following the November 7 election, with the Florida result still in doubt, both political parties unleashed the dogs of law. Squadrons of Democratic and Republican lawyers were deployed, speed-reading the details of Florida's election laws, performing prodigies of brief-writing, meeting legal losses in one forum with an appeal or a new lawsuit in another. As the statutory date for the Florida's selection of electors approached, Democratic lawyers frantically prodded election officials and judges to count disputed votes or ballots. Republican lawyers argued that there was no legal justification or no time to keep counting, successfully delaying manual counts several times. As often occurs in American litigation, the outcome was shaped more by the delays and opportunity costs of extended adversarial legal processes than by authoritative legal judgments about the just result.

To observers from other constitutional democracies, where judges generally are selected through professional, less overtly political mechanisms, it must also have been remarkable that the American judges seemed to be such creatures of politics. As the hydra-headed litigation moved from court to court, journalists pointed out the political party background and connections of particular judges, as if those, and not the law, were likely to shape the court's decision. Indeed, it turned out that the Florida Supreme Court, composed of appointees of a Democratic governor, made two crucial and controversial decisions that favored Gore. The U.S. Supreme Court, made up predominantly of judges appointed by Republican presidents, vacated those decisions, employing legal arguments that surprised (or dismayed) most constitutional scholars. Yet it was not certain ex ante that the judges' political backgrounds would entirely predict their decisions. Generally, American judges are motivated not only by their political predispositions but also by the desire to maintain a reputation for legal craftsmanship and to protect the perceived legitimacy of the courts. Sometimes a judge's individual political views matter a great deal, but sometimes they don't. The Florida Supreme Court decided in Gore's favor in two appeals but against him in several others. A U.S. Court of Appeals, with a majority of Republican judges, rejected a Bush appeal that sought to block the handcounting of ballots—although the predominantly Republican U.S. Supreme Court, in a separate suit, effectively did just that (with two moderate Republican judges dissenting). It is this shifting balance of political and legal factors, combined with the staggering complexity of contemporary American law, that makes a high level of *unpredictability* such a distinctive feature of adjudication in the United States—not just in the election litigation but in general.

Nevertheless, in *this* set of cases, the judges' political leanings seemed to be the deciding factor. Legal scholars, like the public at large, ended up viewing the propriety of each Florida and U.S. Supreme Court decision through sharply divergent partisan lenses, just as the high court itself divided along moderate-conservative lines. Tossed about by these turbulent political waves, the very notion of legal objectivity, already weakened by years of "legal realism," "critical legal studies," and "postmodernism," seemed close to death. In a December 11, 2000, public opinion poll, a majority of respondents (53 percent) said they believed the Supreme Court's decision to stay the Florida manual recount was based on "politics" rather than "law" (34 percent).

The postelection legal battle thus exemplified and intensified America's ambivalence about law and litigation. On one hand, the litigation underscored the nation's fundamental respect for the rule of law and the authority of courts. Just as President Richard Nixon in the Watergate tapes case had bowed to a Supreme Court decision that he knew would doom his ability to remain in office, Vice President Gore, while stating he strongly disagreed with the Court's December 12 decision, was quick to add that he accepted its authority. Throughout the litigation Bush and Gore supporters mounted loud demonstrations outside the key courthouses, but there seemed to be a reservoir of faith and pride that somber legal argument and constitutional procedures, not mobs or raw political power, ultimately would settle the various disputes and produce a smooth transfer of power. On the other hand, many citizens expressed annoyance that dueling lawyers had taken over the selection of the president. Others (including, perhaps, a majority of U.S. Supreme Court justices) worried that the litigation and counterlitigation would spiral out of control, generating not legal finality but a constitutional crisis. The Bush campaign organization found it politically acceptable and even desirable to repeatedly denounce the Florida Supreme Court's attempt to reconcile ostensibly conflicting statutory provisions as "changing the rules after the election was over." Not only the courts but the rule of law itself had become politically contested territory—and not for the first time in American history.

In many respects, therefore, the protracted courthouse struggle following the 2000 election, for all its uniqueness, did typify the American political system, which persistently venerates courts and the rule of law but just as persistently derides the rule of lawyers, judges, and legal excess. "Adversarial legalism," as I call the rambunctious, peculiarly American style of law and legal decisionmaking exhibited in late 2000, has become a common phenomenon in the life of the nation. It recurs in everyday American processes of criminal and civil litigation, and in American methods of regulating police and schools and businesses, of compensating accident victims, and of holding governmental officials accountable.

The elements that fostered adversarial legalism in the 2000 election endgame, this book argues, affect almost every sphere of governmental and economic activity. They include adjudicatory systems that give lawyers for the competing parties a very large and creative role in gathering evidence, formulating legal arguments, and influencing decisions—and hence foster an especially entrepreneurial and aggressive legal profession; a politically selected, somewhat unpredictable, and uniquely powerful judiciary; a fragmented governmental and court system (which often enables losers in one forum to seek a different decision in another); and a system of governmental administration that is more decentralized, more responsive to democratic political pressures, and more generally distrusted than the national bureaucracies and court systems of, say, Western European countries. Florida's election laws were so complex because the legislature periodically had promulgated new, more specific rules to regulate the state's politically selected county election boards. The electoral decisions of Florida's Secretary of State were legally subject to review by courts because she, like her predecessors, was a partisan political official (in this case, a co-chair of Bush's Florida campaign organization) rather than an apolitical, professional bureaucrat. Some U.S. Supreme Court justices voted to stop the manual recount because they indicated that they did not trust Florida election officials or trial judges to conduct the recount in a neutral, consistent, and professional manner. These distrustful attitudes toward a decentralized, politically permeable governmental structure do not affect elections alone. They permeate American politics and governance, making adversarial legalism a pervasive feature of American life.

The passions that trigger adversarial legalism, with its hopes for justice and fears of costly legal excess, usually are not national in scope and attention. Rather, they are local and familiar. They arise in the course of everyday criminal prosecutions, personal injury lawsuits, and disputes over land use. They emerge from environmental controversies, from conflicts between regulatory officials and businesses, between commercial enterprises, and between employees and employers. That is the terrain that this book traverses, exploring the ways in which American adversarial legalism differs from law and governance in other economically advanced democracies, examining why that is the case, and describing its consequences, both positive and negative.

As best I can piece it together, the idea for this book arose during a fellowship I was granted by the Netherlands Institute for Advanced Study in the Social and Behavioral Sciences (NIAS) in 1987. Month after month, I was immersed in discussions of the Dutch and other European legal processes with Erhard Blankenburg, Kees Groenendyk, Albert Klijn, and other sociolegal scholars—conversations in which I had to explore what was different about American legal culture, methods of regulation, and modes of adjudication and why those differences arose and persist.

I also used the NIAS fellowship to begin a comparative study of seaports and intermodal transportation. My goal was to compare Dutch and U.S. legal and regulatory processes in resolving cargo damage claims, promoting safety, managing labor relations, fostering technological innovation, and protecting the environment. In this book one can find traces of my interviews in and around the Port of Rotterdam with regulatory officials, labor unionists, port officials, lawyers, shipping line and terminal managers, marine insurance companies, and freight forwarders. Their day-to-day experiences underscored some distinctive aspects of American legal and regulatory processes, particularly their higher costs, heavier penalties, and greater levels of uncertainty.

In the years that followed, my teaching at the University of California, Berkeley, gave me the opportunity and the incentive to gather sociolegal studies that compare particular legal and regulatory processes in the United States with similar processes in other economically advanced democracies. Like my work on the ports, I found these focused studies far more illuminating than global statistics or generalizations about national legal systems. These studies, summarized in Table 1 in Chapter 1 and referred to throughout this volume, all seemed to tell the same story: American legal and regulatory regimes, compared to their counterparts in other countries, generally are characterized by more detailed and prescriptive legal rules, more litigation, more costly forms of legal contestation, more fearsome legal penalties, more political conflict, and higher levels of legal malleability and uncertainty.

My research on seaports also led to a detailed case study of the legal and regulatory struggles surrounding the efforts of the Port of Oakland, California, to dredge its harbors. To me, the Oakland Harbor story epitomized the way in which adversarial legal struggle has become an ever-present propensity of American governance, often with highly disruptive, inefficient, and unjust consequences. When Martin Levin of Brandeis University invited me to write a paper for a conference on American public policy, I sought to link the Oakland Harbor story (discussed in Chapters 2 and 10 of this book) to a broader account of American law and regulation. My work on that paper was supported by the Center for Advanced Study in the Social and Behavioral Sciences in Stanford, California. In the paper, subsequently published in the *Journal for Public Policy and Management* and in a volume edited by Levin and Marc Landy, I invoked the concept of "adversarial legalism" to distinguish American legal processes from the more hierarchical, less participatory methods of regulation and adjudication used in other countries. In writing that paper, I also came to see more clearly how American adversarial legalism springs from fundamental features of American politics, particularly the propensity to distrust and fragment governmental authority—even as government is asked to become more active in providing justice and reducing risk. At my urging, Kenneth Hanf of Erasmus University and Yoshinobu Kitamura of Yokohama University wrote conference papers comparing the Oakland experience with parallel regulatory processes in the ports of Rotterdam and Kobe, respectively, and their research further highlighted the uniqueness of American adversarial legalism.

I am grateful to Professor Herbert McClosky for urging me to turn my initial article into a book, to Aida Donald of Harvard University Press for additional encouragement, and to a year as visiting professor at the College of Law, Ohio State University, during which I was able to conduct additional research about the role of American lawyers, judges, and legal scholars in fostering adversarial legalism. In 1995–1998 I was given the opportunity to undertake a research project that used the cross-national experience of selected multinational corporations to compare legal and regulatory regimes in the United States with parallel regimes in other economically advanced democracies. The project produced ten detailed case studies, gathered in *Regulatory Encounters: Multinational Corporations and American Adversarial Legalism* (University of California Press, 2000). I am grateful to the case study authors, Lee Axelrad, John Dwyer, Kirsten Engel, Holly Welles, Kazumasu Aoki, John Cioffi, Lori Johnson, Martine Kraus, Laura Beth Nielsen, Charles Ruhlin, Deepak Somaya, Tatsuya Fujie, Marius Aalders, Richard Brooks, and Alan Marco. Their efforts provided findings and analyses that filled important gaps in the comparative literature and that I rely on at several points in this book.

My work on the manuscript benefited greatly from the support of Berkeley's Center for the Study of Law and Society and its staff, particularly Rod Watanabe and Margo Rodriguez. I received superb research assistance from outstanding graduate students, including Todd Lochner, Lori Johnson, Linus Masuredis, Brendon Swedlow, Sara Rushing, and especially Jeb Barnes, who not only found facts and summarized literature but also constantly pushed me to sharpen my arguments. The experience of teaching hundreds of Berkeley students over the last decade has also been immensely valuable, forcing me to view the American legal system afresh each year and to focus on its many strengths as well as its disturbing qualities.

So many valued and able academic colleagues have read and commented on various draft chapters of *Adversarial Legalism* that I fear that I will fail to mention everyone who provided important corrections or encouragement or both. Among the most prominent in my mind today are Sandy Muir, Eugene Bardach, David Vogel, Malcolm Feeley, Tom Burke, Albert Klijn, Harry Scheiber, Lawrence M. Friedman, David Kirp, Margaret Weir, David Johnson, Peter Schuck, William Pizzi, Bud Bynack, and David Levine. There are many more scholars whose careful research and thoughtful analyses provided the bulk of the information in this book; their names are in the table of references at the end.

Most important to me have been those whose love and patience have sustained and strengthened me, even as I withdrew into my study on far too many evenings—Betsy, my caring, lovely, and ever-insightful wife, and my wonderful and amazing daughter Elsie.

I

Adversarial Legalism: Contours, Consequences, Causes

1

The Concept of
Adversarial Legalism

In contemporary democracies law is inescapable. Even in an era of political liberalism and "deregulation," it constrains ever more aspects of social, economic, and governmental activity—usually, even if not always, for good reasons. The rule of law is a very good thing. Different nations, however, implement the rule of law in different ways. Compared to other economically advanced democracies, American civic life is more deeply pervaded by legal conflict and by controversy about legal processes. The United States more often relies on lawyers, legal threats, and legal contestation in implementing public policies, compensating accident victims, striving to hold governmental officials accountable, and resolving business disputes. American laws generally are more detailed, complicated, and prescriptive. Legal penalties in the United States are more severe. And American methods of litigating and adjudicating legal disputes are more costly and adversarial.

To encapsulate some of the distinctive qualities of governance and legal process in the United States, I use the shorthand term "adversarial legalism," by which I mean policymaking, policy implementation, and dispute resolution by means of lawyer-dominated litigation. Adversarial legalism can be distinguished from other methods of governance and dispute resolution that rely instead on bureaucratic administration, or on discretionary judgment by experts or political authorities, or on the judge-dominated style of litigation common in most other countries. While the United States often employs these other methods too, it relies on adversarial legalism far more than other economically advanced democracies.

American adversarial legalism has both positive and negative effects. Viewed in cross-national comparison, the legal system of the United States is especially open to new kinds of justice claims and political movements. American judiciaries are particularly flexible and creative. American lawyers, litigation, and courts serve as powerful checks against official corruption and arbitrariness, as protectors of essential individual rights, and as deterrents to corporate heedlessness. In so doing, they also enhance the political legitimacy of capitalism and of the system of government as a whole.

At the same time, however, adversarial legalism is a markedly inefficient, complex, costly, punitive, and unpredictable method of governance and dispute resolution. In consequence, the American legal system often is unjust—not, by and large, in its rules and official decisions, but because the complexity, fearsomeness, and unpredictability of its processes often deter the assertion of meritorious legal claims and compel the compromise of meritorious defenses. Adversarial legalism inspires legal defensiveness and contentiousness, which often impede socially constructive cooperation, governmental action, and economic development, alienating many citizens from the law itself.

Do the negative aspects of American adversarial legalism "outweigh" its positive features? To pose the question in such global terms is not very useful. There is no way to count up and compare all the social costs and social benefits that a gigantic, multifaceted legal system send rippling through economic, political, and communal life. And even if one could make such a calculation, the question would remain, "Compared to what?" That is, would alternative ways of implementing public policy and resolving disputes yield higher aggregate benefits and lower social costs, or vice versa? That question too defies any easy answer, at least at that sweeping, system-wide level of analysis.

Other economically advanced democracies, particularly in Western Europe, structure legal and regulatory institutions and processes in ways that suggest plausible alternatives to American adversarial legalism. But the practice that works well in Amsterdam or London might not work so well in Seattle or Miami, and it may also entail a "downside" not revealed by current comparative studies. Moreover, adversarial legalism is deeply rooted in the political institutions and values of the United States. Americans are not likely to accept wholesale replacement of familiar legal rights and practices by legal institutions drawn from rather different political traditions. Some Western European legal and regulatory practices may achieve higher levels of legal certainty than American adversarial legalism, without nearly so much expenditure on lawyers and legal conflict, but those practices are nested in political systems that impose high taxes and expect deference to governmental bureaucracies—neither of which has much political appeal in the United States. For good and for ill, adversarial legalism is the American way of law, and it is likely to remain so.

The purpose of this book, therefore, is not to provide a definitive overall assessment of adversarial legalism, nor to call for its burial, nor particularly to praise it. Rather, my principal intent is descriptive and explanatory—to enhance social scientific understanding of American adversarial legalism's characteristic features; to show how and why it differs from the legal and regulatory systems of other economically advanced democracies; and to highlight ways in which, for all its strengths, it also frustrates the quest for justice.

Many lawyers and sociolegal scholars view complaints about law and litigation in the United States as exaggerated (Galanter, 1994) or, more pointedly,
as the laments of conservatives who resent legal changes that help the disadvantaged (Engel, 1984; Daniels and Martin, 1995). But the sociolegal scholars' defense of the American legal system, I suspect, also reflects a political
concern: to acknowledge the system's defects, they fear, may encourage politicians to enact reforms that would throw out the baby of justice along with
the bathwater of legal excess. The concern is understandable, but refusal to
recognize the unique and problematic features of the American legal system
may ultimately endanger the baby even more. As Peter Schuck (2000: 421)
has observed, "Law that arouses and then dashes peoples' hopes discredits
[law's] melioristic impulses, leaving corrosive cynicism and mistrust in its
wake." And that may trigger political assaults that also disable law's best capa-
bilities.

With those concerns in mind, this book offers a critical analysis of the
American legal system, based on a wide array of scholarly literature. The analysis employs a sociolegal, comparative, and political perspective. The sociolegal strand draws on empirical studies of the system as it actually operates—
studies of the law in action, not simply the law on the books, so that our focus
is on day-to-day realities, not merely on legal ideals or on famous court cases.
The comparative strand draws on studies that contrast legal and regulatory
processes in the United States with similar processes in other economically
advanced democracies. The political strand traces the links between the distinctive characteristics of the American legal system and fundamental features
of American political culture, political structure, and political processes.

The discussion bridges categories of American law and policy that typically
are treated as separate and distinct—criminal justice, liability law, environmental regulation, social welfare law, and so on. By viewing these different legal spheres holistically, it becomes clear that the different streams of the
American legal process share a common set of characteristics. That is what
undergirds the claim that adversarial legalism is the American way of law. The
very pervasiveness of American adversarial legalism, moreover, suggests that
it is best viewed not merely as a method of solving legal disputes but as a
mode of governance, embedded in the political culture and political structure
of the United States. In an important sense, therefore, this book can be
viewed as a study of the relationship between law and politics in America, examined in comparative perspective.

The goal of the comparative analysis is not to recommend specific reforms
or transplants from other political and legal systems, for that job is best left to
specialists in particular areas of law and policy. The appropriate analogy is not
transplant surgery but psychotherapy. Like that practice, comparative analysis
attempts to reveal roads not taken, unconsciously maintained patterns, and

sources of resistance to change, thereby encouraging new courses of action that build on existing resources and potentials. My cautious hope is that this analysis will lend support to efforts to bring about change—change that builds on the enduring strengths of American legal institutions, reducing adversarial legal excess while keeping and nurturing those institutions' best features. At the same time, by emphasizing the deeply entrenched political roots of adversarial legalism in the United States, this book will repeatedly remind us that legal and political traditions, like individuals, are not easily changed. Yet within legal and political traditions—and especially within the turbulent politics of American law—meaningful incremental changes can and do occur. This study perhaps will be useful in that process.

American Legal Exceptionalism

Everywhere in the modern world legal control of social, political, and economic life is intensifying (Galanter, 1992; Dewees et al., 1991). Law grows from the relentless pressures of technological change, geographic mobility, global economic competition, and environmental pollution—all of which generate social and economic disruption, new risks to health and security, new forms of injustice, and new cultural challenges to traditional norms. Some citizens, riding the waves of change, demand new rights of inclusion, political access, and economic opportunity. Others, threatened by change, demand legal protection from harm and loss of control. Democratic governments pass laws and issue judicial rulings responsive to both sets of demands (Schuck, 2000: 42; Kagan, 1995).

In some spheres of activity, such as land use regulation and worker protection, Western European polities typically have more restrictive laws than does the United States. Compared to the United States, Japan has a more detailed and extensive set of legally mandated product standards and premarketing testing requirements (Edelman, 1988: 292; Vogel, 1990). Germany has stricter recycling regulations and much tighter legal restrictions on the opening and operating of new retail enterprises (Davis and Gumbel, 1995). Compared to most American states, Sweden has tougher laws, and tougher law enforcement, concerning fathers' obligations to provide child support. The Netherlands regulates how much manure a farmer can spread on his fields (Huppes and Kagan, 1989: 215) and, like Germany, has more stringent emission standards than the United States for some major air pollutants (Rose-Ackerman, 1995: 27–28). An increasing number of nations, as well as the European Union, now have active constitutional courts, supporting Torbjorn Vallinder's (1995: 13) claim of a worldwide trend toward the "judicialization of politics," defined as "(1) the expansion of the province of courts or the judges at the expense of politicians and/or the administrators . . . or . . . (2) the spread of judicial decision making methods outside the judicial province proper."

The United States, however, has a unique legal "style." That is the message of an accumulating body of careful cross-national studies, such as those listed in Table 1. Each study examines a specific area of public policy, law, or social problem-solving in the United States and at least one other economically advanced democracy. The studies focus not merely on the formal law but on how the law is implemented in practice. Cumulatively, the studies compare national systems for compensating injured people, regulating pollution and chemicals, punishing criminals, equalizing educational opportunity, promoting worker safety, discouraging narcotics use, deterring malpractice by police officers, physicians, and product manufacturers, and so on. For one social problem after another, the studies show, the American system for making and implementing public policy and resolving disputes is distinctive. It generally entails (1) more complex bodies of legal rules; (2) more formal, adversarial procedures for resolving political and scientific disputes; (3) more costly forms of legal contestation; (4) stronger, more punitive legal sanctions;[1] (5) more frequent judicial review of and intervention into administrative decisions and processes;[2] (6) more political controversy about legal rules and institutions; (7) more politically fragmented, less closely coordinated decisionmaking systems; and (8) more legal uncertainty and instability.

Comparative studies are hardly necessary, moreover, to show that in no other democracy is litigation so often employed by contestants in political struggles over the delineation of electoral district boundaries, the management of forests, the breakup of business monopolies, the appropriate funding level for inner-city versus suburban public schools, or the effort to discourage cigarette smoking. In no other countries are the money damages assessed in environmental and tort suits nearly so high, or have major manufacturers been driven into bankruptcy by liability claims, or have disagreements over tort law generated such intense interest group clashes in the legislatures. Notwithstanding the aggressive prosecution of governmental corruption by Italian and French magistrates, the United States leads the league of nations in the extent to which political parties' struggles for political advantage regularly include investigations and prosecutions arising from charges that the chief executive, his aides, cabinet members, or legislators have committed criminal violations (Ginsburg and Shefter, 1990). The United States has by far the world's largest cadre of special "cause lawyers" seeking to influence public policy and institutional practices by means of innovative litigation. In no other country are lawyers so entrepreneurial in seeking out new kinds of business, so eager to challenge authority, or so quick to propose new liability-

Table 1 Cross-national studies

Author	Policy area	Countries compared with U.S.
Badarraco (1985)	Exposure to polyvinyl chloride	France, Germany, Japan, U.K.
Bayley (1976)	Police behavior	Japan
Bok (1971)	Selection of labor representatives	Several West European
Boyle (1998)	Litigation in the licensing of nuclear power plants	France, Germany, Sweden
Braithwaite (1985)	Coal mine safety	Australia, Japan, Germany, France
Braithwaite (1993)	Nursing home care	Australia, U.K.
Brickman et al. (1985)	Hazardous chemicals regulation	Several West European
Charkham (1994)	Corporate governance	France, Germany, Japan, U.K.
Church & Nakamura (1993)	Hazardous waste cleanup	Denmark, Germany, Netherlands
Day & Klein (1987)	Nursing homes	U.K.
Feldman (2000)	Blood safety	France, Japan
Glendon (1987)	Regulation of abortion and child support	Several West European
Greve (1989b)	Public interest litigation in environmental regulation	Germany
Hoberg (1993)	Environmental regulation	Canada
Jacob et al. (1996)	Role of courts	France, Germany, Japan, U.K.
Jasanoff (1986)	Carcinogens regulation	Several West European
Johnson (1998)	Criminal prosecution	Japan
Kagan & Axelrad (2000)	Environmental and product safety regulation; patents; labor; debt collection	Germany, Japan, U.K., EU, Canada, Netherlands
Kelman (1981)	Workplace safety	Sweden
Kirp (1979)	Racial discrimination in schools	U.K.
Kirp (1982)	Special education	U.K.
Langbein (1979b)	Criminal adjudication	Germany
Langbein (1985)	Civil litigation methods	Germany
Litt et al. (1990)	Banking regulation	Japan
Lundqvist (1980)	Air pollution regulation	Sweden
Pizzi (1999)	Criminal adjudication	Germany, Netherlands, Norway, U.K.
Quam et al. (1987)	Medical malpractice compensation	U.K.
Schwartz (1991)	Products liability lawsuits	Several West European
Sellers (1995)	Land use decisionmaking	France, Germany
Tanase (1990)	Compensation for vehicle accidents	Japan
Teff (1985)	Pharmaceutical products regulation	U.K.
Vogel (1986)	Environmental regulation	U.K.
Wallace (1995)	Environmental regulation	Japan, several West European
Wokutch (1992)	Workplace safety regulation	Japan

expanding legal theories. Finally, referring merely to the last few years, the United States is remarkable in its propensity to stage highly publicized, knock-down-drag-out legal donnybrooks such as the investigation and impeachment trial of President Bill Clinton, the custody battle over the six-year-old Cuban refugee Elian Gonzales, the antitrust cases against Microsoft, and the multicourt battle over Florida's votes in the 2000 presidential election—struggles that inject huge televised doses of politicized legal argument into the nation's everyday experience.

What Is Adversarial Legalism?

All these legal propensities are manifestations of what I call "adversarial legalism"—a method of policymaking and dispute resolution with two salient characteristics. The first is *formal legal contestation*—competing interests and disputants readily invoke legal rights, duties, and procedural requirements, backed by recourse to formal law enforcement, strong legal penalties, litigation, and/or judicial review. The second is *litigant activism*—a style of legal contestation in which the assertion of claims, the search for controlling legal arguments, and the gathering and submission of evidence are dominated not by judges or government officials but by disputing parties or interests, acting primarily through lawyers. Organizationally, adversarial legalism typically is associated with and is embedded in decisionmaking institutions in which *authority is fragmented* and in which *hierarchical control is relatively weak.*

These defining features of adversarial legalism have two characteristic consequences. The first is *costliness*—litigant-controlled, adversarial decisionmaking tends to be particularly complex, protracted, and costly. The second is *legal uncertainty*—when potent adversarial advocacy is combined with fragmented, relatively nonhierarchical decisionmaking authority, legal norms are particularly malleable and complex, and legal decisions are particularly variable and unpredictable. It is the combination of costliness and legal uncertainty that makes adversarial legalism especially fearsome and controversial.

Table 2 contrasts adversarial legalism with other modes of policy implementation and dispute resolution.[3] The horizontal dimension refers to legal formality—the extent to which contending parties or interests, as well as government officials, invoke and insist on conformity to written legal procedures and preexisting legal rights and duties. At one end of the informal-formal continuum, policy elaboration and dispute resolution can be labeled *legalistic,* in the sense that they are controlled by formal legal rules and procedures rather than by discretionary judgment, bargaining, and informal processes. (This definition encompasses, but is broader than, the common use of "legalism" to refer only to mechanical or rigid adherence to legal rules.)[4]

Table 2 Modes of policy implementation and dispute resolution

Organization of decision-making authority	Decisionmaking style		
	INFORMAL	⟷	FORMAL
HIERARCHICAL ↕	Expert or political judgment		Bureaucratic legalism
PARTICIPATORY	Negotiation/ mediation		Adversarial legalism

The vertical dimension of Table 2 concerns the extent to which the implementation or decisionmaking process is hierarchical—dominated by an official decisionmaker, applying authoritative norms or standards—as opposed to participatory—that is, influenced by disputing parties and their lawyers, their normative arguments, and the evidence they deem relevant. Taking each of these dimensions to their extreme form produces four "ideal types."

Negotiation/Mediation

A process in the lower left quadrant of Table 2 is adversarial in the sense that it is dominated by the contending parties, not by an authoritative governmental decisionmaker. But it is informal or nonlegalistic, since neither procedures nor normative standards are dictated by formal law. One example would be dispute resolution via negotiation, with or without lawyers; another would be policymaking by means of bargaining among politicians representing contending factions. The quadrant would also include mediation, whereby an "official" third party attempts to induce contending parties to agree on a policy or settlement but refrains from imposing a settlement based on law or official policy.

Expert/Political Judgment

The more an official decisionmaker or institution (as opposed to the contending interests) controls the process and the standards for decision, and the more authoritative and final the institution's decisions are, the more "hierarchical" the process. As suggested by the upper left quadrant in Table 2, hierarchical processes can be legally informal. For example, in many Western European countries decisions concerning eligibility for disability benefits and the extent of workers' compensation benefits are made by a panel of government-appointed physicians (or a mixed panel of physicians and social workers) without significant probability of intensive judicial review. In Japan disputes over fault in motor vehicle accidents typically are resolved by special traffic police who rush to the scene, question the parties, "hammer out a consensual story as to what happened," and file a detailed report on their findings (Tanase, 1990: 651, 673–674).

Bureaucratic Legalism

A policy-implementing or decisionmaking process characterized by a high degree of hierarchical authority and legal formality (the upper right quadrant of Table 2) resembles the ideal-typical bureaucratic process as analyzed by Max Weber. Governance by means of bureaucratic legalism emphasizes uniform implementation of centrally devised rules, vertical accountability, and official responsibility for fact-finding. The more hierarchical the system, the more restricted the role for legal representation and influence by affected citizens or contending interests. In contemporary democracies the pure case of bureaucratic legalism usually is softened in some respects, but it is an ideal systematically pursued, for example, by tax collection agencies. Also tending toward this ideal are German and French courts, where bureaucratically recruited and embedded judges—not the parties' lawyers and not lay juries—dominate both the evidence-gathering and the decisionmaking processes (Langbein, 1994). Similarly, in contrast to American criminal prosecutors' offices, in which individual assistant district attorneys usually make their own judgments about which charges to make and bargain with defense counsel about how much to reduce them in return for guilty pleas, prosecutors in Japan are subject to detailed rules and close hierarchical supervision concerning the investigation of facts, determination of the proper charge, and the recommendation of penalties (Johnson, 1998).

Adversarial Legalism

The lower right quadrant of Table 2 includes policy-implementing and decision processes that are procedurally formalistic but in which hierarchy is weak and party influence on the process is strong. American methods for compensating victims of highway and medical accidents, for example, prominently include a decentralized and adversarial tort law system driven by claimants and their lawyers, as contrasted with Western European compensation systems, which operate primarily through social insurance or benefit-payment bureaucracies. In American civil and criminal adjudication, the introduction of evidence and invocation of legal rules are dominated not by the judge (as in Europe) but by contending parties' lawyers. Even in comparison with the British "adversarial system," hierarchical, authoritative imposition of legal rules is relatively weak in the United States (Atiyah and Summers, 1987).

From a comparative perspective, American judges are more political, their decisions less uniform (Levin, 1972: 193–221; Rowland and Carp, 1983: 109–134). Law is treated as malleable, open to parties' novel legal arguments and pleas of extenuating circumstances. Lay jurors, whose decisions are not explained and largely shielded from hierarchical review, still play an important role in the American system, which reduces legal certainty and magnifies the influence of skillful legal advocacy.

Similarly, compared to European democracies, regulatory decisionmaking in the United States entails many more legal formalities—complex legal rules concerning public notice and comment, restrictions on ex parte and other informal contacts with decisionmakers, legalistically specified evidentiary and scientific standards, mandatory official "findings" and responses to interest group arguments. These legal devices facilitate interest group participation and judicial review of administrative decisions. But hierarchical authority is correspondingly weak. Policymaking and implementing authority is often shared by different agencies at the same or at different levels of government, with different interests and perspectives. Agency decisions are frequently challenged in court by dissatisfied parties and reversed by judges, who dictate further changes in administrative policymaking routines. Lawyers, scientists, and economists hired by contending industry and advocacy groups play a large role in presenting evidence and arguments. Overall, the clash of adversarial argument has a larger influence on decisions than in other countries' regulatory systems, where policy decisions are characterized by a combination of political and expert judgment and consultation with affected interests (Badaracco, 1985; Brickman et al., 1985).

No modern democratic legal system is characterized entirely by any of the quadrants in Table 2. National legal styles are not monolithic; ways of making, invoking, and enforcing law vary within nations (especially within the United States) and even across offices of the same legal institution. British libel law is more threatening to the press than American libel law, which has been restricted by judicial interpretations of the First Amendment (Weaver and Bennett, 1993). The German Constitutional Court, interpreting a more recent and detailed constitution than the U.S. Constitution, has been more activist than the U.S. Supreme Court in some important policy areas, thereby stimulating a good deal of constitutional litigation (Currie, 1990; Landfried, 1995: 113). Adversarial legalism can and does occur in more "cooperation"-oriented nations, such as the Netherlands and Japan (Niemeijer, 1989: 121–152; Upham, 1987). Privatization, deregulation, intensified economic competition, and the advent of transnational regulation by the European Union and the European Court of Justice all have increased the role of courts and litigation in the governance of European countries (Kagan, 1997a).

Conversely, Americans often refrain from and disparage adversarial legalism. Contrary to one popular belief, ordinary people often do not demand tougher laws, prosecutions, and lawsuits for every kind of offense.[5] Research indicates that accident victims, disappointed purchasers, and regulatory inspectors who encounter violations generally do *not* resort to lawsuits as their first recourse (Hensler et al., 1991; Miller and Sarat, 1981; Bardach and Kagan, 1982). They often are willing to submit to bureaucratic or expert judgment or negotiate solutions to their legal claims. Politicians and legal elites often devise less adversarial, less costly alternatives to adversarial litigation—juvenile courts, family courts, small claims courts, workers' compensation tribunals, commercial arbitration, mandatory mediation, negotiated regulatory rulemaking and compliance plans, and so on.

American judges and legislatures periodically issue rulings and enact statutes that are designed to *discourage* lawsuits and appeals; the 1980s and 1990s saw a wave of such efforts to dampen adversarial legalism. Moreover, in social arenas in which the processes of adversarial legalism often are invoked, full-scale legal contestation usually does not occur, largely because the extraordinary costs and delays associated with formal adversarial litigation impel most disputants to negotiate an informal plea bargain or settlement—even if it means abandoning valid claims or defenses (Feeley, 1979; Macaulay, 1979). Thus it is helpful to think of "adversarial legalism" as encompassing both *a method of policy implementation and dispute resolution* (characterized by a set of legal institutions, rights, and rules that facilitate or encourage adversarial, party-dominated legal contestation) and *the day-to-day practice of adversarial legal contestation,* a practice whose rate or incidence varies over time and across settings, depending on the motivations and resources of potential disputants. In principle and in practice, institutionalizing the methods or structures of adversarial legalism—that is, establishing the kinds of judiciaries, legal rules, and law firms that facilitate adversarial litigation—does not completely determine how often conflicting parties actually *use* those institutions.

Yet viewed in comparative perspective, the United States is distinctive in both dimensions. It is especially inclined to authorize and encourage the use of adversarial litigation to implement public policies and resolve disputes. And according to the comparative studies of particular policy fields listed in Table 1, adversarial legalism as a matter of day-to-day practice is far more common in the United States than in other democracies.[6] Furthermore, adversarial legalism as a matter of day-to-day practice is far more common in the United States today than it was thirty-five or forty years ago.

The dual aspect of adversarial legalism—as decisionmaking structure or method and as day-to-day practice—is crucial to understanding its social consequences. It means that adversarial legalism's importance cannot be measured by litigation or adjudication rates alone, any more than the significance of nuclear weapons rests on the frequency of nuclear war. For example, even if only a small minority of aggrieved persons or organizations actually file lawsuits that result in jury trials, the mere threat of costly and potentially punitive adversarial litigation can deter malpractice by hospitals, business organizations, and governmental bodies. Even if only a small percentage of those who object to new waste disposal facilities challenge the permits in court, and even if only a handful of businesses mount legal appeals against new regulations, the legal rules and practices that facilitate such adversarial legal actions matter a great deal because the governmental officials who formulate solid-waste permits and new regulations cannot predict either the incidence or the outcomes of such actions. Because its structures always stand ready to be mobilized, adversarial legalism—lawyer-dominated, potentially costly contestation—is a barely latent, easily triggered potentiality in virtually all contemporary American political, economic, and administrative processes. It creates a set of incentives and expectations that have come to loom very large in American governmental, commercial, and social life.

The Roots of Adversarial Legalism

In the most immediate sense adversarial legalism is a product of American legal culture. In most other nations, legal elites place great emphasis on legal consistency and stability. Law is viewed as a set of authoritative rules and principles, carefully worked out over time. In the United States, in contrast, law is more often viewed as the malleable (and fallible) output of an ongoing political battle to make the law responsive to particular interests and values. Many, perhaps most, American lawyers, judges, legal scholars, and politicians (many of whom are lawyers) see adversarial litigation as a vital tool for righting wrongs, curtailing governmental and corporate arbitrariness, and achieving a just society. Every working day, American lawyers talk about law, legal ethics, and legal processes in ways that reemphasize those values—and American lawyers work unusually long days.

But there is a competing strain in American legal culture. Many lawyers, judges, law professors, and politicians disparage and discourage adversarial legalism. They work hard at promoting compromise and encouraging cooperation. They believe in judicial restraint, not activism. Moreover, judges and lawyers who do favor the institutions, rules, and practices of adversarial legalism, even if they are in the ascendance at a particular political moment, cannot work their will, at least for very long, without the support or acquiescence of other political elites and ultimately of the voting public (Peltason, 1955). The deeper roots of adversarial legalism, therefore, derive from broader American political traditions, attitudes, structural arrangements, and interest group pressures.

Students of comparative politics have long observed that in relation to other economically advanced democracies, the United States "has a strong society but a weak state"(Krasner, 1978: 61). Among the rich democracies, American government is the most easily penetrated by organized interest groups and extracts less tax revenue as a proportion of gross national product (Steinmo, 1993; Wilensky, 1975). In a comparative analysis of political cultures, Seymour Martin Lipset (1996: 21) writes that due to its long-standing emphasis on individualism and mistrust of government, "America began and continues as the most antistatist, legalistic, and rights-oriented nation." American government, accordingly, is designed to fragment and limit power. Both the federal and the state constitutions subject governmental power to crosscutting institutional checks and judicially enforceable individual rights. Thus, in comparison with most other economically advanced democracies, the national government in the United States shares more power with states and municipalities, and at every level of government chief executives share more power with legislatures, legislative party leaders with subcommittee chairs and back-benchers, administrative agencies with judges, and judges with lawyers and juries. A decentralized financial system, rooted in autonomous equity markets, deprives the American government of direct controls over the economy that, for good or for ill, many governments elsewhere in the world employ (Levy, Kagan, and Zysman, 1998).

A structurally fragmented state is especially open to popular and interest group demands. And in contemporary societies—far richer, better informed, and with higher expectations than any in human history—citizens demand a great deal of their government. They want and expect justice, economic security, and protection from harmful technologies and pollutants. They want and expect guaranteed health care and financial aid when disability, disaster, or unemployment strikes their families. But getting those things from an institutionally fragmented, tax-averse, "antistatist" political system, as in the United States, presents a problem.

American adversarial legalism, therefore, can be viewed as arising from a fundamental tension between two powerful elements: first, a *political culture* (or set of popular political attitudes) that expects and demands comprehensive governmental protections from serious harm, injustice, and environmental dangers—and hence a powerful, activist government—and, second, a set of *governmental structures* that reflect mistrust of concentrated power and hence that limit and fragment political and governmental authority. Adversarial legalism helps resolve the tension. In a "weak," structurally fragmented state, lawsuits and courts provide "nonpolitical," nonstatist mechanisms through which individuals can demand high standards of justice from government. Lawsuits and courts empower interest groups to prod the government to implement ambitious public policies. It is only a slight over-simplification to say that in the United States lawyers, legal rights, judges, and lawsuits are the functional equivalent of the large central bureaucracies that dominate governance in high-tax, activist welfare states.

Adversarial legalism gives the United States the most politically and socially responsive court system in the world. Compared to most national judiciaries, American judges are less constrained by legal formalisms; they are more policy-oriented, more attentive to the equities (and inequities) of the particular situation. In the decentralized American legal system, if one judge closes the door on a novel legal argument, claimants can often find a more receptive judge in another court. Adversarial legalism makes the judiciary and lawyers more fully part of the governing process and more fully democratic in character. But this kind of "responsive law," in the words of Philippe Nonet and Philip Selznick (1978), is a "high risk strategy" of governance. With its high costs and penalties, and with its responsiveness to private claims, adversarial litigation enables ideologues or opportunists to use the law as a tool for extortion. In its eagerness to put aside legal formalism in order to seek good outcomes, responsive law generates high levels of legal unpredictability, at least when it is implemented through adversarial legalism. Thus adversarial legalism is an extremely inefficient and hence often unfair way of meeting the public's demand for justice and protection. The world's most responsive legal system does not necessarily give Americans the world's most reliable legal system or the world's most responsive system of governance.

The Plan of the Book

The tension between adversarial legalism's desirable and undesirable consequences is framed more fully in Chapter 2, "The Two Faces of Adversarial Legalism." Chapter 3, "The Political Construction of Adversarial Legalism," explains in greater detail why adversarial legalism is more common in the United States than in other democracies, and why, despite a great deal of criticism, it has persisted and even increased in recent decades.

The next three parts of the book circle back and elaborate the themes laid out in this and the following two chapters, demonstrating that the same general contours, causes, and consequences of adversarial legalism recur in four broad spheres of policy—criminal justice, civil justice, social justice, and social regulation. The final chapter speculates about the future of adversarial legalism and the prospects for its "taming" in the United States.

Let me reemphasize that this is not a book designed to prescribe specific legal reforms. Its goals are basically to describe and explain the distinctive features and consequences of the American way of law. My own values, of course, inevitably color my characterization of adversarial legalism's consequences, positive and negative. But my analysis does not fit comfortably either with the views of contemporary liberal Democrats, with their nearly automatic resistance to most critiques of adversarial legalism, or with contemporary Republican conservatism, with its nearly automatic resistance to any effort to create alternatives to adversarial legalism through stronger, better-financed government bureaucracies and welfare state measures. My hopes are directed to a system of law and government that would reduce the inefficiencies and resulting injustices that flow from adversarial legalism, while providing less costly, more reliable administrative mechanisms for deterring official arbitrariness and economic rapaciousness and for compensating the victims of injury, injustice, and bad luck.

2

The Two Faces of Adversarial Legalism

Like the blind men of legend who, feeling different parts of an elephant, described it variously as resembling a tree and a snake, critics and defenders of the American legal system often seem to be referring to entirely different phenomena. In 1996 plaintiffs' lawyers in California supported a ballot measure encouraging securities class actions. Their television ads portrayed elderly investors who claimed that only by virtue of such lawsuits had their life savings been recouped from fraudulent companies. Electronics companies opposed to the measure put forth ads about greedy lawyers who brought "frivolous lawsuits" that extorted settlements from honest companies. Both sides, like the blind men, did have a piece of the truth.

Adversarial legalism encompasses many kinds of legal actions, some socially beneficent, some socially detrimental, some a bit of both. In the aggregate it generates both social benefits and social costs. Analysis must begin by recognizing both faces of adversarial legalism, as exemplified by the following case studies, one involving southern prison reform, and one concerning a legal deadlock over dredging the harbor in Oakland, California. The story of litigation and southern prisons illustrates adversarial legalism's capacity for making law and government more responsive to claims for decency and justice. The Oakland Harbor story shows how adversarial legal structures designed to increase governmental responsiveness can also lead to governmental paralysis and to injustice. Together, they pose two related dilemmas. How can the social costs exemplified by the Oakland Harbor story be weighed against adversarial legalism's virtues, as exemplified by the southern prison litigation? And is it possible to adopt reforms that shed adversarial legalism's justice-defeating costs and pathologies without undermining adversarial legalism's capacity for enhancing justice? This chapter provides no answer to those difficult questions but argues that one important step is to look directly at adversarial legalism's unpleasant face, increasing our understanding of how often and why it shows itself.

Adversarial Legalism in Action: Alabama Prison Reform

In the early 1970s Alabama prisons, in the impassioned words of a public health officer, were "unfit for human habitation." Inmates were packed in crowded, unsupervised dormitories. Fights, stabbings, and brutal sexual assaults were common. Inspecting a punitive isolation unit, an investigator found five black inmates packed into a tiny cell with no mattresses, no running water, and a hole in the floor for a toilet. "It was completely dark. The odor would make one's eyes water and throat burn from BO, feces, urine, and general filth." One of the inmates had been there for fourteen days, two for twenty-one days. Throughout the prison system medical care was intermittent and abysmal: unsupervised prisoners, without formal training, regularly pulled teeth, dispensed medication, and gave injections. Severely disturbed and violent psychotics were placed in the general inmate population. Most mentally disturbed prisoners received no psychiatric treatment at all (Bass, 1993: 232–236).

State correctional officials, despite some prodding, did little to remedy these atrocious conditions. Nor did Alabama's governor, George Wallace. Nor did the state legislature, despite committee reports raising the issue. Nor did the opposition political party or the judges of Alabama's courts. In the decentralized American political system, moreover, there was no congressional law governing state correctional systems, no national official charged with supervising state prisons. In this sorry situation adversarial legalism provided a mechanism for forcing some improvements on the Alabama prison system.

As a result of U.S. Supreme Court decisions, prisoners in state penal institutions could petition federal courts for writs of habeas corpus, challenging the constitutionality of their conviction or confinement. A prisoner's petition, however, did not guarantee a positive response. For years, federal judges had turned away complaints about unbearable prison conditions (Friedman, 1993: 309–313). As long as the legal process that had led to the prisoner's incarceration seemed to be in accordance with due process, the judges saw no constitutional defect in harshly run prisons. But adversarial legalism invites creative legal advocacy. In 1965 J. Smith Henley, a federal district court judge in Arkansas, after hearing testimony about prisoners who were savagely whipped for "infractions of discipline" and for not working hard enough in the fields, endorsed a novel theory—that inhumane prison conditions could be construed to be violations of the Eighth Amendment's prohibition of "cruel and unusual punishment." In 1970 Judge Henley found the whole Arkansas prison system unconstitutional (Feeley and Rubin, 1998). The prisoners' rights movement had been launched. It attracted idealistic lawyers from the civil rights movement. In 1972 the American Civil Liberties Union established the National Prison Project. The Southern Poverty Law Center provided financial help and legal advice to dedicated lawyer-reformers.

In October 1971 Frank Johnson, U.S. district court judge for the Middle District of Alabama, received a handwritten petition signed by N. H. Newman, a prison inmate; it described in shocking detail the inadequacy of medical care in the state prison system. Newman had reached the right judge. Frank Johnson exemplified the political independence, diversity, and individualism of the American judiciary. Johnson was a Republican in Democratic Alabama, a former small-town lawyer appointed to the U.S. District Court by President Eisenhower. Soon after his appointment, during the Montgomery bus boycott, Johnson had struck down the Alabama law that required segregated seating; he ruled that the condemnation of official segregation in *Brown v. Board of Education* applied not just to schools but also to other public services. Earlier in 1971 Judge Johnson had ruled that Alabama's horrible state-run mental institutions were unconstitutional; since they did not provide meaningful treatment, he reasoned, they deprived involuntarily committed patients of liberty without due process of law. The mental institutions case provided Johnson, once he encountered inmate Newman's petition, with a model for prison reform.

Judge Johnson quickly appointed a local lawyer to represent Newman, urging him to bring a civil lawsuit against the state. The judge also urged the U.S. Attorney for Alabama to intervene in the case; the petition, he told him, "raises extremely serious . . . 8th Amendment questions" (Bass, 1993: 325). Previously, some federal judges had dismissed such prisoner petitions, arguing that the cruel and unusual punishment clause of the Constitution had not been intended to guarantee convicted criminals any particular level of medical care. Judge Johnson disagreed, and the case went to trial. Newman's court-appointed lawyer and a Justice Department attorney presented hours of deeply disturbing testimony from experts who (pursuant to court order) had toured the prisons' medical facilities. Judge Johnson held that the prison system's woeful neglect amounted to unconstitutionally cruel and inhuman punishment. He ordered the state to take twenty-four specific corrective steps, including arrangements that would guarantee prompt medical treatment and would bring the infirmary into compliance with federal standards for Medicare-accredited facilities (Bass, 1993: 326–327).

Acting on additional prisoner petitions in 1974, Judge Johnson appointed two other Alabama lawyers to represent the inmates. After consulting with experienced prisoners' rights lawyers from other states, the lawyers filed class actions claiming that the whole Alabama prison system was so thoroughly pervaded by violence, overcrowding, inedible food, and brutal methods of punishment that it was unconstitutionally cruel and inhumane.

Again, the mechanisms of adversarial legalism opened up the prisons to outside scrutiny. A weeklong trial featured detailed testimony by an inmate who had been repeatedly raped and by correction system professionals from other states who had toured the facilities. The state attorney general conceded that the system was legally indefensible. Judge Johnson issued detailed orders closing the current disciplinary cells, demanding reduction of overcrowding, controlling violence, improving sanitation and food, and increasing professional staff (Bass, 1993: 335–339).

Governor Wallace mounted an appeal, stating that his attorney general had been wrong in admitting the Eighth Amendment violations. The court of appeals, however, upheld Johnson's constitutional ruling and most of his specific orders. As had become customary in "institutional reform" cases (such as those demanding school desegregation), the trial judge kept the case alive pending full compliance with the injunction; the state officials charged with compliance thus remained subject to punishment for contempt of court should they engage in overt resistance. Judge Johnson also appointed the newly elected governor, Forest James, receiver for the state prison system; the governor thus was obligated to oversee compliance and report back to the judge. By keeping the case open, the judge enabled the prison reform lawyers to keep adversarial pressure alive—by monitoring prison conditions, meeting with the receiver, and complaining to the judge when they detected noncompliance.

In 1990 the case was closed. Observers still criticized Alabama's correctional system, but they also noted far-reaching, positive changes. Correctional officials and guards "professed astonishment, and no small pleasure, that the prisons had changed so drastically" (Bass, 1993: 343). The minimum standards specified in Judge Johnson's order, prisoners' rights lawyers noted, had led to the development of nationwide professional standards and an accreditation system run by the American Correctional Association. And the widespread publicity generated by Judge Johnson's order helped precipitate a 1980 congressional law that authorized the U.S. Attorney General to bring lawsuits to correct constitutional deprivations in state or local jails, prisons, mental health facilities, and nursing homes (Bass, 1993: 345–346; Feeley and Rubin, 1998).

By 1990 state prisons in forty-one states were operating under court orders that demanded that they remedy unconstitutional conditions of confinement, as were nearly one-third of large county jails.[1] As a result of the prison reform litigation, Malcolm Feeley and Edward Rubin (1998) observe, the federal courts promulgated a comprehensive regulatory code for prison management, covering residence facilities, sanitation, food, clothing, medical care, discipline, staff hiring, libraries, work, and education. And throughout the country, prison systems and individual prisons regularly consult attorneys to ensure that they are in compliance.[2]

The Virtues of Adversarial Legalism

The reforms that dragged Alabama's correctional system into the twentieth century were not developed by a national ministry of justice or corrections, as they might have been in a European country, or implemented through a hierarchically organized bureaucracy. The reforms were thrust on Alabama "laterally" by the mechanisms of adversarial legalism. They were made possible by the fragmented, decentralized structure of the American legal system, its openness to individual legal complaints, its tradition of entrepreneurial legal advocacy, and the creativity and boldness of its politically appointed, diverse judiciary.

The southern prison reform cases can remind us that in the adversarial, nonhierarchical American legal order even the lowest and most despised of citizens, convicted felons, feel entitled to petition a court for relief. Adversarial legalism, in Samuel Johnson's phrase, gives the ordinary individual "adventitious strength" (see Muir, 1973: 112). It encourages Americans, more than the residents of other democracies, to regard themselves as rights-bearing citizens.

They would not do so, however, if American judges were not so open to creative advocacy and so powerful. In the Arkansas and Alabama cases, prisoners' lawyers advanced a novel interpretation of constitutional law, undeterred by the fact that it had been rejected by other judges in the past. (In most other democracies, lawyers tend to stick more closely to precedent and authoritative interpretations of legal texts.) Armed with tools provided by the uniquely adversarial American pretrial and trial processes, the prisoners' rights lawyers could investigate and bring to light the hidden malpractices of closed institutions. As a result of recurrent successes of that kind in a wide variety of types of cases, adversarial legalism energizes the American legal profession as a whole; hence American lawyers are far more entrepreneurial and aggressive than their counterparts in other democracies (Osiel, 1990).

Similarly, because hierarchical constraints on American lower court judges are looser than those that prevail in other judiciaries, individual judges, such as J. Smith Henley in Arkansas and Frank Johnson in Alabama, often enjoy enough legal discretion to reinterpret the law and act on the basis of their moral convictions. Even more startling from the standpoint of legal scholars and judges from hierarchical legal systems, the lower court judges in Arkansas and Alabama had the power to issue detailed legal instructions to elected state governors and legislatures and to create ongoing, lawyer-activated implementation mechanisms.

The southern prison reform litigation exemplifies American adversarial legalism's capacity for heroic moral action. Because of that capacity, American adversarial legalism is in many respects the envy of the world—admired for its openness to new ideas, its ability to challenge governmental and corporate arbitrariness, and its empowerment of political, ethnic, and social minorities. Repeatedly, adversarial legalism has enabled political underdogs in the United States to demand better treatment from the government, first and foremost in the cause of racial equality but also in the quest for more equitable electoral districts, more compassionate welfare administration, and more civilized law enforcement practices. Because of the fierceness of its liability law system, adversarial legalism exposed the tragedy of widespread asbestos poisoning and scared corporations into strengthening internal systems for product design, quality control, and fair personnel management. Responding to the arguments of "public interest" lawyers, courts have compelled more than a dozen state legislatures to restructure public school funding to increase spending on children in tax-poor municipalities (Reed, 1998). Richard Emery, a public interest lawyer in New York City, brought a class action lawsuit that ended a common police practice of conducting humiliating strip searches of persons arrested for minor offenses (Herbert, 1998).

Adversarial legalism facilitates (and hence encourages) new kinds of justice claims, such as the right to resist sexual harassment or to recover damages for negligent infliction of emotional injury. Japanese and European environmentalists look across the ocean jealously, for they see in the United States a legal system that enables community groups and advocacy organizations to haul government planners and private developers into court—and hence to compel redesign of housing projects, highways, dumps, and factories. In the competitive American economic system, open to unscrupulous opportunism as well as to useful creativity, adversarial legalism often enables private litigants to bring dishonest businesses to justice.

At a more mundane level, adversarial legalism, even if only sporadically invoked, makes insurance adjusters, prosecutors, and administrative agencies attend more carefully to the evidence and the equities of individual cases. Midwestern city administrators interviewed by political scientist Charles Epp (1998: 12) complained about the time and money their municipal governments had to devote to defense of civil lawsuits. They acknowledged, however, that to ward off liability their cities engaged in more systematic checks of road conditions and playground equipment, instituted more training for police and other employees who deal with the public, and acted more rapidly to weed out "problem officers." Here are some of the things that three senior city administrators told Epp:

> We're much more responsive to complaints and concerns raised by citizens, apart from the election process, because we know in the back of our minds that the complaint might conceivably become a lawsuit.

> The biggest changes for the better in this city have come as a result of lawsuits or threatened lawsuits, not as a result of political changes in the council or anything else. The courts have done a far better job than politics of improving our policies.

> The rights of citizens and employees are far better protected as a result— and only as a result of litigation, not other changes. And the safety of our citizens is better protected. Remember all that training and inspection I mentioned? It makes a difference. Our roads and streets are safer, our playgrounds are safer, our whole operation is safer.

As these quotations suggest, not only does adversarial legalism, with its tools of contingency fee lawyering, pretrial discovery, and significant monetary penalties, enable citizens to fight city hall by suing it, but it also sometimes compels, and hence enables, government officials to do what they believe to be the right thing. When the Kentucky courts, employing a novel reading of the state constitution, ruled the state's entire public school system unconstitutional, the governor and state legislature, which had previously been deadlocked over school reform for fear of raising taxes, quickly moved to enact a reform project. "It's the law," said the governor (Paris, 1998). Adversarial legalism, therefore, serves as a mechanism for injecting principle into the political process, providing legal legitimacy for politicians to act as leaders and statesmen.

When one focuses on such victories, American adversarial legalism is a bright sun indeed. It is this heroic face of adversarial legalism that Owen Fiss (1984: 1086–1087) in an often-cited article contrasts with paler methods of dispute resolution such as negotiated settlement or mediation (and which also might be contrasted with the straightforward rule-following of judiciaries in systems of bureaucratic legalism):

> There is, of course, sometimes a value to avoidance, not just to the judge, who is thereby relieved of the need to make or enforce a hard decision, but also to society, which sometimes thrives by masking its basic contradictions. . . . But when one sees injustices that cry out for correction—as Congress did when it endorsed the concept of the private attorney general and as the Court of another era did when it sought to en-

hance access to the courts—the value of avoidance diminishes and the agony of judgment becomes a necessity. Someone has to confront the betrayal of our deepest ideals and be prepared to turn the world upside down to bring those ideals to fruition.

The "confronters" in Professor Fiss's world, of course, are activist judges, such as J. Smith Henley and Frank Johnson, the idealistic lawyers who bring the cases to court, and perhaps even the law professors who identify injustices and spell out the legal theories and remedies that judges can cite when turning the world upside down.

Adversarial Legalism's Other Face: Disorder in the Port

Even ice-cream cones are no good if you eat too many of them. Even one is bad if you eat it at the wrong time or place. In some times and places, judges shouldn't turn the world upside down. And if too many judges are striving to turn the world upside down, the world may not work so well. Adversarial legalism's sword, honed by distrust of authority, can be used against the trustworthy too. Adversarial legalism can be invoked by the misguided, the mendacious, and the malevolent as well as by the mistreated. Its complexity, costliness, and malleability can produce injustice as well as justice. The Port of Oakland's frustrating struggle to dredge its California harbor illustrates the other face of adversarial legalism.

In 1988 international shipping lines launched a new generation of huge, efficient, $40 million containerships. The new vessels furthered a technological revolution that in the last two decades has transformed international trade, moving cargo across oceans and continents with dramatically greater speed, reliability, and economy. Today, shoppers in Dutch food stores buy green beans and grapefruits shipped in refrigerated containers from Senegal and Florida. A moving inventory of shirts, jeans, and dresses, packed in containers in a Hong Kong warehouse, whisked from ship to train in Los Angeles, flows to the loading docks of shops in Cincinnati and Atlanta at transportation costs of pennies per garment. Technological change has brought order to the port: today's electronically coordinated, mechanized containerports bear little resemblance to the seaports of the past, notorious for costly delays, labor exploitation, pilferage, drunkenness, and crime. On both sides of the Atlantic and Pacific, local monopolies and stodgy oligopolies are threatened by distant competitors, spurring productivity and innovation (Kagan, 1990b).

In the 1970s the Port of Oakland in San Francisco Bay initiated plans to deepen its harbor to forty-two feet in order to accommodate the larger ships of the future. In 1986 the U.S. Congress, which finances improvements in the national navigation system, authorized funding for the project. For the next eight years, however, a seemingly endless series of regulatory actions and lawsuits blocked the dredging of the harbor.

Before the early 1970s seas and harbors were used as free disposal sites for sewage sludge, garbage, and chemical wastes. Regulatory officials and environmentalists had little input into port expansion decisions. Dredging and disposal operations dislodged chemical wastes buried in urban rivers and bays, destroyed marshlands, and disrupted fisheries (National Research Council, 1985). Today, however, dredging projects require a permit from the U.S. Army Corps of Engineers; pursuant to the National Environmental Policy Act, the Corps must first prepare and circulate a comprehensive analysis of all potential environmental impacts and methods of mitigating unavoidable adverse consequences. The Corps of Engineers' decisions, in turn, are checked by other governmental bodies—the U.S. Fish and Wildlife Service, the National Marine Fisheries Service, the relevant state department of fish and game, the U.S. Environmental Protection Agency, the state agency charged with protecting water quality, and the relevant state coastal zone management agency. Each of these agencies, responsible for enforcing a specific environmental statute, is legally instructed to object to or block dredging projects that fail to meet those statutory standards. There is a third level of legal control: citizens, local politicians, and environmental advocacy groups who think that the Corps or the other agencies have not fulfilled their statutory responsibilities are legally empowered to file a lawsuit and seek judicial review of their decisions.

In the Port of Oakland case, the Army Corps of Engineers issued an Environmental Impact Statement (EIS) in 1986. It approved disposal of the dredged harbor floor sands at an established dumping site in San Francisco Bay, near Alcatraz Island. Environmentalists, fishing interests, and state regulatory officials raised concerns about damage to water quality and fisheries. The Corps, in response, conducted further sediment tests and in September 1987 released a Supplementary EIS comparing various alternatives. It called for "special care" disposal and "capping" methods for about 21,000 cubic yards of sediment (less than 1 percent of the total project) to be dredged from certain contaminated areas, but concluded that in-Bay disposal of the bulk of noncontaminated sediments would have no adverse environmental effects. State and local regulatory agencies, however, had legal power to block in-Bay disposal under state environmental law, and they preferred disposal in the deeper waters of the Pacific Ocean.

Confronted with this regulatory deadlock, Port of Oakland officials in January 1988 proposed disposal at an ocean site designated 1M, although that would double the cost of dredging. New regulatory hurdles then arose. Fishermen claimed that disposal at 1M would harm ocean fisheries. The Corps prepared another Supplementary EIS, which disputed the fishermen's claims. Nevertheless, the U.S. Environmental Protection Agency, statutory guardian of ocean waters, refused to issue a permit for 1M, and an environmental advocacy group (that had opposed disposal at Alcatraz) prepared to bring a lawsuit challenging the Corps' Supplementary EIS; the environmentalists said the sediments should be dumped beyond the Continental Shelf, fifty miles out at sea. The Corps responded that it was legally precluded from authorizing disposal beyond the Continental Shelf because that would cost at least twice as much as 1M without being demonstrably better in environmental terms. Prodded by increasingly anxious Port of Oakland officials, in March 1988 the Corps and the EPA negotiated a compromise, also agreed to by environmental groups and a federation of Pacific fishing associations. Ocean site B1B, ten miles off the coast, would be used for the first 500,000 cubic yards of the dredged material (except for sediments from the clearly contaminated area); further testing and study would precede any decision concerning disposal of the remaining 6.5 million cubic yards. The dredging machinery and barges moved into place.

When access to court is easy, however, compromise is unstable. In mid-April of 1988, just before the dredging commenced, the Half Moon Bay Fishermen's Marketing Association brought suit in federal court, alleging that the B1B disposal decision violated a number of federal regulatory provisions and would disrupt fisheries. The U.S. district court judge, and then the federal court of appeals, rejected the fishermen's legal claims. The dredging machinery completed one day of digging. Then, on May 16, 1988, a state court judge, responding to a new lawsuit based on another legal argument, held that the dredging permit had been issued without a requisite certification from the California Coastal Commission. The dredging stopped.

By that time, shipping lines using the Port of Oakland were screaming for deeper water. Desperate port officials announced an alternative plan to dispose of the first 500,000 cubic yards of dredged material in the Sacramento River Delta, where it would be used to reinforce levees. Local regulatory processes then creaked into action. The Port prepared a new EIS. After a year or so, a California regional water quality agency approved the plan, but the Contra Costa Water District challenged the Port's EIS in state court. Yet another year later, in July 1990, the court upheld the Delta plan. At that point, however, the Port of Oakland declined to go forward, since regulatory conditions designed to safeguard Delta water quality had pushed estimated disposal costs to $21 per cubic yard, ten times the cost of disposal at Alcatraz.

As Oakland officials searched for other disposal alternatives, new legal obstacles arose. The Water Quality Control Board for San Francisco Bay explicitly banned deposit of all new dredge project spoils in the Bay, as did the National Marine Fisheries Service, which cited dangers to already diminished salmon populations. Officials from the National Marine Sanctuaries program and other environmental groups objected to ocean disposal off the Continental Shelf. The EPA, having been burned by litigation, retreated into legalistic defensiveness, refusing to approve any new ocean disposal site. It noted that federal law required agency officials to make scientifically grounded findings about the environmental impact of ocean disposal, and yet the requisite mapping of the ocean bottom and currents had not even been initiated until 1990. No decision that would hold up in court, EPA indicated, could be made before 1994.

All this time, while possible environmental harms were debated and investigated, very tangible economic and social harms mounted. The powerful and costly hydraulic dredging equipment stood idle. Big ships that sought to call at Oakland, nearly scraping bottom (and thereby risking truly significant environmental harm), had to carry reduced loads and wait for high tides. Schedules of container trains and waiting warehouses and factories were disrupted. Shipping companies, facing higher costs and customer complaints, scrapped plans to expand operations at the Port of Oakland. The previously successful port lost money, and hence the municipal government lost revenues it needed to maintain social services. Port-related employment was adversely affected.

Finally, political pressure mounted, new studies were funded, new impact statements were prepared, and more regulatory hearings were held. In late 1992 partial "Phase I" dredging, encompassing 500,000 cubic yards of sediment, was at last permitted. The contaminated sediment (21,000 cubic yards) was deposited in a lined upland site. Regulation officials allowed the port to dump the other half-million cubic yards near Alcatraz in San Francisco Bay—just where the Port and the Corps of Engineers had first proposed in 1986 (U.S. Army Corps of Engineers, 1992a). (In the interim, additional sampling and testing costs incurred by the Port of Oakland and the Corps of Engineers had reached almost $4 million, or $8 a cubic yard for Phase I— more than double the cost of the actual barging and disposal operation.) For the next six million cubic yards, a final decision did not come until late 1994, after a multimillion-dollar research and analysis program. The relevant agencies endorsed a much more expensive disposal plan: some dredged sediments would be barged by sea to the edge of the Continental Shelf, and some (in order to win the support of environmental groups) would be used to create new wetlands far up the Sacramento River Delta. Funding the wetlands disposal project required a $15 million appropriation from Congress and an additional $5 million from the California legislature—at an estimated cost of about $20 per cubic yard. In 1995 the port finally was dredged to the planned forty-two-foot depth (Busch, Kirp, and Schoenholz, 1999: 193–194; Kagan, 1999b).

The Pathologies of Adversarial Legalism

The legal procedures that for eight years blocked dredging in Oakland Harbor reflect fundamental ideals of pluralistic democracy—that public policy should be formulated and implemented only after full and fair deliberation; that meaningful attention should be given to the claims of the individuals and groups who are not politically powerful (such as the Half Moon Bay fishermen); that environmental protection should be given special weight in planning currently urgent development projects that might deprive future generations of irreplaceable ecological amenities; and that to vindicate those values, a variety of interest groups and agencies should be able to challenge official assumptions and judgments in court. But in the Port of Oakland story, the procedures designed to protect those values seemed to fall into the hands of the Sorcerer's Apprentice, multiplying themselves beyond control. Month after month, regulatory officials, scientists, and lawyers, arguing first in one legal forum, then in another, debated the propriety of decisionmaking procedures, the adequacy of sediment samples and tests for chemical contamination, and the reliability of environmental impact models. No proceeding produced any definitive finding that the proposed disposal plans were environmentally dangerous. But neither could any single court or agency authoritatively designate a single environmentally acceptable, economically sensible alternative.

In the Port of Oakland case, adversarial legalism's legal flexibility—which in the Alabama prison case permitted a bold judge to create new rights and remedies—produced only a legal mess. The governing body of law, detailed and complex, generated only uncertainty, inconsistency, and legalistic defensiveness. When one agency found a plan legally acceptable, another would disagree. When one court upheld a regulatory decision, another overturned it. No agency could ever be sure that its legal rulings would hold up in court. The mere threat of adversarial litigation, with its capacity to impose further crippling delays, induced both the Port and the Corps of Engineers to accept successively more remote (and far more costly) disposal sites and methods, regardless of the merits of the objections. In the tangled web of adversarial legalism, mollusks received far more protection than human communities.[3]

Rotterdam, Europe's largest seaport, must deal with far larger volumes of far more seriously contaminated dredged material. The Netherlands, like the United States, adheres to the London Dumping Convention preventing ocean disposal of toxics. There is a strong "green movement" that pushes officials to comply with national environmental laws, which, like those in the United States, call for detailed impact analyses and detailed mitigation plans. Thus the Port of Rotterdam has dealt with its massive dredging and disposal problems in an environmentally responsible manner. It has done so, however, far more expeditiously than the Port of Oakland, without resource-draining and dispiriting adversarial litigation (Hanf and Smits, 1991). The deadlock in Oakland, the Rotterdam experience suggests, is not inherent in the task. It stemmed from a particular institutional structure, characterized by fragmented authority, complex and constrictive legal rules, wide access to litigation, and unpredictable risks of judicial reversal.

Because it derives from basic structures of American government, the Oakland story is far from unique. The same kind of expensive, time-consuming, legally unpredictable, extortive, and economically destructive legal wrangling is a common occurrence in the United States. Virtually every major port-dredging plan, on the East Coast as well as the West, must slog though the quicksand of litigation or invest huge sums in "mitigation projects" extorted by the threat of litigation.[4] Adversarial legalism recurs, imposing similar risks and costs and concessions, in virtually every kind of large-scale development or construction effort—from siting garbage dumps (Welles and Engel, 2000) to building highways (Detlefsen, 1995), factories (Harris, 1995), and housing projects (Frieden, 1979). The complexities and costly delays of adversarial legalism burden commercial disputes, criminal prosecutions, and rulemaking by regulatory agencies. Adversarial legalism slows down and imposes large expenses on American processes for compensating injured people, drawing electoral district lines, battling discrimination, caring for the mentally ill, choosing labor union representatives, preserving wildlife habitats, financing businesses, running hospitals and schools, and cleaning up chemical waste sites. No other country comes close.

The U.S. Superfund program for cleanup of hazardous waste disposal sites, one study noted, generates so much time-consuming litigation among former chemical waste disposers that "by mid-1990 . . . after 10 years of program operation, only sixty-three of the more than twelve hundred National Priorities List sites had been cleaned up" (Church and Nakamura, 1993). As several studies of regulatory rulemaking have shown, new rules concerning workplace health risks (Mendeloff, 1987), hazardous air pollutants (Dwyer, 1990), and motor vehicle safety features (Mashaw and Harfst, 1987) were bogged down in the federal bureaucracy for years, while administrators called for additional scientific research, economic analyses, and legal opinions, hoping to ward off judicial reversal—a threat that their counterparts in other economically advanced democracies do not experience (Badaracco, 1985; Brickman et al., 1985). European and Japanese multinational corporations often maintain larger staffs of in-house attorneys in their U.S. subsidiaries than in their corporate headquarters and other subsidiaries combined, and they spend more in the United States for reporting, record-keeping, testing, and certifying to regulators (and potentially to courts) that their companies are complying with the law (Kagan, 2000; Kagan and Axelrad, 1997). In lawsuits seeking damages for personal injuries, lawyers for both sides absorb an astonishing 40 or 50 percent of the sums that liability insurers expend on claims (Kakalik and Pace, 1986; Abraham and Liebman, 1993: 108)—far more than is absorbed by the "transaction costs" of injury compensation systems in Western Europe or Japan.

In the Oakland Harbor saga, the American legal and regulatory system was not malfunctioning. It was being used as directed, or at least as officially permitted and encouraged. Each regulatory agency and interest group whose legal actions postponed harbor dredging was invoking regulatory standards, procedures, and analytical requirements that are written into law. The redundant reviews by a multiplicity of specialized agencies, along with the laws that enabled fishermen and county water districts to haul government officials into court, were consciously designed bulwarks against environmental heedlessness. Each of those laws, viewed on its own, seems rational and balanced, attentive to economic as well as to environmental values, well grounded in democratic opinion. Nevertheless, the cumulative outcome was irrational, unjust, and lamentably inefficient. And that is because the mechanisms of American adversarial legalism—the very kinds of mechanisms that sometimes block environmentally obtuse development projects, that yielded *Brown v. Board of Education* and the prison reform decisions, and that sometimes free the unjustly accused—produce irrational, unjust, and inefficient outcomes as well. Adversarial legalism is Janus-faced.

That the same thing can produce both good and evil should not be regarded as a paradox. Bureaucracies repeatedly are created because they provide higher levels of honesty and consistency than other modes of administration, but bureaucracies repeatedly are reviled for their frustrating caution and red tape. The busy hospital that relieves the suffering of the diseased and wounded also produces dangerous wastes and instances of medical malpractice. The welfare system that generously assists the needy also generates a certain amount of fraud, dependency, and irresponsibility. "For every jury that departs from the law in order to acquit Vietnam War resisters," George Fletcher (1994: 35) observed, "another convicts the Scottsboro boys."

In the same way, the heroic image of adversarial legalism is not false. It is only incomplete. As a system for administering criminal justice and resolving civil disputes, the engines of American adversarial legalism can and often do advance the cause of justice in uniquely progressive ways. But the engines don't always work well or work the same for everyone. And even when they operate as advertised, they are so complex, expensive, slow, and erratic that they generate deeply distressing side effects. To offer one more metaphor, American adversarial legalism is like a baseball slugger who leads the league in magnificent home runs—but who also misses routine plays in the outfield, often arrives late to the game, and demands such a large salary that many fans can't afford to come to the ballpark.

Of course, in most cases adversarial legalism produces neither home runs nor terrible errors, neither the heroic justice of the southern prison cases nor the counterproductive legal warfare of the Oakland Harbor story. Because full-scale adversarial legalism is so cumbersome, time-consuming, and costly, disputants usually seek informal compromise rather than all-out adversarial conflict. In many other cases, the outcome is mixed: adversarial legalism does produce justice but at a disturbingly high price in time and money.

Focusing on Adversarial Legalism's Costs

Let us stipulate, then, that adversarial legalism sometimes works well, yielding social benefits that far outweigh its costs; that it sometimes works badly, generating social costs that outweigh its intended benefits; and that sometimes it produces a difficult-to-evaluate mix of social costs and benefits. In principle, a comprehensive evaluation of adversarial legalism would attempt to work out an overall ledger. But gathering the data, coding the outcomes, and comparing incommensurable consequences (better prison conditions versus the toll on economic well-being due to legally imposed opportunity costs) all present unfathomable problems. In the alternative, one might focus only on the system's successes as an inspiration or model for future cases—for there surely are many situations in which heroic litigation would be highly desirable. But this book concentrates, by and large, on the social costs of adversarial legalism.

Why emphasize the Oakland dredging story rather than the Alabama prison reform litigation? Why focus on adversarial legalism's dark shadow rather than on its luminous successes? Indeed, why concentrate on the extreme cases that lie within either tail of the distribution, rather than on the American legal system's more typical cases? One reason is that in institutional analysis, as in medicine, pathological cases have diagnostic value, revealing fundamental systemic mechanisms. If we understand the reasons for the adverse effects of legal institutions and practices, they perhaps can be altered for the better. Second, the pathologies of adversarial legalism are of immense social importance, for they are both unpredictable and enormously debilitating. They engender costly "defensive medicine," deter the assertion of just claims and defenses, distort and delay the implementation of government programs, undermine faith in the justice system, and invite political overreaction. If we are to retain the system's virtues, it is important to understand and hence to tame its vices. And to do that, it is necessary to explore the reasons why adversarial legalism has come to loom so large in the American system of justice.

3

The Political Construction of Adversarial Legalism

The Netherlands is a pluralistic, intensively regulated nation. Nevertheless, sociologist Erhard Blankenburg found that Dutch civil litigation rates are much lower than those in neighboring Germany and Belgium. The reason is that "Dutch jurists have found many ways to avoid handling conflicts in a legalistic way. A rich supply of institutions offers legal aid, legal protection, and conflict resolution alternatives" (Blankenburg and Bruinsma, 1991: 51). In this lies an important lesson: institutional alternatives to courts, not cultural dispositions toward "litigiousness," shape the propensity to rely on litigation to resolve disputes.

Similarly, adversarial legalism in the United States does not arise from a deep-rooted American propensity to bring lawsuits. Many, perhaps most, Americans are reluctant to sue, even when they have grounds to do so, and they often disparage those who do.[1] Rather, American adversarial legalism arises from political traditions and legal arrangements that provide incentives to resort to adversarial legal weapons. Such weapons are used far less frequently in parliamentary democracies with different institutional mechanisms for addressing social problems. Put another way, American adversarial legalism arises from the relative *absence* of institutions that effectively channel contending parties and groups into less expensive and more efficient ways of resolving disputes, ensuring accountability, regulating business, and compensating victims of injury or economic misfortune (Wilensky, 1983).

Glance again at the list of comparative studies in Table 1 in Chapter 1. In virtually every policy area studied, the other democracies, rather than relying on adversarial legalism, tend to implement public policy and resolve disputes by other means. These include powerful national bureaucracies or corporatist bodies[2] in which internal administrative or political mechanisms, rather than lawsuits and judicial review, provide the primary mode of accountability for regulatory and other policy decisions. The other countries have more comprehensive social insurance programs, which serve as the primary recourse for injured persons and victims of misfortune; accordingly, liability law recoveries in court are limited. In most other democracies judiciaries are professionally (not politically) selected and are deferential to parliamentary decisions. Judges and law enforcement bodies engage in proactive (rather than lawyer-driven and adversarial) fact-finding, and they are dedicated more to achieving legal consistency than to social problem-solving. Those kinds of institutional arrangements, however, do not grow easily in the shifting sands of American politics.

Adversarial legalism does. Its roots are nurtured, as already noted, by a political culture that demands comprehensive governmental protections from harm, injustice, and environmental dangers—and hence a more powerful, activist government—but that also mistrusts governmental power, and hence fragments political authority and seeks to keep it accountable through lawsuits and judicial review. This chapter shows how American political culture and its governmental structure shaped adversarial legalism, why it increased dramatically in the years since 1960, and why it persists despite widely heralded efforts to curtail it.

Something Old, Something New

We nod with familiarity when modern authors cite Alexis de Tocqueville's observation that in the United States of the 1820s and 1830s, most major political issues became judicial issues. The Supreme Court's Dred Scott decision helped precipitate the Civil War. In the late nineteenth century and the first third of the twentieth, business interests often resorted to adversarial legalism, urging the courts to strike down prolabor statutes and to issue injunctions against striking workers. It took twenty-one days just to pick a jury in the 1886 trial of eight radicals in Chicago who were charged with throwing a bomb that killed police officers in Haymarket Square (Friedman, 1993). An 1895 editorial in the *Street Railway Journal*, Lawrence Friedman (1978) reports, referred to accident liability lawsuits as a "nightmare" and a "sword of Damocles," while railroad executives complained about ambulance-chasing lawyers. Wigmore's treatise on the law of evidence, published in 1904, consumed five thick volumes (id. at 248).

One might be led to conclude, therefore, that there is nothing new about contemporary American adversarial legalism, since it has always been woven into the fabric of American life and politics. But that would not be quite correct. It is true that early in the nation's history, four basic engines of adversarial legalism were already in place: litigant-dominated modes of adjudication; a politically selected judiciary, with powers to reverse legislative and administrative decisions; a highly entrepreneurial legal profession; and trial by jury. Compared to their counterparts in England and Western Europe, nineteenth-century Americans probably were more likely to use law and litigation to maintain a sense of moral order. They lived in a more pluralistic, more transient, society, with weaker institutions of social control. Free from traditions of deference to kings and priests and guilds, Americans have long been inclined to challenge authority in an adversarial manner. David Bayley's (1976) observation, even if a bit of an overgeneralization, captures a common strain in American culture: "An American accused by a policeman is very likely to respond, 'Why me?' A Japanese more often says, 'I'm sorry.' The American shows anger . . . [and] contests the accusation and tries to humble the policeman; a Japanese accepts the accusation and tries to kindle benevolence."

Yet the adversarial legalism that has pervaded the United States in the last few decades is both more extensive and more intense than that of the nineteenth century and the first half of the twentieth (Kagan, 1991a). The dramatic increase began in the mid-1960s. Before then, there were few legal struggles akin to the Alabama prison reform case and the endless battle over dredging Oakland Harbor. In 1960 standing to sue governmental agencies was more restricted; "public interest" groups did not routinely appear in court. Massive class actions against business corporations and welfare departments were rare, as were damage suits against police departments. The average civil and criminal trial was far shorter than today's. Before the late 1960s, American administrative agencies, school boards, highway planners, and zoning boards were much less likely than their contemporary counterparts to be challenged in court. In 1960 the threat of litigation was not an omnipresent consideration, as it is today, in corporate finance, electoral redistricting, seaport planning, and the practice of medicine. Nominations to the Supreme Court did not unleash intensely partisan, interest group conflicts of the magnitude that swirled around Robert Bork and Clarence Thomas—partly because the Supreme Court had not yet issued rulings establishing, and then threatening to restrict, women's constitutional right to abortion.

In 1960 there was one lawyer for every 627 people in the United States. By 1995 the ratio had doubled to 1:307 (Curran and Carson, 1994). Between 1960 and 1987, *expenditures* on lawyers in the United States grew *sixfold*, from $9 billion annually to $54 billion (in constant 1983 dollars), almost tripling the share of GNP consumed by legal services (Sander and Williams, 1989: 434–435). Between 1960 and 1980, federal court appellate cases involving constitutional issues increased sevenfold (Kagan, 1987). Between 1970 and the late 1980s, federal indictments of public officials swelled from less than 100 per year to almost 1,000 per year, which, as Ginsberg and Shefter (1990: 5–7) point out, "suggests growing use of criminal investigation of public officials as a mode of partisan struggle for political advantage."

Medical malpractice suits, rare in 1960, reached 4.3 per 100 insured physicians in 1970 and 18.3 per 100 in 1986 (Quam et al., 1987: 1529–1531, 1597–1600; Dewees et al., 1991). The volume and rate of state appellate and federal court cases involving public schools, roughly stable from 1920 through 1960, doubled in the 1967–1981 period (Tyack and Benavot, 1985). In the decades following the California Supreme Court's 1971 decision in *Serrano v. Priest*, litigants filed more than sixty cases in forty-one states challenging the constitutionality of school finance methods, and in many states litigants and judges assumed a significant ongoing role in reshaping school-funding policy (Heise, 1995). In 1990 a former CEO of a major American bank told me, "I sit on a lot of corporate boards of directors. I started using my stopwatch to see how much of each board meeting is taken up by lawyers. Years ago it was about 5 percent. Recently it has gone up to 40 or even 50 percent."

The period before 1960 was not a Golden Age. It was harder to challenge governmental and economic power, and power was not always benign. Racial, ethnic, and gender discrimination usually went unchallenged. Government controls on pollution were weak or nonexistent. Many regulatory agencies were soft on the industries they were supposed to control. Citizens, especially poorer citizens, often had little recourse when highways were thrust through their neighborhoods, when chemical waste sites were located near their homes, or when policemen, school principals, or bureaucrats treated them arbitrarily. The point is that the 1960s initiated a period of striking change in the level and reach of adversarial legalism. Something new had been added to the stew of American law. It became much more spicy. It was served up more often and in larger portions. It nourished more people— while giving more indigestion to others. To understand these changes, we must explore the mind-set of the cooks and the ways in which the structure of the kitchen and the demands of the diners channeled their choices.

The Demand for "Total Justice"

Most obviously, the increases in adversarial legalism reflected an outpouring of new legal rules, rights, and obligations. State courts made sweeping changes in tort law, making it easier for injured people to sue and obtain substantial damage awards from doctors and landlords, manufacturers and municipal governments. The Supreme Court's "due process revolution" enlarged the legal rights of criminal defendants, prisoners, and welfare recipients. Judicial decisions and congressional statutes established government-funded public defenders' offices for criminal cases and legal services offices for the poor. Between the mid-1960s and mid-1970s, federal and state governments enacted an unprecedented wave of regulatory statutes concerning pollution control, land use, consumer protection, and nondiscrimination in employment and education. They also mandated a more legalistic and punitive approach to regulatory enforcement, not only by regulatory officials but also by advocacy groups acting as "private attorneys general" (Ackerman and Hassler, 1981; Bardach and Kagan, 1982).

But why was there such an outpouring of new law? The proximate causes were the powerful political movements that swept through the United States in the 1960s. Beginning midway in that decade, the United States experienced what political scientist Samuel Huntington labels a period of "creedal passion." During such recurrent episodes in American history, he argues, many citizens become outraged by the gap between America's liberal, egalitarian political creed and the inequalities that stem from contemporary institutional practices (Huntington, 1981). Caught up in the politics of creedal passion, citizens leap the channels of electoral politics and turn to demonstration and protest, as in the case of the populist agrarian rallies of the 1880s or the sit-down strikes and marches by the labor movement and the unemployed during the Great Depression. Similarly, in the 1960s the moral passion, street demonstrations, and civil disobedience of the civil rights movement—and then the anti–Vietnam War movement—overwhelmed the incremental processes and compromises of "normal politics." These movements energized and provided a model for others, such as environmentalism and feminism. Active, specialized "public interest groups" were organized to demonstrate and lobby on behalf of consumer safety, the aged, the poor, tenants, children, the handicapped, welfare recipients, and so on. Cumulatively, they demanded major transformations in established social and economic patterns and a major expansion of the role of the federal government.

Policy entrepreneurs in Congress and the judiciary were extremely responsive (Wilson, 1980b). Southern states were commanded to register black voters en masse. "Technology-forcing" statutes instructed industry to control pollution and prevent accidents. The Supreme Court banned prayer in public schools, ordered reapportionment of state legislatures, and gave women the right to obtain abortions. Judges ordered school districts to bus school children across town to achieve racial balance. Others ordered the "deinstitutionalization" of mental patients. State court judges reshaped tort law in order to compel businesses, professionals, and local governments to develop better safety precautions.

To some observers, moreover, the legal revolution of the 1960s and 1970s reflected not merely a periodic burst of idealism and political activism but a more enduring change in American political culture. To Aaron Wildavsky (1990), it suggested an upsurge in an "egalitarian" spirit among American political and cultural elites—critical of inequalities of wealth and power, and impatient for governmental action against the technological risks and economic vicissitudes unleashed by powerful corporations (Polisar and Wildavsky, 1989). Lawrence Friedman (1985), surveying American legal culture, pointed to rising popular expectations of "total justice"—the notion that because rich societies now have insurance and other ways of compensating victims of unfair treatment, personal injury, and unexpected health care costs, they should be required by law to do so.[3] In contrast to their more fatalistic forebears, Friedman noted, late-twentieth-century Americans see that modern societies can devise means to prevent misfortune and mistreatment—regulatory inspections, double hulls for oil tankers, tests to detect carcinogens, better education and nutrition for poor children. If those techniques exist, it is unjust not to use them. The law, therefore, should require them. Such ideas, Friedman (like Wildavsky) suggests, penetrated the thinking of many, if not all, members of the law-shaping governmental elite—law professors, appellate court lawyers, judges, legislative staffers, lobbyists, and journalists. Hence the judges' expansion of liability in tort law. Hence elite endorsement of stringent environmental and safety regulation and broader antidiscrimination laws.

These changes in political and legal culture, however, are not quite enough to explain the intensification of adversarial legalism. Popular demands for governmental social engineering and for "total justice" are not unique to the United States. In the 1960s Western European democracies extended preexisting governmental protections against misfortune and added new ones to limit environmental degradation and unfair treatment. Like the United States, they liberalized divorce laws, created women's rights to obtain abortions (Glendon, 1987), banned discrimination in employment, and expanded long-standing national social insurance and health care schemes (Wilensky, 1975; Kamerman and Kahn, 1988). European "Greens" battled successfully for pollution controls, restrictions on nuclear power, and limits on hazardous chemicals that compare in stringency with those of the United States (Vogel, 1986; Brickman et al., 1985; Lundquist, 1980). Western European laws protecting employees from arbitrary termination, restricting urban sprawl, and guarding tenants' interests generally are much stricter than those in the United States.

The expansion of entitlements and regulation in Western Europe, however, did not produce American-style adversarial legalism.[4] There, national governmental bureaucracies and corporatist bodies implement ambitious regulations and welfare state entitlements without much reliance on—and hence without much interference from—courts and lawyers. American-style securities class actions, mass "toxic tort" cases, and court-ordered institutional reform plans are virtually unknown. Fierce controversies sometimes erupt, as in the case of siting decisions for development projects, but they usually are resolved in political and administrative forums, not in courts. Outcomes rarely are shaped, as in the Oakland Harbor dredging story, by the sheer costs and delays of legal procedures.

In sum, similar winds of change blew through both Western Europe and the United States. The difference is that the winds were filtered through sharply contrasting political structures and traditions. Somewhat similar basic policy norms emerged, therefore, on both sides of the Atlantic, but the national methods of establishing and implementing those norms were markedly different. To fully understand the intensification of adversarial legalism in the United States, we must adopt what is currently called a "new institutionalist" approach (Ikenberry, 1988; McCann, 1999), examining how political pressures for total justice interacted with and were shaped by inherited legal structures and modes of government.

Fragmented Governmental Authority and Adversarial Legalism

To state the argument briefly, adversarial legalism in the United States has been stimulated by a fundamental mismatch between a changing legal culture and an inherited set of political attitudes and structures. Americans have attempted to articulate and implement the socially transformative policies of an activist, regulatory welfare state through the political and legal institutions of a decentralized, nonhierarchical governmental system. In the absence of cohesive political parties, a strong national bureaucracy, and a widely trusted social insurance system, proponents of regulatory change and social welfare measures fought for citizens' rights to obtain benefits and influence policy through litigation.

Damaska's Typology

In *The Faces of Justice and State Authority* (1986), Mirjan Damaska formulates a typology of legal processes built on two dimensions. The first dimension contrasts *hierarchical* with *coordinate* modes of organizing administrative and legal processes. The hierarchical model, toward which continental European states incline, emphasizes strong, highly professional national bureaucracies, directly responsible to a parliamentary cabinet. Fidelity to official policies and uniformity of case-by-case decisionmaking are the reigning ideals of hierarchical law and administration. Legal and administrative officials are relatively insulated from the potentially corrupting influence of local politicians, wealthy citizens, and public opinion. American legal and administrative processes, on the other hand, lean toward what Damaska labels a coordinate organization of authority that seeks to counteract the potential for tyranny or political bias inherent in centralized political and legal authority. The power to make and apply policy and law, therefore, is fragmented among many governmental bodies and courts, staffed by officials primarily responsible to local political constituencies. Coordination is exercised horizontally, through one governmental body's capacity to check another and through citizens' rights to challenge governmental decisions in court.

The second dimension of Damaska's typology contrasts two polar visions of the proper role of government. At one extreme is the *activist state,* dedicated to the aggressive management, mobilization, or transformation of the national economy and society. At the other pole, the political culture supports a *reactive state,* expected only to provide an orderly framework for private economic and social interaction. The reactive state formulates and implements policy primarily by resolving conflicts generated by competing interests.

There are obvious affinities between an activist state and a hierarchical organization of authority, with its centrally managed bureaucracy and judiciary, willing and able to implement official policy. Similarly, a reactive state fits nicely with a coordinate organization of authority, with its wide openings for civilian influence, its skepticism about state-enforced norms, and its reliance on adversarial argument. In the reactive, conflict-resolving state, when government is involved in a dispute with citizens, the government official stands on the same plane, in theory, as the individual; he represents just another competing interest. A judge attentive to individual rights must have the last word, not (as in the activist state) the government official bent on policy implementation.

Reactive Government and Coordinate Authority

Through the nineteenth century and well into the twentieth, the United States blended a reactive state and coordinate authority. Both flowed naturally from the political liberalism that animated the American Revolution and constitutional founding (Hartz, 1955).[5] In the liberal vision, governmental power must be limited and restrained by law, invoked and applied by rights-bearing citizens.

American political culture has also harbored a turbulent "populist" strain, deeply mistrustful of accumulations of economic power, quick to believe that government officials will engage in self-dealing or will be corrupted by business interests (Goodwyn, 1978). If powerful men cannot be trusted, power should be fragmented, held accountable to watchful local electorates and to the rule of law, invoked and applied in courts staffed by ordinary people serving as judges and jurors. Conversely, American business interests have been mistrustful of the motives and competence of democratically elected politicians. Hence business has also favored constitutional and other legal controls on government, enforceable in the courts.

These basic political attitudes were embodied in constitutions, state as well as federal, that splintered governmental authority among separate "branches," establishing legal constraints on each. The federal Constitution compelled the national government to concede much governing power to the states, while state constitutions guaranteed generous measures of "home rule" to local governments (Briffault, 1990). Both federal and state constitutions included a government-limiting Bill of Rights, enforceable in local courts at the behest of ordinary citizens.

With a tradition of limited, decentralized government, the United States developed what some students of comparative politics have called a "weak state," highly responsive to popular opinion and organized private interests, as opposed to a "strong state," capable of dominating and transforming civil society through powerful bureaucratic structures (Krasner, 1978: 55–70; Huber et al., 1994). In contrast to Western European nations, where strong royal bureaucracies preceded the development of democracy, nineteenth-century American government was dominated not by legislatures and bureaucrats but by decentralized political parties and locally selected judges (Skowronek, 1982; Shefter, 1994). State legislatures met for limited terms and for limited pay, which further encouraged judges to become active policymakers (Horwitz, 1977)—albeit in a highly decentralized, incremental, and "reactive" or "conflict-resolving" mode. Hence de Tocqueville's (1835) observation that in America important political issues repeatedly were transmuted into judicial questions and that politics and social life were pervaded by the vocabulary of the law.

Decentralized, "coordinate" governmental structures reinforced a reactive approach to governance. Separation of powers, bicameral legislatures, and fragmented political parties created a large number of "veto points" at which special interests could strive to block governmental action that displeased them. Decentralized government favored political parties built by the dispensation of patronage to local supporters. Professional governmental bureaucracies were thus slower to develop in the United States than in Europe, while American state and city governments were often corrupt and distrusted.

In the late nineteenth century and early in the twentieth, business interests turned to the courts, successfully in many cases, to obtain constitutional decisions limiting national governmental authority over local business and employment practices; this further retarded expansion of national regulatory bureaucracies. It took almost twenty years and a constitutional amendment to overturn an 1895 Supreme Court decision invalidating a federal income tax *(Pollock v. Farmers' Loan and Trust Co.)*. Politically conservative judges also struck down many state regulatory programs and taxes. To be sure, the courts did not strike down *most* regulatory statutes (Friedman, 1973: 396–405). During the Progressive Era, city, state, and even federal bureaucracies grew rapidly. But American government remained much smaller, less centralized, and less dominant in society than the governments of such countries as Germany, France, and Japan. Compared to Western Europe, economic life in the United States—not only in the nineteenth century but in the twentieth as well—was more fully the province of private business firms and less subject to governmental financing, control, and guidance. Business relationships, labor relations, and business-government interactions were policed primarily by litigation and by judge-made rules that favored entrepreneurial energy, freedom of contract, and private property (Hurst, 1956; Horwitz, 1977). This too reinforced a reactive, conflict-resolving approach to governance.

Activist Government and the New Deal

In all industrialized democracies, twentieth-century political demands have pushed governments to become more activist—to steer and stabilize the economy and to provide a measure of economic security to injured workers, the unemployed, and the aged. In the United States, however, those political demands were channeled through the political structures that fragmented and decentralized power. And as Damaska (1986: 13) pointed out, "A state with many independent power centers *and* a powerful desire to transform society can be likened to a man with ardent appetites and poor instruments for their satisfaction." When that hungry man was an American political activist in the 1960s, he grabbed the "instrument" that best seemed to address his dilemma—adversarial legalism. In the 1930s an even hungrier man tried something else.

Confronted with the crisis of the Great Depression, Franklin Roosevelt's New Deal directly addressed the tension between fragmented government and demands for transformative governmental action. To the New Dealers, "a system of centralized and unified powers, bypassing the states and the judiciary, seemed indispensable to allow for dramatic and frequent governmental regulation" (Sunstein, 1990: 23). The Roosevelt administration strengthened the central government and extended its administrative reach, substituting national, bureaucratically administered programs for markets and state law. The president and Congress established public works programs, agricultural stabilization programs, national bank insurance, and the social security retirement program, all administered by federal agencies. The National Recovery Act (NRA), in a move evocative of European corporatist arrangements, mandated nationwide price-and-wage stabilization agencies for each industrial sector (Hawley, 1966).

The Supreme Court, a "coordinate-model" institution dominated by defenders of the inherited reactive regime, held that the NRA and several other major New Deal statutes were unconstitutional. The New Dealers, in response, reenacted those statutes in different form and tried to push the courts out of the ring. Congress forbade judicial injunctions against strikes. It shifted legal disputes about antiunion practices from the courts into an administrative tribunal, the National Labor Relations Board. Although President Roosevelt had to abandon his plan to expand the Supreme Court and "pack" it with supportive Democrats, the Court backed down and upheld most major New Deal laws. Roosevelt, followed by President Truman, reshaped the judiciary; they appointed federal judges who believed in judicial deference to federal legislation and to the decisions of federal administrative agencies. Through the 1950s, the new constitutional and administrative law doctrines forged by the New Deal judges squelched litigation by business interests who opposed the expansion of federal regulation and taxation.

The huge increases in federal taxation, spending, and military procurement that occurred during World War II, together with the federal bureaucracies they spawned, persisted into the Cold War. The postwar federal government continued to assume responsibility for national economic policy. Thus from the New Deal on, the American state no longer could be characterized as mostly "reactive." It was characterized by a large measure of activism and a greater degree of centralized governmental control.

Total Justice + Fragmented Government = Adversarial Legalism

Notwithstanding the centralizing impact of the New Deal, World War II, and the Cold War, in the 1950s and early 1960s government in the United States, viewed in comparative terms, remained structurally and politically fragmented (Wilensky, 1965: xvi–xix). Most realms of law, policy, and administration—policing and criminal law, education, land use control, family, tort, and commercial law, welfare administration, and antidiscrimination policy—were still the province of state and local governments and courts. A number of important federal programs, such as unemployment insurance, disability insurance, and Aid for Dependent Children, were actually administered by state and county agencies; procedures and some standards differed from state to state and county to county (Mashaw, 1971, 1983). National political party unity was fragile. Members of Congress were responsive to pressures from local constituencies and particularized interest groups. In consequence, the federal government often appeared paralyzed, even in the face of demands for aggressive central-governmental action to advance social justice. It was that collision—between politically fragmented government and urgent political demands for action—that ignited the fires of adversarial legalism.

To take just one example, partly because of the claims to democratic virtue engendered by the Cold War, American national political elites in the 1950s had become acutely sensitive to the contradiction between the egalitarian "American creed" and the ugly reality of southern apartheid (Dudziak, 1988; Rosenberg, 1991). Hampered by the constitutional limits of federalism, however, the national government could not displace local democratic control of public school policy and law enforcement. There was no national Minister of Education or Minister of Justice who could give instructions to segregationist local school officials or racist sheriffs, or replace them if they were recalcitrant. Because American political parties were not hierarchically controlled, southern Democrats in the Senate repeatedly blocked congressional civil rights legislation.

The coordinate structure of American government, on the other hand, encouraged civil rights leaders to circumvent the legislative deadlock by turning to the courts. Civil rights lawyers argued that because legislatures, federal and state, had persistently failed to act against a nationally recognized injustice, it was incumbent on the courts to step into the breach. Such an argument might not have swayed an apolitical judiciary, such as Great Britain's or France's, committed to legal formality and disinclined to engage in social problem-solving. But the American judiciary, staffed with ex-politicians (Goldman, 1967),[6] was open to arguments based on substantive justice. (When lawyers cited an ostensibly dispositive legal precedent, Chief Justice Earl Warren, a former governor of California, was said to have responded, "Yes, but is it fair?") Thus in 1954 the Supreme Court, arguing that prior precedents were based on flawed sociological assumptions, held that legally segregated schools violated the equal protection clause *(Brown v. Board of Education)*.

The NAACP had cast its argument and requested remedy in the form of a constitutionally grounded legal right. This meant—at least in the American political tradition—that the policy could be invoked by ordinary citizens and citizens' groups (like the NAACP) and could be enforced by ordinary judges, state or federal, in hundreds of county courthouses. Thus private enforcement of public law by means of litigation—a major feature of adversarial legalism—became a primary mode of implementing national antisegregation policy (although an only moderately effective one).[7] And henceforth the African-American struggle for equality tended to revolve around the formal legal category of nondiscrimination, as exemplified by the rhetorical emphasis on "civil rights" (Sarat, 1997).

The 1960s "due process revolution" in criminal procedure repeated this pattern. The national legal elite, prodded by the civil rights movement, had become increasingly dismayed by abusive police practices in segregated southern states and in crime-ridden northern cities. Yet Congress and the Department of Justice did not have clear hierarchical authority to impose reforms on hundreds of local police departments and courthouses. The only viable strategy for change seemed to be a further elaboration of *coordinate* controls, using the tools of adversarial legalism—lawyering, litigation, and judicial policymaking.

Responding to particularized petitions for review, the Supreme Court during Chief Justice Earl Warren's tenure set aside legal precedents and reinterpreted the Constitution. The Court elaborated new nationwide rules to regulate pretrial detention, interrogation of suspects, searches for evidence, station-house lineups, and jury selection. In addition, the Court mandated *adversarial* enforcement mechanisms for those new legal standards—free counsel for indigent defendants and an "exclusionary rule" for evidence obtained in violation of the Supreme Court's rules. Again, because these new policies and procedures were cast as constitutional rules, they were largely insulated from reversal or amendment by legislatures or police administrators, state or federal. This ensured that policy development and implementation would remain in the province of adversarial legalism. Defense lawyers' motions to suppress illegally obtained evidence and confessions became a routine practice in local criminal prosecutions,[8] and the appellate courts, not state legislatures, laid down the principles for determining when police need a warrant, when they can search a suspect's car trunk, and so on. The result has been a moderately effective but unusually adversarial, confusing, and politically controversial way of regulating local criminal justice officers (Walker, 1993; Bradley, 1993).

Fragmented Government and the Politics of Rights

Congress was just as active as the federal courts in promoting adversarial legalism. In the 1960s Democratic majorities faced the same structural problem that confronted New Deal reformers: how to implement socially transformative legislation in a coordinately organized, decentralized political system. The New Deal tried to consolidate and extend the powers of the central government and its new bureaucracies, displacing state governments and the courts. In the 1960s and 1970s, in contrast, Congress embraced adversarial legalism.

Between 1964 and 1977, in a truly extraordinary surge of activity, Congress passed twenty-five major environmental and civil rights acts, plus far-reaching statutes regulating workplace safety, consumer lending, product safety, private pension funds, and local public education.[9] At the same time, Congress was reluctant—for political, fiscal, and constitutional reasons—to create huge federal bureaucracies, with offices in every metropolitan area, to enforce all these demanding regulatory programs. In many cases, therefore, Congress assigned primary enforcement responsibility to state and local governmental officials. But then how could reformers and their congressional allies be sure that the new federal norms would be faithfully implemented? Adversarial legalism provided one answer. Regulatory reformers couched their goals in the form of sweeping legal rights—to equal treatment, a safe workplace, clean water, clean air (Melnick, 1995; Landy and Levin, 1995). Armed with those rights, individual victims of injustice and energetic reform lawyers could act as "private attorneys general," bringing lawsuits against state and local governments for half-hearted implementation of federal laws, or they could sue regulated businesses directly. To energize the private attorneys general, Congress enacted scores of one-way fee-shifting statutes, which enabled successful plaintiffs to recover lawyers' fees from governmental and corporate defendants but did not require them, if they lost, to pay the defendants' lawyers' bills (Greve, 1989a; O'Connor and Epstein, 1985).

In sum, whereas European polities generally rely on hierarchically organized national bureaucracies to hold local officials accountable to national policies, the U.S. Congress mobilized a distinctly American army of enforcers—a decentralized, ideologically motivated array of private advocacy groups and lawyers. For example, the landmark federal Education for All Handicapped Children Act (EAHCA), enacted in 1975, required local public schools to provide all children, regardless of handicap, an "appropriate public education." Rather than creating a federal enforcement bureaucracy, Congress imposed detailed due process procedures on local educators and gave parents of handicapped children legal rights to appeal, first administratively, then to court, from educational plans with which they disagreed. Predictably, adversarial, legalistic hearings became common (Neal and Kirp, 1986), and federal courts became the principal forums for defining "appropriate public education"(Melnick, 1995).[10]

Congress also invited private attorneys general to police policy implementation by *federal* agencies. The public interest movement of the 1960s and 1970s, Michael McCann (1986) has shown, wanted to expand the regulatory power of the federal government but remained deeply suspicious of centralized power. Books published by consumer advocate Ralph Nader argued that regulatory agencies were all too easily "captured" by powerful regulated businesses and their allies in government. The reformers' solution was to subject the more powerful federal regulatory state to the checks of coordinately organized adversarial legalism. In McCann's phrase, they sought to institutionalize a "judicial model of the state."

The national legislature was sympathetic. Especially after 1968, when the executive branch was controlled by Republicans, a Democratic Congress willingly gave citizen watchdog groups and courts more leverage over administrative policymaking and enforcement. In contrast to New Deal regulatory statutes, which granted administrative policymakers a great deal of discretion, the regulatory statutes of the late 1960s and 1970s set forth detailed rules and strict deadlines. Legislative specificity enabled advocacy groups to challenge administrative leniency or inaction as illegal, and gave courts grounds to reverse agency decisions (Melnick, 1992a, 1992b). Regulations promulgated by administrative agencies, the new statutes also said, had to be made through formal, adversarial procedures reviewable in court: no more backroom deals with regulated businesses (Shapiro, 1988). In the same spirit, judges often discerned "implied" statutory rights to sue government and to bring private enforcement actions, even when the original legislation was silent on the subject.[11]

Lawsuits against the federal government and appeals of governmental decisions, not surprisingly, increased apace. By the early 1980s, more than 50 percent of the Environmental Protection Agency's new major regulations were blocked, at least temporarily, by court challenges (Coglianese, 1997). Lawsuits and appeals also blocked or delayed virtually every U.S. Forest Service management plan, (*The Economist*, 1990: 28), new motor vehicle safety regulation (Mashaw and Harfst, 1991), federal lease for offshore petroleum exploration (Lester, 1992), and seaport dredging plan (Kagan, 1991b).

During the late 1960s and early 1970s, even as the reach and power of the federal government was expanding, the American electorate became more mistrustful of government (Griffin, 1991: 701–709), and political leaders seemingly became more mistrustful of each other. Voters more often elected legislatures and chief executives of different parties (Fiorina, 1991: 646–650; Thurber, 1991: 653–657). The civil rights and anti–Vietnam War movements splintered the authority of political party leaders, instigating a more decentralized political primary and fund-raising system (Polsby, 1983). The power of congressional committee chairmen was redistributed among a multiplicity of subcommittees (Davidson, 1981). Campaign finance reforms intensified each legislator's search for independent sources of funding and support. Taking all these changes together, political party leaders were stripped of a considerable measure of control over policy formulation (Huntington, 1981; Polsby, 1983; Ranney, 1983). The resulting "hyperpluralism" further promoted adversarial legalism. Here is why.

In political systems without "dominant disciplined political parties" it makes sense for interest groups and momentarily strong political coalitions to demand enactment of highly detailed laws, enforceable in court, for that will help insulate today's policy victories from reversal following tomorrow's electoral loss (Cooter and Ginsburg, 1996: 305; Moe, 1989; Landes and Posner, 1975). Thus in the United States, beginning in the late 1960s, politically divided government and fragmented political parties encouraged and enabled organized interest groups—representing particular localities, industries, or ideologies—to demand statutory amendments that would help them exert influence on policy implementation and challenge unsympathetic administrative officials in court (Moe, 1989). American statutes have always been less carefully drafted, and hence less coherent, than those of, say, the British Parliament, in which cohesive majority governments need not compromise with the current minority (Atiyah and Summers, 1987). But in an era of divided government and weak political party unity, American legislation got worse. In Congress, statutes had to be painfully stitched together by shifting, issue-specific coalitions. Legislative proponents and presidents could gather support for their bills only by adding a variety of loopholes and side-payments demanded by a multitude of stakeholders. Individual senators and House subcommittee chairs often added hastily drafted last-minute amendments (Smith, 1989). Divided government did not block congressional lawmaking (Mayhew, 1991) but it made legislation more complex, lengthy, and confusing. Multisubject omnibus acts—the impenetrable Employee Retirement Income Security Act (ERISA), the 400-page 1990 Clean Air Act, and their ilk—resembled incoherent patchwork quilts, laden with legally contradictory or incomprehensible provisions. This style of legislation magnified legal uncertainty, virtually demanding subsequent litigation and judicial reconstruction of congressional policy.

Tax legislation provides a striking example. Comparing American, British, and Swedish taxation systems, political scientist Sven Steinmo (1993: 38) observes:

> The American tax system is by far the most complex system in the world. There are myriad special exemptions, deductions, credits, adjustments, allowances, rate schedules, special tariffs, minimum and maximum taxes designed to affect certain classes, groups, regions, industries, professions, states, cities, companies, families, and individuals. No other tax system in the industrialized world comes anywhere close to the degree of specificity found in the U.S. Federal Revenue Code.

Steinmo (1993: 141) notes that British and Swedish politicians, like their American counterparts, are under constant pressure to make tax adjustments in the name of equity or efficiency or special need. But Great Britain and Sweden, with their unified political parties and strong parliamentary governments, are better at containing interest group pressures. The mind-boggling complexity of American tax law, says Steinmo, directly reflects the fragmentation of power in Congress and in American political parties, which "made an already overly open process even more open and made an already porous system even more loophole-ridden." Compared to other democracies, not surprisingly, the implementation of tax law in the United States is far more burdened by expenditures on tax lawyers and consultants and far more prone to adversarial legalism.

Beginning in the 1960s, as courts were drawn further into the policymaking process, judge-made law similarly became more complex, uncertain, and malleable—thereby inducing more litigation. As some judges responded to popular demands for "total justice," political divisions within the American judiciary became sharper. Supreme courts, both state and federal, were riven by higher dissent rates (Friedman et al., 1981). Political struggles over judicial selection intensified. The resulting changes in judicial personnel often led to rapid shifts in legal doctrine. The ever-changing Supreme Court rulings on search and seizure law left police officers and lower court judges confused (Bradley, 1993). Again, the consequence was more adversarial legalism: when legislation is unclear and court decisions unpredictable, then disputants have more incentive to hire lawyers and seek to reshape the law to their own ends.

Political Conservatives and Adversarial Legalism

For all their criticism of "excessive litigation," Republican presidents and legislators have also been active supporters of measures that promote adversarial legalism, which helps explain its persistence even in the more conservative 1980s and 1990s. While the liberal "public interest movement" harbored some mistrust of the federal agencies created in the 1960s and 1970s for fear that they might betray reformist goals, political conservatives feared that the bureaucrats might be too zealous, hostile to business and economic growth. Hence Republicans also fought for legislative provisions that restricted administrative discretion and subjected it to legal challenge. Unable to block regulatory legislation, they tried to ensure that regulatory statutes would insist on high standards of economic and technological rationality. This gave business firms leverage for attacking regulatory decisions in court, which they did with considerable regularity.

Similarly, conservatives exploited the populist strain in American political culture—eager for the benefits of "total justice," perhaps, but also mistrustful of "big government" and hostile to tax increases. In consequence, Republicans helped craft regulatory schemes that called for private litigation, rather than public expenditure, to accomplish collective goals. For example, conservative senators' reluctance to fund a federal enforcement bureaucracy led liberal sponsors of the 1968 Truth-in-Lending Act to enact an enforcement system that relied primarily on private lawsuits against lenders (Rubin, 1991). Similarly, in 1991, as case backlogs swelled at the understaffed Equal Employment Opportunity Commission, the response of Republican president George Bush (and the Democratic Congress) was not to bolster the EEOC but to encourage more private lawsuits to implement antidiscrimination laws. The Civil Rights Restoration Act empowered plaintiffs to obtain higher money penalties, including punitive damages, in lawsuits against employers—a strategy that requires few new federal bureaucrats and no new taxes (Potter and Reesman, 1992).

In addition, public interest law firms financed by political conservatives pushed for a conservative brand of judicial activism. Conservative lawyers persuaded the Supreme Court to expand constitutional rights against regulatory restrictions on (or "takings" of) private property and to strike down race-based preferences in affirmative action programs. Activist Court rulings on both topics propelled judges throughout the country into the business of adjudicating the validity of university student admissions policies, governmental "set-asides" for minority-owned (or ostensibly minority-owned) contractors, and the decisions of local and regional zoning boards. Conservative judges loosened constitutional restrictions on police searches, forged exceptions to the exclusionary rule, and moderated other Warren Court criminal procedure precedents, but this made legal doctrine so contradictory, complicated, and uncertain that continued litigation on the same issues persists and even increases (Bradley, 1993).

Even the conservative "tort reform movement" has done relatively little to displace adversarial legalism as a method of compensating accident victims. Rather than seeking to supplant the adversarial tort/jury system with social insurance plans and administrative tribunals, the reformers' goal has simply been to make it harder for plaintiffs to obtain large damages (which tends to disadvantage the most severely injured accident victims) or to encourage more cases to settle. The basic structure of the tort liability system, permeated by adversarial legalism, has remained intact.

Fragmented Economic Power and Adversarial Legalism

While fragmentation of governmental authority is the principal causal factor, adversarial legalism also arises from the economic structure of the United States. American capitalism, resistant to control by guilds and governments, has always been more decentralized and open than European market-oriented economies. Constitutional restrictions on protectionist measures by local governments, together with common law doctrines forged by nineteenth-century probusiness judges, promoted competition. Compared to Europe and Japan, American markets have less often been dominated by cartels, centralized banks, governmental ministries, or nationalized companies (Levy, 1997; Roe, 1991; Katzenstein, 1978). In the American tradition of limited government, private enterprise has performed many social functions—the operation of railroads and utilities, the provision of health insurance and pensions, and more—that long were dominated by government or corporatist bodies in Europe.

In the competitive American economy, business factions have often sought to use law and litigation to disadvantage their economic enemies. For example, in the late nineteenth century small American merchants and shippers helped enact antitrust laws, enforceable in the courts by private lawsuit as well as by public prosecution. Local American bankers, exploiting populist aversion to Wall Street, lobbied for laws that forbade interstate banking and blocked banks from owning controlling shares in corporations. Hence the ownership and finance of American corporations, viewed in comparative perspective, are unusually fragmented and dependent on a competitive stock market (Roe, 1991). Corporations in the United States, therefore, are controlled not by a handful of bankers or by a governmental finance ministry but by the shifting pressures of aggressive investors and markets, and they rely more on lawyers and litigation to resolve conflicts.

Because the American economy has remained particularly decentralized and open, it is particularly penetrable by buccaneers, con men, and rugged individualists. Compared to British business leaders, David Vogel (1986) points out, American businessmen have tended to be suspicious of government and antagonistic toward governmental controls,[12] partly because American governments, unlike European states, historically did not play a large role in financing and organizing industrial development. Similarly, American businesses have not found it necessary or desirable to submit to governance by private industrial associations of the kind that thrive in the Netherlands and Germany. In Japan, the Ministry of Trade and Industry (whose bureaucrats move into high positions in leading corporations) works closely with tightly organized national trade associations *(keidenren)* and interlinked industrial-financial conglomerations of companies *(keiretsu)*. Hence Daniel Okimoto (1989: 158) observes that there "government-business relationships are informal, close, cooperative, flexible, reciprocal, nonlitigious, and long-term in orientation." In the United States, in contrast, Okimoto describes most business-government relations as "formal, distant, rigid, suspicious, legalistic, narrow, and short-term minded" (ibid.). In the United States, opportunism, financial problems, and conflict among business firms cannot be resolved informally by powerful bankers, dominant industrial groups, or business-government control systems. Instead, regulation of commercial relations (and business-government relations) is left more fully to the realm of defensively worded contracts and the threat of litigation. Martin Shapiro (1993: 42) suggests:

> America may use so many lawyers in business and governmental dealings less because we have a special affection for lawyers, than because economic and political power has been widely dispersed among scattered, disparate elites who cannot get together at their club or country house, because they do not have one, and who would find that they had little in common upon which to build mutual trust even if they did have a meeting place. Where there are no gentlemen, there have to be contracts, rather than gentlemen's agreements.

The fragmented, competitive American business structure also has made government regulation more adversarial and legalistic. In the 1960s and 1970s, when the federal government enacted demanding environmental and safety laws, there were few powerful trade associations with whom regulators could negotiate and implement specific regulations and compliance plans. Consequently, in comparison with comparable bodies of law in Japan and in Europe, American corporation law, securities regulations, and safety and environmental regulations are formulated in an arm's-length, legally formalistic, and adversarial manner (Badarraco, 1985; Brickman et al., 1985). Laws and regulations are more detailed and are enforced more legalistically. All this breeds more legalistic resistance from business and more appeals to the courts (Braithwaite, 1985; Bardach and Kagan, 1982; Kelman, 1981).

Business-labor relations in the United States also occur in an organizational context that is particularly fragmented. In many Western European countries, collective bargaining occurs at the national level, among peak associations of labor and industry. Agreements cover most workers and employers, whether they are union members or not. Key benefits (holidays, vacations, severance pay, retirement benefits) are frequently embodied in nationwide laws. In the United States, in contrast, the National Labor Relations Act (1935) encouraged plant-level union-management conflict.[13] Industrywide bargains are the exception rather than the rule, and government-legislated benefits, in comparison with European governments, are sparse. Industry-specific unions fight for their own advantage, regardless of effects on workers in other unions (Rogers, 1990; Kagan, 1990a).

Lacking hierarchical systems of governance, American labor-management relations, viewed in comparison to those of European countries and Japan, are more pervaded by adversarial legalism. Labor lawyers guide employers' antiunion campaigns. Union elections are routinely appealed to the National Labor Relations Board (NLRB) (Flanagan, 1987). In Japan, labor commissions, established to hear claims of unfair labor practices, hear between 500 and 1,500 cases a year, most of which are settled by conciliation. In the United States, between 30,000 and 45,000 unfair labor practice cases are filed with the NLRB each year (Sanders, 1996: 379; Gould, 1984: 48). Both organized labor and business interests struggle to control presidential appointments to the NLRB, whose regulations, not surprisingly, end up following the election returns (Moe, 1989).

Because American pension, workplace-injury insurance, and health care systems are left far more fully to the private sector than in Europe, and because providers of these benefits are more fragmented and competitive, providers in the United States have stronger incentives to maintain a hard line on claims and qualify their obligations in contractual fine print. In consequence, although hard evidence is lacking, litigation in court over benefits and coverage almost certainly is far more common in the United States. Similarly, governmental regulation of the privatized, employer-dominated American system for employee pension funding and pension rights is legalistic, complex, and frequently litigated.

Put the more fragmented, more competitive American economic system under greater financial stress and adversarial legalism increases. In recent decades, a more competitive world economy has generated rapid shifts in corporate management, corporate downsizing, and contracting-out, and more risky, high-stakes relationships among strangers. In response, American legislatures and courts formulated new regulations and rights of action aimed at financial deception, insider trading, and unjust employee dismissals. In consequence, since 1970, the United States has seen sharp increases in class-action stockholder lawsuits against corporate managers (Romano, 1991: 65), more lawsuits between business debtors and creditors (Nelson, 1990), more suits between insurance companies and their insureds (Dunsworth and Rogers, 1996), and more lawsuits by dismissed employees (Dertouzos et al. 1988). During the wave of hostile corporate takeovers that swept the restructuring U.S. economy in the late 1970s and 1980s, law firm partners deployed teams of young lawyers like squadrons of fighter planes, bombarding their corporate adversaries with preemptive lawsuits, demands for truckloads of documents, and pretrial motions, trying to spend and to stall their adversaries into submission (Stewart, 1983: 146). In Europe and Japan there have also been sharp increases in competitive pressures, but adversarial legalism among businesses, and between business and government, is much less frequent than in the United States (Kagan, 1997a).

Lawyers, Legal Culture, and Adversarial Legalism

One further contributing cause of American adversarial legalism must be mentioned—the legal profession and the legal culture it generates. Beginning in the 1960s, the advent of a distinctively American brand of activist government—one that seeks "total justice" through decentralized governmental and economic institutions, legalistic regulation, adversarial legal challenge, and citizen-initiated lawsuits—vastly increased the demand for lawyers. Within a few decades there were far more of them, housed in larger organizations. There were many more economically and politically important cases of the kind that warrant big investments in creative, aggressive lawyering. In no other country were lawyers so entrepreneurial in seeking out new kinds of business, so eager to challenge authority, and so quick to propose new liability-expanding legal theories.

Lawyers themselves have not been the primary cause of the expanding domain of adversarial legalism. Broader political currents and interest groups, as suggested earlier, were the sorcerers that called forth adversarial legalism—thereby generating demands for more legally trained apprentices. The sorcerers' apprentices, however, soon became richer, better organized, more energetic. While many judges and lawyers strive to dampen adversarial legalism (Kagan, 1994; Suchman and Cahill, 1996), thousands of lawyers who believe in or profit from litigation exploit every opportunity to extend it further and to thwart the sorcerers' occasional efforts to rein it in. Organized networks of activist lawyers—such as the National Prison Project in the Alabama reform case, plaintiffs' lawyers who focus on particular hazardous products (e.g., asbestos, tobacco, breast implants), and conservative organizations opposed to affirmative action—systematically push courts to extend the realm of adversarial legalism. The American Trial Lawyers Association and lawyers who make a good living from class-action litigation assiduously lobby legislatures and mobilize very large campaign contributions to block reforms that would reduce adversarial legalism (Kagan, 1994; Heymann and Liebman, 1988: 309).

Moreover, American lawyers and law professors, in sharp contrast to their counterparts in other democratic nations, have created and defended a body of legal ethics that exalts adversarial legalism. In the United States (far more than elsewhere) lawyers' codes of ethics endorse zealous advocacy of clients' causes, short of dishonesty, but without regard to the interests of justice in the particular case or broader societal concerns (Osiel, 1990: 2019). American lawyers' professional culture is unique in permitting and implicitly encouraging them to advance unprecedented legal claims, coach witnesses, and attempt to wear down their opponents through burdensome pretrial discovery. In the hands of some practitioners—not all, but not merely a few—entrepreneurial, manipulative, and superaggressive modes of getting clients and litigating push the limits of adversarial legalism even further (Kagan, 1994: 1, 53–58).

Perhaps most important, American law professors, judges, and lawyers have elaborated legal theories that actively promote adversarial legalism not as a necessary evil but as a desirable mode of governance. Their heroic view of the judiciary's role in government—exemplified by Professor Owen Fiss's statement quoted in the previous chapter[14]—has not been uncontested in the law schools or in the judiciary. But on balance, in the last few decades American legal scholars and judges have become more supportive of a "social engineering" or even a political vision of law and the judicial role. In a comparative study of public interest litigation to shape public policy, Michael Greve (1989b: 231) observed: "In the United States, there has been a broad consensus for public interest litigation among legal scholars, judges, and the legal establishment in general. In the Federal Republic [of Germany], there is a similarly broad consensus against it. Judges on the Federal Constitutional Court and the Federal Administrative Court voiced their opposition to association lawsuits not only on the bench but in legal periodicals and in public."

Whereas European legal scholars speak of law as a logically coherent set of authoritative principles and rules, American legal scholars often speak of law as a manifestation of the ongoing struggle among groups and classes for political and economic advantage, or as a manipulable set of tools for achieving better government (Kagan, 1988: 728–730; 1994: 24–27). In contrast to Great Britain, Atiyah and Summers (1987: 404) observe, "American law schools have been the source of the dominant general theory of law in America . . . 'instrumentalism' . . . [which] conceives of law essentially as a pragmatic instrument of social improvement." Thus the language of the American law school classroom is the language of policy analysis. Law reviews bristle with arguments for new legal rights, not for legal stability. American legal scholars tend to celebrate those American judges who, like the Supreme Court justices in *Brown v. Board of Education* or Frank Johnson in the Alabama prisons case, feel authorized or even obligated to "do justice" when the other bodies of government have "failed" to take action against social problems. The dominant strain in the legal culture of American law teachers supports easy access to courts, along with policy solutions that take the form of judicially enforceable individual rights, harsh penalties for violations, and tight legal controls on official discretion.

As law school graduates move on to legislative staff positions, governmental policymaking jobs, bar association committees, advocacy organizations, and the judiciary, they tend to be supporters of adversarial legalism as a mode of governance. The federal Superfund Act, intended to clean up hazardous waste disposal sites, reads in key parts as if it were drafted by a plaintiff's tort lawyer.[15] A cross-national comparison of styles of statutory interpretation classified the American judiciary as the most freewheeling and creative (Summers and Taruffo, 1991). Thus American judges have encouraged adversarial legalism by finding "implied" private rights of action in statutes and constitutional provisions, from the National Environmental Protection Act to the Fourth Amendment, thereby opening up new spheres of litigation against government officials by citizens and advocacy groups. More generally, American judges have encouraged the litigation of policy issues by treating an extraordinarily large range of public policy issues—from the adequacy of funding for public schools to the design of electoral districts—as appropriate for judicial resolution.

American legal culture is far from monolithic in its endorsement of adversarial legalism. In recent years, as a result of more Republican appointments of conservative judges to the federal bench and some state judiciaries, courts have chipped away at the structure of adversarial legalism in some respects. U.S. Supreme Court rulings have called for greater judicial deference to administrative agency decisions, put some limits on standing to sue government agencies, and made it significantly harder for criminal defendants to overturn their convictions on constitutional grounds. Legislatures in many states have enacted restrictions on tort litigation. Congress enacted restrictions on class-action securities litigation. Corporations and their lawyers have devised arbitration schemes and contractual provisions that help keep them out of court.

Nevertheless, these restrictions have not substantially changed the basic structures or curtailed the incidence of adversarial legalism in the United States. The basic causes of adversarial legalism—popular demands for fair treatment, recompense, and protection, combined with mistrust of government and fragmentation of political and economic power—remain unchanged and perhaps unchangeable. Indeed, three decades of expanded adversarial legalism have deeply imprinted the ideas of American *legal* culture on the country's political culture as a whole. As political scientist Michael McCann (1999: 87) has pointed out, such salient political issues as "discrimination against women, ethnic minorities, gays and lesbians; the incendiary abortion issue; pornography and hate speech; campaign finance regulation; the relationship between religion and public education; gun control; restrictions on police abuse; [and] death penalty policy . . . have been understood and contested in distinctly legal terms delineated by the federal courts over time." In consequence, he adds, "Even those citizens who oppose prevailing court constrictions and legal frames typically [must] pose their own counterclaims in terms of legal traditions authorized by the courts."

*　　*　　*

In the last half of the twentieth century all economically advanced democracies have experienced political demands for governmental action to enhance economic security, promote equal opportunity, provide for the injured, reduce the risk of harm, protect the natural environment, and safeguard human rights. The United States is unique, however, in the extent to which the governmental response has resulted in increased levels of adversarial legalism. The fundamental reason, we have seen, lies in the collision between demands for more active government and some enduring features of the American political system—political structures that fragment governmental power, a political culture that mistrusts "big government," an increasingly competitive but disaggregated business system, and a legal culture that promotes and validates adversarial legalism. The catalytic reaction of these seemingly incompatible progovernmental and antigovernmental elements has produced an approach to governance that is active but decentralized, legally constrained, and litigious. Political and economic factions, fearing that their adversaries will have too much influence on federal bureaucracies and local governments, have insisted that regulatory and law enforcement agencies, as well as large corporations, should be held accountable via detailed laws and procedures, lawsuits, and courts. In addition, an entrepreneurial, politically active legal profession, professoriat, and judiciary all have promoted the desirability of adversarial legalism as a response to policy problems and injury compensation, successfully foreclosing attempts to seriously curtail the powers of judges, lawyers, and juries in governance and dispute resolution.

In consequence, as new demands for governmental problem-solving are pressed onto the American political agenda, adversarial legalism tends to spread and intensify. Succeeding parts of this book will show how the patterns summarized in this chapter recur in many broad spheres of governance, from criminal justice to civil adjudication, social welfare, and governmental regulation of business.

II

Criminal Justice

4

Adversarial Legalism and American Criminal Justice

In the United States, as the index of reported crime per 100,000 population tripled between 1960 and 1980, fear of violence drove much of the middle class to the suburbs, robbing many cities of their economic and cultural vitality. In England the index of indictable crimes increased tenfold between 1955 and 1991. In 1955, according to Gertrude Himmelfarb (1994: 62), England was so civil that "football crowds [were] as orderly as church meetings," whereas a couple of decades later, "those games became notorious as the scene of mayhem and riots." While homicide rates in the United States remain much higher than in other economically advanced democracies, by the end of the 1980s or the early 1990s reported burglary rates in Australia, Great Britain, Denmark, Sweden, and the Netherlands exceeded the rate in the United States, and car theft was more common in France than in America (Marshall, 1996; *The Economist*, 1996a: 23–25; Wilson, 1994: 25).

Perhaps people in fatalistic societies bear the risk of criminal victimization silently. But in rich, democratic societies, citizens expect government to protect them, even from environmental hazards and products that entail a low probability of harm. Not surprisingly, therefore, the demand for crime control soared toward the top of the political agenda. National responses to demands for security and justice, however, are not identical. The American response differs from those of other economically advanced democracies along two broad dimensions. Substantively, the criminal law of the United States is distinctive in its greater punitiveness, political volatility, malleability, and inconsistency. Procedurally, American criminal justice is structured and pervaded by adversarial legalism—lawyer-driven legal contestation in a relatively nonhierarchical, organizationally decentralized system.

Adversarial legalism provides powerful tools for challenging bias, abuse of power, and error by law enforcement authorities. But adversarial legalism's procedural tools do not significantly temper the distinctive harshness of the American system of criminal justice, and they exacerbate its potential for inconsistency and unequal treatment. This chapter provides an overview of ways in which the American criminal justice system differs from those of other democracies and why the American criminal justice system is so pervaded by adversarial legalism. The next chapter will delve further into adversarial legalism's consequences, particularly in the routine disposition of criminal cases.

Adversarial Legalism in Action: The McCleskey Cases

In 1978 Warren McCleskey, an African-American, entered a store in Marietta, Georgia, together with three armed accomplices. Brandishing a gun, McCleskey commanded all the customers to lie face down on the floor while his accomplices robbed the store manager at gunpoint. Responding to a silent alarm, Frank Schlatt, a white police officer, entered the store. Two shots rang out. Officer Schlatt was killed. The county prosecutor charged McCleskey with murder and armed robbery. McCleskey denied having fired the shots, but at trial the prosecutor introduced evidence indicating that at least one of the fatal bullets was fired from a gun of the type that McCleskey had carried during the robbery. In addition, two witnesses (one a codefendant, one an inmate in the county jail in which McCleskey was held) testified that they heard McCleskey admit to the shooting. The jury found McCleskey guilty. A Georgia statute provides that homicide in the course of an armed robbery and the killing of a police officer are "aggravating circumstances" that warrant capital punishment. Based on that law, McCleskey was sentenced to be executed.

McCleskey appealed. His lawyers alleged that he had been denied due process of law in various ways.[1] But on January 24, 1980, the Georgia Supreme Court affirmed the conviction and the sentence. McCleskey's lawyers then asked the U.S. Supreme Court to review the case, but the petition was denied (like all but about 1 percent of the several thousand that reach the Court each term). McCleskey's lawyers then petitioned another Georgia court, asserting over twenty legal arguments, but in April 1981 the court denied relief. McCleskey appealed. In June 1981 the Georgia Supreme Court turned down McCleskey's request for review. McCleskey's lawyers again sought review by the U.S. Supreme Court; that petition was denied in November 1981.

On December 30, 1981, McCleskey, still incarcerated, filed a petition for habeas corpus in federal court. His lawyers made eighteen separate arguments concerning the unconstitutionality of his conviction and sentence. One claim, soon abandoned, was that McCleskey's right to counsel had been infringed. The claim that the lawyers pushed hardest was that the Georgia capital sentencing process was administered in a racially discriminatory manner. McCleskey's lawyers relied on a statistical study of Georgia murder cases in the 1970s. The study, funded by the NAACP and conducted by Professor David Baldus and others, indicated above all the fateful importance of prosecutorial discretion in homicide cases. In more than 2,000 murder cases, only about 5 percent of defendants were sentenced to capital punishment. Even in the 463 cases in which the defendant was "death eligible" due to the presence of statutorily specified "aggravating factors," only 100 defendants (22 percent) had received a death sentence, mostly because prosecutors often did not ask for the death penalty.

If county prosecutors in Georgia sought capital punishment in only a minority of "death eligible" cases, what guided their decisions to do so? Those decisions, the Baldus study suggested, were influenced, consciously or unconsciously, by race. Surprisingly to many, the data did not show that prosecutors discriminated against black defendants. Overall, fewer black defendants (4 percent) than white defendants (7 percent) were sentenced to die. Rather, the race of the *victim* seemed to matter. In "death eligible" cases, the prosecution sought the death penalty in 70 percent of cases in which black defendants had killed white victims, but did so only in 32 percent of cases in which white defendants had killed whites, in 15 percent where black defendants had killed blacks, and in 19 percent where white defendants had killed blacks (*McCleskey v. Kemp*, 1987). The disparities persisted when the researchers controlled for the number of aggravating factors. In the end, Georgia defendants charged with killing white victims, and especially blacks who killed white victims, were significantly more likely to receive a death sentence, while black killers of blacks (one of the largest categories of cases) were least likely to receive a death sentence (Baldus et al., 1983).[2]

In 1984 the U.S. District Court ruled that the study did not support McCleskey's claim that the entire system was so tainted by racial discrimination that it was unconstitutional. McCleskey's lawyers appealed that decision. On January 29, 1985, the U.S. Court of Appeals affirmed the district court decision. McCleskey again petitioned the U.S. Supreme Court for review, and this time the Court accepted the case. In 1987 the Court, by a bare 5–4 majority, affirmed the district court ruling. The majority opinion argued that "discretion is essential to the criminal justice process" and that the statistical evidence fell short of proving that "the decisionmakers in McCleskey's case acted with discriminatory purpose" (*McCleskey v. Kemp*, 1987).

In July 1987, five days before his scheduled execution, McCleskey's lawyers, perusing records obtained as a result of a change in Georgia's open-records law, discovered that the jail inmate who had originally testified against McCleskey had in fact been a government informant, planted in an adjoining cell by law enforcement officials. The defense lawyers filed another petition for habeas corpus in the U.S. District Court in Georgia, arguing that the use of an informant constituted a violation of McCleskey's Sixth Amendment right to have an attorney present during pretrial interrogation. The district court agreed and scolded the prosecution for misconduct (Kaplan, 1991: 68). The state of Georgia then appealed. In December 1989, the federal court of appeals reversed the district court, holding that McCleskey had abandoned his Sixth Amendment claim in his December 1981 petition for habeas corpus, and hence could not now argue it again (notwithstanding his claim that his lawyers then had no knowledge of the government's deliberate use of an informant).

McCleskey appealed that decision to the U.S. Supreme Court, which again accepted his case, now labeled *McCleskey v. Zant*. In 1991 the Court held, by a 6–3 vote, that second and subsequent habeas corpus petitions could properly be dismissed as "abusive" unless the defendant could show that his counsel had been impeded from raising the same claim earlier and that the claimed constitutional error probably affected the outcome of his trial and sentencing (*McCleskey v. Zant*, 1991). By these standards, the Court held, McCleskey's Sixth Amendment claim, even if legally supportable, had been properly dismissed.

The Georgia authorities prepared to carry out McCleskey's death sentence. His lawyers petitioned the Georgia Board of Pardons and Paroles for clemency. On September 24, 1991, the board turned down this appeal. McCleskey's execution was scheduled for 7 P.M. that day. At once, McCleskey's attorneys filed nearly identical appeals in Georgia and in federal courts. The state court immediately rejected the Georgia appeal; McCleskey's attorneys quickly appealed that decision to the U.S. Supreme Court. At 10 P.M. the Supreme Court, by a 6–3 vote, denied the appeal from the Georgia court.

Meanwhile, in the federal appeal, U.S. District Court Judge Owen Forrester summoned attorneys and witnesses to an emergency hearing. He issued an order staying the execution until 7:30 P.M., then until 10 P.M., and then until midnight in order to hear further evidence (Montgomery and Curriden, 1991; Applebome, 1991: 18; Harris and Curriden, 1991). At 11:20 P.M. Judge Forrester denied McCleskey's petition but stayed the execution until 2 A.M. to permit McCleskey's lawyer to file an appeal. At 1:50 A.M. the federal court of appeals affirmed Judge Forrester's denial of McCleskey's claim and lifted the stay of execution. At 2:17 A.M. McCleskey was placed in the electric chair. Three minutes into his final statement, the warden informed him that the U.S. Supreme Court was considering his case. McCleskey was removed from the chair. At 2:42 A.M. the Supreme Court issued a ten-minute stay of execution. At 2:52 A.M., it denied the last of McCleskey's twenty appeals. At 3:06 A.M. on September 25, 1991,

Warren McCleskey was electrocuted, thirteen years after the killing of Officer Schlatt.

In 1910 a Warren McCleskey might well have been lynched.[3] In 1950 he might have been physically coerced into confessing before trial. If there had been a trial, it would have been conducted before an all-white jury and a judge who had been put in office by white local politicians. Upon conviction, McCleskey would have been executed promptly. By 1978, however, adversarial legalism had changed the criminal justice system of Georgia and the nation, providing poor defendants with lawyers and providing defense lawyers with new opportunities to challenge criminal charges and law enforcement methods in court. That in turn forced prosecutors, police, and judges to attend more closely to the law. Supreme Court constitutional rulings had narrowed the range of persons subject to capital punishment and reduced the risk of discrimination based on the race of the defendant. Despite the Court's rejection of McCleskey's racial discrimination argument, courts and prosecutors throughout the country nevertheless became more attentive to the subjective attitudes that might explain the race-of-victim effects demonstrated by Professor Baldus and others.

On the other hand, the McCleskey case also brings into sharp relief some of the American criminal justice system's equally unique but more troublesome features: its tendencies toward punitiveness, cumbersomeness, inconsistency, inequality, and political volatility—tendencies that pervade the handling of crimes other than homicide as well.

Punitiveness

In the end, Warren McCleskey was electrocuted. While a minority of American states do not employ the death penalty, and in states that do, only a relatively small minority of "death eligible" murderers actually are sentenced to die,[4] the United States stands alone among economically advanced democracies in employing capital punishment (Zimring and Hawkins, 1997: 33–39). Even aside from the death penalty, penal policy in the United States is distinctively harsh. In 1995 its incarceration rate—565 per 100,000 people—was more than five times as high as in other rich democracies (*The Economist*, 1997: 46, 1995: 25). The disparity is due not so much to differences in the crime rate but to the much longer prison terms doled out by American courts for felonies (Frase, 1990: 658; Selke, 1991), including for the sale of psychoactive drugs, and to America's greater propensity to impose jail sentences for "victimless" infractions such as disorderly conduct, prostitution, and public drunkenness (Frase and Weigend, 1995: 320–321).[5] American police are more likely than their French or German counterparts to arrest and lock up crime suspects rather than simply issuing a summons, and American defendants are more likely to be held in jail until both their first court appearance and the final decision (Frase and Weigend, 1995: 329; Frase, 1990: 599–601).

In one respect, American criminal law is less harsh and restrictive. Warren McCleskey and his companions in crime carried guns. If the United States made guns as hard to get as other countries do, Officer Schlatt might not have been shot, the law enforcement establishment might have been less vengeful, and McCleskey might not have been executed. The liberality (or laxness) of United States gun control laws, viewed in comparative perspective, helps explain why the United States suffers much higher levels of *lethal crime* than other economically advanced democracies with high crime rates (Zimring and Hawkins, 1997: 33–39). American robbers are much more likely to use guns,[6] as are people involved in fights and acts of revenge. At the same time, weak restrictions on gun ownership and possession mean that American police officers face potentially armed citizens much more often then their counterparts abroad—which gives them greater incentives to approach suspects defensively and to engage in aggressive searches for possible weapons, which increase the incidence of legal conflict over alleged police malpractice.

Cumbersomeness

With its extended, agonizing legal jousting, the McCleskey case reflects adversarial legalism's capacity to drag the legal process into a costly and protracted procedural morass. The prosecution and trial of a capital case have become so legally complex that appellate courts have found defense lawyers, prosecutors, and judges guilty of reversible legal error in two out of three death penalty appeals (Butterfield, 2000b). As a result of sequential appeals stretching over years, each execution in the United States has been estimated to cost at least $2 million in public and private legal expenses—three or four times the cost of life imprisonment (Chiang, 1996a: A1).[7] Adversarial legalism makes other aspects of the criminal justice system extremely cumbersome as well. Even in ordinary, noncapital cases, the routine criminal jury trial is so complex, slow, and costly that it can only be used sparingly: 90 percent of felony prosecutions are resolved through negotiated guilty pleas that are hurried, low visibility, and unreviewable (Langan and Grazadei, 1995: 9).

Inconsistency

Had Warren McCleskey not lived in a southern state where the death penalty is employed far more frequently than elsewhere in the United States, his execution would have been far less likely.[8] Moreover, within the thirty-six states that impose capital punishment, the propensity of locally elected prosecutors to seek the death penalty—and hence the risk that an accused murderer will get a death sentence—varies markedly from county to county (Paternoster, 1991: 176–180).[9] Had a Warren McCleskey been tried in Bronx County Courthouse in New York City, where predominantly minority juries have at times acquitted black felony defendants at almost three times the national acquittal rate (Holden, Cohen, and de Lisser, 1995), he might have gone free. Had he been tried in Alabama rather than in Georgia, the trial judge might have imposed a death sentence even if the jury had decided to show mercy.[10] The same kind of cross-jurisdiction variation pervades the decentralized American system of criminal justice in the handling of routine felonies as well as homicides, which opens the door to inconsistency in enforcement, prosecution, case processing, and sentencing, and hence to significantly different legal outcomes for similar offenses (Levin, 1972; Eisenstein et al., 1988).

Inequality

Warren McCleskey's legal fate was shaped in large part by the state-appointed defense counsel assigned to his case, for in the procedurally complex, adversarial American justice system, lawyers bear primary responsibility for challenging the evidence and violations of the defendant's legal rights. In the postconviction stage, McCleskey's lawyers were extraordinarily persistent. But at the crucial initial stages of many cases, and at trial, overworked public defenders or poorly compensated state-appointed defense counsel sometimes do not mount an aggressive investigation and defense, even in capital cases, and are compelled to do even less in routine felonies.[11] Prosecutors too are often inexperienced or overloaded. Therefore, to a far greater degree than in most democratic nations' criminal justice systems, outcomes in the United States are shaped by the shifting and often unequal balance of competence, commitment, and resources between prosecuting attorneys on one side and defense lawyers on the other. Adversarial legalism is good for establishing rights to challenge police and prosecutorial procedures, but it is a weak mechanism for ensuring that governmentally supported defense and prosecutorial offices will be supported at levels that guarantee energetic and competent assertion of those rights (Stuntz, 1997).

Political and Legal Volatility

McCleskey v. Zant, the second Supreme Court opinion in McCleskey's case, was a judicial "boy who cried wolf" response to adversarial legalism in capital cases. Reacting against sequential appeals and midnight requests for stays of execution,[12] a politically conservative Supreme Court majority began in the 1990s to impose limits on appeals and habeas corpus petitions, reversing liberal precedents established not many years earlier. In 1996 Congress limited the ability of state prisoners to file more than one habeas corpus petition in federal courts,[13] and in 1998 eliminated funding for defense lawyers to help defendants in capital cases pursue federal appeals. In recent years the courts have sometimes rejected appeals by defendants who belatedly turn up evidence pointing toward their innocence—even though there are "wrongful conviction" needles to be found in the haystack of capital case litigation.[14]

The restrictions on appeals in capital cases reflect the uniquely politicized American system for making and remaking criminal law and procedure for all kinds of offenses. In most other economically advanced democracies, penal policymaking is dominated by a professionalized national ministry of justice, and judges are appointed and promoted almost exclusively on the basis of professional qualifications and performance. In the United States, in contrast, individual politicians compete by proposing ad hoc legislative measures that are "tough on crime." Hoping to soften the law's harshness, defense lawyers, as in McCleskey's case, take the political struggle to the courts. Often they lose but sometimes they win because the American judiciary is politically diverse, independent, and creative. Since the courts play a significant role in reshaping criminal law and its administration, judges' decisions often generate further political controversy. The United States, in consequence, is distinctive in the extent to which judges are nominated (and in some states elected) on the basis of their attitudes toward crime control and defendants' rights. This makes the criminal law politically malleable. A legal expert on death penalty jurisprudence noted that Supreme Court "decisions decided no more than a year apart often seem to manifest totally different priorities" (White, 1987: 21). In cross-national perspective, American criminal law is perpetually enmeshed in political and legal challenge.

Why is American criminal law distinctively punitive and politicized? Why are its procedures, shaped and pervaded by adversarial legalism, so cumbersome and susceptible to inconsistent and unequal implementation? To address these questions, we must look to the basic political structures of the United States, first as they affect the making of the criminal law, then as they affect the law's implementation.

Making Criminal Law: Political Permeability and Penal Policy

In the 1980s convicted burglars and thieves in the United States spent three or four times as many months in prison than did their counterparts in Denmark (Selke, 1991) and other Western European countries. Since then the gap undoubtedly has been expanded by the mandatory sentence enhancements (greatly extended prison sentences for third felony convictions, use of firearms in a crime, and narcotics dealing) that were enacted by Congress and by many American state legislatures in the 1990s (Lowenthal, 1993).

American penal laws may be harsher, one might speculate, because the voting public in the United States demands tougher penalties.[15] Crime rates in Copenhagen are comparable to those in Indiana (Selke, 1991: 232–233) and burglary rates in London exceed those in New York, but street crime in gun-ridden American cities is much more deadly (Zimring and Hawkins, 1997). Americans, bombarded with news of violent crime by competing commercial television stations, are significantly more likely than Western Europeans to endorse imprisonment and longer prison terms (Savelsberg, 1994: 929–930).

Popular sentiment, however, does not automatically produce tougher penalties. "In many countries besides America," *The Economist* (1990: 25) observed, "public opinion strongly supports capital punishment. . . . The difference is that, in America, politicians are more likely to follow public opinion . . . not try to change it." Leading politicians in Great Britain and New Zealand sometimes have emphasized the crime problem during election campaigns. But the much-publicized "tough on crime" measures enacted by Tory governments in Great Britain during the 1980s and 1990s did not come close to matching the large increases in punitiveness and incarceration rates in the United States during those years. The "central difference," writes James Q. Wilson (1997: 81), "is that the gap between public opinion and official governance is wider in England than in America." That gap, in turn, reflects Britain's more hierarchical governmental structure, in which the ruling political party is tightly disciplined and in firm control of governmental policy and its implementation until the next election (usually a five-year period), and the judiciary is deferential to Parliament.

Moreover, in most other rich parliamentary democracies, policymaking on crime-related issues is generally dominated by professionals in the Ministry of Justice and by respected academic experts. The United States does not lack for experts, both in and out of government. But in the United States, far more than in other rich democracies, the making of criminal law often proceeds along a different, more populist, political track, spurred by interest groups and ambitious politicians reacting to highly publicized crimes. The populist track is kept busy by fragmentation of political authority. Criminal law is forged by fifty state legislatures as well as by Congress. In contrast to parliamentary systems, in which individual representatives defer to their party's leadership, American legislators, largely on their own in raising campaign funds and building constituent support, face stronger incentives to introduce or support legislation that will demonstrate they are not "soft" on crime. In a number of American states "law and order" advocacy groups can put initiatives and referenda concerning crime policy directly to the electorate. In California, for example, following a highly publicized kidnap-murder, California voters (ignoring the objections of many law enforcement professionals) passed a sweeping "three strikes and you're out" ballot initiative in 1994, mandating life imprisonment for a third felony conviction (even if the third felony is not a violent crime).

In this political environment American politicians often are unwilling to defer to criminologists, bar associations, law professors, or judges who argue that harsher methods will be ineffective, impossible to implement, or unjust.[16] Instead, politicians fall over each other in the scramble to "deal with" the crime problem by enacting new laws. A study of nine states indicated that legislatures passed several new criminal statutes virtually every year, almost always pushing penal policy in a more legalistic and punitive direction (Jacob, 1984: 143–147; Berk et al., 1977: 182). In 1984 Congress sought to rationalize the federal criminal penalty structure by establishing a professional sentencing commission, but in 1986 Congress responded to mass media accounts of a crack cocaine epidemic by rushing through the Anti-Drug Abuse Act, which mandated sentences for selling crack that were vastly harsher than those for selling powder cocaine.[17] In the years that followed, Congress ignored the U.S. Sentencing Commission's argument that the disparity between crack and powder penalties was unjustified, and it ignored too the enormous sentence disparities between whites and blacks convicted of cocaine trafficking (since blacks constituted the overwhelming majority of those convicted of crack sales).[18] A surge of adversarial legalism resulted, as hundreds of defense lawyers (and some lower court judges) challenged the constitutionality and enforcement of the federal crack cocaine law (Provine, 1998).

In sum, compared to other democracies, the permeable American political structure generates more frequent, more punitive, and more uncoordinated changes in the criminal law. The consequences include not only heavier penalties for offenders but also more adversarial legalism.

Implementing Criminal Law: Two Models of Authority

Criminal justice systems empower police officers to capture and subdue those who resist their commands, to search for evidence, and to lock suspects in jail. For democratic nations the perennial and pressing problem is guarding us from the guardians, preventing abuse and error by those who exercise officially granted coercive powers. One fundamental mechanism of control is the rule of law; another is democratic accountability. Most democracies seek a measure of both, but the two principles coexist in uneasy tension.

Recall Mirjan Damaska's (1975) distinction between "hierarchical" and "coordinate" models for organizing governmental authority. The hierarchical model, which Damaska abstracts from the systems of Western Europe, centralizes political control of law enforcement and adjudicative processes. It is designed first and foremost to minimize the inconsistency, bias, and injustice that can stem from local, parochial influences on criminal justice system officials. If the hierarchical model could dream, its nightmares would be populated by the corrupt local police chief, the ideological judge who disregards national policies he dislikes, and the jury that acquits or convicts because of the defendant's race. Hence the hierarchical model strives to substitute the rule of law for the rule of men. It emphasizes apolitical professionalism in the recruitment and training of police, prosecutors, and judges. It organizes them in carefully structured bureaucracies and subjects their performance to close hierarchical supervision and review. To the same end, hierarchical systems grant a minister of justice far-reaching powers to guide and discipline local officials and supervisors. Democratic responsiveness is focused at the top of the hierarchy of offices—not at the level of frontline, local officialdom—by making the minister of justice directly accountable to the national government and to the parliamentary opposition.

Damaska's "coordinate model" erects a different set of defenses against a different set of injustices. Its "nightmares" would feature an overly powerful centralized government that uses the criminal code as an instrument of political repression or makes laws that, even if not meant to be repressive, are too harsh and unbending, too unresponsive to the values of minority subcultures or to the equities of particular cases. The coordinate ideal, accordingly, emphasizes the fragmentation of power and grassroots democratic responsiveness. Police, prosecutors, and judges are selected and held accountable by local political processes. Politically independent defense lawyers are empowered to dispute the state's evidence, to expose misbehavior by enforcement officials, and to question the fairness of the law itself. Hence the coordinate model exalts the techniques of adversarial legalism—party-influenced (as opposed to hierarchically controlled) legal contestation—to provide legal coordination and ensure accountability.

No nation's criminal justice system conforms entirely to either the hierarchical or coordinate model. Germany, for example, employs nonprofessional lay judges who sit alongside professionals (although the latter are clearly dominant) (Machura, 2000; Casper and Zeisel, 1972). Conversely, there are some hierarchical elements in the United States: trial court decisions can be appealed up the ladder of courts, as in the McCleskey case; the U.S. Supreme Court's constitutional rulings are binding on state and local officials; large urban police departments and prosecutors' offices employ bureaucratic modes of supervision and coordination. Still, the Japanese and most European criminal justice systems lean much more strongly toward the hierarchical ideal (Damaska, 1975: 487, 488; Bayley, 1979),[19] while the criminal justice systems of the United States approximate the coordinate model—and do so far more than their British parent or their Canadian and Australian cousins.

In the United States authority over the making, enforcement, and adjudication of criminal law is scattered over the fifty states and their many political subdivisions. There is no comprehensive nationwide criminal code and no truly national police force (Bayley, 1979).[20] The authority of the U.S. Attorney General in Washington extends only (and only weakly) to the ninety-four locally based U.S. Attorneys who prosecute federal crimes, and hardly at all to the several hundred locally elected district attorneys who prosecute state crimes or to the *thousands* of municipal police chiefs and county sheriffs. In contrast to their counterparts in Japan, France, Germany, or the Netherlands, American trial court judges, police chiefs, sheriffs, and district attorneys have not been selected, socialized, and supervised by an overarching state bureaucracy that administers entrance exams, provides systematic training, coordinates policy, rewards the diligent, and weeds out the incompetent. Rather, American law enforcement officials and judges are elected by local constituencies or appointed by local political leaders—a practice that reflects the coordinate model's concern for independence and political responsiveness rather than for carefully honed legal craftsmanship or fidelity to legal rules.

"Becoming a prosecutor in France," writes Richard Frase, "is a long-term career choice," whereas the average tenure of prosecutors in the United States is relatively short. And compared to the French system, "procedures for training American prosecutors are rudimentary at best" (Frase, 1990: 562–563). In the Netherlands five senior prosecutors meet twice monthly to discuss and revise nationwide guidelines governing the waiver of prosecution for different kinds of offenses and offenders (Downes, 1988: 15). Conversely, "in most American states, prosecutors are locally elected officials with surprisingly great and virtually uncontrolled authority" (Damaska 1975: 502, 512). Hierarchical supervision of individual prosecutors' case-by-case discretionary decisionmaking is weak. Compared to their Japanese counterparts, David Johnson found that assistant prosecutors in the United States have much more leeway to act on the basis of their own individual judgment, yet their judgments are more subject to the influence of complaining victims, grand juries, defense lawyers, and criminal defendants themselves (Johnson, 1998: 247).

Similarly, compared to European (or British or Japanese) judiciaries, American judges have remarkably diverse social, educational, and career backgrounds. Selected for political reasons rather than on the basis of prior experience, a tort lawyer can end up on the bench in family court, and a prosecutor or politician who has never been a trial judge can be catapulted onto the state supreme court or even the U.S. Supreme Court (Kagan et al., 1984). Newly appointed American judges do not receive the intensive, specialized training required of new European judges. One consequence is the variability that is the hallmark of the American judiciary. Some American judges are gifted, some well prepared, some neither (Atiyah and Summers, 1987: 345, 357). Some judges are tough sentencers, while others are much more lenient. Judges differ in individual personality, political philosophy, and local political culture, and those differences have been shown to affect their decisions (Levin, 1972; Gaylin, 1974; Gibson, 1980). Notwithstanding a New Mexico statute that mandated imprisonment for drunk-driver recidivists, a study found that at least half of New Mexico judges did not incarcerate repeat offenders—sometimes because they disagreed with the legislative mandate or resented the legislature's attempt to limit their discretion—while other judges faithfully followed the statute (Ross and Foley, 1987).

In the adjudicative process a still more diverse and localistic institution, the jury, tugs against rule-of-law ideals. Guilt or innocence is determined by a small group of legally untrained citizens drawn from the local community, who hear a single case and then disperse. In German criminal adjudication lay citizens serve on panels with professional judges, but the lay people serve for a period of time, thereby gaining some experience. Moreover, in every case in Germany a professional judge writes an opinion explaining and justifying the panel's decision (including the sentence), which makes the decision reviewable by an appellate court. American juries, in contrast, decide in secret. If jurors acquit, they do not have to explain in an intellectually defensible way that their doubts about the prosecution's case were "reasonable." If they convict, they need not explain why they found the defense unpersuasive. Juries' decisions are essentially impervious to post hoc rational analysis or hierarchical legal review. The American jury's unreviewable powers mirror the powers of American police, prosecutors, and judges to make discretionary decisions—particularly decisions to drop or reduce criminal charges—without meaningful possibility of legal review.

From the perspective of a Japanese or a European criminal lawyer steeped in the values of the hierarchical model, the American criminal justice system is an uncoordinated, weakly supervised, potentially inconsistent mess. The co-ordinate model, however, deliberately sacrifices some legal regularity in order to make the criminal process more responsive to popular notions of justice.

Thus Michigan jurors could decline to convict a physician who helped termi-
nally ill patients commit suicide. Ordinary American trial court judges can
declare statutes unconstitutional and impose novel conditions of probation
on convicted persons. Juries have declined to convict women who attacked
or even killed husbands who previously had physically abused them. As political opposition to the Vietnam War increased in the late 1960s and early
1970s, juries often acquitted young men charged with draft evasion (Levine,
1992: 114–115).

But the coordinate model also means that a criminal defendant's fate may
rest on contingencies such as where and by whom he is tried. Some judges
are known to be biased in favor of the prosecution (Brill, 1989). Conviction
rates are higher in politically conservative than in politically liberal counties
(Levine, 1983). The white Los Angeles police officers who were captured on
videotape brutally beating Rodney King (an African-American) after a high-
speed car chase were acquitted by a jury in a white suburban community
(triggering a violent riot by African-Americans), but were convicted by a predominantly minority jury when reprosecuted in federal court in downtown
Los Angeles (Holden, Cohen, and de Lisser, 1995: A1, A5). Jurors can (and
sometimes do) vote for conviction and even the death penalty based on mis-
understandings of the evidence, of the judges' instructions, or of the operations of the legal and penal system (Paduano and Stafford-Smith, 1987: 211;
Garvey et al., 2000).[21]

Regulating the Coordinate Model: Adversarial Legalism

Americans may value the democratic responsiveness inherent in the coordinate model, but they also believe that similar cases should be treated similarly,
and that official power should be constrained by law. The decentralized coordinate model accordingly seeks to add a dose of legal regularity by means of a
sequence of "lateral" legal checks. American prosecutors can reject charges
pushed forward by the police when the evidence is inadequate to support a
conviction. Judges have the authority and obligation to reject charges made
by prosecutors when a preliminary hearing indicates insufficient evidence or
legal grounds to proceed against the suspect. There are some hierarchical
checks as well, triggered by defendants' appeals to higher courts. In principle,
and to a considerable degree in practice, each decisionmaker anticipates the
possibility of rejection by the next one in the sequence and thus will avoid legal errors or factually weak cases that may result in dismissal at the next stage.

Defense lawyers are the enzymes that catalyze the coordinate model's sequential checking system. Their job is to slow the rush to judgment, direct-
ing judges' or prosecutors' attention to police malpractice or to weaknesses

in the prosecutor's case. At trial, defense lawyers cross-examine police and other witnesses (a job that falls primarily to the judge in continental European systems).[22] American defense lawyers remind the judge about legal precedents, build a record that can sustain an appeal, and summarize the evidence for the jury, a job done by the judge in British jury trials.

Suppose, however, that a criminal suspect does not have a defense attorney, or that his lawyer is inept, lazy, or overburdened. In such cases the coordinate system's checking mechanisms can easily lie dormant. In Philadelphia on a February morning in 1954, soon after the police (responding to political pressures) had opened a drive against "vagrants and habitual drunkards" in the central city, officers herded fifty-five defendants before a magistrate. As Caleb Foote described the court, there were no prosecuting attorneys and no defense lawyers. Within fifteen minutes, the magistrate discharged forty defendants and found fifteen guilty, sentencing each of the latter to three-month terms in the House of Correction. Foote (1956: 603) wrote: "Four of these committed defendants were tried, found guilty and sentenced in the elapsed time of seventeen seconds. . . . The magistrate merely read off the name of [each] defendant, took one look at him, and said, 'Three months in the House of Correction.' As the third man was being led out he objected, stating, 'But I'm working . . . ,' to which the magistrate replied, 'Aw, go on.'" In the Philadelphia magistrate's court and thousands like it, in 1954 and in previous decades, whenever defendants were not represented by counsel—as was common for the poor—little adversarial legalism prevailed in practice (Friedman and Percival, 1981). The method of adjudication in actuality was judge-dominated, yet without the same level of commitment to norms of legality that are inculcated in highly professional, hierarchically organized European judicial systems.

Professor Foote's account, published in a law review, was designed to force legal elites to recognize the huge gap between the ideals of the judicial system and its tawdry reality, especially as it applied to poor Americans. But how could that gap be closed? In theory, after reading about the Philadelphia magistrate's disregard of legal norms, reformers might have called for nationwide or at least statewide professional standards for recruiting, training, and supervising judges, along the lines employed in Great Britain and continental European democracies. No more political cronies of the mayor on the bench. Alternatively, reformers might have urged welfare bureaucracies to provide noncriminal alternatives for dealing with panhandling vagrants and alcoholics—such as government-provided shelter, aid, and treatment—rather than arrest and jail.

In the politically decentralized United States, however, neither Congress, the president, or the U.S. attorney general had the political authority to seek to change fifty state judicial recruitment systems, each of which would be defended, in any case, by the bonds of local political patronage. Nor was there a national social welfare department with funding or authority to induce scores of municipalities to provide shelters and treatment facilities. The predominant strategy of American legal reformers, therefore, was to sharpen the weapons of adversarial legalism, that is, to arm "vagrants" and other victims of unprofessional local judiciaries with stronger legal rights and with free legal advocates, capable of challenging and resisting governmental control. The achieve these goals, the reformers turned to the sole national institution with a modicum of hierarchical control over local courthouses—the U.S. Supreme Court, interpreter of the U.S. Constitution, the self-proclaimed "supreme law of the land." In a series of cases in the 1960s and 1970s the Supreme Court held that individual rights to liberty were violated by laws that made it a crime to be drunk in a public place, absent proof that the defendant actually was disturbing the peace.[23] In *Argersinger v. Hamlin* (1972), the Supreme Court announced a constitutional right to free counsel for indigent defendants in any prosecution that might result in substantial imprisonment, even for misdemeanors such as "disturbing the peace." *Argersinger,* along with the Supreme Court's 1963 *Gideon v. Wainwright* decision, transformed the institutional landscape of American criminal justice, inducing cities and urban counties to establish offices of full-time "public defenders" or to fund court-appointed lawyers for indigent criminal defendants (Spangenberg and Beeman, 1995: 31).[24]

In the early 1970s Malcolm Feeley studied a lower criminal court in New Haven. In contrast to Philadelphia in 1954, public defenders were consistently present in the court and so were prosecuting attorneys, for Connecticut had been compelled to provide prosecuting lawyers to match the state-funded defense lawyers. The prosecutors in turn demanded more systematic, documented evidence of guilt from the police; there was a written file and police report for each case. Feeley (1979: 184) observed that while approximately 40 percent of New Haven misdemeanor defendants were not represented by counsel (usually because they said they didn't want one), they benefited because others did have lawyers: "By pressing their clients' interests, occasionally raising legal defenses, and pressing for openness and trust between themselves and the Prosecutor's Office, defense attorneys have helped carve out the factors which enter into the assessment of the case. . . . Once they are established, these norms . . . are applied more or less equally to all."

In the 1960s legal reformers also pressed for nationwide legal controls over repressive and often racist local police practices. Again, in a politically decentralized, "coordinate" system, neither the president nor his attorney general had constitutional authority to fire a racist chief of police in Birmingham, Alabama. Moreover, Congress, hamstrung by federalism and by Democratic Party division, was of little help. But confronted with television pictures of southern sheriffs beating civil rights marchers, national political, journalistic, and legal elites came to believe that something had to be done. Adversarial legalism again was the answer. It provided the tools for circumventing the power vacuum on Capitol Hill and for asserting "hierarchical" federal controls over politically autonomous local police departments and courts.

In a series of appeals from state court decisions, the Supreme Court reinterpreted the Constitution, applying to the states the criminal procedure provisions of the Bill of Rights, which traditionally had been understood to operate as a check on the federal government, not the states. Case by case, the Court elaborated detailed nationwide rules concerning pretrial detention, interrogation of suspects, and police searches for evidence; required local judges to exclude evidence obtained by means of illegal searches or interrogations (as defined by the Supreme Court); expanded opportunities for locally convicted defendants to seek collateral review in lower federal courts (as exemplified by Warren McCleskey's habeas corpus petitions); and opened the door for federal reprosecution of racist law enforcement officers who had been acquitted by local juries in state courts, again expanding the number of checks in the coordinate system (and making possible the federal reprosecution of the Los Angeles officers who beat Rodney King).

Finally, federal courts expanded opportunities for victims of police misconduct to bring lawsuits for money damages against individual officers and police departments. Between 1961 and 1977 "constitutional" tort suits against government officials in federal courts increased from 296 to over 13,000 annually (Skolnick and Fyfe, 1993: 300–305; Schuck, 1983: 41–51, 200–201). In 1990 lawsuits against the Los Angeles Police Department cost the city about $11.3 million in settlements and verdicts (Skolnick and Fyfe, 1993: 202). In the wake of a $25 million verdict against the Torrington, Connecticut, police department for failing to arrest a repeatedly violent and abusive husband, 84 percent of urban police departments adopted policies calling for mandatory or preferred arrest policies in cases of domestic violence (Sherman, 1992).[25]

What Adversarial Legalism Cannot Do

Adversarial legalism is not the only set of tools that the United States employs to foster the rule of law. In larger American law enforcement organizations, legal professionals, fighting the centrifugal tendencies of the coordinate model, develop regulations and guidelines designed to enhance legal uniformity. For example, the district attorney's office in Los Angeles convenes a weekly "Special Circumstances Committee," which reviews homicide cases and strives to impose normative coherence on the decision whether to seek the death penalty, and New Jersey created a statewide office to train, assign, and oversee defense lawyers who handle capital cases for indigent defendants (Lewin, 1995).

To some extent, moreover, adversarial legalism has accelerated the development of such internal bureaucratic controls. As a result of the Supreme Court's exclusionary rule and the adversarial challenges to illegally seized evidence that it makes possible, most municipal police and federal law enforcement officers now receive extensive (and by most accounts effective) training in the law of search and seizure (Bradley, 1993: 37; Walker, 1993: 46–53; Orfield, Jr., 1987). Similarly, judicial decisions making it easier to sue police departments for damages have compelled many municipalities to codify policies on use of force and to work harder at training police officers and weeding out bad ones (Skolnick and Fyfe, 1993: 203; Epp, 1998).

Nevertheless, the centrifugal tendencies of the coordinate model are still very powerful. In comparative perspective American police officers, prosecutors, and trial judges are remarkably independent-minded and often resistant to hierarchically imposed administrative controls (Heilbroner, 1990). Adversarial legalism has distinct limits in imposing normative order in a politically fragmented system. A criminal suspect's or defendant's fate still depends significantly on *where* he is. According to Eric Schlosser (1994: 54–55), "If you are caught with three ounces of marijuana in Union City, Ohio, you will probably be fined $100. But if you are caught in the town of the same name literally across the road in Indiana, you could face nine months to two years in prison, a fine of up to $10,000, a felony record, suspension of your driver's license, forfeiture of your car." Within the same state individual locally elected or appointed county prosecutors often "will treat the possession of a small amount of cocaine, a first time property offense, or drunk driving differently" (Pizzi, 1993: 1344).

The weaknesses of adversarial legalism as a regulatory mechanism are products of its limited reach, its inefficiency, and its counterproductive effects, which include the politicization of the criminal justice system. A few words on each topic will illustrate the point.

The Limited Reach of Adversarial Legalism

Adversarial legalism exerts little control over the *discretionary* decisions that constitute the most frequent, crucial, and potentially discriminatory actions by law enforcement officials, such as district attorneys' determinations concerning when to decline to prosecute, or for whom to demand high bail, or in which cases to file multiple as opposed to single charges. Thus the United States still contrasts sharply with hierarchical prosecutorial systems, which have well-developed mechanisms for subjecting individual prosecutors' decisions to the rule of law (Johnson, 1998: 255–257; Pizzi, 1993: 1337). Nor can adversarial legalism impose much legal uniformity on police officers' decisions about whom to stop and question, whom to arrest (Stuntz, 1997: 5, 50), or whether to disclose potentially exculpatory evidence.[26] Similarly, because the juvenile justice system, designed as an alternative to adversarial legalism, operates in a more informal, discretionary manner, adversarial legalism has not been capable of eliminating the substantial differences in outcomes for African-American youth, who, according to a Department of Justice report, are significantly more likely than young white offenders to be arrested, held in jail, sent to either juvenile or adult court for trial, convicted, and sentenced to long periods of incarceration (Butterfield, 2000a).

Adversarial legalism's protections are invoked by the defendant, not imposed automatically as a matter of hierarchical legal command. Hence those protections often remain dormant when a gullible or scared criminal suspect chooses not to invoke them. Police investigators therefore have incentives to persuade suspects in custody to waive the right to silence and to legal counsel guaranteed by the Supreme Court's *Miranda* decision, and the police in some cities have become very adept at doing so, obtaining waivers and admissions in some two-thirds of all interrogations (Leo, 1996). Few observers, and even fewer American black males, would disagree with comparative legal scholar William Pizzi's judgment that "mistreatment of citizens by police remains a serious problem in the United States" (Pizzi, 1999: 108).[27]

Constitutional law, and hence adversarial legalism, also has little influence on many crucial decisions by the fifty state legislatures—such as how much funding to provide to public defenders' offices, which in turn strongly influences how often the protections against police and prosecutorial misconduct established by the courts actually are invoked (Stuntz, 1997). Similarly, adversarial legalism has had relatively little effect on the *substance* of criminal law and penal policy. By and large, American courts have not been able to stop or even slow the populist political drive to increase prison sentences and to criminalize narcotics, marijuana, and other social problems. The Supreme Court has compelled states and localities to improve criminal *procedures,* particularly in capital cases and other felonies, but with few exceptions, neither it nor other courts have claimed the legal or political authority to override elected politicians' decisions to make American criminal law distinctively punitive.

Inefficiency

As a mechanism of legal accountability, litigation is far more costly than bureaucratic supervision. As will be discussed more fully in Chapter 5, adversarial legalism has also made the American criminal trial a distinctively inefficient method of deciding disputes, a method so complex and costly that it has become a relatively uncommon event. By making courts the primary lawmakers, adversarial legalism has produced a confusing and erratic body of procedural rules, especially when compared to the professionally drafted codes and guidelines implemented by European Ministries of Justice. As lawmakers, American courts proceed reactively case by case, making rules in the form of highly contextualized judgments about which appellate judges themselves often disagree (Bradley, 1993). Hence Supreme Court rulings concerning car searches, or the waiver of *Miranda* rights, are commonly misunderstood and misapplied by police officers and lower court judges alike (id. at 47–49).[28] Of course, legal confusion and malleability breed more costly litigation as well as inconsistent treatment.

The Politicization of Criminal Procedure

Viewed in comparative perspective, adversarial legalism's techniques of legal challenge seem to turn the processing of criminal cases into a legal slalom course in which a rule violation by the police or a "prejudicial" statement by the prosecutor, the trial judge, or a juror results in the exclusion of incriminating evidence, a mistrial, or an appellate court reversal. When the legal error seems disproportionate to the seriousness of the criminal offense, the public, like Charles Dickens's Mr. Bumble in *Oliver Twist,* is then likely to view the law as an ass, focused on "legal technicalities" rather than on the truth or falsity of the criminal charge. Hence adversarial legalism has been a politically controversial mechanism for increasing accountability in the criminal justice system.

Once liberal reformers made constitutional litigation a primary strategy for imposing nationwide standards on local police, courts, and prosecutors, conservative interest groups and politicians turned their attention to the judiciary, trying to stack the courts with judges inclined to reverse or restrict "liberal" judicial precedents. On the U.S. Courts of Appeals, where judges sit in panels of three, judges appointed by Republican president Ronald Reagan disagreed with colleagues appointed by Democratic president Jimmy Carter in almost one of four criminal appeals during the 1980s (Gottschall: 1986: 52). In 1986 political conservatives, complaining that the California Supreme Court had reversed the trial court in sixty-four of sixty-eight appeals in capital punishment cases, mounted a successful electoral campaign to oust the chief justice, Rose Bird, and two liberal colleagues (Wold and Culver, 1987). In the next decade, with a new cast of Republican judges, the California court *upheld* most of the death sentences it reviewed—much more often, in fact, than almost every other state supreme court (Kamin, 1999). In Congress and in some states liberals have fought back, battling to block conservative judicial appointments and to put politically liberal judges on the bench. In many states "judicial election campaigns have come to resemble other races, complete with attack advertising and multimillion-dollar war chests" (Glaberson, 2000). America's uniquely partisan political struggle to control the courts thus has exacerbated the malleability, inconsistency, and indeterminacy of criminal procedure in the United States.

Adversarial legalism does fill an organizational void. It has prodded a highly decentralized, politically responsive criminal justice system toward the uniform application of legal rights and penalties. It enables dedicated lawyers and judges to expose malpractice or legalistic inflexibility on the part of police and prosecutors and to employ imaginative constitutional interpretation to make improvements in the justice system. But it is an indirect, incomplete, and inefficient mechanism of control and legal coordination, compared to the professionalized and bureaucratic police, prosecutorial, and judicial systems of many parliamentary democracies. Adversarial legalism also has made American criminal procedures distinctively cumbersome, inconsistent, and confusing. And those characteristics, as we will now see, exacerbate the risk of injustice in the disposition of individual cases.

5

Deciding Criminal Cases

In the eighteenth century, English juries sitting in the Old Bailey tried between twelve and twenty felony cases a day (Langbein, 1979a: 262). In the late nineteenth century, jury trials in Oakland, California, probably averaged half an hour at most (Friedman, 1979). But during the twentieth century, writes Albert Alschuler (1986: 1825), "the American jury trial . . . has become one of the most cumbersome and expensive fact-finding mechanisms that humankind has devised."

In 1968 felony trials in Los Angeles averaged 7.2 days. A detailed study of nine county courts in the mid-1980s found that the median jury trial in felony cases (excluding trials in which the death penalty is at issue) took more than fourteen hours (National Center for State Courts, 1988: 19).[1] Since actual "trial days" averaged less than 3.5 hours (id. at 9), the median trial probably was spread out over four days. In Oakland, California, the study also revealed, homicide trials, which accounted for a third of all criminal trials in the county, averaged forty-four hours (before jury deliberations)—probably at least two weeks (id. at 30).[2] In North Carolina the average trial in a capital murder case in 1991 cost the state about $80,000, and some cost more than $150,000. Lawyers' fees in some cases, including but not limited to the infamous O. J. Simpson trial, have run into the millions of dollars.[3] "England may be the cradle of the adversary system," Graham Hughes (1984: 568) observes, "but the child it reared never grew to the giant proportions of the sibling who crossed the Atlantic."[4]

The expansion of the American criminal trial springs from the intensification of adversarial legalism. Litigation and court rulings have generated a set of constitutional rights and legal practices that encourage criminal defendants to remain silent and empower criminal defense lawyers to challenge the prosecution's evidence, the composition of the jury, and the conduct of the adjudicatory process. Each right was elaborated in hopes of reducing the risk of unjust conviction. But the pumped-up adversarial jury trial has become so complex, legalistic, and costly that, in the words of comparative legal scholar

John Langbein (1979a: 265), it is "unworkable as an ordinary or routine dispositive procedure." Average citizens sense this too: in many cities a large proportion of people summoned for jury duty fail to show up in court.[5] After comparing criminal trials in the United States to those in the Netherlands, Germany, Norway, and England, William Pizzi (1999: 74, 184) concluded that American trials are much more susceptible to variability in the intensity of adversarial advocacy and are a more uncertain mechanism for determining the truth—exacerbating the risk of both unjust conviction and unjust acquittal. Indeed, Pizzi notes, defense lawyers and judges in the United States commonly refer to trials as "crapshoots" and go to great lengths to avoid them.

Instead of trial, therefore, the overwhelming bulk of criminal charges are decided by defendants' guilty pleas. In Phoenix, Arizona there were approximately 20,000 felony convictions in the 1983–1986 period. Only 4.27 percent were tried; the rest were disposed of by guilty plea (Lowenthal, 1993: 80). Trial rates of less than 5 percent also have been found in Los Angeles, Denver, and Manhattan (Boland et al., 1990: 91–97). Nationwide, it is estimated that more than 90 percent of all criminal convictions are obtained via guilty pleas (Stuntz, 1997: 24; Alschuler, 1983: 935). According to Thomas Weigend (1980: 411), a German comparative legal scholar, "The admirable American preoccupation with safeguarding the individual's procedural rights has backfired. By affording the whole collection of procedural rights to a small minority of defendants, the system deprives the great majority of rights [particularly the right to a meaningful day in court] available to the accused in most civilized countries."

Adversarial Legalism's Ugly Child: Plea Bargaining

Plea bargaining isn't a new practice (Friedman, 1979),[6] and most nations, Weigend observes, have established a simplified, speedy, and inexpensive dispositional system for the majority of criminal cases—those in which the evidence is strong and defendants do not have any plausible defense. Full-scale, labor-intensive adjudication, replete with opportunities for the defendants and their lawyers to challenge the prosecution's case, tends to be reserved for serious cases and those in which defendants strongly claim to be innocent.

The key normative issues revolve around the character of the simple model and how much pressure is exerted on defendants to be "cooperative"—to confess. In Germany and France, Weigend (1980: 420) notes, the simple model involves either a less complicated, quicker trial in a lower court or a payment of a fine in return for dismissal of criminal charges as in American traffic courts. But, and this is the critical point, in Germany and in France "the cost of choosing the more complicated model is not prohibitive." In the

United States, however, the "situation is dramatically different." Compared to a rapid plea negotiation (the simple model in the United States), the American jury trial is vastly more complex, labor-intensive, expensive, and anxiety-provoking. Unlike a plea negotiation, Weigend notes (id. at 420–421), an American jury trial not only requires the lawyers to spend many days in court but imposes the following chores on them:

> finding, interviewing, and coaching witnesses; submitting briefs on, and arguing, pretrial motions to suppress evidence; fighting over discovery and inspection rights; devising tactics for questioning witnesses and generally for the conduct of the trial; analyzing and challenging the composition of the jury; preparing lengthy opening and closing arguments; presenting the evidence in a fashion understandable to uneducated and ignorant laypersons; arguing, again and again, about objections to particular lines of questioning and to the introduction of evidence; attacking the credibility of the opponent's witnesses and preparing drafts of jury instructions.

[handwritten margin note: jobs of lawyers if trial goes to court]

"It is the disproportion in America between the simple and the complicated models of adjudication," Weigend concludes (id. at 421), "which induces the American system to use coercion and deceit in order to reach the quick dispositions it has come to depend on for survival."

Weigend overstates the point a little. In the United States most guilty pleas are not the product of coercion, and many do not stem from the disparity he refers to. Rather, guilty pleas often reflect straightforward confessions by defendants caught dead to rights, and the ensuing sentence reflects a "going rate" well understood by the courthouse community.[7] Many other guilty pleas reflect negotiations between prosecutors and defense counsel that probe the evidence, assess the defendant's record and degree of culpability, and tend to arrive at sensible and fair dispositions (Utz, 1978). On the other hand, many guilty pleas *do* reflect the extraordinary legal complexity and stressfulness of adversarial jury trials, which cast fear into the heart of the unpracticed defense lawyer and vastly increase the difficulty of a prosecutor's and a trial judge's job. In the criminal process, as in other spheres of American law, adversarial legalism enables disputing parties to threaten their adversaries with very large costs and delays, which encourages case disposition by means of informal (and often extortionate) bargaining.

Defense lawyers in the United States are keenly aware that prosecutors and judges, obligated by law to dispose of criminal cases within a few months, cannot afford to mount many seven-day trials. Hence, whereas Japanese defendants are encouraged to confess and apologize (Foote, 1992),[8] American defense lawyers routinely encourage even clearly guilty defendants to maintain a stony silence and to plead not guilty,[9] for the lawyer can then threaten, implicitly or explicitly, to insist on trial unless the prosecutor offers concessions. Prosecutors, in turn, feel compelled to reduce charges (and hence penalties) in order to elicit guilty pleas, thereby avoiding a laborious, schedule-wrecking trial. Judges also encourage the aversion to adjudication. In many jurisdictions, researchers have shown, judges give defendants who insist on trial stiffer sentences than those imposed on comparable defendants who plead guilty (Brereton and Casper, 1981: Uhlman and Walker, 1979).[10] By emphasizing the "trial penalty" (or, from the prosecutor's standpoint, the guilty-plea discount), defense lawyers pressure at least some defendants who might prefer a trial to plead guilty to a lesser offense (Lynch, 1994: 127).

The risk that innocent (or legally acquittable) defendants will be coerced into pleading guilty has been intensified, many observers assert, by the enactment of "sentence enhancement" statutes, which mandate extremely long prison terms for offenses involving certain circumstances, such as use of a firearm or conviction for a third felony. These statutes raise the stakes for defendants. Consequently, they are more inclined to insist on trial, which threatens to overwhelm both the courts and the prosecutors' offices.[11] But the huge penalties also enable prosecutors to avoid trial by offering not to charge the aggravating circumstance (thereby offering an enormous reduction in the prison term) if the defendant will plead guilty to a lesser offense (Lowenthal, 1993; 80).[12] For an alleged burglar with a prior record, faced with life imprisonment if convicted, the prosecutor's offer can be very hard to refuse—even if the defendant is inclined to contest the charge.

Plea bargaining is troubling on other grounds as well: for the guilty, it transforms the act of confession from a ritual of moral and social healing into a cynical game, reinforcing the criminal's alienated view of society (Casper 1972: 80–81). American prosecutors, unlike their European counterparts, can freely reduce charges at any time; hence in a regime of plea bargaining, prosecutors have a strong incentive to inflate and multiply the initial charges to fortify their bargaining position (Frase, 1990: 621; Alschuler, 1983: 939).[13] Even if many ethically committed prosecutors resist this temptation, not all of them do. In any event, actual control over sentencing shifts from judges to prosecutors because they control the ultimate *charge*. Yet in the United States, in contrast to Western Europe and Japan, prosecutors receive little formal training in sentencing theory; often they decide the fates of defendants rapidly and intuitively, without obligatory coordinating guidelines and without any institutionalized requirement to explain and compare their decisions in a reviewable manner (Lynch, 1994: 125–126).[14] American also spend less time and effort than Japanese prosecutors, for example, probing the facts of each case and assessing the proper legal disposition. Consequently, David Johnson (1998) concluded, outcomes for similar offenses and offenders in the United States are far less uniform—and in that sense, less just—than in Japan. Also, even more than at trial, where at least there is a supervising judge, in a regime of plea bargaining defendants' fates are deeply affected by differences in bargaining skills among attorneys (Lynch, 1994: 130–131).

Ironically, then, the rules and structures of adversarial legalism, because they generate such a cumbersome and costly mode of dispute resolution, produce *too little* adversarial legalism in practice—a pattern that recurs in many areas of American law.

Criminal Case Disposition in Comparative Perspective

Most European democracies firmly forbid large sentencing differentials between defendants who confess and those who insist on trial, or at least carefully limit such disparities (Myhre, 1968: 650; Alschuler, 1983).[15] Most strictly forbid prosecutors to bargain over reductions in charges; with some sub rosa slippage, that seems to be the practice as well.[16] Many legal systems insist, in fact, that a confession should not preclude a trial, both as a safeguard against coerced confessions and for reasons suggested by Alschuler's assertion that plea bargaining "is inconsistent with the presumption that a decent society should want to hear what an accused person might say in his defense" (Alschuler, 1983: 933–934).

Many European legal systems can attain or at least approximate those goals because in contrast with the radically decentralized and adversarial American system, their prosecutorial and judicial systems and processes are hierarchically organized, and their adjudicatory processes are vastly more efficient. Germany, John Langbein (1979b: 204–225) asserted in an illuminating article, is a "land without plea bargaining." This is no longer entirely true, particularly in complex cases involving economic, environmental, and narcotics charges (Pizzi, 1993: 1325) but also in routine cases, in which prosecutors offer to file only a "penal order" (which entails a fine, not incarceration) in return for defendants' acquiescence to the charge (Dubber, 1997: 559).[17] Langbein's article has been criticized, moreover, for idealizing the German system a bit (Dubber, 1997). Nevertheless, knowledgeable comparativists insist that plea bargaining in Germany, compared to the more prevalent American version, is "less likely to cause major sentencing disparities, to encourage initial overcharging, or to create undue risks of convicting the innocent" (Frase and Weigend, 1995: 354). Charging decisions by German prosecutors are constrained by written guidelines, and prosecutors are part of a carefully trained and hierarchically supervised career bureaucracy. But most importantly, Langbein pointed out, German prosecutors, compared to their American counterparts, have less *need* to bargain because German criminal trials are short. According to a 1970 study, they averaged a day in length for major trials, about two hours for average cases (Casper and Zeisel, 1972: 149–150).[18] In the 1990s Germany experienced a fair number of strongly contested "monster trials," in which a sequence of hearings spread out over months or even well over a year. Still, a systematic 1989–1990 study found that trials for the most serious crimes (two judge-three lay judge panels) averaged 2.8 days, in somewhat less serious cases (one judge-two lay judge panels) 2.4 days (Dubber, 1997: 569). Why are German trials substantially shorter than American trials?

No Juries

In Germany adjudication is entrusted to a panel of judges and lay persons.[19] As we have seen, the court's decision (including the sentence) must be explained in writing and is subject to searching appellate review. Since there are no juries, with their unexplained and unreviewable verdicts, German criminal trials have no need for the time-consuming "prophylactic procedures" the United States employs to prevent juror bias or error. These American procedures include lengthy interrogation of prospective jurors,[20] disputes concerning "the vast exclusionary apparatus of the law of evidence" (Langbein, 1979b; Damaska, 1997b),[21] and adversarial debates over the proper wording of jury instructions.

Less Adversarial, More Focused Trials

In Germany (as in France and several other continental European democracies), defendants have a right to remain silent, and the judge reminds them of it, but defense lawyers rarely advise their client not to answer the judge's questions. In contrast with the United States, where defense lawyers often preclude a defendant from testifying at trial, the defendant in Germany generally tells his version of the story and is then questioned by the judge (Van Kessel, 1992: 421; Frase and Weigend, 1995: 343; Langbein, 1979b: 208).[22] As in England and other European countries, the defendant typically is the *first* witness, which immediately focuses the trial on the most important points at issue (Langbein, 1979b: 208–209). The U.S. Supreme Court actually held unconstitutional a state law requiring the defendant to testify first (Pizzi, 1999: 165–168). Because the defendant testifies last, or not at all, in the United States, the prosecution must painstakingly prove every potentially contestable point since it doesn't know which will be contested. In Germany the defendant and other witnesses are questioned by the presiding judge, who then "invites his fellow judges (professional and lay), the prosecutor, the defense counsel, and the accused to supplement his questioning" (Langbein, 1979b: 207).[23]

The Pretrial Investigation

At trials in Germany (and in the Netherlands and Norway) (Pizzi, 1999: 112–113), the questioning of the defendant and other witnesses is based on a detailed file of pretrial statements and other evidence gathered by police, prosecutors, or investigating magistrates. Well before trial, the file is made available to the defense—which can suggest further, potentially exculpating lines of inquiry by prosecutors, who are obligated to investigate such leads. According to Langbein (1979b: 208), "This thorough, open, and impartial pretrial preparation effectively eliminates surprise and forensic strategy from the trial," while enabling the judge to zero in on the real issues, avoiding the repetitive and often trivial testimony that characterizes American trials.[24]

Because of the thorough pretrial investigation, in fact, many German trials are essentially uncontested. One study found that German defendants made a "full confession" during their testimony in 41 percent of trials, and another 26 percent offered "partial" confessions (Casper and Zeisel, 1972: 142–147). In the Netherlands, a British scholar observed, the facts are "mainly established at the investigating stage, so that . . . the Dutch public trial is mainly a check on whether the investigations have been properly carried out." The primary focus of the trial judge (as opposed to the investigating magistrate) is developing an understanding of the defendant's motivations and degree of culpability (Downes, 1988: 94–97).[25]

Americans may be inclined to characterize such trials as little more than a "slow plea"—the equivalents of the many cases resolved in the United States by guilty plea because they are essentially uncontested. But the short European trials are vastly different from American plea bargaining. The short European trials take place in open court, the defendant speaks for himself, and most important, his fate is decided by a judge (or panel of judges), who must explain and justify the decision orally and in writing. The decision in one case can be compared to the decision in others, and it can be appealed. American plea bargaining, in contrast, is a low-visibility process; the decisions it reaches are unexplained and essentially unreviewable.

The dominance of the investigatory phase in criminal justice processes in Europe does not mean that there is no scope for adversarial argument. In the Dutch process, for example, where all evidence collected by prosecutors or investigating magistrates must be shared with defense counsel, "the investigation *by* the examining magistrate" can be "turned into a procedure *before* the examining magistrate," introducing a *trial* element into the pretrial phase (Peters, 1992: 259–298). The defense lawyer often takes a role in the building of the file, which ultimately contains testimony from witnesses suggested by the defense and reports by forensic social workers and psychiatrists (id. at 285, 288).[26] Within a judge-dominated structure, however, adversarial interaction by attorneys rarely devolves into the contentious adversariness often employed by American defense counsel and prosecuting attorneys, in which each often strives to prevent the other from ascertaining evidence that would detract from the goal of "winning" (Pizzi, 1999).

Of course, it is not easy to imagine "transplanting" European methods of criminal adjudication to the United States. Nor is that the point of this comparison, which is only to highlight the structural causes and the consequences of American adversarial legalism. A hierarchically supervised investigatory system and a short, less adversarial criminal trial seem to avoid, or to at least mute, the more coercive and tawdry effects of unrecorded and unreviewable plea bargaining—the ugly but affordable offspring of the woefully costly and inefficient American jury trial.

London and New York

Criminal case disposition under American adversarial legalism remains distinctive even when compared with England, the birthplace of trial by jury and the "adversarial system." British prosecutors and courts, like their American counterparts, have had to cope with rising urban criminal caseloads. A form of "implicit plea bargaining" is not uncommon; defendants' lawyers let them know that a substantial penalty reduction is available if they plead guilty (Hughes, 1984). But British criminal defendants have another option. For a large range of serious crimes, British defendants can decline to plead guilty and can demand a prompt, nonjury trial in a magistrate's court rather than a jury trial in Crown Court. The magistrate's court also deals with misdemeanor cases; hence "roughly 98 percent of all criminal matters are handled in magistrate's courts" (Pizzi, 1999: 105).[27]

In the 1980s Graham Hughes (1984: 606) compared lower criminal courts in New York City with London's magistrate's courts. In the New York courthouse, he wrote:

> The physical plant is run down . . . , with sickening rancid bathrooms. . . . A general air of seething disorder, verging on chaos prevails. Officials appear harried and angry and information is almost impossible to obtain. Clerks are bored and patronizing, police are cynical and indif-

ferent. In the courtrooms . . . a hum of noise prevails. . . . Events taking place before the bench are meaningless to all except a few insiders. A series of rapid and muttered colloquies take place . . . between lawyers [for defense and prosecution] and judges with a mute defendant physically present but rarely involved. . . . When judges can be heard at all they often appear angry and at times abusive.

In the London magistrate's court, Hughes observed that the proceedings are dominated not by the prosecutor and the defense lawyer but by a professional magistrate. In American lower courts, the opposite is true because only a tiny proportion of misdemeanor prosecutions result in trials; as Malcolm Feeley (1979) explained in *The Process Is the Punishment*, to most defendants the delays and other costs of a jury trial make it an unattractive option.[28] Not so in the London magistrate's court. The trials often last only an hour and "rarely last more than a day" (Hughes, 1984: 600). As Hughes saw it:

London's magistrate's courts also have an air of . . . considerable bustle. But the business and bustle usually appear to be under firm control by the magistrates and the police who are in charge of he courts. . . . The proceedings are conducted smoothly with some formality, a great deal of decorum, general civility, and an air of considerable authority. The prevailing tone is one of benevolent paternalism coupled with recognition of defendants' procedural rights. Magistrates are almost unfailingly polite to defendants, and this appears . . . to express itself in an institutional concern that the defendant is aware of the nature of his situation and can appreciate his choices and exercise his rights. The police behave in court . . . in a strongly authoritative but not unkind way to defendants. The proceedings are easily audible and make sense to even the casual, untrained observer.

. . . [D]efendants participate in the process more than in a New York court. They are spoken to directly by the clerk and the magistrates in clear and simple language which is repeated until there is confidence that the defendant has understood. The defendant is listened to carefully and any ambiguities . . . in his responses are usually examined. . . . At the end of the proceeding, most defendants appear to be satisfied that they have taken part in a reasonably fair process in which they were treated in a dignified fashion and given an opportunity to express choices on significant questions.

Hughes was by no means an unqualified admirer of the English system, and his comparison, focusing on two courts at a particular moment in time, may not be fully representative. Except in British urban centers, for example, magistrates are lay persons, advised by a lawyer-clerk (Pizzi, 1999: 105).[29] For our purposes, the primary value of Hughes's account is to highlight the difference between two ways of enhancing protection for defendants in routine criminal cases. The American approach, imposed via the Supreme Court's constitutional decisions, is to emphasize adversarial legalism, guaranteeing defendants the right to a jury trial and to representation by defense counsel. Fairness increases, but so do the costs and delays of trial, so that, as noted earlier, most cases are resolved by informal, lawyer-dominated bargaining. The British, in contrast, seek to enhance both efficiency and fairness by muting adversarial legalism and by concentrating more power in a reasonably well-staffed, apolitical judiciary.[30] As Hughes (1984: 608–609) puts it:

> The virtues of these English magistrate's courts are, in the end, those of benevolent authority and paternalistic order. The strong control of the court by the magistrate, the firm control of the defendants and the public by the police, the relative dearth of lawyers and their deference and brevity of speech when they appear at all, converge to produce this picture. Questions of defendants' rights are certainly not absent, but raising them will often depend on the magistrate himself, and, if defendants are treated fairly and all the norms of procedure and substantive criminal law are followed with decent fidelity, it is often not because of the vigilance of any representative of the defendant, but because of the traditional behavior of the courts.

The contrast between the American emphasis on lawyer-driven adversariness and British judicial paternalism is also reflected in comparisons of felony cases that go to full-scale jury trial. For example, in the United States adversarial rights to purge racial and other forms of bias from jury selection have become routinized into what Alschuler (1986: 1824) justifiably labels a "prolonged, insulting, privacy-invading jury selection process,"[31] as prosecutors and defense lawyers strive "to kick people they don't like off the jury" (Pizzi, 1999: 18). In Los Angeles criminal trials in 1984, jury selection averaged five hours (Kakalik et al., 1990). In England criminal juries usually are impaneled in a matter of minutes (Alschuler, 1983: 971; Hughes, 1984: 590). Similarly, in the United States adversarially invoked rights to prevent unfair trial practices generate lengthy in-court wrangles over evidentiary issues. Jurors periodically are marched in and out of the courtroom like children kept from hearing their parents' arguments. In English criminal trials lawyers rarely tie up proceedings with objections and disputes about the admission of evidence,[32] partly, William Pizzi (1999: 176, 180) argues, because British appellate courts are less likely than American appeals courts to reverse a trial court's decision for procedural error, unless it appears to have resulted in a "miscarriage of justice."[33]

Hughes (1984: 589–599) remarks on the muted adversariness of the average British barrister, as compared to the typical American criminal lawyer.[34] American lawyers feel no compunction about "coaching" friendly witnesses before trial (which British barristers would not do) or about using facial expressions to signal to the jury that a hostile witness's testimony should not be believed. In some cases the American adversary system's competitive ethos leads prosecutors to engage in heavy-handed or even illegal tactics, such as withholding exculpatory evidence.[35] Encouraged by the adversarial ethic, American prosecutors and defense lawyers engage in "frequently repetitive (as well as pointless and degrading) cross-examination" (Alschuler, 1986: 1824) punctuated with objections and arguments from opposing counsel about the cross-examiner's questioning style. This rarely occurs in English criminal trials, where, Hughes (1984: 589) observed, "judges are forthright and dominating" and opposing counsel are "correspondingly restrained"— again, partly because British judges are considerably less likely to be reversed on appeal for a remark or ruling that an appellate court regards as prejudicial to the defendant's interests (id. at 109). In contrast to American judges (Friedman, 1993: 387–388), British judges in jury trials summarize and comment on the evidence (Wolchover, 1989). In American trials that task is left entirely to the competing lawyers, who have leeway to resort to obfuscation and appeals to general values rather than to close analysis of the evidence. Finally, following a parliamentary statute enacted in October 1994, British judges and juries have been authorized to draw inculpatory inferences from a defendant's refusal to answer questions or explain his actions, either to the police or in court (Schmidt, 1994: A17).[36] The United States, in contrast, continues to encourage a radically adversarial posture on the part of defendants (in the police station as well as at trial) by banning such inferences and by preventing prosecutors from calling the jury's attention to the defendant's refusal to offer a defense in his own words. By making proof more difficult, the adversarial stance encouraged by the American interpretation of the Fifth Amendment's privilege against self-incrimination also leads police in the United States to resort to psychological trickery in order to induce defendants to waive their right to silence (Leo, 1996; Parloff, 1993: 58–62).

In sum, British trials, while adversarial, entail a much larger dose of hierarchical control, hence more constraints on party-driven adversariness, than criminal adjudication in the United States. That does not mean that English tribunals are kangaroo courts; acquittal rates in British Crown Courts are considerably higher than in American jury trials. It does mean that British trials are shorter and less costly. And that moderates incentives to resolve cases via the kind of low-visibility, sometimes extortive, sometimes coercive plea negotiation that occurs in American criminal courthouses.

Unequal Justice

No criminal justice system can always provide equal justice. Compared to the usual defendant, wealthier, better-educated, better-connected defendants enjoy many advantages. Typically, they have a larger number of respectable friends who might be able to provide favorable evidence (Cooney, 1994: 833–858). Typically, they have a shorter criminal record. They are more likely to be able to refer to the good deeds they have done, which can then be weighed against the bad. They get better lawyers. But *costly* systems of justice exacerbate these inequalities.

In regimes that lie closer to the ideal type of bureaucratic legalism, the prosecutor and judge are the dominant figures; they can be trained and reviewed in ways that can offset social inequalities in the defendant population. But in a regime of adversarial legalism, the parties' *lawyers* are the crucial actors. Hence, compared to European criminal justice systems, outcomes in the United States are far more sensitive to variations in the energy and skill of particular defense counsel and prosecutors, and especially to any *imbalance* of effort and competence between the two sides. Moreover, those imbalances are common, partly because full-scale adversarial legalism is so slow, complex, and costly that advantages flow to those who can best afford the battle.

When asked in opinion surveys if there is a different system of justice for the rich and the poor, Americans tend to say, "Yes, indeed" (McClosky and Brill, 1983: 150–151).[37] They are right. The difference does not show up clearly in scholarly comparisons of the fate of white and black criminal defendants, whose sentences (controlling for prior record and seriousness of offense) are remarkably similar; after all, the overwhelming majority of criminal defendants of both races are poor.[38] Rather, the inequality arises from the capacity of well-financed defendants, or of especially dedicated defense lawyers, to create an entirely different kind of legal proceeding by mobilizing all the weapons afforded by adversarial legalism.[39]

In white-collar crime cases, for example, well-paid defense lawyers often get involved early, maneuvering to restrict the prosecution's access to information and negotiating with prosecutors even before the indictment is handed down (Mann, 1985; Penner, 1992: 3). Well-financed defense counsel hire consultants to help them select sympathetic juries or try out arguments before mock juries (Adler, 1994). To enhance defense witnesses' ability to withstand adversarial cross-examination, well-financed defense counsel spend hours coaching them—other legal systems forbid witness coaching and encourage witnesses to tell their stories in their own words (Pizzi, 1999: 197–198). At complex trials, American jurors are sometimes befuddled by the complexity of evidence and by the tactics of skilled defense lawyers, whose reputations in turn rest on "winning," not merely (as in other countries) on ensuring that defendants reliably get a fair trial.[40] But poorly financed public defenders' offices cannot come close to consistently mounting full-scale aggressive defenses in capital cases,[41] and particularly in noncapital cases (Stuntz, 1997). Even the most competent public defender lacks the time and resources for requisite factual investigation, research, and legal argument for every plausible claim in each defendant's case (ibid.). The poor defendant thus gets fewer legal arguments made on his behalf than the rich defendant, and some poor defendants get less than others.

Although most (not all) state legislatures have steadily increased appropriations for public defenders' offices and assigned criminal defense counsel, these expenditures have not kept pace with the volume of criminal cases. Reviewing the available data, William Stuntz estimates that *in constant dollars* public expenditures *per case* on defense lawyers for indigent defendants "declined significantly" between the late 1970s and the early 1990s—"a period in which the law of criminal procedure mushroomed" and hence in which litigation costs ought to have *risen* (Stuntz, 1997: 9–10). Numerous studies have concluded that public defenders, while hardworking and generally competent, are "terribly overburdened" (ibid.; Hanson et al., 1992; McIntyre, 1987). Stuntz cites a New York City study that found that court-appointed defense lawyers filed written pretrial motions on procedural issues in only 11 percent of nonhomicide felony cases, but even this exceeded the proportion of cases in which appointed defense lawyers visited the crime site (4 percent), interviewed witnesses (4 percent), and used experts to challenge the prosecution's evidence (2 percent) (McConville and Mirsky, 1986–1987: 762–767).

Resource inadequacy affects prosecutors' offices as well. When caseloads are high, prosecutors, who operate under legal mandates to try or dispose of criminal cases within a few months, tend to treat defendants more leniently. Law professor Randy Barnett (1994: 2595–296) writes:

> In 1976, when I was a law clerk for the State's Attorney's Office of Cook County [Chicago], the average caseload per judge was well over 400. In those days, plea bargaining was notorious. . . . Rapes routinely were reduced to aggravated battery. Car thieves and burglars had to be convicted dozens of times before being imprisoned. It simply was not possible to bring even a small fraction of cases to trial, and defense lawyers knew it. So most cases ended with extremely lenient deals.
>
> . . . By the time I returned to the felony trial courts as an Assistant

State's Attorney in 1979, the caseload in each courtroom was down to between 125 and 135 [due to federal funding assistance]. This meant that I could credibly threaten to try any case . . . and could offer plea bargains that were in my judgment correct sentences. . . . By the 1990s, [due largely to the "War on Drugs"] the caseload had once again climbed to over 400, even though the number of courts had greatly increased. Give-away plea bargaining was once again rampant, especially for those accused of property crimes.[42]

Going to trial is the most labor-intensive and hence expensive choice a public defender can make. And in a regime shaped by adversarial legalism, trying a case before a jury has become an especially complex and stressful performance. Recalling his first few jury trials, an American public defender provided the following description of the formidable demands American trials place on lawyers, not all of whom, we can be sure, rise fully to the occasion:

> During the government's direct exam you must listen to what the witness is saying; take copious notes; make objections before—not after—the answers are given; refine and replan your cross-examination; and watch the jury's reaction. I repeatedly found my mind wandering and had no idea what the witness had said. When I did focus carefully on what the witness was saying, I forgot to make objections. When I managed to listen and make objections, I found that I had taken no notes (and thus had only the vaguest recollection of the testimony). (Bellows, 1988: 78)

Yet in a regime of adversarial legalism, the quality of justice is especially dependent on equality in the quality of the duelling lawyers. In a study of death penalty litigation, Samuel Kamin (1999: 124) writes:

> Experts with whom I've spoken have generally agreed that the most important variable in determining whether a capital defendant will be sentenced to death is not the details of the crime, the locale in which the case will be tried or the race of the defendant but rather the competence of the defendant's attorney in trying death cases. This opinion is shared by death penalty scholars as well.

Some of the unequal outcomes generated by the American criminal justice system stem from its deliberate emphasis on *political responsiveness* rather than on legal uniformity. Thus legal penalties for similar crimes differ from state to state, or from time to time within the same state, as legislatures respond to public opinion or organized interest groups. But those inequalities in outcome are not regarded as wholly improper, for they are legitimated, at least in part, by democratic processes. Similarly, American reliance on locally selected police chiefs and prosecutors, who make discretionary decisions about enforcement priorities and charging policies, suggests that similar offenders in different communities will often be treated differently. Reliance on trial by panels of randomly selected citizen jurors, whose decisions are unexplained and unreviewable, virtually guarantees unequal outcomes.

Such county-to-county, jury-to-jury inequalities, justifiable or not (and they're surely troublesome in terms of the ideal of equal treatment under the law), were deliberately built into the system long ago. They are the inherited legacy of a polity that feared a government strong enough to impose legal uniformity across a whole continent or even a whole state.

Inequalities that stem wholly from the expense and complexity of highly adversarial criminal trials, however, are of a different order. Those inequalities arise from the relegation of most criminal case dispositions to informal, legally unreviewed negotiations between weakly supervised individual prosecutors and defense lawyers who vary in quality and resources. They are the *unintended* consequence of judicial decisions that by arming all defendants with lawyers and legal rights, and by devising more rules to control bias or error by juries, were designed to promote more *equal* justice. Adversarial legalism has been the American substitute for hierarchical methods of guaranteeing the rule of law. In a politically fragmented system, it has provided legal weapons for combating blatantly unjust laws and law enforcement processes. But adversarial legalism is far less effective for achieving equal justice in everyday criminal legal processes. It is too costly, cumbersome, and complicated for everyone to wield it equally. It undermines, rather than promotes, the belief that in the United States decisions in criminal cases are based on law, accurately applied to the facts of each case (Johnson, 1998). Perhaps the most serious unintended consequence of adversarial legalism, therefore, is that it erodes the legitimacy of the criminal justice system.

III

Civil Justice

6

Adversarial Legalism and Civil Justice

Anthropologists tell us that before systems of criminal justice, before police departments and jails, human societies established systems of *civil* justice. Victims of theft, violence, and betrayal could assert their claims before political and legal authorities; persons charged with those acts could offer denials, excuses, and counterclaims; the authorities adjudicated and imposed penalties, typically involving restitution or other compensatory payments (Schwartz and Miller, 1964; Hoebel, 1964). Contemporary governments too, as part of the implicit bargain on which their claim to legitimacy rests, establish courts that decide disputes over property, allocate responsibility for injuries, and compel the payment of debts. Criminal law, by and large, is used only for offenders who cannot afford to pay restitution (hence most often against poor offenders), for certain offenses that are deemed politically dangerous, and for those serious offenses for which compensation is deemed morally inadequate.

In large pluralistic societies, however, the civil law is complex. Jurisdictional rules and formal requirements are daunting and confusing. Litigants need lawyers, and lawyers are expensive. Courts often are overburdened; justice is delayed and hence denied. The "true facts" of a dispute often are hard to determine. Established legal rules may not quite fit the protean variety of particular situations. Dealing with these problems—accessibility, affordability, delay, effective fact-finding, adaptability—is the day-to-day challenge faced by every contemporary civil justice system and a periodic political challenge for every democratically elected government. The United States, however, meets those challenges in distinctive ways.

This chapter shows that, compared to other economically advanced democracies, the American system of civil justice, like its system of criminal justice, adheres more closely to an organizationally fragmented "coordinate model" (Damaska, 1975) than to a governmentally guided "hierarchical model." The United States has been less aggressive than many countries in mobilizing governmental resources to provide alternatives to litigation and

99

to reduce the private costs of civil justice. The American system is shaped more by an exceptionally large, entrepreneurial, and politically assertive legal profession, and less by national ministries of justice. A wider range of problems are taken to court in the United States, and as this chapter shows, its civil justice system has swallowed much larger doses of adversarial legalism. The chapter that follows this one explores in more detail adversarial legalism's effects in the realm of tort law, the most controversial form of civil justice in the United States.

The Two Faces of Adversarial Legalism in Action

By placing powerful tools of pretrial discovery in the hands of entrepreneurial lawyers, adversarial legalism provides more probing forms of fact-finding than do other civil justice systems, and it provides more flexible and potent remedies. The politically responsive American judiciary is quicker than its counterparts in other countries to endorse new causes of action and more willing to craft legal techniques with which to call governmental bodies and corporations to account for unjust decisions or heedless practices. On the other hand, adversarial legalism makes American civil litigation especially costly, unpredictable, and alienating.

Adversarial legalism's attractive face is illustrated by *Gilmore v. Columbia Falls Aluminum Company*. By 1985, according to a lengthy *New York Times* article by Jim Robbins (1998), Columbia Falls Aluminum Company, located in northwestern Montana, had become a perennial money loser. Its corporate owner, Atlantic Richfield Company (ARCO), sold the company to Brack Duker and Jerome Broussard for $1, plus $3 million for unsold inventory. As part of the deal, the parties agreed that Columbia Falls workers would be entitled to "at least 50 percent" of any future annual profit, an agreement referred to in a letter from ARCO to Duker. After taking over Columbia Falls Aluminum, Duker and Broussard embarked on a major cost-cutting program, persuading hundreds of workers to accept a 15 percent pay cut in return for the promise of a 50 percent share of future profits. Faced with the alternative—shutting down the plant—the workers consented. Beginning in 1986, Columbia Falls Aluminum started making money. The new owners split the $2.6 million in profits with Columbia Falls employees. Robbins goes on:

> But over the next five years, rather than splitting the take, [Duker and Broussard] funneled much of the money into offshore bank accounts. Before they cut off their union and salaried employees altogether, the

two men had awarded $84 million to them and $231 million to themselves. . . .

. . . In 1989, Mr. Duker and Mr. Broussard dismissed their chief financial officer after he raised concerns about their financial practices. . . . [Later] a 39-year-old accountant at the plant named Roberta Gilmore challenged the company's bookkeeping practices and was promptly told, she says, to keep her mouth shut.

Instead, after fuming for a couple of years, she filed a [class action] lawsuit. . . . At one point, the two small-town lawyers she hired showed up in Federal Court in Missoula, Mont., wearing polar fleece jackets and Sorel boots. They were greeted by Mr. Duker—flanked by three bodyguards and 13 lawyers in finely tailored suits.

Clearly, Mr. Duker had the upper hand in any [legal] war of attrition. And yet, five years and 10 months after the suit was filed [and after pretrial discovery and other investigation by the plaintiff's lawyers unearthed the diversion of funds noted above, plus a letter from ARCO memorializing the profit-sharing requirement] he threw in the towel. Just two weeks before Ms. Gilmore's lawsuit was scheduled for trial, he agreed to pay the [approximately 1,000] workers $97 million. . . . When she heard the news, Ms. Gilmore broke into sobs.

Gilmore's lawyers—who at one point had to take out an $800,000 bank loan to pay their expenses—were to receive $6 million of the $32 million settlement for salaried employees, and labor union lawyers were to receive 10 percent of the $65 million settlement for hourly employees. Duker's lawyer sued him, claiming that Duker had refused to pay a promised bonus of $3 million for holding the final settlement to $100 million or less (Robbins, 1998: 11).

Gilmore v. Columbia Falls Aluminum Company exemplifies the strengths of American adversarial legalism. By validating class actions and thereby offering the prospect of very large fees to plaintiffs' lawyers, the American civil justice system taps the energy of entrepreneurial lawyers, enabling legally inexperienced citizens such as Roberta Gilmore to pursue legal claims against economically powerful "repeat players." By authorizing wide-ranging, lawyer-guided pretrial discovery, adversarial legalism enables plaintiffs' lawyers to uncover even carefully concealed evidence of malfeasance. Gilmore and her lawyers gained courage from the distinctive "American rule" concerning attorneys' fees and court costs, for it holds that even if they had lost, they would not be responsible for Mr. Duker's massive lawyers' bills. In sum, in giving ordinary people extraordinary legal weapons, American adversarial legalism contrasts with civil justice systems that are cheaper and more expeditious but less creative and less threatening. Doris Marie Provine (1996: 239) writes:

> France has taken considerable pains to keep the fees for civil litigation at a reasonable level. A 1991 law, for example, makes civil litigation free to those who cannot afford it. The system encourages laypersons to represent themselves and a significant minority do, especially before administrative tribunals. Even when people do hire lawyers, self-imposed and court-imposed restrictions on the scope of their activities tend to keep the fees much lower than in the United States. What the system does *not* provide, however, is a check on the excesses of powerful institutions. The problem, as Cappelletti and Garth observe, is that "a right of individual access, however liberally granted, does not necessarily lead to the vindication of new rights on a very large scale."

Consider, however, the less attractive face of adversarial legalism, exemplified by *Johnson v. Johnson.* In 1983 Seward Johnson, heir to the Johnson & Johnson health care products fortune, died at the age of eighty-seven. Johnson's will, drafted in the last months of his life, left the bulk of his $400 million estate to his third wife, Basia. In 1968 Basia, a recent immigrant from Poland, had come to the Johnson home as a kitchen employee; three years later she married Johnson, forty years her senior. Johnson's will left nothing to his six children, from whom he had long been estranged (apparently for good reason); years earlier, however, he had given each child a trust containing tens of millions of dollars' worth of Johnson & Johnson stock (Margolick, 1993).

Seward Johnson's children challenged the validity of his will in the New York Surrogate's Court, claiming Basia—who had become increasingly imperious as Seward declined—used undue influence in getting Johnson to change the will in her favor. Their case, according to David Margolick's detailed account, was legally (as well as morally) weak: in a sequence of earlier wills, Johnson had similarly left nothing to his dissolute children on grounds that their trust funds were enough, and he had made successively more generous bequests to Basia (Margolick, 1993: 198, 268). But Johnson's children employed smart, aggressive lawyers from a big New York City firm. They conducted marathon pretrial depositions of Basia, the children, and Seward Johnson's lawyer (Goldsmith, 1987) and concocted enough of an argument, in the judge's view, to get a jury trial. Before and during the over-three-month trial, the presiding judge displayed "astonishing partiality" toward the claimants (Langbein, 1994: 2041). Before the trial ended, Basia agreed to a settlement that gave about $40 million of the estate to the Johnson children and paid their legal fees. The legal fees for both sides amounted, amazingly, to $25 million (Goldsmith, 1987)—enough to pay the annual salaries and benefits of at least 500 new police officers, nurses, or schoolteachers.

Reviewing Margolick's account of the Johnson litigation, John Langbein (1994: 2043) points out that litigation based on claims of undue influence or unsound mind, "which occupy so prominent a place in American probate law, are virtually unknown both on the Continent and in English and Commonwealth legal systems."[1] "Anywhere else in the Western world," Langbein continues (id. at 2045), "the Johnson children's lawsuit would have been suppressed in short order. In the United States, it became a license to exploit the shortcomings of the procedural system. Skilled plaintiffs' lawyers extorted a multimillion-dollar payoff for themselves and their unworthy clients." The Johnson will litigation, with its huge stakes, is far from a typical case. But its costliness, legal unpredictability, and arbitrary outcome, Langbein suggests, are the legacies of two distinctive features of the American system of civil justice that characterize ordinary cases as well: a lawyer-dominated, intensely adversarial, and often manipulative system of evidence-gathering and presentation; and trial by jury and by politically appointed, highly autonomous judges.

Johnson v. Johnson does hint at some positive features of American adversarial legalism as well. In some European civil law systems courts are reluctant to look behind the words of a formal legal document (Hazard and Taruffo, 1993); adversarial legalism, with its potent weapons of pretrial discovery, wielded by self-interested and aggressive private attorneys, gives litigants more opportunity to uncover the human truths that lie behind the documentary mask. It is not difficult to find cases in American law reports in which courts thwarted a fortune hunter who really did subvert an ailing testator's mind, hoping to cheat deserving children of their birthright.[2] American judges, less carefully socialized to the bench and less closely supervised than their counterparts in many other countries, may be less predictable, but they also tend to be more flexible, more oriented to practical problem-solving.

Johnson v. Johnson reminds us, however, that adversarial legalism can be used by the unscrupulous, as well as against them, and that a politically selected judiciary, trial by jury, entrepreneurial lawyering, and aggressive pretrial discovery also have four disturbing implications. Viewed in comparative terms, litigation in the United States is extraordinarily *costly* to the parties, and it entails more legal *unpredictability*. Costliness and legal uncertainty often result in *injustice*, as parties (like Basia Johnson) feel compelled to abandon legally justified positions in order to avoid the costs and risks of adjudication. Another result is *inequality*: parties who can better withstand the costs and risks of litigation and can obtain better lawyering enjoy a greater advantage in the United States over parties who cannot.

These characteristics disturb even those who are sometimes in a position to benefit from them. In 1994 John Lande surveyed 143 American business executives, corporate "inside counsel," and "outside counsel." Asked to assess how the court system has been working on a five-point scale, half the executives and one-third of outside counsel said "poorly." A majority expressed severe doubts about its capacity to determine the truth correctly (Lande, 1998). It is important, therefore, to look more deeply into the dynamics of costliness, unpredictability, injustice, and inequality in American civil justice.

Adversarial Legalism and the Cost of Civil Litigation

If one were starting from scratch, it would be difficult to imagine, much less design, a mode of adjudication that, as in *Johnson v. Johnson,* would spend $25 million on lawyers to resolve a single dispute. The absolute size of the legal fees in the Johnson conflict was very unusual, to be sure; the fact that the "legal transaction costs" of both sides exceeded the amount actually paid to the claimant was not. In the average American product liability lawsuit, lawyers' fees for both sides, added together, are larger than the amount received by the plaintiff. Even in routine auto accident lawsuits, payments to lawyers account for more than 40 percent of total liability insurance payouts (Hensler et al., 1987: 27–28). The Wisconsin Civil Litigation Project, examining a systematic sample of 1,649 lawsuits in federal and state courts in the 1970s, found that in cases in which the plaintiffs' recoveries were less than $10,000, the median plaintiff's legal costs amounted to some 35 percent of the recovery when her lawyer took the case on a contingent fee basis and 46 percent when she paid her lawyer on an hourly basis (Trubek et al., 1983: 111). Defendants' legal fees generally are almost as large, which indicates that total transaction costs for both sides amount to well over 50 percent of the total settlement.

One 1988 study indicated that when employers were sued in wrongful discharge cases, their legal defense costs alone averaged over $80,000 (Dertouzos et al., 1988), those costs increasing to $124,000 in a 1994 study (Maltby, 1994: 107). The American Intellectual Property Law Association estimated in 1994 that in patent infringement cases the median litigation cost for each side was $280,000 through pretrial discovery and $518,000 through trial (Gerlin, 1994a: B1). According to a 1993 survey, in defending stockholders' fraud claims against their officers and directors, corporations paid law firms an average of $967,000 per case, this average including the "less expensive" cases that the responding companies won without paying a settlement (Lambert, 1995: B6). Why does American adversarial legalism generate such enormous legal bills? Some cross-national comparisons will provide a large part of the answer.

Lawyer-Dominated versus Judge-Dominated Litigation

While interviewing Dutch representatives of cross-Atlantic shipping lines and marine insurance companies, I asked if the legal resolution of disputed cargo damage claims differs when the cargo damage is discovered in Rotterdam, and hence is subject to Dutch courts, rather than in New York. "Oh yes," I was invariably told. "You have to pay a great deal more in lawyers' bills if the cargo is in the United States." This was not merely because American lawyers charged higher hourly rates but also because they put in far more time—and hence more billable hours—on each case.

American lawyers do more because American judges do less. In civil cases filed in Rotterdam or in other continental European cities, the *judge* is primarily responsible for interrogating parties and witnesses, selecting expert witnesses, demanding production of relevant documents, identifying the relevant law, and summarizing the evidence. In American litigation those burdens are shouldered by opposing counsel. In continental Europe legal advocates for the contending parties play only a supporting role, identifying witnesses to be interrogated by the judge and suggesting avenues of inquiry or legal analysis the judge may have omitted (Langbein, 1985). Thus in comparative perspective continental European legal systems are "judge-heavy," while the American system is "lawyer-heavy" (id. at 846). A 1973 study indicated that California had about 18 practicing lawyers for each judge, compared to 8 in Italy, 3 in France, 2.5 in Germany, and 2 in Sweden (Council on California Competitiveness, 1992: 88).[3] The Swedish and West German governments spent more on courts, prosecutors, and legal-aid lawyers than their citizens spent on private legal services, but "public sector expenditures in the United States were about one-fourth to one-fifth of private expenditures" (Johnson and Drew, 1978: 10, 55).

Although there are no systematic comparative data, the European practice of allocating many costs of litigation to judges almost certainly results in a much less costly civil adjudication system not only for disputing parties but for society at large (Brookings Institution, 1989: 6). Richard Hulbert (1997: 747), who has practiced law both in the United States and in Paris, writes that when viewed from an American perspective, the French system of civil justice "is cheap. It is quick. It produces judgments that overall seem to be satisfying." In a widely cited article, John Langbein (1985) argued that compared to civil justice in the United States, Germany's adjudicatory system is both cheaper and quicker, mainly because its fact-gathering process is far more efficient. "Probably no unbiased observer would disagree," says Herbert Bernstein (1988: 594), holder of law degrees from both countries. That conclusion is bolstered by considering some of the striking differences in European and American methods of civil litigation.

Redundancy

In strongly contested cases in the United States, separate lawyers for all parties participate in lengthy pretrial depositions, where parties and witnesses are first questioned by one lawyer, then cross-examined by another. In cases that go to trial, the lawyers, parties, and witnesses repeat virtually the same interrogation in open court. In high-stakes cases, lawyers meet with "their" parties and witnesses both before depositions and before trial for another run-through—a rehearsal of the anticipated interrogation (Reitz, 1990: 989). German civil litigation is remarkably different. Langbein (1985: 826) notes that "there is no distinction between pretrial and trial. . . . Trial is not a single continuous event. Rather, the court gathers and evaluates evidence over a series of hearings, as many as the circumstances require." The lawyers for each side nominate the witnesses they wish the judge to question (Bernstein, 1988: 592–593). Hence in contrast to American litigation, German parties and witnesses testify just once, when interrogated by a judge (Reitz, 1990: 989). Because witnesses are not coached in advance by lawyers and it is the judge's responsibility to assess the evidence, there is far less emphasis than in the United States on adversarial challenge—and hence less necessity to have lawyers for both sides present (and paid for) each time a piece of evidence is examined by or presented to the judge (Damaska, 1997a: 846).

All-at-Once versus Episodic Trials

American pretrial discovery is complex and costly, Langbein observes (1985: 831), partly because the sharp division between pretrial and trial encourages American lawyers to "investigate everything that could possibly come up at trial." Once trial begins, lawyers "can seldom go back and search for further evidence." In contrast, the episodic character of German fact-gathering, unfettered by the need to accommodate the jury, means that "if the case takes an unexpected turn, the disadvantaged litigant can count on developing his response in another hearing at a later time."

Dueling Expert Witnesses

In complex cases in which expert technical assessments are required, contending American litigants each hire and carefully coach their own expert witness; in a more hierarchical system such as Germany's, the court appoints a single "neutral" expert witness, who is not coached in advance by anyone (id. at 835–840).[4] A corporate counsel experienced in intellectual property disputes writes that "although European litigation also involves the use of experts, in the U.S. there are experts, experts, and still more experts" (Pantuliano, 1983; see also Somaya, 2000). Thus, according to patent attorney James Maxeiner (1991: 601, 604), "expert testimony in U.S. patent litigation is much more costly than in Germany." In French courts, practicing attorney Richard Hulbert (1997: 749) tells us, the judge appoints an expert for "controverted issues of fact, particularly facts of a technical nature." Then:

> The appointee will conduct an investigation outside the courtroom, under no formal rules of evidence or relevance, at sessions to which the parties are convoked with full freedom to present their views and those of their experts or other representatives, orally or in writing. The results of the *expertise* is a report that in principle the judge need not accept, but in the absence of other evidence, it is difficult to see how it could be rejected, provided that the judge is satisfied that the *expert* [whose investigative and reporting procedures are regulated by law] has done what he was commissioned to do and that no material procedural irregularities have been committed.

Trial by Jury

European courts (including British courts, which have abandoned the jury in most civil cases) avoid the extraordinary inefficiencies of the American civil jury trial, such as lengthy, adversarial jury selection (National Center for State Courts, 1988: 110; Kakalik et al., 1990) and legalistic wrangling over what evidence and arguments must be suppressed because they might mislead amateur decisionmakers. Civil trials in the United States that are conducted by only a judge tend to be at least 50 percent shorter than jury trials.[5] And because American jurors, in contrast to judges in Europe, are not given written summaries of the issues and evidence in advance, the whole story of the dispute must be presented to them orally. Each witness is questioned first by one set of lawyers, then cross-examined by another. Unlike a European judge, American jurors cannot comment during trial or indicate that they are satisfied on a certain point. Hence lawyers, uncertain which issues will be regarded as crucial, must cover all issues and, playing it safe, often call "extra" witnesses to testify (Reitz, 1990: 989; Langbein, 1985: 830). Overall, therefore, the average urban jury trial in the United States—in all likelihood a fairly routine motor vehicle accident or other personal injury case—takes about 13.5 hours, spread over several days, to conduct (National Center for State Courts, 1988). (The median for contract and nontort cases is about 14.5 hours.) In 1984 half of all jury trials in Los Angeles and Oakland, California, lasted more than thirty hours, spread over seven days (Kakalik et al., 1990: 110).[6]

Pretrial Discovery

In more than 95 percent of American civil lawsuits there is no trial (Heise, 2000: 823; Ostrom et al., 1996: 234), partly because trials are so costly. In many cases information gathered in pretrial discovery becomes the basis for a settlement. As the *Columbia Falls Aluminum* case teaches, adversarial pretrial discovery is a powerful tool for unmasking phony defenses and for undermining spurious claims. Nevertheless, even when it works well, the adversarial American pretrial discovery and negotiation process is costly, inefficient, and slow. Second Circuit Court of Appeals judge Ralph K. Winter (1992: 264), a member of the federal courts' Advisory Committee on Civil Rules, lamented: "In private conversations with lawyers and judges, I find precious few ready to argue that pretrial discovery involves less than considerable to enormous waste. . . . [The Advisory Committee found] a no-stone-left-unturned . . . philosophy of discovery governs much litigation and imposes costs, usually without corresponding benefits. . . . Second, discovery is sometimes used as a club against the other party . . . solely to increase the adversary's expenses."

Delay

Besides adversarial legalism's direct costs, American litigants must endure its extraordinary delays if they insist on a jury trial. According to Albert Alschuler (1990: 6), "the average civil case tried during 1988 in the Circuit Court of Cook County [Chicago] had been filed more than six years before." In Los Angeles the median time between filing and trial of a civil action, only 4.2 months in 1942, grew to 19 months in 1962 and 41.5 months (almost three and a half years) in 1982 (Selvin and Ebener, 1984: 27). More typically, in a 1987 study of thirty-seven urban jurisdictions, the median time from filing to jury trial was slightly more than two years, although in Detroit, it was more than three years, and in Providence, Rhode Island, almost five

(Goerdt, 1991: 296; Ostrom et al., 1996: 24).[7] In Germany half of civil court plaintiffs have a decision within six months, three-quarters within nine months, and summary proceedings are even faster (Blankenburg, 1994: 806).

The Decline of Adjudication

As a result of the costs and delays associated with adversarial legalism, only a small percentage of American litigants actually get their day in court or have their cases decided by the application of law to the facts by a judge or jury, except for cases that fall within the tight monetary limits for small claims courts. As noted, the percentage of civil cases resolved by trial (as opposed to settlement, withdrawal, or dismissal) is less than 5 percent. Alschuler (1990: 4) concludes: "The civil trial is on its deathbed, or close to it, because our trial system has become unworkable. The American trial has been bludgeoned by lengthy delays, high attorneys' fees, discovery wars, satellite hearings, judicial settlement conferences, and the world's most extensive collection of cumbersome procedures. Few litigants can afford the cost of either the pretrial journey or the trial itself."

The decline of adjudication, as Sam Gross and Kent Syverud (1996: 62) argue, stems from a political and legal system more intent on elaborating the tools of adversarial legalism than on investing in inexpensive, more expeditious methods of civil dispute resolution:

> The essence of adversarial litigation is procedure. . . . When we want to improve our judicial system we pass a procedural reform, which invariably means elaborating old procedural rules or adding new ones—rules that govern the presentation of evidence and arguments, rules that create opportunities to investigate and prepare evidence and argument. . . . The upshot is a masterpiece of detail, with rules on everything from special appearances to contest the jurisdiction of the court, to the use of exhibits during jury deliberation. But we cannot afford it. As litigants, few of us can pay the costs of a trial; as a society, we are unwilling to pay even a fraction of the cost of the judicial apparatus that we would need to try most civil cases. We have designed a spectacular system for adjudicating disputes, but it is too expensive to use.

What is left is a system of civil dispute resolution by negotiation between lawyers, in which nonlegal factors such as cost and delay and the parties' relative ability to sustain them play a major role. And even that system is too expensive for many.

Adversarial Legalism and Legal Unpredictability

In all legal systems most civil cases are settled before trial, as the litigants, advised by their lawyers, come to recognize what their chances would be in court. The cases that go to adjudication are likely to be those in which the litigants can't agree on the likely outcome. Hence in all countries the cases that reach adjudication involve a relatively large amount of legal uncertainty. Yet it appears that legal unpredictability in the civil justice systems of the United States, as exemplified by the *Johnson v. Johnson* case, is greater than in many other economically advanced democracies.

Johnson v. Johnson is far from unique in that regard. On January 4, 1984, Getty Oil and Pennzoil Corporation, a Houston-based company, announced Pennzoil's purchase of three-sevenths of Getty's stock for $112.50 per share; the press release described the proposed sale as an "agreement in principle" that was "subject to [the] execution of a definitive merger agreement" (Petzinger, 1987: 198; Mnookin and Wilson, 1989: 301). Pennzoil, however, apparently refused to withdraw its original tender offer of $100 per share until a final agreement was signed, sealed, and delivered (Baron and Baron, 1986: 256), and Getty Oil's bitterly divided board of directors continued to seek out a "white knight" who would not only increase the purchase price but would also support current management in its battle with minority shareholders. After being assured by leading corporate takeover professionals that Getty Oil was "free to deal," Texaco offered to buy all of Getty Oil's outstanding stock for $125 per share. Texaco's offer was formally accepted by the relevant parties on January 7, 1984.

Pennzoil sued Getty Oil in Delaware, but the judge declined to block the sale to Texaco. Pennzoil then filed a new lawsuit against New York-based Texaco in Houston, seeking a staggering $14 billion in compensation. Legal analysts agree, based on an independent analysis of the court file, that (1) no contract existed between Pennzoil and Getty under the law of New York, where the Texaco-Getty deal was negotiated; (2) even if Texaco were liable, under either New York or Texas law, Pennzoil's damages should not have exceeded $422 million (id. at 269, 279). Nevertheless, a Houston jury awarded Pennzoil $7.5 billion in "actual damages" and $3 billion in punitive damages. A Texas appeals court reduced the punitive damages to $1 billion, but even Texaco couldn't write an $8.5 billion check and filed for bankruptcy—which was temporary but resulted in a fire sale of $5.1 billion in assets, deeply strained business relationships, and the near collapse of a company that employs thousands of workers (Brown, 1988: H1, H7).

How could a sophisticated company such as Texaco, with its cadre of experienced attorneys and investment bankers, fail by such a wide margin to discern the legal risks to which it was exposed? The answer is that in the decentralized American legal system, constantly being shaped and reshaped by adversarial argument, the legal terrain is often unstable; the ostensibly solid path mapped by one's lawyer can suddenly turn to quicksand. This is not an endemic feature of all legal regimes. When asked about transatlantic cargo damage disputes that reach adjudication, the shipping line and insurance firm representatives whom I interviewed all asserted that results in the courts in Rotterdam are far more predictable than when the litigation occurs in the United States.

After analyzing the record in the Johnson estate case, Professor Langbein, along with David Margolick, the experienced legal correspondent who chronicled the litigation, felt certain that the Johnson children's case lacked legal merit (Margolick, 1993: 198, 268). But the lawyers representing the Johnson estate apparently were not sure that the court would recognize the legal merits of their defense, and Johnson's widow Basia acceded to the children's legal gamble, buying them off with a $40 million settlement. Langbein traces the source of this legal uncertainty (and the defendant's consequent vulnerability to extortionate demands) to two factors: the relatively nonprofessional, political character of the American judiciary, and the unique American insistence on using untrained citizen-jurors to resolve civil cases.

Professional versus Political Judiciaries

German courts have a specialized chamber that deals with commercial disputes and another that deals with patent disputes, along with specialized labor courts and specialized tribunals that deal with disputes concerning social benefits.[8] In the Netherlands cargo damage disputes are channeled into a chamber of the court system staffed by judges who specialize in maritime cases. The United States has specialized federal courts for bankruptcy and for patent appeals, but most litigation is before "generalist" judges. The U.S. District Court judge who hears a cargo damage dispute or a patent infringement case may not have dealt with such cases recently—and perhaps never.[9] She relies on the litigants' attorneys to point out the relevant statutes, precedents, facts, and arguments. Supported by a pragmatic, results-oriented legal culture, the "generalist" American judge is more likely to rely on her own judgment to reach a result that she thinks is just (Atiyah and Summers, 1987). That may sound appealing, but it also adds to legal uncertainty and unpredictability.

In the Netherlands (and in other hierarchically organized European legal systems) judges are recruited, socialized, and supervised in a manner explicitly designed to maximize adjudicative predictability. After a closely supervised apprenticeship, open only to law graduates who have done very well on a nationwide exam,[10] a young judge's progress to more responsible and prestigious posts depends on merit ratings she receives from senior judges in the chambers through which she rotates, as well as on periodic evaluations by the ministry of justice (Meador, 1983: 22–23).[11] The goal of this bureaucratically organized career-management system is to homogenize the judiciary, to make its decisions legally competent, uniform, and predictable.

The American judiciary is professional too, in its own way. All judges have had legal training. They almost uniformly state that their obligation as judges is to apply the law uniformly to all, regardless of their own beliefs. They are constrained by the possibility of appeal and reversal by higher American judges, or by criticism by lawyers and other judges for failure to apply the law in accordance with the conventions of legal reasoning (Cross and Tiller, 1998). Millions of potential disputes are resolved, therefore, when American lawyers tell their clients, with a high degree of conviction, that they will lose if they go to court. The point is not that American law is wholly unpredictable, but that its level of unpredictability is greater than in economically advanced democracies whose judiciaries are selected in a nonpolitical manner. Unlike their counterparts in England or Western Europe or Japan, American judges come to the bench after prior careers as practicing lawyers, prosecutors, or political activists.[12] Some have had little courtroom experience. In most American states, new judges get little formal training, and there is no systematic merit-oriented promotion system (Meador, 1983: 26). Compared to their European counterparts, American judges enjoy far more autonomy vis-à-vis their judicial superiors, both with respect to their career prospects and to their day-to-day legal decisionmaking, and most of the countless procedural decisions that American judges make in the course of pretrial hearings and trials are de facto unreviewable.

There is a method to this ostensible madness. Free from the homogenizing professionalism of hierarchically organized European legal bureaucracies, the American judiciary, precisely because it is politically responsive and less formalistic, is more pragmatic, quicker to invent new rights and remedies, and more willing to adapt the law to changing circumstances and new justice claims. But there is a madness to the method as well; its symptom is susceptibility to comparatively higher levels of legal inconsistency and unpredictability.

Comparing trial judges in England with their politically selected counterparts in the United States, Atiyah and Summers (1987: 164) observe: "It cannot be doubted that in England the judge brings on average a higher level of competence to the entire trial process. The judge is invariably a former barrister of many years' experience and high standing at the bar. . . . In

America . . . the situation is much more variable" (see also Hazard and Taruffo, 1993: 68). As shown by an observational study of small claims courts, some American judges are narrowly legalistic, while others tend to act as mediators, and still others tend to decide cases according to their own notions of fairness and desert (Conley and O'Barr, 1987). Decisions by U.S. District Court judges appointed by Democratic presidents are demonstrably more liberal than those appointed by Republican presidents (Rowland and Carp, 1983), and similar findings recur for studies of other courts, both state and federal (Pinello, 1999; Cross and Tiller, 1998). Not surprisingly, American lawyers, as documented by Sarat and Felstiner's (1986) study of divorce lawyers, often tell their clients that the legal outcome will depend on which judge ends up hearing the case. Dutch divorce lawyers, a similar study showed, simply tell their clients what the law prescribes and hence what they can expect in court (Griffiths, 1986).

What's more, stories of seriously biased and incompetent American judges are far from rare (Brill, 1989). The Texas trial judge who instructed the jury in the Pennzoil-Texaco case acknowledged afterward that "there is a good chance that perhaps I read the cases wrong and not have applied [the law] correctly." In fact, he had adopted Pennzoil's proposed jury instructions nearly verbatim while ignoring Texaco's submissions (Petzinger, 1987: 463, 453). Similarly, day by day, the Johnson estate's lawyers saw what seemed to be an airtight case crumble, as the trial judge, a politically active former personal injury lawyer, repeatedly acted in a biased and improper manner (Margolick, 1993: 301–313). "Americans can only look with envy," Langbein (1985: 2044) asserts, "to the esteemed and meritocratic chancery bench that conducts probate adjudication in English and Commonwealth jurisdictions." The American judiciary, far from homogenized, is not even reliably pasteurized, and it is not always the cream that rises to the top. The result is a higher level of legal unpredictability.

Juries

"American law is unique," says Langbein (1985: 2043), "in undertaking to resolve will contests by means of civil jury trial" in which skillful lawyers strive "to evoke the jurors' sympathy for disinherited offspring and to excite their likely hostility towards a devisee such as Basia, who can so easily be painted as a homewrecking adventurer." Ironically, some scholars suggest, Americans have emphasized trial by jury because they fear the biases and inconsistencies of a politically appointed, nonprofessional judiciary (Schuck, 1993: 310). But the cure may be worse than the disease.

As George Priest (1993: 130) puts it, "The civil jury is an engine of inconsistency." In the jury system judgment is entrusted to an ever-changing cluster of individuals who are not told about the applicable rules of law until the trial is over, nor instructed how similar cases have been decided by other juries. Jurors are not expected to explain and justify their decisions, and thus one jury's decisions cannot be systematically compared with another's. That is not to say that juries usually or even frequently ignore the judge's instructions, or that they often reach decisions on the basis of emotion rather than evidence. On average, researchers have found, jurors regard plaintiffs' claims for money damages with some skepticism. Marc Galanter (1993: 70) concludes: "The literature, on the whole, converges on the judgment that juries are fine decisionmakers. They are conscientious, collectively they understand and recall the evidence as well as judges, and they decide on the basis of the evidence presented."[13] When researchers presented similar tort cases to over 500 mock juries, they found that individual jurors drawn from different states, ethnic groups, income levels, and age groups tended to make remarkably similar average judgments about the defendant's moral culpability and the severity of the harm (Schkade et al., 2000: 1156).Jury decisions thus are not random (Osborne, 1999). But that does not mean that the jury system yields legal predictability.

In the University of Chicago Jury Project in the 1950s, researchers asked judges who had presided over jury trials how they would have decided the case had it been a bench trial. The judge agreed with the jury's decision on liability in 79 percent of the cases (Kalven, 1964; Kalven and Zeisel, 1966: 56; Galanter, 1993).[14] That is only moderately encouraging. Legal uncertainty stems from two looming problems: first, one cannot tell in advance whether any particular jury will be the one in five or so that decides idiosyncratically, and second, the idiosyncratic judgment is likely to go uncorrected. A Philadelphia judge, referring to two asbestos cases he had presided over, commented: "[T]wo men had similar physical problems. They each had pleural thickening and some shortness of breath. In the case involving the man who counsel believed to be the sicker of the two, the jury awarded $15,000. For the other plaintiff, the jury awarded $1,200,000. These results make this litigation more like roulette than jurisprudence" (Hensler, 1985: 65).[15] To a legal scholar from another country, the striking point would be not only that the juries decided inconsistently, but that there was no mechanism for reconciling their judgments.[16]

Peter Huber (1990: 290) compared verdicts by different juries in a sequence of cases concerning claims of harm from Bendectin (a morning sickness drug), in another sequence of cases involving an alleged defect in Audi motor cars, and in sequences of cases involving several other allegedly dangerous products. Most juries, in accordance with the weight of the scientific evidence presented, found that the product in question was not defective or not responsible for the plaintiffs' injuries. But, as Huber noted, "Every new case has a new jury, and one jury's finding is not binding on the next's." In each sequence of trials concerning a particular product, one or a few juries, hearing the same evidence as those that found no liability, decided otherwise and awarded the plaintiff massive compensatory and punitive damages. The modal jury award was nothing at all, but the mean award was in the millions of dollars. For each manufacturer in question, the result was inescapable legal uncertainty and enormous litigation expenses (id. at 278; Sugarman, 1985b: 599–602; Bork, 1996: A15).

In the above-mentioned study of more than 500 mock juries, the researchers found that in deliberating over the appropriate *monetary damage* award, juries were unpredictable, producing a wide range of results; moreover, jury deliberations often yielded awards far larger than the evaluations that most individual jurors had made before deliberation began, and sometimes larger than any juror had made before deliberating (Schkade et al., 2000: 1139). Judges ultimately reduce jury awards as legally unjustified in 20 to 25 percent of cases, more often for large verdicts (Peterson, 1983: ix–x; Broder, 1986); Ostrom et al., 1993; Adler, 1994: 244; Vidmar et al., 1998). But this does not produce legal predictability. The judges do not *always* reduce damage awards. Their decisions in that regard are not subject to definitive legal rules and are rarely reversible on appeal. Compounding the legal uncertainty, judges almost never reverse a jury decision for awarding *insufficient* damages or no damages at all.

Examining the inconsistent outcomes in the Bendectin trials, Joseph Sanders (1993) locates the problem not in the jury per se but in the organization of a jury-focused trial system dominated by the parties' lawyers. Information on causation was provided by conflicting, lawyer-coached expert witnesses, presenting different kinds of scientific evidence, not back-to-back but at widely separated points in the trial. The lawyers' cross-examination of the witnesses was designed more to generate contradictions and to obfuscate than to inform. No wonder, Sanders concludes, the result was a body of testimony that failed to enable the lay fact-finders to weigh properly the quality of experts or the scientific findings on Bendectin's effects.

Guessing what a jury will do is made even more difficult by the infrequency of jury decisions. Since only a tiny percentage of civil cases go to verdict, the jury system sends only weak and static-filled signals to the trial bar.[17] News media coverage of trial verdicts is selective, oversampling very large jury verdicts or cases in which juries find liability in unlikely situations (MacCoun, 1993; Aks et al., 2000). The result, as indicated by a number of studies summarized by Galanter (1993: 81–86), is that lawyers come up with widely divergent pretrial estimates of a case's likely outcome at trial. When Douglas Rosenthal (1974) asked five experienced New York trial lawyers to read the files and estimate the recovery value of fifty-nine settled cases, their predictions were way off. The median recovery was about 75 percent of the experts' estimates, and 40 percent of recoveries were less than two-thirds of the experts' estimates. And in a study of 443 back and neck injury cases, Philip Hermann (1962) found that only one-sixth of the final demands and offers by plaintiffs and defendants came within 25 percent of the jury's actual verdict.

One might argue that these and similar studies (Danzon, 1985: 50; Kritzer, 1990: 31; Clermont and Eisenberg, 1992: 1170–1172; Priest, 1993: 129) reflect the incompetence of the average lawyer rather than any defect in the jury system. But a legal system in which the average lawyer is very poor at predicting outcomes, for whatever reason, is an unpredictable legal system. One might argue too that these studies focus on personal injury cases, in which both the substantive law and the law of damages are unusually vague, even by American standards, and in which clever appeals to jury sympathy might (but might not) sway the verdict. But legal uncertainty, as indicated by *Pennzoil v. Texaco* and *Johnson v. Johnson,* reigns in other spheres of civil litigation as well. An analysis of a broad sample of cases found substantial variation between attorneys' expectations and actual awards after trial by judges and juries (Osborne, 1999: 193).[18] Kent Syverud (1997: 1943) points to "the almost universal election of businesses and governments to opt out of fact finding by a civil jury when they are civil plaintiffs," because they perceive "that there is less predictability . . . in fact finding by a civil jury than in dispute resolution by other methods."

Legal unpredictability also pervades American family law (Ellman, 1999), in which judges, not juries, decide alimony, child custody, and marital property distribution disputes. The authors of a study of divorce and custody litigation in Wisconsin note: "Several of the lawyers we interviewed report that they have difficulty in discerning court standards and that they cannot predict the outcomes of court processes. . . . Even the lawyers . . . who do think there are set standards and who do say they can predict outcomes differ in their opinion of the content of those court standards" (Erlanger et al., 1987: 599). In a survey of attorneys (Lande, 1998: 32), one typical respondent said:

I started out as a plaintiffs' trial attorney with a strong belief in the jury system. . . . I don't believe that anymore. I think . . . it behooves you to do anything possible to avoid it. . . . You can go through all of the different systems, whether it be family law through divorce, products claims, malpractice claims, securities litigation, you know, virtually every category of major litigation. . . . Is it predictable, reliable in terms of a rule? Are the transaction costs reasonable in terms of a result? Does it provide guidance for the future? Not a single one of these systems would even get a passing grade.

Because of the costs and delays of trials, many busy court systems have encouraged "managerial judging," whereby judges pressure the parties' lawyers to settle cases before trial. But this too adds to legal uncertainty, for judges differ in the intensity with which they apply pressures to settle and in their knowledge of the facts (Frankel, 1975: 1042; Resnick, 1982; Yeazell, 1994; Molot, 1998: 992). In European civil justice systems, where judges dominate the fact-gathering processes, settlement negotiations occur under the nose of a third party who is deeply familiar with the case. In both kinds of legal systems, pretrial settlements occur "in the shadow of the law." But the greater predictability of European adjudication means that the boundary of the shadow is far clearer.

Injustice

By making litigation and adjudication slow, very costly, and unpredictable, adversarial legalism often transforms the civil justice system into an engine of injustice, compelling litigants to abandon just claims and defenses. Dixie Flag Manufacturing Company, a firm in San Antonio, Texas, with sixty-three employees, makes and sells American flags. In 1991 Dixie Flag was sued by a person who had seen some men lowering a large flag in a parking lot, and then volunteered to help so that the flag would not touch the ground. As the volunteer grasped the flag, according to his subsequent legal complaint, a gust of wind billowed the massive banner high into the air. The plaintiff, apparently more patriotic than he was quick-witted, failed to let go, and the flag pulled him high off the ground. *Then* he let go. He crashed to the ground and was injured. His patriotism now tempered by avarice, he sued Dixie Flag for compensatory damages. The company's president spent considerable time combing old company records but could find no evidence that his company had even made that particular flag. Nevertheless, Dixie Flag's liability insurance carrier paid the plaintiff $6,000 to settle the suit, much to its client's outrage. The insurers explained that it would have cost $10,000 in attorneys' fees to prevail in court (Van de Putte, 1995: A14).[19]

The Dixie Flag settlement is far from unique. In a 1992 survey of 234 municipal government attorneys, "over 80% acknowledge that on occasion they settle cases that would be winnable . . . just to save money in the short term" (McManus, 1993: 835). Conversely, the costs and unpredictability of adversarial legalism induce potential plaintiffs to back away from asking the courts to vindicate entirely just legal claims when they are met with questionable but costly-to-rebut legal defenses. California collection agencies, the president of their trade association estimated, take no more than 20 percent of their debt default cases to court, largely because of litigation expenses, complexities, and delays (Kagan, 1984: 338). Charles Ruhlin found that a major multinational bank with credit card operations in the United States and Germany is more reluctant to sue delinquent debtors in the United States because German courts deal with collection cases far more efficiently and reliably (Ruhlin, 2000). The bank ends up writing off a significantly larger proportion of unpaid debt here than it does in Germany.

Manipulative Lawyering

As the Dixie Flag and the Johnson estate cases suggest, adversarial legalism's expense and unpredictability also encourage and reward manipulative lawyering and extortive demands. An experienced corporate counsel, comparing patent litigation in the United States and in Europe, observed that one is much more likely to encounter hyperaggressive lawyering and obstructionist defenses in the United States (Pantuliano, 1983). Dutch and American shipping company and insurance officials told me that if settlement negotiations in cargo damage claims take place in the shadow of Dutch courts, they are "more logical" than negotiations that occur in New York, where the lawyers are more likely "to see what they can get away with" or to take an uncompromising stand based on a legalistic reading of the bill of lading. The American lawyer's goal, in the claims agents' view, was not to work out a reasonable agreement based on the facts and the law but to manipulate the law and its cumbersome processes so as to extort concessions from the other side.

In terms of personal character, Rotterdam lawyers may be no less Machiavellian, on average, than are New York lawyers. But compared with the United States, professional codes of ethics in the Netherlands, as in England and other countries in Western Europe, more strongly enjoin lawyers to temper one-sided advocacy in the search for objective legal truth (Osiel, 1990: 2019; Atiyah and Summers, 1987: 163). Moreover, in the decentralized, adversarial American court system—with its long delays before adjudication, its weak hierarchical controls over lawyer-controlled pretrial discovery, its legal uncertainty, and its opportunities for forum shopping—lawyers have much stronger *incentives* to "see what they can get away with" than they do in Holland. Because litigation in Holland is less costly and more legally predictable, Dutch litigants have less reason to succumb to a settlement that departs from the law solely in order to avoid the costs of further pretrial discovery and the risks of going to trial.

To be sure, manipulative American lawyers run some risk that their adversaries will haul them before a judge, where they can be sanctioned for pretrial discovery abuse or for making factually unfounded legal claims. Within some tight-knit communities of lawyers, reputational networks discourage excessively adversarial litigation activity (Gilson and Mnookin, 1994). In cases in which the monetary stakes are small, neither side, typically, invests much in legal maneuvering (Trubek et al., 1983). Many, perhaps most, American lawyers prefer an ideal of gentlemanly interaction to that of the warrior litigator (Kagan and Rosen, 1985). Nevertheless, studies suggest that superaggressive, manipulative lawyering—explicitly designed to increase the other side's litigation bills and thereby to induce them to compromise their claims or defenses—is sufficiently common that any potential litigant would rationally be afraid of encountering it (Garth, 1993: 939–945, 949). Chicago lawyers who frequently are involved in large-stakes litigation admitted to a researcher that they had used discovery tools in 40 percent or more of their cases simply to impose work burdens or economic pressure on their adversaries. More than 80 percent said they had sometimes done so, employing discovery tactics in order to slow down the progress of the suit, shipping huge numbers of documents to opponents in hopes of obscuring crucial information, or tutoring witnesses to give evasive answers in depositions (Brazil, 1980a: 857).

It is all quite logical. The more a disputing party has to spend in defending or asserting a just position, the greater her incentive to compromise her legal claims or defenses and make concessions to settle the case, simply to avoid further legal costs. In a regime of adversarial legalism, disputing parties' litigation costs are higher than in more hierarchically organized, less adversarial legal systems; hence the incentives to compromise just claims and defenses are greater. In the United States, moreover, because even a party who wins at trial generally must pay her own legal fees, lawyers and disputing parties have greater incentives to inflict litigation costs or delays on their adversaries in order to induce them to make greater concessions. In the absence of a "loser pays" rule, lawyers also have incentives to make and cling to legally weak claims and defenses, for even weak legal arguments force one's adversary to expend resources to rebut them, and hence may have some "settlement value" (Molot, 1998: 992).[20] In consequence, in the United States, parties' relative capacity to bear the costs of litigation plays a much larger role in case disposition than in judge-dominated adjudicatory systems.

Large Stakes and Extortive Settlements

The extortive settlement in *Johnson v. Johnson* did not stem from one party's eagerness to avoid pretrial discovery burdens or other *litigation* costs. Rather, it stemmed from the explosive combination of very large financial stakes ($400 million) and adversarial legalism's legal unpredictability, as embodied in a biased, amateurish judge and a potentially swayable jury. This extortive potential arises in other high-stakes lawsuits as well, as in the realm of class actions by consumers, investors, and tort claimants. The class action is a distinctively American legal invention, generally eschewed by other political systems but quite congruent with American political propensities.[21] During the 1970s consumer and environmental advocates, judges, and politicians saw in the class action a mechanism for imposing higher normative standards on big business without having to rely on expensive government bureaucracies. The class action offered entrepreneurial American lawyers potentially very large fees for successfully suing offending business corporations on behalf of all the company's consumers, stockholders, female employees, neighbors, or so on. By accumulating all claimants' alleged losses into one gigantic claim, the lawyer could threaten companies with potentially enormous money damages—a threat that presumably would deter them from engaging in fraudulent, unfair, or hazardous business practices. It seemed like a good idea. *Columbia Falls Aluminum* illustrates the virtues of the class action device, as do a significant number of class actions based on claims of racial or gender discrimination in employment (Gaiter, 1996: A1, A11). The powerful class action weapon, however, can be used for ill as well as for good, especially when the potentially huge penalties are combined with a highly unpredictable adjudication system.

Reviewing a large number of cases, John C. Coffee, Jr. (1995: 1347–1348) notes that "the modern class action . . . has long been a context in which opportunistic behavior has been common and high agency costs have prevailed. Settlements have all too frequently advanced only the interests of plaintiffs' attorneys, not those of class members."[22] For example, after learning of a government investigation of alleged price fixing by major airlines, attorneys filed twenty-one cases on behalf of 12 million passengers. After three years the consolidated cases were settled for $458 million in cash and discount coupons, and $14.4 million in fees for the plaintiffs' lawyers—even though the presiding judge said he "would assess the chances of the plaintiffs recovering as not good" and that he believed "the case would have a hard time surviving a motion for summary judgment" (*Wall Street Journal*, 1993: A14). But it made sense for the defendants to settle once they hit on the idea of paying the actual plaintiffs in discount coupons worth 10 percent off purchased tickets for off-peak travel. As in many class actions, the plaintiffs' attorneys got a big payoff while providing their "clients"—those who bother to go to the trouble of proving they fall within the affected class and collect the coupons—with minimal benefits.

Similar cases of extortion by litigation arise under consumer protection laws (Moses, 1992: B8; Geyelin, 1994: B1);[23] under securities laws, where certain lawyers routinely file class actions against "high tech" companies whose stock values have fallen (Alexander, 1991; Romano, 1991);[24] and in "toxic tort" class actions, where defendant corporations faced with enormous potential damages sometimes feel compelled to settle despite the absence of proof of harm to human health stemming from the chemical exposures in question (Peterson and Selvin, 1991: 227, 231, 241; Huber, 1988). In the Agent Orange case, seven chemical companies settled the claims of tens of thousands of Vietnam veterans for $180 million, even though the trial judge indicated that no persuasive causal connection had been shown between the plaintiffs' ailments and exposure to Agent Orange (Schuck, 1986; Sugarman, 1985b: 597–598).[25] But the defendants had already spent roughly $100 million on their legal defense, with more to come at trial, and faced a risk, however small, of losing a jury verdict for more than a billion dollars (id.; Peterson and Selvin, 1991: 231, 241; Rabin, 1989: 818). Similarly, confronted with 12,359 individual lawsuits, filed in the wake of multimillion dollar verdicts for a few plaintiffs, Dow Corning and three other manufacturers of silicone breast-implants offered a $4.23 billion settlement, notwithstanding scientific studies that found no causal link between the implants and the plaintiffs' claimed immune system diseases (Coffee, 1995: 1405–1410; Angell, 1996). The settlement agreement later collapsed and Dow Corning filed for bankruptcy, only to settle remaining claims for $3.2 billion in 1998—even though by then the scientific evidence failing to find any causal relationship had become even more convincing (Bandow, 1998: A23; Kolata, 1998: A1; Bernstein, 1999).

Some judges, recognizing the potential of class actions to induce a "blackmail settlement," have refused to certify class actions based on tenuous liability claims.[26] Those decisions are left largely to the trial court judge's discretion, however, and so the likely legal outcome in such high-stakes cases often is overshadowed by uncertainty.

Inequality

Adversary theory suggests that the detrimental effects of manipulative lawyering will even out as each side's lawyers fight fire with fire. But that faith seems justified, at best, only when both sides can afford and are willing to engage in a full-scale firefight. That type of strict equality of wealth and motivation seems unlikely in most cases. Under adversarial legalism, where privately hired lawyers perform the demanding tasks of interviewing and cross examining witnesses, devising litigation tactics, and conducting trials, it is quite likely that these tasks will not be performed adequately and equally for all parties (Johnson and Drew, 1978). Great Britain strives to even out the quality of advocacy by limiting trial practice to a specialized corps of barristers whose links to particular clients are attenuated and who are constrained by strong legal constraints on overzealous action. Atiyah and Summers (1987: 162–163) observe, "There are . . . cases in the American courts in which the opposing lawyers are strikingly mismatched. . . . Such gross mismatches rarely occur in England."

In a lawyer-dominated litigation system even small differences in opposing counsel can make a big difference. Gerald Williams (1983: 7) divided forty Iowa lawyers into pairs, gave them identical case files (and photocopies of comparable jury awards from the Des Moines area), and asked them to negotiate a settlement. Among the fourteen pairs who completed the exercise and were willing to submit a signed statement of results, settlements ranged from $15,000 to $95,000, and none were within 20 percent, plus or minus, of the average settlement. And when Robert Condlin (1985: 66) examined transcripts of arguments by 100 teams of law students in a simulated lawsuit negotiation, he concluded that negotiators' experience, preparation, and intellectual abilities, "along with tolerance for conflict, stamina, ruthlessness, oratorical skill and emotional force, play as large a role in determining the extent to which norms are invoked and elaborated as do qualities inherent in the norms themselves."[27]

Unequal legal representation in the United States does not occur randomly, of course. Rich litigants generally can hire better lawyers than opponents who are not rich, and they can buy the services of consultants to help them choose a favorable jury and test out arguments before mock juries (Alschuler, 1998: 410–411; Adler, 1994). In Marc Galanter's (1974) well-known formulation, "repeat players," on average, get better lawyering than inexperienced "one-shotters." The repeat players do better at the difficult job of shopping for lawyers, marshaling evidence, producing supportive witnesses, and preparing the contracts and record-keeping systems that will strengthen their legal position (Galanter, 1974; Cooney, 1994). Even if parties can *afford* equal lawyering, their capacity to endure the lengthy, frustrating process of litigation often varies. In a study of divorce cases in Wisconsin the authors concluded that "instead of reflecting the parties' interests, settlements most typically reflect the parties' relative stamina and vulnerability to the pressures of a prolonged dispute" (Erlanger et al. 1987: 592). In a more hierarchical, judge-dominated civil litigation system, these differences in capacity of parties probably matter to some degree but almost certainly not as much as they do in the United States.

Perhaps the saddest inequality imposed by adversarial legalism, however, afflicts those who must acquiesce in violations of their legal rights because the cost of civil litigation exceeds the monetary value of their losses. For losses under $1,500 or so (depending on state law), American claimants can pursue their legal rights in small claims courts, where the trappings of adversarial legalism (juries, lawyers, pretrial discovery) are banned—and hence justice is affordable. For tort cases, if the claimant's damages are large enough to make it worth his time, a lawyer might be found to take a small-stakes case on a contingency fee basis, that is, in return for a third of the winnings. But for countless moderate-stakes commercial, contract, or property disputes, the court system is simply out of reach—not only because adversarial legalism is expensive but because under the "American rule," even if a court upholds your claim, you, and not the guy whose legally unfounded defense forced you to trial, must pay your lawyer's fees. The best that can be done is to find a lawyer who will see what can be accomplished by means of a threatening demand letter or telephone call (Macaulay, 1979). The "loser pays" rules that prevail in England and in Europe are criticized for deterring justifiable lawsuits by risk-averse disputants who cannot afford even a small possibility of losing and having to pay the other side's legal fees. It seems likely, however, that those kinds of injustices, however troublesome, are not as large and pervasive as the injustices that stem from the American rule.

Other economically advanced democracies, such as the Netherlands and Great Britain, attempt to minimize the legal effect of economic inequality by ensuring that not only the poor but a substantial proportion of the working and middle classes are eligible for government-reimbursed legal services.[28] The United States, despite its commitment to lawyer-dominated methods of litigation, provides governmental support for civil legal services only to the poor and gradually has been shrinking the level of support.[29] Moreover, Japan, the Netherlands, and the United Kingdom also deal with the problem of inequality by providing a richer array of free or inexpensive "precourt" dispute resolution institutions for "personal plight cases"; these include legal advice clinics as well as administrative tribunals for landlord-tenant conflicts, employee dismissal issues, and consumer complaints, in which lawyers are not needed (Kritzer, 1996; Blankenburg, 1994; Tanase, 1990; Rosch, 1987).

Sophisticated "repeat players" in the United States often can avoid the expense and unpredictability of adversarial legalism by purchasing more efficient "alternative" dispute resolution by private third parties. Arbitrators, for example, decide without juries; some American arbitration proceedings look a bit like European civil adjudication. Arbitration clauses have become standard in architectural and construction contracts, industrial supply contracts, and real estate transactions. Experienced companies have come to recognize, as Hazard and Taruffo's comparatively oriented study of American civil procedure acknowledges, that "arbitration required by contract . . . usually affords better justice than a prohibitively expensive right to litigate" (Hazard and Taruffo, 1993: 171).

Ordinary citizens are far less likely than sophisticated business firms to plan their way into "alternative dispute resolution" (ADR) systems. Increasingly, however, legislatures and courts are compelling litigants to submit to arbitration or mediation before granting them a trial (Alschuler, 1990: 17). In fact, plaintiffs, defendants, and their attorneys, whether winners or losers, tend to be extremely satisfied with court-annexed ADR (Hensler, 1990: 417; Brazil, 1990) probably because, as compared to the usual disposition by bargaining through lawyers, they often participate directly and get a respectful hearing (Alschuler, 1990: 24). Less happy, however, are many ordinary American citizens who are forced into industry-dominated ADR programs. Seeking to avoid the costs and unpredictability of litigation, stock brokerage firms, health maintenance organizations, banks, and many corporate employers compel new customers and employees to sign away their rights to a jury trial and accept arbitration instead. But the securities industry, for example, sets the basic rules and chooses the pool of arbitrators.[30] Customers not infrequently complain that the process is not entirely fair (Jacobs and Siconolfi, 1995: A1, A9). Likewise, female employees have complained that sexual harassment complaints do not get a fair hearing from business-oriented arbitration panels (Jacobs, 1994: B2; Meier, 1997: A1). Consumer advocate Ralph Nader, who lobbied against a provision for mandatory arbitration in President Clinton's 1993 proposed national health care package, has called ADR clauses a "systematic attack on the law" (Winninghoff, 1994: 30; Menkel-Meadow, 1991).

A civil justice system bloated by adversarial legalism thus is a twofold source of inequality: sophisticated litigants gain an advantage not only because they are better at withstanding the costs and uncertainties of adversarial litigation but also because they are better able to devise ways of circumventing it. More fundamentally, knowledge that the court system is too costly, complicated, slow, and uncertain to vindicate many legal rights and defenses must surely have a deeply corrosive effect on American citizens' faith in the justice system. The average citizen thinks it favors the rich. The average businessperson, like the owner of the Dixie Flag Company, sees the feckless and the unscrupulous aided by the cost and uncertainty of adversarial litigation, and feels that the system is unfair to the honest. Both are right—not all the time, but all too often.

In the 1970s an extensive academic study and a congressionally established reform commission recommended that routine bankruptcy cases be diverted from federal courts into an administrative agency, which, it was argued, could process them nonadversarially, more efficiently, and more cheaply (Barnes, 1997). Federal bankruptcy judges and bankruptcy lawyers reacted by lobbying hard against the proposed reform bill. They succeeded. Congress enacted instead the "Judges' Bill," which kept bankruptcy cases in the courts. The reform bill died, Jeb Barnes has explained, not merely because American lawyers, as such, are politically influential or because so many key members of Congress (and of leading consumer advocacy groups) are lawyers. The reform bill was also opposed by the American Bankers Association, the National Consumer Finance Association, the Department of Justice, organized labor, and congressional leaders of both parties. These politically diverse opponents all expressed misgivings about creating a "new federal bureaucracy," which they feared might disfavor their constituencies' interests.

For all its cost and inefficiency, therefore, a system structured by adversarial legalism persisted. It persisted because of a political tradition that is mistrustful of bureaucratic authority—preferring to fragment authority and to hold it legally accountable through individually activated rights and adversarial litigation. American politicians, interest groups, and broad swaths of the American public may complain bitterly about adversarial legalism, but they have trouble accepting any alternative that smacks of hierarchically organized bureaucratic legalism or expert judgment. They all are left, therefore, with more reliance on legal rights, more unpredictable methods of contestation, and higher lawyers' bills than those who seek civil justice in other economically advanced democracies.

7

The Tort Law System

In the 1970s and 1980s the incidence of asbestos-related diseases among Dutch workers was five to ten times as high as in the United States. As of 1991 almost 200,000 asbestos-based tort cases had been filed in the United States. Fewer than *ten* had been filed in the Netherlands, although Dutch law authorizes tort claims against employers. The primary reason for the huge discrepancy in tort claims, according to Harriet Vinke and Ton Wilthagen (1992: 12, 17), is that "in the Netherlands employees get reasonable benefits in a non-confrontational way"—that is, through the social security system. Disabled Dutch workers are entitled to all needed medical care and lifelong benefits equal to 70 or 80 percent of their lost earnings, without having to prove that an employer or product manufacturer did anything wrong. In the Dutch nonfault collective system, compensation is modest in amount but far more certain and consistent than in the adversarial American tort system (id. at 21).[1]

The asbestos litigation exemplifies both the strengths and the weaknesses of American adversarial legalism. Energized by the prospect of large contingency fees, and armed with the adversarial weapons of pretrial discovery, entrepreneurial plaintiffs' lawyers uncovered evidence that asbestos manufacturers had failed to tell workers all they knew or at least suspected about the health risks associated with inhalation of asbestos dust (Rosenberg, 1986). Politically responsive American judges, willing to innovate, allowed claimants to circumvent the workers' compensation system (which only allowed claims against employers, and for limited damages) by bringing tort suits against asbestos manufacturers and obtaining money damages for their "pain and suffering" as well as punitive damages. By driving at least eleven of the twenty-five major asbestos manufacturers into bankruptcy (Coffee, 1995: 1386),[2] the tort system sent a loud deterrent message to all American business executives and did so far more powerfully than any governmental regulatory agency could have done.

On the other hand, one might question the deterrent efficacy of the powerful American tort system. In the 1950s and 1960s, even as warning signs were rising, it had failed to compel companies that mined, made, or used asbestos to do adequate research about the risks of asbestos exposure and to provide adequate protections to workers. Moreover, as a mechanism for compensation, adversarial legalism proved to be costly, inconsistent, and inequitable. Studies indicated that close to two-thirds of insurance company expenditures in asbestos suits (including cases settled before trial) ended up in the pockets of lawyers and experts for both sides rather than in those of asbestos victims and their families (Kakalik et al., 1984: vviii).[3] Judicial decisions and jury awards in asbestos cases varied from state to state and case to case; hence some victims obtained far less compensation than others with similar illnesses and losses, and many victims whose claims were harder to prove got nothing (Sugarman, 1989: 46).[4] In a multiplaintiff asbestos case in Texas, five different juries, after hearing exactly the same evidence, reached substantially different decisions after being asked to rule on a series of specific issues relating to causation and liability (Bell and O'Connell, 1997: 22; Green, 1989: 221–223, 228–235). Claimants swept up in later class settlements were restricted to substantially lower recoveries than those who sued on their own or were agglomerated in earlier class settlements (Coffee, 1995: 1384–1396).[5] Furthermore, appellate courts invalidated some huge class action settlements as legally improper (Schuck, 1992b: 553–568; Brickman, 1992; Kakalik et al., 1983).

In the early 1980s Congress considered but failed to create a fund that would compensate asbestos victims without the need for costly civil litigation (Anderson, Warshauer, and Coffin, 1983). In the late 1990s, as tens of thousands of asbestos cases lingered on in the courts, and still more large companies lurched toward bankruptcy, a bipartisan group of senators and representatives again proposed an administrative compensation program, but the idea was again fiercely and successfully opposed by plaintiffs' lawyers, newly enriched and politically strengthened by multimillion-dollar fees obtained in tort litigation against tobacco companies (Jenkins, 1999).

The asbestos story reflects a broader pattern in American governance. Compared to other economically advanced democracies, the United States is distinctive in the relative prominence of private tort actions, rather than social insurance and bureaucratic mechanisms, for seeking compensation for personal injuries and environmentally caused illnesses. The United States is also distinctive in the severity of the legal sanctions (large money damages) available through tort litigation, and in the unpredictability and costliness of its lawyer-driven, jury-centered methods of adjudication. The United States employs a wider array of litigation-encouraging procedural mechanisms—contingency fees to finance tort litigation, extensive lawyer-controlled pretrial discovery, large class actions, and the rule that losing litigants generally need not reimburse the winner's legal fees. No other country comes close to matching the organizational and political energy of American personal injury lawyers, who aggressively seek out cases, disseminate litigation technologies, dream up new causes of action, and fiercely resist litigation-reducing reforms. And in no other nation is tort law so enmeshed in political controversy, as politicians are besieged by competing pro-and-anti tort reform lobbyists—rendering the substantive law even more changeable and inconsistent.

Tort Law or Social Insurance, Courts or Bureaucracies?

Throughout most of the nineteenth century, sunken ferries and exploding boilers evoked little legal response. Accidents "just happened" (Friedman, 1978: 374). By the end of the century, however, legal culture was changing. Fatalism declined. Reformers asserted that if engineers could make locomotives that roared along at fifty miles an hour, they also could make better braking and signaling and coupling systems; if they didn't, corporate officials, not God, were responsible for train wrecks and their human carnage (id. at 376). The rise of mass markets for casualty insurance meant that courts could compel business firms to compensate the victims of their technologies without bankrupting useful companies (Friedman, 1986). At a sharply increasing rate, therefore, accident victims brought tort suits against factory owners, railroads, and streetcar companies.[6]

But tort law called for detailed factual and moral inquiries, tailored to the particular case. Didn't the plaintiff know some danger would be involved? Was his own negligence a contributing cause? How fast was the train really moving? What could the defendant company reasonably have done to reduce the risk, short of eschewing the accident-causing activity altogether? Did the plaintiff have a bad back before the accident? Confronting these issues, the legal rules and adjudicatory processes of tort law grew ever more complicated. Legal complexity made the relative economic capacity and legal sophistication of the contending parties just as important as the law itself in determining which accident victims would be compensated and in what amounts. Examining California trial court records of the late nineteenth century, Lawrence Friedman (1978: 367) found that although some accident victims obtained substantial recoveries, "it is likely that nothing was paid—not a penny—to most victims and their families." Railroads systematically coerced workers into relinquishing injury claims (id. at 370–371). Nonetheless, railroad executives complained about ambulance-chasing lawyers and the fraudulent claims they arranged through "rascally confederates in the medical profession" (id. at 373).

In the decade after 1910 American state legislatures began to carve one major type of dispute out of the tort law/jury system. They made employers absolutely liable for medical expenses and for about two-thirds of lost earnings resulting from work-related injuries. The injured worker no longer had to prove the employer was at fault, and the employer no longer could escape liability by blaming the employee's contributory negligence or claiming that the worker had voluntarily "assumed the risk." Employers were required by law to carry workers' compensation insurance. Disputes about the extent of accident-related disability were diverted from costly jury trials to less formal administrative tribunals in which lawyers' fees were limited. Workers' compensation was to be the exclusive remedy in most cases.

Western European democracies also adopted collective approaches to compensating workplace accident victims, although they were more inclined to rely on payroll taxes on both employers and employees, rather than on employer-provided private insurance, to fund compensation systems (Williams, 1991: 117–197). Since World War II many European democracies have expanded coverage beyond the workplace, further restricting the role of tort law. In Germany, for example, mandatory industrial accident insurance has been extended to cover injuries to students as well as accidents in the course of travel to and from work and school; it thus covers at least one-third, possibly half, of all traffic accident injuries—including the substantial proportion of injury accidents to drivers who have no one to blame but themselves and hence for whom tort law is useless (Nutter and Bateman, 1989). Switzerland extended workers' compensation insurance coverage to injuries at home and at play (Duffy and Landis, 1988). Disputes are resolved not in court but in specialized administrative tribunals.

Further, in most post–World War II Western European welfare states, medical care for victims of any kind of accident or chemical exposure has been provided through tax-supported universal public health care programs. Lost wages are replaced in large part by tax-funded disability plans. Tort law damages are limited to economic losses that are not covered by such medical and social insurance programs; noneconomic damages are legally specified and moderate in amount. Consequently, most disputes concerning compensation for injury are decided not by courts but by bureaucratic agencies and panels of medical and occupation experts.[7]

New Zealand represents the purest version of the collective responsibility/ social insurance approach. A governmentally operated social insurance scheme, funded by levies on employers, motor vehicle owners, and general taxes, provides moderate but certain compensation—the cost of medical attention and rehabilitation, plus 80 percent of lost earnings—for all personal injuries arising out of accidents, including medical mishaps, regardless of fault

(Gellhorn, 1988: 188–212).[8] For unintentional injuries the tort law system is marginalized. In contrast to the enormous litigation costs of adversarial legalism in the United States, in New Zealand "about 90 percent of expenditures go to or on behalf of injured people; administration and other transaction costs claim only 10 percent" (Sugarman, 1989: 40).[9] Moreover, surveys indicate that New Zealanders are overwhelmingly supportive of their current tort-free regime (Gellhorn, 1988: 194).

The American Pattern: Social Insurance *and* Adversarial Legalism

The United States has also gradually extended reliance on a collective responsibility/social insurance model for compensating victims of harm, but its moves in that direction have been much more tentative and limited, and it has been less willing to restrict the role of tort law and adversarial legalism. Workers' compensation coverage has not been extended beyond the workplace. The workers' compensation process, originally designed to provide insured benefits to injured workers without costly legal conflict, has become intensely adversarial and legalistic (Nonet, 1969; Schroeder, 1986: 151).[10] A study of workers' compensation claims for permanent partial disability indicated that in Maryland, New Jersey, and some categories of cases in Wisconsin, "dueling adversary experts" were employed in 63 percent, 79 percent, and 63 percent of cases, respectively, and that legal "friction costs" added up to 38 percent, 46 percent, and 42 percent of the total disability payments awarded (Workers Compensation Research Institute, 1988). In workers' compensation tribunals in Great Britain and Western Europe, in contrast, governmentally appointed physicians and other experts (not American-style "dueling doctors") make disability analyses (Kritzer, 1993: 16).

Nevertheless, even in the United States the collective responsibility/social insurance model of injury compensation has steadily expanded its importance as a mode of compensation. An extensive 1988–1989 survey found that the overwhelming majority of Americans who experience personal injuries do not file tort suits.[11] They seek payment for their medical bills and lost wages from employer-provided health insurance, workers' compensation insurance, government-provided Medicaid, disability insurance, and so on (Hensler et al., 1991). Only about 10 percent of injured people each year—mostly motor vehicle accident victims—obtain compensation via the fault-based tort liability system. The tort system ends up compensating only 7 percent of total *economic* loss resulting from injuries, and 11 percent if one includes payments for "pain and suffering," but 33 percent of all compensation received for motor vehicle accident injuries (id. at 18).

Although the American fault-based tort system occupies only a secondary place as a monetary source of compensation for injuries, it remains legally and conceptually primary. For example, except in a few states that have recently modified the "collateral source rule," tort case juries are not supposed to be told if the plaintiff's medical expenses or earnings losses are covered by health or disability insurance. Revealing that information to the jury, the argument goes, would erode the moral and deterrence rationales for tort damages, which require negligent defendants to pay for the full measure of the harm they cause. Thus, Stephen Sugarman (1989: 40) points out, "When payments for losses already covered by collateral sources and for pain and suffering are subtracted, one finds that only about 10–15 percent of the costs of the tort system go to compensating victims for out-of-pocket medical expenses, lost income and the like."[12]

Intensifying Tort Law

During the 1960–1980 period, as Western European democracies were bolstering their social insurance programs and marginalizing fault-based tort law, the United States, always ambivalent about "big government," diverted the political demand for "total justice" (Friedman, 1985) into a different channel, dramatically expanding tort law's coverage and potency. Beginning in the 1960s reform-minded judges sharply modified the common law rule that tort claimants are barred from recovery by their own contributory negligence (Ursin, 1981: 243–244), abolished governmental and charitable institutions' legal immunity from tort liability, changed evidentiary rules for medical malpractice cases, and imposed "strict liability" for product defects—all making it far easier for plaintiffs to win. Judges expanded the right to recover compensation for accident-related emotional distress (id. at 244), made it easier to sue out-of-state businesses in the injured party's county courthouse, and enabled entrepreneurial lawyers to aggregate the claims of large numbers of accident or defective product victims into massive class action suits (Coffee, 1995: 1356–1358; Priest, 1985: 461). The doctrinal changes did not induce a universal litigation explosion; for many categories of accidents and in some regions, the rate of tort litigation grew only modestly.[13] Nevertheless, tort litigation gradually became an enormous presence in American life. In 1989, 447,374 tort cases were filed in state courts (National Center for State Courts, 1991: 3). Medical malpractice tort claims increased from 1 per 100 American physicians in 1960 (when malpractice suits, however justifiable, were very difficult to win) to 10.6 per 100 in 1980 and then to 17 per 100 in 1986. (By way of comparison, there were only 1.8 malpractice claims for every 100 Canadian physicians in 1986, and the average American physician's medical malpractice insurance bill was eleven times that of her Canadian counterpart) (Dewees, Trebilcock, and Coyle, 1991: 219, 221; Danzon, 1990: 56; Nutter and Bateman, 1989). Tort claims against officials of municipal and county governments in the United States grew dramatically (Tort Policy Working Group, 1986).

European and Japanese tort law governing liability for physicians and product manufacturers also changed in the 1980s and 1990s, coming "reasonably close to American doctrine" (Schwartz, 1991: 28; Gifford, 1991: 10); still, "the rates of litigation and the costs of liability in those countries," writes Gary Schwartz (1991: 28, 47–51), "are only a small fraction of what they are here." Dow Chemical reported that in 1986 it incurred $100 million in legal and insurance expenses for product liability in the United States, compared to $20 million for such expenses on a comparable volume of manufacturing and sales elsewhere, and was engaged in defending 456 lawsuits in the United States, compared to only four elsewhere (Chinloy, 1989: 57; Nutter and Bateman, 1989). The asbestos class actions provided a precedent for other "mass tort" cases in which tens of thousands of claims were aggregated into a single lawsuit calling for millions or even billions of dollars in damages on behalf of individuals who claimed that their maladies stemmed from pharmaceutical and chemical products (such as Bendectin and Agent Orange), silicone breast implants, and intrauterine birth control devices (Coffee, 1995).

Perhaps most controversially, American courts expanded the moral boundaries of responsibility in tort law, perhaps not in the routine case but in some subsets of cases that jarred traditional expectations. Motorists and pedestrians injured in auto or sidewalk accidents sued municipal governments for not making traffic signs more visible or walkways smoother. Shoppers who had been mugged in shopping center parking lots sometimes recovered from the center, arguing that management should have posted security guards there (Lee, 1997), and some tenants victimized by crime sued landlords on the same grounds (Woo, 1993).

But despite cases of this nature, the new American tort law did not really achieve the ideal of enterprise liability, under which—as in American workers' compensation law or Swedish pharmaceutical accident insurance—any injury arising out of an enterprise's activity is compensable without proof of the enterprise's fault. American tort plaintiffs still must present evidence indicating that the defendant company or governmental body was in some sense at fault (Bell and O'Connell, 1997: 32). That means that lawsuits are contentious, costly, and risky to pursue. That, in turn, means that most victims of medical malpractice or product injuries or parking lot muggings do not file claims and do not recover anything (Saks, 1992: 1147; Abel, 1987: 448–451). And that means that the tort system does not compel negligent injurors as a class to bear anywhere near the full economic cost of the harms they inflict on their victims.

The Tort Industry

For all its weaknesses as a compensation system, American tort law became enormously threatening to actual and potential defendants. Juries are granted wide discretion to assign monetary values to the plaintiff's "pain and suffering" and to impose very large punitive damages without explaining why (Blumstein et al., 1990). Between 1960 and 1980 a substantial majority of jury verdicts in product liability and medical malpractice cases in Chicago went against the plaintiff, but average awards in cases that plaintiffs *won* increased more than tenfold—more rapidly than the consumer price index and the price of medical care. Verdicts in which damages exceeded $1,000,000 grew from 0.1 percent of all trials in 1960–1964 to 3.5 percent in 1980–1984, and those million-dollar verdicts accounted for 85 percent of the money awarded in all 1980–1984 trials (Peterson, 1987: 22, 33, 35, 51). An insurance industry study of large product liability claims revealed an increase in payments of $1 million or more from none in 1975 to 13 percent of all claims closed in 1985 (Soular, 1986: 3).

Like government lotteries with growing jackpots, the large-recovery cases, even if statistically infrequent, acted like magnets, drawing new cases into the liability system. With the prospect of collecting one-third of the awarded damages through contingency fees—a practice prohibited in most other countries—American plaintiffs' lawyers geared up to seek out accident victims and to aggregate cases. An intensely competitive litigation industry developed. The Supreme Court held that laws and regulations that barred advertising by lawyers amounted to unconstitutional restrictions on freedom of speech (*Bates v. State Bar,* 1977). Ads for tort lawyers blossomed on bus-stop benches and late-night television.[14]

Entrepreneurial plaintiffs' lawyers developed sophisticated methods of "ambulance chasing," such as holding press conferences near the sites of dramatic plane crashes and chemical spills and deploying representatives to advertise for and sign up potential claimants. The American Trial Lawyers Association (ATLA), the Public Citizen Health Research Group, and the Center for Automotive Safety created databases, lists of expert witnesses, and "litigation kits" for plaintiffs' lawyers, helping (and encouraging) them to bring lawsuits concerning harms caused or allegedly caused by particular automobile models, medical products, lead paint, and silicone breast implants (Rabin, 1993: 128; Stipp, 1993; Kolata, 1995). Conversely, liability insurance companies and other defendants learned to contest large tort claims all the more fiercely, throwing costly legal obstacles into the path of serious claims (Lohr, 1995: 19; Opatrny, 1995: C1), including many that might have been entirely valid. Overall, as the financial stakes rose in tort litigation, so did the level of adversarial legalism, the transaction costs, and the unpredictability of outcomes.

The American tort industry reached its twentieth century zenith in litigation against major tobacco companies. For years, American juries in scores of lawsuits declined to find the tobacco companies liable, apparently feeling unsympathetic to smokers who did not quit after tobacco's hazards became widely known.[15] After all, by the 1980s some fifty million smokers in the United States had quit. Polls indicated that 90 percent of respondents know that cigarette smoking can cause lung cancer (Viscusi, 1990; 1992), and a majority said that smokers, not tobacco companies, are primarily responsible for the adverse health consequences of smoking cigarettes (Kagan and Nelson, 2000). Nevertheless, plaintiffs' lawyers who had made millions of dollars in mass tort actions against asbestos companies had the skills, the resources, and the incentives to keep trying.

In the mid-1990s plaintiffs' lawyers persuaded several state attorneys general to hire them, on a contingency fee basis, to file lawsuits against the tobacco industry on behalf of the state governments (Mather, 1998). Each action, emphasizing the tobacco companies' years of cynical denial that cigarette smoking is addictive and carcinogenic, demanded compensation for billions of dollars that the states had paid for the care of tobacco-related illnesses pursuant to Medicaid programs. As the publicity mounted, virtually every state attorney general filed a parallel suit. The tobacco companies could argue that there was no evidence that their denials had actually misled the smokers; that the state governments, knowing the risks, had allowed cigarettes to be marketed, while profiting from tobacco excise taxes; and that even before taking those tobacco tax revenues into account, government benefit programs actually *save* money on smokers, since they die earlier and with lower medical costs than nonsmokers (Viscusi, 1997: 27–32). No judge had validated the legal arguments of the attorneys general (Mather, 1998: 920), but faced with trillions of dollars of total claims and an unpredictable court system, the tobacco companies agreed to a massive $368 billion settlement of the states' lawsuits in exchange for relief from further liability.

The U.S. Congress, whose legislative authorization was required to provide immunity from future liability, sought to increase the settlement amount to $516 billion and declined to provide any legal immunity. The tobacco companies then bolted. The congressional bill died, but the lawsuits did not. In 1998 the tobacco companies settled the state lawsuits for $246 billion, without a promise of exemption from liability in other cases. The settlements encouraged the filing of still more individual and class action suits against the major tobacco companies, including one by the U.S. Department of Justice. As in the asbestos story, no American legislature enacted a replacement measure, that is, a law that bans the seemingly endless round of tort cases in return for creation of a fund, financed by cigarette taxes, that ensures uniform, moderate medical insurance and income replacement for victims of tobacco-related diseases and their families or that subsidizes smoking cessation programs. And American use-discouraging taxes on cigarettes remain far lower than those in many other economically advanced democracies.

The Critique of American Tort Law

By the 1980s increases in adversarial legalism had made American tort law the world's most politically controversial liability law system, generating heated legislative battles, ballot propositions, and controversies about judicial appointments. The political attack was initiated by organizations that directly face the costs and uncertainties generated by adversarial litigation—insurance companies, physicians' associations and hospitals, product manufacturers, municipalities, and school districts. They funded the American Tort Reform Association (ATRA), which mounted a costly mass media advertising campaign that focused on the theme of "lawsuit abuse" (Bell and O'Connell, 1997: 188–189). The arguments that ATRA and other tort critics have made in the political arena have often been one-sided, based on unsupported statistical claims and on the unrepresentative cases that circulate like viruses in the business press (Daniels and Martin, 1995; Galanter, 1998). Sociolegal scholars have made much of the conservative critics' exaggerations. Nevertheless, it is entirely understandable why American tort law has become politically controversial. As we shall see, a body of academic analysis and cross-national comparisons suggest that a tort law system shaped by adversarial legalism is a very inefficient and inconsistent means of compensating accident victims and that its contribution to deterrence and safety are erratic.

Inefficiency

The costly inefficiency of the American tort system is revealed most strikingly by comparing it to a more efficient one. In Japan, as noted by Takao Tanase (1990), fewer than 1 percent of automobile accidents involving death or an injury result in tort litigation. In the United States the comparable figure is 21.5 percent. The disparity does not stem from passivity on the part of Japanese accident victims. They commonly make claims based on tort law and they receive compensation from negligent drivers and their insurance companies.[16] The litigation rate is low because Japan provides nonlitigious methods of assessing fault, advising victims of their legal rights, and determining the appropriate level of compensation. It is instructive to examine how this is accomplished.

First, Japan invests heavily in *official investigation of accidents* to determine the facts and the relative responsibility of the parties. Accidents must be reported to the police immediately; this obligation is widely obeyed, Tanase reports, partly because insurance companies may refuse to pay compensation to motorists who fail to report. Members of a large cadre of police officers who specialize in traffic accidents come to the site rapidly, question parties and witnesses, "and hammer out a consensual story as to what happened to which the parties agree and formally endorse by signing." These police reports are given great weight and rarely are challenged in court (Ramseyer and Nakazato, 1989: 673–674). In addition, in assessing an accident victim's medical bills and permanent injuries, insurance companies and courts rely heavily on the victim's own treating physician, who is trusted because a "Compulsory Insurance Investigative Bureau" employs medical consultants to reexamine dubious reports and crack down on hospitals or physicians who seem out of line. Overall, in terms of the typology outlined in Chapter 1 of this book, Japan's method of investigating the facts is both more hierarchical and more reliant on expert judgment than the American system, where fact-gathering and assessment are dominated by adversarial investigation, pretrial discovery, and negotiation by contending parties (drivers versus insurance companies) and their lawyers.

Second, before a court case is filed in Japan, contested claims generally are resolved by *nonlitigious dispute resolution mechanisms*. These include Traffic Accident Dispute Resolution Centers, which along with courts, provide mediation services, as well as a network of consultation centers operated by governments, the bar association, and insurance companies. The consultation centers provide free advice on legal rights from special counselors (nonlawyers, who mostly are retired government officials) (Ramseyer and Nakazato, 1989: 675–677). The mediation services and advice centers work effectively because the Japanese legal system works hard at developing *clear rules that guarantee virtually automatic, predictable, and moderate compensation* for most accident victims. In the 1960s Japanese judges took the lead in developing fixed formulae for determining damages and assessing liability.[17] Special "traffic sections" in the Japanese judiciary continue to produce, update, and disseminate legal standards for compensation. Ministry of Finance regulations, compulsory loss-sharing arrangements, and other governmental controls strive to standardize the damages offered by insurance companies.

In court, decisions are made by judges, not juries, and these decisions are subject to review for conformity to the traffic and compensation law (Tanase, 1990: 667–673). To return to the typology in Chapter 1, the establishment of standards for compensation approaches the ideal of bureaucratic legalism, as contrasted with the more flexible and powerful but less predictable adversarial legalism of the American system.

In Japan probably fewer than 2 percent of accident victims hire lawyers (Tanase, 1990: 660). The Japanese auto accident victims referred to above need not hire a lawyer and go to court because they and the defendants' insurance companies can agree what the court decision will be.[18] In contrast, in civil cases tried in Chicago between 1960 and 1980, George Priest (1990: 196) found that the majority of jury time was spent on routine, small-stakes auto accident or slip-and-fall cases "[b]ecause the difficulty of predicting how Chicago juries will decide makes it impossible for the parties to agree on a settlement amount to save litigation costs." Tanase estimates that in Japan legal fees comprise only 2 percent of the total compensation paid to injured persons and that mediating and claims process costs amount to about 0.2 percent of the total amount paid to injured persons. In the United States, according to an in-depth survey in the late 1980s, 24 percent of individuals hurt in motor vehicle accidents involving potential defendants hire a lawyer, which generally compels the defendant to employ a lawyer too; the figure goes up to 57 percent of claimants with "serious injuries"(defined as fractures, burns, or worse) (Hensler et al., 1991: 124). When persons with serious motor vehicle injuries hire lawyers, more than half file lawsuits (id. at 116, 122). The resulting costs are shocking. According to a Department of Transportation nationwide study of motor vehicle accident tort claims (not just lawsuits) in 1968, lawyers for both sides were paid almost $1 billion, which equaled *47 percent* of the total personal injury benefits ($2,059,100,000) paid by liability insurers to third party accident victims (Bombaugh, 1971: 229–230). Similar results emerged from a RAND Civil Justice Institute study in the mid-1980s (Kakalik and Pace, 1986: 70–72). In the words of Peter Bell and Jeffrey O'Connell (1997: 67), "No one wants to compensate injured people with a bucket brigade of money that wastes every second bucket."

As always, the economic costs of adversarial legalism have unintended adverse consequences. The average driver's automobile liability insurance policy cost 250 percent more in 1990 (in constant dollars) than the same coverage cost in 1980 (RAND Institute, 1995; Carroll, Abrahamse, and Vaiana, 1995). In consequence, huge numbers of poorer motorists—up to a quarter of all drivers in California—have been tempted into outlawry, driving illegally without insurance.[19] Others can afford only minimal coverage; hence many victims of underinsured motorists' negligence have little hope of obtaining meaningful compensation through the tort system (Sugarman, 1993a).

Injustice

All that expense might be tolerable if it produced just decisions and reliable, meaningful levels of compensation for the injured. But here too study after study seems to support the conclusion that the American tort system does not attain those goals (Abraham and Liebman, 1993; O'Connell, 1979). Summarizing several studies concerning motor vehicle cases, Robert Rabin (1988: 34) wrote: "Research has shown that the tort system only erratically compensates the victims of traffic accidents, often undercompensating the most seriously injured, overcompensating others, and spending more money on litigation costs than on payments that end up in injured plaintiffs' pockets."[20]

Both the American adjudicative system and the law of damages encourage that kind of inconsistency. Whereas the Japanese make clear, specific laws and organize the judiciary to maximize uniformity and reliability of compensation, the American tort law system seems designed to encourage the opposite. Decisions are entrusted to amateur juries, who are uninformed about decisions in comparable cases, are not compelled to explain their decisions or coordinate them with those of other juries, and are subject to the competitive tactics of truth-manipulating lawyers, who all too often are unequally matched. The law of damages, particularly with respect to the crucial category of compensation for "pain and suffering" (which accounts for 30 to 40 percent of all compensation awarded), is completely vague (Blumstein, Bovbjerg, and Sloan, 1990: 174–176; Geistfeld, 1995). In a typical jury instruction, the judge tells the jury that it may award the plaintiff compensation for past and future physical pain stemming from the defendant's wrongdoing, but "there are no objective guidelines by which you can measure the money equivalent of this element of injury; the only real measuring stick, if it can so be described, is your collective enlightened conscience" (Douthwaite, 1988: 274).

The law of punitive damages is also vague, making it difficult to predict whether juries will award them (fewer than 10 percent do) (Eisenberg et al., 1997; Polinsky, 1997: 666; Ostrom et al., 1996: 237–238), how high those damages will be (Sunstein et al., 1999), or whether appellate courts will reduce them.[21] Studies show that injury severity explains only about 40 percent of the variation in pain-and-suffering awards (Bovbjerg et al., 1989: 923–924; Sloan and Hsieh, 1990: 1025), and that plaintiffs with similar painful and debilitating injuries are often awarded significantly different amounts of damages (Geistfeld, 1995: 784; Leebron, 1989: 310). Experienced medical malpractice insurance companies, one careful study of their files showed, were "seriously off the mark" in estimating the amount of damages a jury would award and "failed to establish anything like a going rate" (Metzloff, 1991).

The cumbersomeness, costliness, and legal unpredictability of the American tort system also mean that compensation payments to injured claimants are strongly affected by factors that have nothing to do with the legal validity of a claim or a defense. For example, jury awards tend to be substantially smaller if the case is tried in a small county rather than a big city (Danzon, 1984: 143). Moreover, as Stephen Sugarman (1989: 38) notes, these questions make a significant difference: "Was your injuror insured? Do you happen to have (or did the other side make or destroy) the right evidence? Do you have the right lawyer, the right expert, and the ability to endure the settlement process? Do you look like you will make a good witness? Who happens to be the insurance adjuster or lawyer with whom the settlement is being negotiated?" The result, Sugarman says, is a system in which "lawyers' talents, plaintiffs' demeanor, defendants' grit, and the idiosyncrasies of jury composition hand similar victims altogether dissimilar results" (ibid.).

That the American tort system fails to compensate or undercompensates many legally deserving accident victims is best revealed by the extensive research on malpractice litigation. Partly because of the costliness and uncertainty of the tort system, the great majority of patients injured by medical malpractice do not even file claims (Danzon, 1985: 42; Bell and O'Connell, 1997: 105).[22] Among those who *do* file claims or bring suit, many victims give up and recover nothing once they confront the problems of obtaining expert witnesses and overcoming legalistic resistance (Munch, 1977: 76).[23] At trial, liability verdicts are difficult to predict. When a panel of eleven expert anesthesiologists was asked to evaluate malpractice case files, the physicians' judgments on liability coincided with the actual jury verdicts in only 57 percent of the cases (Liang, 1997: 125–126; Sanders, 1998: 360). Even in a sample of cases in which a physician evaluator employed by the defendant's insurance company had rated the defendant's behavior "indefensible," juries decided against plaintiffs in 42 percent of malpractice trials (Targin et al., 1992: Sanders, 1998: 360).

At the same time, the American tort system often results in *overcompensation*. One reason is that defendants often pay damages to tort victims for losses that had been covered by other sources (Sugarman, 1989: 40). Another reason is that the tort system not infrequently rewards legally doubtful claims. In the study mentioned above, medical malpractice plaintiffs won at trial in 21 percent of cases had been rated "defensible" by physicians whom the defendant's insuror had retained to evaluate malpractice claims (Targin et al., 1992; Sanders, 1998: 360). The Harvard Medical Malpractice Study showed that while most patients hurt by substandard care did not file legal actions, more than 80 percent of patients who *did* bring suit had *not* received substandard care (Huber, 1997). Those patients brought suit, notwithstanding the questionable validity of their legal claim, because they stood to gain by doing so. As indicated by a number of careful studies, insurance companies, faced with an expensive and legally uncertain adjudicative system, seem willing to buy off many tenuous medical malpractice claims with small settlements.[24]

The insurers (like other "repeat player" defendants such as municipalities and mass transit systems) prefer to devote their legal firepower to fighting claims by victims with the most serious injuries, for those could result in million-dollar jury awards. But that fierce resistance tends to result in *undercompensation of the most seriously injured*. To be sure, some victims of very serious and disabling medical accidents succeed in obtaining very large jury awards. That happens often enough to frighten doctors (because of the tort system's unpredictability) (Weiler, 1991: 6; Songer, 1988; Kennedy, 1985) and to drive up the level of malpractice insurance premiums (for the "big cases" account for almost half the total compensation paid) (Sugarman, 1989: 39). Nevertheless, more than two of every three jury decisions go *against* the plaintiff (Eisenberg et al., 1995; Moller, 1996). Just as significantly, victims of serious injuries often are desperate for money and cannot afford the delay of waiting for a trial (which always entails a risk of losing). Thus research shows that most malpractice claimants with legally strong claims receive much less than full compensation of even their economic losses (Sloan and Van Wert, 1991: 158; Weiler, 1991; Munch, 1977: 80).

In other spheres of tort law, Bell and O'Connell (1997: 63–64) summarize the research as similarly indicating that "persons with minor injuries on average receive a much higher percentage of their economic loss from a tort claim than do persons with serious injuries." The measure of justice also depends on whom one gets to sue. Controlling for severity of injury, jury awards in medical malpractice cases are several times higher than awards in auto accident cases, according to a study based on jury verdict reporters in five states in the 1980s.[25] And in the 1960–1980 period, Chicago juries awarded plaintiffs who had fallen in a building owned by a corporation significantly higher damages than plaintiffs who had fallen on government-owned property, and three times as much as those who fell in a private dwelling (Chin and Peterson, 1985).[26] Had those injured claimants received similar injuries in falls at their own workplaces, they would have been barred from the tort system but would have been able to obtain much smaller awards (with more certainty) by filing workers' compensation claims.

Uncertain Deterrence

With its energetic plaintiffs' lawyers—fueled by contingency fees, far-reaching powers of pretrial discovery, and the prospect of large money damages—American tort law is uniquely capable of exposing and penalizing those responsible for unsafe products and negligent practices (Speiser, 1980). It stands to reason, defenders of the system argue, that "reforms" that diminish tort law's fierceness or replace it with a more efficient, nonfault-based compensation system would weaken tort law's regulatory and condemnatory function and therefore make life in the United States more dangerous. Accurately assessing the regulatory effects of American tort law, however, is not easy. As Stephen Sugarman (1989) has pointed out, besides the threat of tort liability, individuals and organizations are simultaneously subject to other, often more salient, inducements for safe and responsible behavior. Pilots and motor vehicle drivers are motivated by the instincts of *self-preservation*. The precautions taken by physicians and product engineers are motivated primarily by *professional ethics*. For airlines and product manufacturers, *market forces* provide strong inducements to construct multiple layers of precautions because serious fatal accidents, dramatized on television news programs, can destroy a company's reputation and market share. Finally, *direct governmental regulation,* with its roadway speed limits, factory inspections, and permit systems (plus the threat of criminal penalties for willful violations that result in accidents), provides more immediate and more specific instructions than tort law on how to prevent harm.

Moreover, Sugarman argues, *the liability system's deterrent threat is muted by liability insurance and by the uncertainty and delayed effects of tort liability.* Then there is the stubborn persistence of human incompetence, inattentiveness, and calculated corner-cutting, which lead truck drivers, emergency room doctors, and the crew of the Exxon *Valdez* to make mistakes, no matter how large the potential tort liability. After surveying American corporate product design staffs, George Eads and Peter Reuter (1984: 263–294) wrote, "Although product liability exerts a powerful influence on product design decisions, it sends an extremely vague signal. Because the linkage between good design and a firm's liability exposure remains tenuous, the signal says only, 'Be careful, or you will be sued.' Unfortunately, it does not say how to be careful, or, more important, how careful to be."[27]

Consequently, efforts to sort out how much tort law really adds to the regulatory equation generally have been rather inconclusive (Schwartz, 1994:

379; Deweese and Trebilcock, 1992: 59–60; ALI, 1991: 32). For example, a comprehensive study concluded that American tort law had stimulated "broad-based improvements in the institutional environment and procedures through which medical care is delivered" (Weiler, 1991: 91). Physicians report having adopted new standard procedures following well-publicized court cases (Weiler, 1991: 127; Givelber et al., 1984; Wiley, 1981). Indeed, some studies indicate that American malpractice law sometimes may "overdeter," leading not only to sensible extra precautions but also to unnecessary hospitalizations, lab tests, and other defensive procedures.[28] On the other hand, Dewees and Trebilcock (1992: 83) observe that while the level of medical malpractice claims in Canada is 20 percent that of the United States, "there appears to be no evidence that Canadian physicians are more careless than their U.S. counterparts." Yet no detailed study analogous to those conducted in the United States has examined the incidence of medical malpractice in Canada or Western Europe. For the same reason, disagreement arises about whether the substitution of social insurance for medical malpractice law in New Zealand adversely affected the quality of care.[29]

Overall, it is by no means clear that life is more dangerous in economically developed countries where tort suits are far less common and less fearsome than in the United States. Nor do other democratic countries, comparing their accident and injury rates with those in the United States, seem inclined to emulate American adversarial legalism. Yet it is hard to believe that the deterrence argument is wholly wrong. Some safety-enhancing measures in the United States—such as warning beepers on trucks and construction machines that are put in reverse gear, improved helmets for football players, softer surfaces under climbing structures in children's playgrounds—probably were stimulated by tort cases that imposed liability on companies or municipalities that had failed to institute those improvements. Recall the midwestern city managers quoted in Chapter 2, who recounted improvements in municipal safety inspections, personnel training, and supervision that had been stimulated by lawsuits (Epp, 1998). In a 1987 study by an international consulting firm, more than half of 101 top corporate executives surveyed said that their companies had added safety features to their products as a result of the threat of lawsuits (Zehnder, 1987; Schwartz, 1994: 480).

Yet systematic studies of particular industries have found little evidence that American tort law consistently or significantly affects product design or safety. In the 1970s and 1980s crashes of small airplanes almost routinely led to lawsuits against the aircraft manufacturers, alleging that the crash stemmed from product defects. Two analyses of safety improvements in small aircraft, however, concluded that litigation and escalating liability insurance costs did not lead to improved aircraft design or lower accident rates (Martin, 1991;

Craig, 1991).[30] Meanwhile, sales plummeted, and by the late 1980s domestic production of light aircraft had virtually ceased. Thousands of workers were laid off. Flying probably became riskier, not safer, since users kept flying (rather than retiring) older used planes. Finally, in 1994 Congress enacted the General Aviation Revitalization Act, which limited lawsuits involving planes more than eighteen years old.[31]

Multinational motor vehicle manufacturers claim that no other country comes close to the United States in terms of the incidence and cost of product liability litigation (Kagan, 2000). A major Japanese auto manufacturer asserted that with twice as many of its cars on the road in Japan than in the United States, "[i]ts American operations lead to about 250 product liability claims against the company each year. By contrast, in Japan the number of annual product liability filings averages about two" (Schwartz, 1991: 51). But two careful analyses of the development of particular safety improvements in motor vehicles (ergonomics, braking, lights, crashworthiness) contend that American product liability law—as compared to direct government safety regulation—has made only negligible or, at best, secondary contributions to better design (Graham, 1991; Mackay, 1991). By the time a company's engineers hear that an American jury has found "defects" in their design for a model currently on the road, they usually have completed work on new designs and safety features for subsequent model years.[32]

On the other hand, as in the small aircraft example, American tort law sometimes "overdeters," inducing precautions that make products and services unnecessarily expensive or suppressing the provision of products and services that would actually reduce the risk of harm. In the mid-1980s lawsuits led some manufacturers of the DPT vaccine to exit the business, threatening the supply of a product that has all but wiped out childhood diphtheria, whooping cough, and tetanus, diseases that killed thousands of children in previous generations (Burke, 2001).[33] According to a 1992 survey of 500 public accountancy partnerships in the United States, more than half had limited their audit services, or had shunned certain clients engaged in higher risk markets, in order to protect themselves from lawsuits by disappointed investors (Berton and Lublin, 1992; Berton, 1995).[34] At a congressional hearing a lawyer for Wyeth, a manufacturer of birth control pills, testified that the threat of liability lawsuits was the primary reason that it and other companies had been unwilling to market a "morning after" birth control pill in the United States (although these companies have done so for years in Europe) (Lewin, 1996: A1, A10).[35] A 1995 survey by the Society for Resource Management found that 63 percent of personnel managers declined to make negative evaluative comments when asked for an assessment of a former employee, for fear of landing in court (Louis, 1987: C1).[36]

Overall, therefore, the spotty existing evidence suggests that American tort law has an erratic effect on safety. Potential target groups vary in their attentiveness. Some manufacturers, physicians, corporate personnel officers, and others *overestimate* the actual risk of being sued, perhaps because of the publicity accorded unrepresentative jury verdicts (Bailis and MacCoun, 1996: 419–429; Edelman et al., 1992: 47–83; Songer, 1988: 585–605), but others do not. Hence tort law sometimes deters. Sometimes it overdeters, compelling adoption of precautions that reduce overall social welfare. Often tort law is too uncertain and unpredictable to affect behavior very much at all, or is far less salient than other inducements to responsible behavior. All in all, therefore, critics of the system have argued that American tort law's regulatory effects are too mixed, uncertain, and scattered to justify an adversarial system that generates large economic costs, pours a great deal of money into lawyers' bills, and fails to provide just and reliable compensation.

The Tort System and Popular Morality

Tort litigation provides Americans with a steady stream of morality tales. In contrast with nonfault-based accident compensation schemes, tort litigation enables ordinary individuals to take forceful public action against powerful organizations. Tort case verdicts express a jury's moral judgment about what behavior is blameworthy. But American tort law has become politically controversial because for many citizens it seems to have lost its moral resonance. The disjunction reflects tort law's ambivalent doctrinal drift toward enterprise liability, or "system blame," to use Aaron Wildavsky's term—a drift not fully endorsed by Americans who adhere to traditional notions of *individual* responsibility (Polisar and Wildavsky, 1989; Sanders, 1987; Engel, 1984). The latter shake their heads when they read about the automobile passenger who was badly burned after leaving a McDonald's takeout window because she put a hot cup of coffee between her legs and it spilled—but then won a $2.9 million verdict (including $2.7 in punitive damages) against McDonald's. Her lawyer's argument was that the fast food chain deliberately served unusually hot coffee and failed to cool it down or warn customers about it (Gerlin, 1994b; Rhode, 1999: 143–144).

To those Americans who are inclined toward what Wildavsky calls an "egalitarian" political culture, the McDonald's decision is entirely defensible; in their view, businesses ought to be held accountable for avoidable harms that flow from their profit-making activity. Thus some legal scholars have been keen to point out that McDonald's had refused to reduce the temperature of its coffee even after other previous patrons had been scalded, and that the plaintiff had initially requested payment only for her medical and attendant expenses (about $11,000), a request McDonald's had refused (Galanter, 1998: 732).[37] Moreover, the tort system's defenders point out, the public has been getting distorted messages from the media, leading them to a false impression that the system is morally "out of control." Most newspaper accounts of the McDonald's hot coffee verdict fail to note that the judge subsequently reduced the award to $500,000 (ibid.). Nor did news media give much prominence to a U.S. Court of Appeals decision that *rejected* the claim of a plaintiff who had sued a manufacturer of coffee-making machines after spilling hot coffee on herself in a moving car (*McMahon v. Bunn-O-Matic Corp.*, 1998). The news media are far more likely to report jury verdicts *favoring* tort plaintiffs—especially those involving quirky claims or huge punitive damage awards—than verdicts for defendants (Bailis and MacCoun, 1996; Chase, 1995).

Hence the public at large, in contemplating the McDonald's coffee case, probably does not consider the fact that most tort claims are morally uncontroversial and that juries often regard plaintiffs' claims with skepticism (Hans and Lofquist, 1992; MacCoun, 1996). To many legal scholars, therefore, the common view that the tort system is morally out of control stems from distorted reporting and from propaganda spread by a business community seeking to avoid its social responsibilities (Rhode, 1999; Daniels and Martin, 1995). Similarly, David Engel (1984) has suggested that hostility to the tort system arises because litigation challenges traditional patterns and privileges, giving voice to social "have nots."

Perhaps there is a grain of truth to those diagnoses, but they miss the genuinely philosophical basis of much of the political reaction. Notions of individual responsibility are just as ingrained in Americans' beliefs as populist, egalitarian notions of enterprise liability are. As noted earlier, in the late 1990s a majority of survey respondents asserted that cigarette smokers, not tobacco companies, should be responsible for the health care costs stemming from smoking-related diseases (Kagan and Nelson, 2000). To believers in individual responsibility, no amount of rationalization or subsequent reduction of the verdict can obliterate the deep sense that the woman who foolishly put a cup of hot coffee between her legs was primarily to blame and that imposing legal responsibility on McDonald's violates basic principles.

The tort system also seems morally unhinged to many Americans because of the common knowledge that it rewards and encourages corruption. In 1991 the vice president of State Farm Insurance noted that "the ratio of bodily injury claims to property damage claims [in auto accident cases] has increased about 50 percent over the last 10 years . . . at a time when automobiles have become safer and there should be fewer bodily injury accidents" (Sloane, 1991: 15). The rise of such claims is concentrated in major urban centers: in 1991 the ratio of bodily injury claims to accidents was less than 13 percent in Harrisburg, Pennsylvania, but 75 percent in Philadelphia (Brickman et al., 1994: 33). A RAND Institute for Civil Justice report observed that "the availability of general damages ('pain and suffering') and the fact that they are usually calculated as some multiple of economic losses provide the incentive to submit claims for nonexistent injuries and to build medical costs." Researchers found that motor vehicle accident claimants represented by attorneys accumulate significantly more visits to doctors and chiropractors than similarly injured claimants who do not retain attorneys; and other studies also provide strong suggestive evidence of lawyer-driven medical bill padding (RAND Institute, 1995: 32–33). The RAND scholars' analysis led them to the astonishing estimate that "about one-third of the automobile industry accident costs submitted to insurers appear to be excess" (id. at 1; Carroll et al., 1995; Grady, 1996). Sociolegal scholars point out that there is a great deal of "underclaiming" as well as "overclaiming" by accident victims (Saks, 1992). But the tort system's "overclaiming" shadow, bloated by padded claims, is morally troublesome and more politically explosive.

Many Americans also accuse the tort system of undermining traditional notions of responsibility by encouraging legal blaming. According to an extensive survey, more than 90 percent of American drivers injured in two-car accidents blamed someone else for the crash, as did 37 percent of drivers involved in *one-car* accidents (Hensler et al., 1991: 159). Comparing these results to a similar survey of British accident victims, Herbert Kritzer (1991: 400–427) noted that Americans were considerably more likely than the British to blame someone else for an auto accident, and among motorists who blamed the other driver, Americans were considerably more likely to demand compensation. Kritzer speculates that the difference is at least partly attributable to the incentives provided by the American tort system. Similarly, a tort system shaped by adversarial legalism seems to encourage legal defensiveness. American drivers repeatedly are instructed not to apologize when they get into a collision, so as not to compromise their bargaining position in a subsequent lawsuit.[38] Americans are accustomed to encountering business enterprises that decline reasonable requests by saying, "Sorry, our insurance company won't let us." For years, tobacco company executives publicly denied that cigarettes are addictive and hid their research because they feared that any admission would be used in pending and future lawsuits (Jenkins, 1996; Kluger, 1996).[39] The many citizens who are disturbed by these law-induced tendencies to dissemble, shift blame, and act callously are potential members of the political constituency for tort reform.

The Politics of Tort Reform

In the 1980s and early 1990s critiques of American tort law spilled out of the law reviews, appellate courts, and the business press into the broader political arena. Business groups urged state and federal legislatures to curtail judge-made liability rules. Republican candidates for office courted votes by calling for limits on tort litigation. Ballot initiatives in California twice asked the electorate to approve plans substituting "no-fault" self-insurance for tort suits arising from motor vehicle accidents; each time, opponents and proponents spent tens of millions of dollars on television commercials designed to sway the voters, who ended up rejecting both initiatives. On several occasions the U.S. Supreme Court reviewed the constitutionality of unlimited punitive damages. State supreme courts were asked to invalidate state laws that imposed "caps" on jury awards.

The political attack on tort law made some headway. Between 1985 and 1991 forty-one state legislatures enacted changes in tort law (Lipsen, 1991: 248–249), mostly what Tom Burke (2001) labels "discouragement" measures—enactments designed to inhibit lawsuits by making it more difficult for plaintiffs to sue, to win, and/or to win a lot, but which keep the basic adversarial, court-based tort law system intact. But, except for a handful of narrowly targeted measures, there was little movement toward wholesale "replacement" reforms—legislative enactments that bar adversarial tort claims and jury trials, offering in their stead a compensation system that provides automatic, moderate benefits without any need to prove fault, and that relies on administrative dispute resolution. Thus as of the end of the 1990s, the adversarial character, inefficiency, and general fearsomeness of American tort law remained essentially intact. Yet because of all the political activity, the tort law of the United States, which is intrinsically more inconsistent and malleable than the tort law and compensation regimes of other democracies, became even more unstable and unpredictable.

Replacement Reforms

State workers' compensation schemes, enacted earlier in the twentieth century, represent the classic "replacement reform." Injured employees were barred from bringing tort suits against their employers but were guaranteed moderate recovery for workplace injuries in administrative tribunals, without regard to their employers' or even their own negligence. In 1969 Congress enacted a special compensation fund, financed by taxes on all coal mine companies, for coal miners suffering from black lung disease. But with a few special exceptions,[40] American legislatures have shown little willingness to extend the workers' compensation or the black lung program models more broadly to replace the tort system for other kinds of injuries, such as medical accidents, asbestos disease, adverse reactions to pharmaceuticals, or tobacco-related illnesses—all of which remain the province of contingency-fee tort litigation and erratic compensation.

In both state and federal legislatures, well-financed lobbying organizations of plaintiffs' personal injury lawyers fiercely opposed proposals for no-fault self-insurance plans to replace tort suits for motor vehicle accidents. Often, the proposed no-fault bills died in lawyer-dominated legislative committees (Heymann and Liebman, 1988). The bills that did pass, with few exceptions, were watered down by low "thresholds" that preserved the right to bring tort suits for the most significant injuries (U.S. Department of Transportation, 1985; Foppert, 1992). As part of its ill-fated 1993 health care reform package, the Clinton administration proposed insulating doctors from direct liability for malpractice claims while imposing "enterprise liability" for medical accidents on health insurance plans and health maintenance organizations. But faced with opposition not only from plaintiffs' trial lawyers but also from physician-owned malpractice liability insurance companies, the proposal was quickly abandoned (Rogers, 1993: A16).

Discouragement Reforms

In 1986 some 800 civil justice reform bills were introduced in state legislatures, followed by 1,000 in 1987 and 1,400 in 1988 (Nutter and Bateman, 1989: 16). Generally, these bills sought to limit defendants' liability and to raise higher obstacles to questionable suits. But there was no quid pro quo: the proposals did not promise accident victims guaranteed, moderate, collectively financed payments without having to prove anyone at fault. These "discouragement"-oriented bills typically sought to modify joint and several liability rules so that "deep pockets" that were only partly responsible for injuries would not be stuck with the whole cost of compensation. The bills also sought to shorten statutes of limitations, placed caps on "pain and suffering" and punitive damage awards, and changed the collateral source rule under which tort victims can claim damages even for losses covered by their own insurance. Other bills called for penalties on refusals to accept early settlement offers, for limits on contingency fees, and for arbitration or mediation as a prerequisite to a jury trial.

The discouragement-type proposals were opposed by the American Trial Lawyers Association (ATLA) and its state-level affiliates. Yet by the late 1980s ATLA no longer could be assured of prevailing in state legislatures. Scores of reform laws were enacted (Blackmon and Zeckhauser, 1991: 274),[41] and some did have some dampening effect on litigation rates and award levels (Danzon, 1986).[42] Nevertheless, the trial lawyers often limited their losses, weakening reform bills or bottling them up in lawyer-dominated legislative committees (Spitzer, 1993). In at least seventeen states the plaintiffs' bar successfully took the battle to the courts, persuading judges to hold that tort reform statutes, particularly those imposing caps on damages, are unconstitutional under state law (Nutter and Bateman, 1989: 16–18).

At the federal level, beginning in the mid-1980s ATLA and its allies in the Democratic Party year after year blocked "discouragement"-oriented product liability reform bills in Congress (Nelson, 1983: 1; Heymann and Liebman, 1988; Kagan, 1994). The Republicans swept into control of both houses in 1994 after offering a "Contract with America" that included a promise to restrict tort law, but in March 1996 President Clinton successfully vetoed a Republican bill that would have capped punitive damage awards and eliminated joint and several liability in product liability cases (Schmitt, 1996; Lewis, 1996). In 1994 ATLA did sustain one defeat: Congress passed the previously mentioned General Aviation Revitalization Bill, which prohibited lawsuits against manufacturers of older piston-powered small planes (Weintraub, 1994b; Bryant, 1995). And after the 1994 elections, a Republican Congress enacted a law, over President Clinton's veto, that imposed some constraints on securities-fraud class action lawsuits.[43]

The battle over tort reform also led to partisan political battles over the staffing of state supreme courts. Business interests made sizable contributions supporting a 1986 ballot measure that called for the ouster of liberal California Supreme Court justice Rose Bird, whose retention campaign received $400,000 from plaintiffs' tort lawyers (Wold and Culver, 1987). In 1996 a member of the plaintiffs' bar commented that Bird's conservative replacement, Chief Justice Malcolm Lucas, had been "more effective than any Republican legislator in the past 10 or 15 years" in curbing civil litigation. In 1988 Lucas wrote an opinion that overturned a 1979 decision that had facilitated injury victims' suits against insurance companies for "bad faith" resistance to compensation claims. Similarly, Lucas wrote an opinion limiting the damages employees can collect in "unjust termination" cases (Chiang, 1996b).

California has not been alone in this regard. Since the 1980s judges across the United States have issued rulings that have tended to slow the growth of tort liability—limiting damages, pulling back from notions of strict liability, and construing causation more narrowly (Schwartz, 1992; Eisenberg and Henderson, 1992; Sanders and Joyce, 1990). The U.S. Supreme Court ruled that huge punitive damage awards that are unrelated to the seriousness of the harm can be held unconstitutional (*BMW of North America v. Gore*, 1996) and urged federal trial court judges to exclude the testimony of expert witnesses who relied on uncorroborated "junk science" to draw causal connections between defendants' products and claimants' maladies (*Daubert v. Merrill Dow Pharmaceuticals,* 1993; Sanders, 1998). And, behind the scenes, as in the Bird campaign in California, business groups have spent fortunes in campaign contributions to the election campaigns of state supreme court judges they believe will roll back tort law, while plaintiffs' lawyers have contributed lavishly to "pro-plaintiff" judicial candidates.

The Limits of Tort Reform

By the end of the 1990s the conservative push for tort reform had produced only a moderate diminution of the intensity of American tort litigation. The new "discouragement" measures deter some lawsuits and curtail damages, especially for the most severely injured plaintiffs, but the reforms have not changed the basic shape of adversarial legalism. In contrast to other democracies, the United States still has few constraints on contingency fees and has not moved to a "loser pays" system with respect to attorneys' fees. Viewed in cross-national comparison, the American reforms (aside from some caps on punitive damages in some states) have not significantly constrained trial court (or jury) discretion in awarding money damages. They have not significantly reduced the cost of litigation or displaced the cumbersome jury system. And they have not offered injured persons more comprehensive, reliable, inexpensive, collectively financed compensation mechanisms that *replace* inefficient and inequitable tort litigation.

Indeed, perhaps the most important legacies of the political struggle over tort law have been greater *instability* in the law of personal injury and greater *inconsistency* in compensating similarly injured accident victims. Once politicians leapt into the fray, interest group politics, lobbying clout, campaign contributions, and partisan electoral campaigns—rather than lawyers' debates over principles of justice—have played a larger role in reshaping tort law. New elections brought big legal shifts. In 1999 a newly elected Democratic governor in California, prodded by the trial lawyers' association, signed legislation reinstating an injury victim's right to sue her injuror's insurance company for "bad faith" in contesting her claim (overriding Judge Lucas's 1988 decision) and authorizing medical malpractice lawsuits against health maintenance organizations for unreasonably denying or delaying coverage. Hence an accident victim's chances of obtaining compensation and the level of compensation she will get (as well as an insurance company's chances of being found liable) are likely to vary not only from state to state and case to case but from year to year, depending on shifts in political party control of the legislature and the state supreme court.

The Persistence of Adversarial Legalism

Notwithstanding its shortcomings as a mechanism for compensating the injured, its randomness as a regulatory instrument, and its problematic relationship to popular morality, American tort law has proved remarkably resistant to fundamental reform. One might point to three basic reasons for its persistence—the political influence of American lawyers, the legal culture they generate, and, most important, the political structures and beliefs that shape public policymaking in the United States.

Interest Group Politics and the Role of Lawyers

In no other economically advanced democracy do plaintiffs' tort lawyers play a powerful political role. The reason is largely structural. In parliamentary democracies with cohesive political parties, the policymaking process is dominated by party leaders in the ruling party or coalition, along with the top civil servants in the relevant ministries, leaders of major business federations, and, when socialist or labor governments are in power, leaders of national labor union federations. Changes in the codes of civil justice are enacted only after long deliberation and consultation among legal experts, jurists, relevant central government bureaucrats, and cabinet ministers.

In the United States, however, where political power is fragmented across the branches of government, across states, within legislatures, and within the political parties, no single national or state bureaucracy, no party leader, no business or labor confederation, no high legal commission, and no court controls policy development in civil justice—or in most other policy realms. Interest groups of many political stripes, liberal and conservative, contend for influence on legislative committees. They channel campaign contributions to candidates for office, including judgeships (Glaberson, 2000). They fund research and disseminate the views of their favorite law professors.

Political scientists' standard analyses of policy formulation hold that the demands of intense, well-organized interest groups often win out over the more broadly held but less intense preferences of unorganized like-thinking citizens. Hence the particularly important role, in the politics of tort reform, of the American Trial Lawyers Association (ATLA) and its state-level affiliates. These organizations, which are unique to the United States, lobby legislatures and serve as conduits for political contributions for some 60,000 plaintiffs' personal injury lawyers. Both the economic well-being of the plaintiffs' lawyers and their professional ideology are intimately connected with the perpetuation of legal rules that permit or enshrine contingency fees, expansive tort liability, high money damages, and the jury system. Between January 1989 and December 1994 campaign contributions by ATLA and individual plaintiffs' lawyers to congressional and state candidates for office amounted to some $56 million, an amount that exceeded the $30 million contributed by the five largest labor union contributors, the $2.2 million from General Motors, Ford, and Chrysler, and the $7 million from the ten largest oil and gas companies (Bell and O'Connell, 1997: 183).[44]

Business interests, including insurance firms and the medical profession, also have been politically active, generating publicity for unrepresentative tort "horror stories" (Galanter, 1998; Aks et al., 2000) and lobbying legislatures. Sometimes ATLA and its state-level organizations have lost particular legislative battles over laws designed to limit liability and damages, but more often the plaintiffs' lawyers have blocked or watered down such incremental changes. And most important, they have warded off attempts to enact or even to propose fundamental legal changes, such as sharply restricting contingency fees, instituting a loser-pays rule, systematizing noneconomic damages, or substituting more comprehensive, automatic, moderate, and administratively operated compensation programs for tort law and the jury system.

American Legal Culture and Adversarial Legalism

European comparativists often observe that surprisingly few American judges, lawyers, legislators, and law professors have even a rudimentary knowledge of the systems of injury compensation and adjudication in other economically advanced democracies (Stiefel and Maxeiner, 1994: 155; Schlesinger, 1977: 363). Journalists who write about the "tort crisis" in the United States almost never discuss the injury compensation and regulatory systems of other economically advanced democracies or discuss alternatives to the tort system (Aks et al., 2000). By and large, therefore, American legal elites wholeheartedly endorse the fundamental rules and institutions of the American civil liability system: the primacy of tort law as a mode of recourse against injustice; the desirability of broad access to courts, juries, and adversarial lawyers to resolve disputes and enforce safety standards; and a familiar panoply of litigation-encouraging practices—contingency fees, punitive damages and awards for pain and suffering, class actions, and so on. With their vision restricted by these distinctive American legal traditions, legal elites in the United States generally are resistant to "replacement"-type reforms.

The same failure of imagination afflicts politically conservative legal critics of the tort system, who tend to blame the pathologies of the tort system on irresponsible lawyers and runaway juries rather than on the fundamental structures of adversarial legalism within which the lawyers and juries work. Hence their reform proposals tend to focus on incremental "discouragement" changes that leave the basic structures of adversarial legalism intact, diminishing injured persons' legal rights while offering nothing in return. They fight adversarial legalism in an adversarial way. The mainstream legal defenders of the tort system react defensively. In 1991 Vice President Dan Quayle, venturing into the American Bar Association convention, complained that the United States had 70 percent of the world's lawyers (which is not true) and criticized the "staggering expense and delay" of the American civil justice system (which is true). Quayle's reform proposals consisted of a rather mild set of discouragement measures. John Curtin, president of the ABA, reacting as if the vice president had proposed burying all American lawyers in an underground disposal site in Nevada, retorted: "Any one who believes a better day dawns when lawyers are eliminated has the burden of explaining who will take their place. Who will protect the poor, the injured, the victims of negligence, the victims of racial discrimination, and the victims of racial violence?" (Geyelin, 1991: B1).

European lawyers and legal scholars might respond that there *are* ways—well established in their countries—of protecting the poor, providing income replacement to the injured, providing guarantees against unjust dismissal, and regulating hazardous products and activities, and that those ways are more efficient, effective, and comprehensive than lawyer-dominated American adversarial legalism. The actual merits of that response, of course, may be debated. But it is clear that legal elites in Western Europe and the British Commonwealth have a less heroic vision of the individual lawyer's role in society and hence a less apocalyptic view of modes of implementing public policy in which lawyers and litigation play a less dominant role.

To Americans who might be skeptical about adversarial legalism, no well-developed countervailing ideal is offered by the legal culture created and perpetuated by American lawyers, judges, and law professors. In public debates critics of tort law argue that it is costly and enriches tort lawyers. But those are crimped, negative arguments, devoid of the high-sounding values that permeate the arguments in favor of rights and adversarial legalism. A countervailing legal ideal would entail greater emphasis on reliable, collectively provided social security than on individual vindication and vengeance; on legal stability, predictability, and uniformity rather than ad hoc legal responsiveness; and on the notion that professional administration of democratically endorsed regulatory rules usually will be better than litigation in guaranteeing safety and protecting the public interest. But that is not what one generally encounters in American legal scholarship and bar association meetings (Glendon, 1991). In American elite legal culture, therefore, the proponents of adversarial legalism, like ABA president Curtin, place themselves on the moral high ground.

Political Culture

Legal culture is never sealed off from the rest of society. Even ATLA has not been able to keep tort reform off the political agenda, and the trial lawyers could not win legislative and electoral battles if political majorities didn't at least acquiesce. Hence one additional abiding source of adversarial legalism's persistence is its general consonance with the broader American political culture.

In 1996 California voters were presented with three ballot initiatives designed to curtail adversarial legalism. One would have instituted no-fault compensation for motor vehicle accidents, displacing tort law. Another sought to discourage extortive stockholder class actions. A third called for limits on contingency fees in quickly settled cases. Opponents of the measures, led by the California trial lawyers' association, bombarded the electorate with television commercials that showed ravenous-looking wolves on the hunt, while a voice-over warned voters not to vote for ballot propositions that would benefit "corporate wolves." Another commercial, portraying a female motorist whose car suddenly was hit by a reckless driver, proclaimed: "Under no-fault, it's always your fault." All three ballot measurers were defeated at the polls.

The trial lawyers' commercials skillfully tapped two enduring strains in American political culture, populism and individualism (Lipset, 1996: 20). Populism is ever-suspicious of the corporate wolves, from Wall Street to the insurance company boardroom, and of the politicians and bureaucrats who are thought to be under the baleful influence of the wolves. American individualism has long emphasized the right of the individual to define and pursue his own interests, and also to seek justice in the courts (which are distrusted less than other governmental institutions) against those who wrongfully impinge on one's liberty or property. Both strains are suspicious of collectivist methods of compensating accident victims, especially if they totally displace individual rights to sue and strong legal sanctions against corporate wrongdoers.

Of course, in the broad bay of American politics there are yet other currents that are more supportive of collective income security programs, such as aid for farmers (a legacy of the Populist movement) and social security. Adherents of this tradition endorse the basic propositions of "total justice"—the idea that government bears responsibility for ensuring that the innocent victims of misfortunes and injustices (and especially their families) should not be plunged into destitution. But many Americans do not quite trust the government to implement that responsibility properly. Democrats, who generally support active government, worry that government-funded compensation programs will be subjected to Republican budget-cutting pressures and be besieged by business lobbyists, so that eventually they will shortchange powerless injured individuals and their families. The course of state workers' compensation programs—in some states, during some eras—provides some support for this concern. Republicans worry that Democratic administrations will turn collectivist accident-compensation programs into undisciplined, fraud-ridden boondoggles, engines for increasing benefit payments and higher tax or insurance charges. The course of state workers' compensation programs—in some states, during some eras—and of the federal black lung compensation program provides some support for this concern too.

Thus political mistrust of government and politics itself leaves adversarial legalism, for all its flaws, as an accepted method for seeking to help the victims of accidents and injustice—perhaps not the only game in town but a very important one. And that is sad, for it is a very expensive and unpredictable game, the lawyers who run it take an unreasonably large share of the pot, and it leaves neither most players nor attentive bystanders satisfied that justice is being done or safety guaranteed.[45]

IV

Public Law:
Social Justice and Regulation

8

Adversarial Legalism and the Welfare State

In France governmental efforts to trim costly welfare state benefits are regularly met by mass demonstrations in the streets. In the United States a different mode of protest prevails. In August 1999 the *New York Times* reported: "Just this week, a group of welfare recipients filed suit against the State of Florida, contending that the state had illegally cut off their Medicaid benefits when it ended their cash assistance. In January, a Federal district judge ruled that New York City had improperly denied Medicaid to poor people who failed to comply with work requirements of the city's welfare program" (Pear, 1999).

The Florida and New York City lawsuits were not unique. The American welfare state differs from those of most economically advanced democracies. Substantively, social provision in the United States is less comprehensive and less generous. Structurally, the American welfare state is marked by the fragmentation of authority among federal, state, and local government in the formulation and administration of social policy, and the United States relies more on *private* provision of social insurance and social services. To coordinate and control this fragmented system, American social programs tend to rely on detailed legal rules and rights, enforceable in court. One consequence is that litigation, courts, and adversarial legalism play a much more significant role in shaping and administering social and educational policy in the United States than in other countries.

This chapter describes the distinctive prominence of adversarial legalism in the American welfare state, explains that prominence, and examines some of its consequences.

The American Welfare State in Comparative Perspective

The "welfare state" is one of the most striking public policy developments of the twentieth century, representing both a political and a humanitarian strategy for softening the harsh edges of capitalism. In country after country, governments have imposed taxes and created programs to buffer families from the devastating effects of illness, sudden economic loss, and poverty. Germany's 1920 Weimar constitution declared a right to social insurance. Chile's 1925 constitution "guarantees to all the inhabitants of the country . . . social security, especially regarding healthy housing and economic conditions of life such that each inhabitant . . . would have a minimum of welfare for his needs and that of his family."[1]

Neither Weimar Germany nor Chile truly fulfilled their constitutional promises, of course, but the aspirations expressed in such documents have been of great political and practical importance. By the last third of the century, most economically advanced democracies had guaranteed their citizens free public education and medical care. They had enacted laws assuring families a meaningful level of income replacement in the event of a breadwinner's unemployment, injury, disability, or retirement, and even in the event of marital separation or divorce. Many nations provide or subsidize day care for preschool children of working mothers, mandate paid vacations and maternity leaves for workers, provide job training for the unemployed, and construct low-cost housing for poor families.

In the United States governments have been subject to similar political pressures to improve economic opportunity, reduce economic inequality, alleviate misfortune, and provide a social minimum to all residents. American governments, therefore, have participated in the construction of the welfare state. But they have done so less enthusiastically and more haltingly than other economically advanced nations. Early on, American state and local governments provided universal public education. The United States has been a leader in subsidizing mass college-level education. In the depths of the Great Depression newly elected president Franklin Roosevelt declared that ensuring the economic security of all Americans should be the highest priority of government. In his 1944 "Four Freedoms" speech Roosevelt declared that "individual freedom cannot exist without economic security and independence" (Goldman, 1977: 287, 386).

Yet in the United States the welfare state idea has always been controversial. Neither the federal nor state constitutions establish rights to social welfare. Compared to their counterparts in Western Europe and Canada, American political elites and the public at large have been quicker to express concern about the "moral hazard" and fraudulent claims generated by governmental giveaways. Americans have been more reluctant to sustain the high tax burdens required by generous cradle-to-grave coverage and more reluctant to live with the labor market rigidities, inefficiencies, and unemployment associated with mandatory job protection and benefits. Thus the American welfare state is less comprehensive than the governmental programs of post–

World War II Western Europe, and many American programs are considerably less generous (Esping-Anderson, 1990; McFate et al., 1995).

Among economically advanced democracies the United States stands out in declining to guarantee universal health care. The federal government compels governmentally subsidized hospitals to provide emergency care to all and, through the tax code, provides incentives for employer-provided health insurance. But legally prescribed benefits are limited to the elderly (Medicare), the very poor (Medicaid), and military veterans.[2] American minimum wage laws are set much lower. Unskilled male workers in the United States earn less and enjoy fewer legally mandated benefits than their counterparts in Western Europe (Freeman, 1994).[3] Compared to Western Europe, legally mandated unemployment benefits in the United States are available for a much shorter period and replace a smaller percentage of the laid-off employee's wages (McFate, 1995: 636).[4] Labor law in Western European countries and Canada provide workers with rights to severance payments in the event of layoffs or dismissals; American labor law does not (Freeman and Katz, 1994; Abraham and Houseman, 1993). Except for Italy, the United States spends far less than other rich countries, as a percentage of GDP, on public employment services and job training for unemployed workers (McFate, 1995: 641, 644).

In a study of fourteen economically advanced democracies, the United States ranked a distant last in terms of legislation mandating maternity leave benefits and job protection for employed mothers-to-be (Gornick et al., 1997: 138; *The Economist,* 1998: 110). In comparison with virtually all Western European countries, American public policies have done far less to prevent or ameliorate poverty among single mothers and their children, either by direct income transfer programs or by programs encouraging employment, such as subsidized child care (Gornick et al., 1997). Overall, the United States taxes its citizens less and spends less on social benefits, as a percentage of GDP, than comparably rich countries. In the 1980s and 1990s the American economy, less burdened by taxes and restrictive labor laws, has been more successful than most European welfare states in generating jobs and reducing unemployment, and that surely has been a very meaningful "antipoverty program." Nevertheless, income inequality remains significantly greater in the United States, as does the severe poverty of many inner-city areas.

The American welfare state also has a distinctive political and organizational structure. Viewed comparatively, social welfare benefits and services in the United States tend to be administered or delivered in a more politically decentralized fashion. Public education is governed and largely funded by *municipal* governments, supplemented by the states. So are many other aspects of social welfare policy. Since the 1930s the federal government has formulated a number of nationwide programs, but many—Social Security Disability Insurance, Medicaid, unemployment insurance, Aid for Dependent Children (renamed TANF in 1996)—are administered not by federal bureaucracies but by state and local governments. Moreover, the central government often provides only partial funding; state and local governments retain considerable discretion in setting spending and eligibility levels. Compared to Europeans, moreover, American citizens rely much more heavily on private insurance companies, employers, and nonprofit organizations (rather than on government agencies) for health care coverage, compensation for workplace injuries, treatment of the mentally ill and the elderly, and retirement pensions.[5] In the United States provision of low-income housing has relied much more on governmental subsidies to private developers and nonprofit organizations.

These structural arrangements affect the legal character of welfare state administration in the United States. Because benefit provision is entrusted to far-flung (and sometimes financially hard-pressed) county governments, private insurance companies, school districts, private nursing homes, and employers, the United States, in contrast with more statist European welfare systems, typically employs *detailed, judicially enforceable legal regulations and procedures* to ensure that those benefits are made available uniformly and fairly. The House of Representatives report on the 1977 amendments to the federal Food Stamp Act filled 869 pages and "contained advice on such matters as how late intake offices should be open and which court decisions had identified the proper method for counting the income of migrant workers" (Melnick, 1993: 34; Katzmann, 1995).

In the 1974 Education for All Handicapped Children Act, Congress provided sweeping rights to an "appropriate education" in public schools but provided only limited funding to local schools required to absorb the high costs of implementing those rights. To promote compliance, therefore, Congress also armed parents of handicapped children with legal rights to contest school administrators' decisions. In contrast to Great Britain, which also adopted ambitious "special education" policies, litigation by dissatisfied parents has been a common feature of the "special ed" programs in the United States (Kirp, 1982). American (but not British) judges regularly have ended up deciding what an "appropriate education" entails for particular children or categories of children (Melnick, 1995). Similarly, to ensure that pensions and other benefit plans promised by private employers are adequately funded, Congress in 1974 enacted the enormously complicated Employee Retirement Income Security Act (ERISA); one consequence has been "the continuing explosion of ERISA litigation" (King, 1991) as courts are asked to resolve conflicts between ERISA and employee claims or employer defenses based on state labor law, bankruptcy law, and collective bargaining agreements (Kukanza, 1997).

Furthermore, compared to European welfare states, governmental benefit programs in the United States are more often *"means tested,"* that is, they are provided only for poor persons rather than for all households.[6] Means testing gives applicants incentives to understate their economic resources—which in turn generates political pressures from taxpayers who become incensed about "welfare fraud," which in turn generates counterpressures for legal rules that require administrators to treat applicants fairly. For this reason too, in making eligibility and benefit determinations, American welfare agencies, compared to their counterparts in Europe, are more tightly restrained by detailed, judicially enforceable legal rules and procedures.

The United States, in consequence, is unique in the extent to which individuals and advocacy groups appeal to courts to challenge individual decisions concerning social provision, asking the judges to elaborate and enforce norms of social and procedural justice. In other economically advanced democracies, litigation and courts play some role, perhaps an increasing one, in policing the fairness of decisions by welfare state bureaucracies, but the litigation has a different character. Germany diverts complaints by patients who are denied special medical services into free "social courts," where they are decided by panels staffed by a professional judge who specializes in such cases, a lay judge who represents the patient, and another lay judge who represents the employer or doctor (Jost, 1998).[7] Great Britain provides a system of relatively informal administrative tribunals in which citizens can dispute bureaucrats' decisions concerning entitlements. But neither these tribunals or regular courts, Herbert Kritzer (1996: 135, 147, 174) observes, "exercise the kind of direct control over other governmental institutions that courts in the U.S. have done repeatedly over the past several decades." The same is true in France, which operates an extensive administrative court system for processing individual complaints against government agencies, but which excludes the judiciary from significant influence on governmental policy (Provine, 1996). Moreover, in response to American judicial decisions that alter rules concerning social provision, legislatures and agencies in the United States make statutes and administrative rules that are yet more detailed and complex, prompting further litigation. Thus the American welfare state has been uniquely pervaded, and sometimes reshaped, by adversarial legalism.

Adversarial legalism has lent strength to segregated black schoolchildren, welfare mothers, handicapped children, pregnant teenagers who desperately want abortions, the children of illegal immigrants, and arbitrarily treated nonunionized workers. Advocates for members of these and other groups have used the courts to challenge and sometimes to reverse public policies and administrative practices that reflect racist attitudes, repressive moralism, or bureaucratic callousness. On the other hand, adversarial legalism is a highly imperfect tool for realizing the ideals of social justice. The remedies that courts provide generally are *procedural:* they have reduced arbitrariness in the administration of public policy, but they have not been able to fill the wide substantive gaps in the American welfare state.

In short, as stressed earlier, adversarial legalism is Janus-faced. It makes American government more responsive to individualized claims of justice and to the arguments of the politically less powerful, but it is also, as the following case study suggests, a peculiarly cumbersome, erratic, costly, and often ineffective method of policy implementation and dispute resolution.

Adversarial Legalism in Action: Naming Deadbeat Dads

The strengths and limits of adversarial legalism in the realm of social justice are exemplified by the legal struggle over the thorny social problem of absent fathers. American states, like governments in most economically advanced democracies, legally require divorced or absent men to provide financial support for children they have fathered. As noted by Stephen Sugarman (1985) (whose excellent analysis this section recounts), state governments traditionally defer to the custodial mother if she declines to enforce her children's rights to paternal support.[8] The policy considerations are somewhat different, however, when the mother is on welfare, for if the father can be compelled to pay child support, the state's AFDC obligation is reduced or disappears entirely. In the late 1960s, as the number of unmarried mothers on AFDC rolls expanded dramatically, some states decided to compel mothers, as a condition of receiving AFDC, to disclose the father's identity to welfare administrators, enabling the state to enforce his legal child support obligations. Forcing absent fathers to recognize their illegitimate children, it was argued, would also have beneficial psychological effects for the family, establish the child's inheritance and social insurance rights, and deter both men and women from having babies they were not prepared to support on their own. Moreover, disclosure might deter welfare fraud: in some cases the father may be providing child support and the mother wishes to cover up that source of income in order to qualify for AFDC.

Without disparaging those concerns, welfare rights activists argued that in some cases a mother on welfare might have good reasons for not seeking support payments from the father or for not divulging his name to state authorities. She might be afraid that the father will be abusive toward her or the child. She might believe that the father will marry her and help support the child, but that governmental demands will drive him away. She might have other, more personal reasons to conceal the father's identity, or fear that disclosure would be psychologically harmful for the child. In any event, welfare rights advocates argued, an innocent child should not be denied assistance because his mother refuses to accede to the local welfare officials' demand for information about the father. In 1968 an unmarried "welfare mother" in Connecticut, defying state regulations, refused to name the father of her illegitimate child, "Scott Doe." Connecticut, as its regulations prescribed, terminated both Scott's and his mother's AFDC benefits. Scott's mother sued the state. Welfare rights lawyers championed her case, seeing it as a vehicle for advancing their legal reform agenda. Understanding Doe's legal argument requires some further background.

The AFDC program, initiated as a minor part of the historic Social Security Act of 1935, arose from a plan to revive insolvent state pension funds for widows or children with absent or disabled fathers. Bowing to pressure from state governments (which wanted both federal money and continued political autonomy), New Deal reformers crafted a joint federal-state AFDC program. The federal government provided matching funds for state-administered programs that aided single-parent families; state governments were allowed to set both benefit levels and eligibility requirements "under the circumstances of each State." Within states, welfare administration typically was further decentralized to city and county governments. Intercounty differences in attitudes toward welfare and welfare recipients compounded interstate differences, leading to sharp variations in the application of eligibility rules and in levels of aid to needy families (Mashaw, 1971: 818–839).

By 1967, however, state and local government control over AFDC rules and welfare administration had become enmeshed in controversy and in adversarial legalism. In the 1960s, as welfare rolls swelled, political conservatives complained that the AFDC system was riddled with fraud, that it encouraged sexual and financial irresponsibility, and that it led to dependency. Some states, particularly in the South, required the agencies that administered AFDC to deny benefits to applicants who failed to provide a "suitable home" for the aided children. Welfare authorities conducted so-called midnight raids to find out if there was a "man in the house," who was presumed to be an undeclared source of support. Welfare rights lawyers—led by attorneys in the federally funded Legal Service Program and Legal Services "backup centers"—claimed that many such state rules were motivated by racism and systematically challenged those rules in federal courts (Davis, 1993; Lawrence, 1990).

The federal judiciary was remarkably responsive. In a flurry of decisions beginning in the late 1960s, they transformed AFDC from a program grounded in state and local discretion in setting eligibility and benefit policies into a system of entitlements subject to federal legal supervision (Melnick, 1993: chs. 4, 5). For example, some states, such as California and New York, which provided comparatively generous AFDC payments, had enacted regulations imposing one-year residency requirements before immigrants from other states (such as southern states that provided much lower AFDC benefits) could qualify for aid. In *Shapiro v. Thompson* (1969), however, the Supreme Court (following the lead of nine lower federal court opinions) held that the Constitution contained a fundamental (albeit nontextual) "right to travel," which it interpreted as overriding California's one-year residency requirement. And in *Goldberg v. Kelly* (1970), the Court, asserting that welfare was not a privilege but a right, held (as had eight lower federal courts) that before a state or local government could terminate aid on grounds of a recipient's ineligibility, the government is constitutionally obliged to provide the AFDC recipient a right to a hearing before a neutral administrative adjudicator.

In the 1968 case of *King v. Smith,* the Court dealt with an Alabama regulation providing that if a single mother had a "regular boyfriend" she was ineligible for AFDC assistance; the Court held that certain congressional amendments to the AFDC law had restricted states' rights to establish eligibility requirements and that the Alabama rule was invalid since it conflicted with federal law. "Immorality and illegitimacy," the Court pronounced, "should be dealt with through rehabilitative measures rather than measures which punish dependent children" (Davis, 1993: 68). In *Townsend v. Swank* (1971) and *Carleson v. Remillard* (1972), the Court, rejecting eligibility rules promulgated by Illinois and California, asserted that states could not exclude AFDC applicants who were eligible under federal guidelines and that in enacting the AFDC program, Congress, far from allowing states discretion (as had been generally assumed), "intended to provide a program for the economic security and protection of *all* children." Thus federal court judges were able to impose national rules (and reject more conservative local governments' policies) on a wide range of issues—such as what resources should be counted in determining an AFDC applicant's eligibility, AFDC recipients' obligations to seek employment, and whether children in college or still in the womb should receive benefits (Melnick, 1993: 97).

Now we can return to the Connecticut case of young Scott Doe. In August 1969 in *Doe v. Shapiro,* a U.S. District Court judge in Connecticut, citing *King,* ruled that Connecticut's law, by cutting off benefits to AFDC children if mothers declined to name the father, was unlawful. Connecticut appealed, but the court of appeals refused to hear the case because state lawyers had filed the appeal a day after the prescribed deadline. Connecticut policymakers were unwilling to abandon the basic principle of parental responsibility, however, and amended their regulations, stating that an AFDC *mother's* (rather than her children's) benefits would be cut off for failure to cooperate with welfare officials in seeking paternal support payments. Welfare rights lawyers brought suit again. In this case, *Doe v. Harder,* the U.S. District Court held in March 1970 that Connecticut's partial cutoff violated federal law and the spirit of the *Doe v. Shapiro* decision (Sugarman, 1985a: 377). The state's welfare commissioner was held guilty of contempt of court. Connecticut appealed directly to the U.S. Supreme Court. This time its appeal was again rejected on technical grounds; apparently Connecticut's lawyers should have sought review in the court of appeals. Connecticut responded by enacting a new law in 1971, providing that an AFDC mother who refused to identify her child's father could be taken to court, and if she still refused, the judge could jail her for contempt. While in jail, the mother and her child would continue to receive AFDC benefits. Not surprisingly, reform lawyers attacked this law in court, in a case designated *Roe v. Norton.*

Roe v. Norton took more than ten years to resolve. A small army of lawyers generated novel legal arguments—that Connecticut's contempt provision violated a constitutional right of "family privacy" or the mother's right against self-incrimination; that it unfairly singled out poor mothers in imposing the obligation to seek paternal support payments; that disclosure of the father's name was not always in the best interests of the child, so that a case-by-case determination should be required. In response, Connecticut's attorney general argued that judges did have discretion not to use the contempt penalty in those cases in which disclosure of the father's identity threatened harm. The case was first heard in early 1973 by a three-judge U.S. District Court panel; one judge had participated in *Doe v. Shapiro.* Nevertheless, in April the court unanimously upheld Connecticut's law. Doe's lawyers took the case to the U.S. Supreme Court, which quickly granted review. The Children's Defense Fund filed an extensive amicus curiae brief challenging Connecticut's contempt rule and helped persuade twenty-six other organizations, ranging from the American Academy of Child Psychiatry to the Salvation Army, to join as fellow amicus curiae. In its brief the Children's Defense Fund added new constitutional arguments, for example, that the law violated the equal protection clause by discriminating against the indigent, and that jailing the mother imposed a cruel and unusual punishment on her children.

Meanwhile, the *Doe v. Shapiro* decisions (along with similar court decisions invalidating coerced maternal cooperation rules in other states' AFDC programs)[9] aroused congressional interest in the policy issue. Senator Russell Long of Louisiana, the influential chairman of the Senate Finance Committee, had long been opposed to liberalizing AFDC requirements with respect to absent fathers' obligations. In 1974, before the Supreme Court decided *Roe v. Norton,* Long pushed through a congressional law requiring all states to terminate AFDC benefits for mothers who refused to name the fathers of their illegitimate children. The Supreme Court then remanded *Roe v. Norton* to the lower courts for evaluation in light of the new congressional act.

In 1975, however, prodded by lawyers for the Children's Defense Fund and the Welfare Rights Center, Congress amended the 1974 law, adopting a "good cause" exception to the cutoff rule. The exception was not to come into effect, however, until its details were specified in regulations to be drafted by the Department of Health, Education, and Welfare. The Republican Ford administration's HEW moved slowly in drafting those regulations, declaring that in the interim states should follow the 1974 rules, which authorized coerced maternal cooperation in virtually all cases. But in the remanded *Roe v. Norton* case, U.S. District Court judge Joseph Blumenfeld, interpreting the 1975 law, held that Connecticut must withhold all sanctions from noncooperating mothers until HEW defined "good cause." Connecticut appealed to the U.S. Supreme Court. Meanwhile, welfare rights lawyers sued HEW, demanding that it revise its interim regulations to extend Judge Blumenfeld's ruling nationwide. When a U.S. District Court ruled against the plaintiffs, they too appealed to the Supreme Court. Before the Court heard the case, Democrats won an electoral victory and a reconstituted HEW urged states to issue their own good faith exception regulations, pending final HEW rules.

In June 1977 the Supreme Court again remanded *Roe v. Norton,* noting that Connecticut had adopted its own good cause provision. The plaintiffs agreed to abandon *Roe v. Norton* in 1981, after the HEW good cause exception rules became final. The regulations provide that an AFDC mother can be excused from identifying her child's absent father if she can show at a hearing that disclosure would create a risk of serious physical or emotional harm.

The net result of thirteen years of litigation, Stephen Sugarman (1985a: 380) observed, is that "the law on maternal cooperation is not very different from Connecticut's policy in 1968 before the lawyers ever got involved." True, he noted, there is now a narrow set of formal excuses for noncooperation, and only the mother's share of AFDC is at risk. But those excuses are not easy for her to establish (id. at 430). In 1979, among some 50,000 cases in which Connecticut mothers were asked to name the father, 236 mothers refused to cooperate and only 21 established good cause. At the same time, it is equally far from clear that the struggle was worth it for Connecticut. In 1978 and 1980, Sugarman noted, the support payments that Connecticut managed to get "deadbeat dads" to pay amounted to 6 and 7 percent, respectively, of all AFDC payments—about 4 or 5 percent after subtracting the state's collection costs—and it is not clear how much of that came from coerced identification as opposed to identification that would have been made voluntarily, absent the legal requirement (ibid.). In the 1990s, notwithstanding the issues raised by the *Roe v. Norton* litigation, a new federal welfare law ordered states to produce annual increases in the percentage of unwed fathers acknowledging paternity in order to avoid losing substantial amounts of federal welfare money (Jacobs, 1997).

The Positive Effects of Adversarial Legalism

From one perspective, the "naming deadbeat dads" story illustrates how adversarial legalism enables idealistic American lawyers and judges (unlike their professional counterparts in most other democracies) to help shape the welfare state. Adversarial legalism provides a public forum for challenging legislative and bureaucratic malpractice, for exposing the prejudices or lack of imagination that may be embodied in statutes and regulations, and for arguing that considerations of social justice sometimes should outweigh fiscal concerns and considerations of bureaucratic efficiency. Whereas legislation states general rules, litigation forces judges to focus on the plight of particular individuals whose situation may differ from the typical "problem situation" envisaged by legislators. Thus in *Roe v. Norton* the lawyers pointed out that in some cases it is *not* in the best interests of a child for the state to require AFDC mothers to identify the child's father and to compel him to meet his support obligations. In such cases the legislature's assumption—that the "welfare mother" who declines to identify the father is socially and morally irresponsible—is incorrect. Ultimately, the *Roe v. Norton* litigation and the debate it generated led to a nationwide HEW regulation authorizing an AFDC mother who can show good cause to decline to identify the father.

Similarly, in the other welfare rights cases mentioned—*King v. Smith, Goldberg v. Kelly, Shapiro v. Thompson*—adversarial legalism enabled advocates for single welfare mothers to challenge public policies that reflected overbroad, and sometimes racist, assumptions. The Supreme Court's decision in *Goldberg v. Kelly* compelled thousands of counties and municipalities to conduct "fair hearings" when claimants argued that the agency had erred in terminating benefits, thereby requiring agencies to substitute legal proof for potentially arbitrary administrative judgments. Public interest litigation on behalf of handicapped children enabled educational reformers to expose the fallacy (or the heartlessness) of state policies that assumed it was too difficult or too costly to provide a public education for handicapped children or to integrate them into the regular school program; these lawsuits precipitated enactment of federal legislation that mandated an appropriate public education for handicapped children (Melnick, 1995).

Perhaps most important, adversarial legalism has provided a vital mechanism for raising issues of social justice that had simply been ignored by the elected branches, which are more responsive to the demands of better organized or politically potent interests than to the claims of politically disorganized or marginalized minorities. In the years during which African-Americans were disenfranchised, litigation in the federal courts was the only effective means of challenging legally mandated racial inequality, for southern legislators, both in state legislatures and in Congress, blocked any serious efforts at reform. Similarly, adversarial legalism has been vitally important in asserting and vindicating the rights of other groups who are literally disenfranchised—such as prisoners and involuntarily committed mental patients held in underfunded and understaffed institutions (Rothman and Rothman, 1984), children of illegal immigrants who were excluded from the public schools (*Plyler v. Doe*, 1982), and refugees seeking political asylum.

The availability in the United States of class action litigation, which encourages lawyers to file cases on behalf of large numbers of similarly situated individuals (e.g., women, African-Americans, or the handicapped), makes American antidiscrimination laws far more potent than comparable laws in nations that do not foster the private enforcement of public law. Thus in *Feminism and Politics,* Joyce Gelb (1989: 206) concludes that the availability in the United States of powerful forms of litigation on behalf of women's rights has provided a more secure foundation for equal opportunity than in Great Britain and Sweden, where feminist activists, lacking tools such as class action suits and aggressive pretrial discovery, are far less likely to use the courts to enforce claims or to advance novel ones. In a political system that for a variety of structural and cultural reasons has been reluctant to establish comprehensive, well-funded social welfare programs comparable to those provided by other economically advanced democracies, adversarial legalism has often been the only game in town as far as reformers were concerned, or at least the game that could best put social provision on the political agenda.

The Negative Effects of Adversarial Legalism

Consider the "naming deadbeat dads" story again, but this time from the perspective of one of its less auspicious consequences—perpetuating legal uncertainty. Notwithstanding litigation that lasted more than ten years and involved dozens of arguments and decisions by different courts, adversarial legalism could never really impose a definitive legal solution on the coerced maternal cooperation controversy and failed to produce significant procedural or substantive changes in policy outcomes. Judicial decisions, far from providing authoritative legal guidance, succeeded only in stimulating legal and political counterattacks. When a U.S. District Court judge rejected Connecticut's cutoff of AFDC funds to children of "uncooperative" mothers, Connecticut responded by recasting its rules to cut off only the mother's benefits. When a court said that too was unlawful, Connecticut passed a law calling for the jailing of noncooperative mothers; *this* law was *upheld* by a three-judge federal court, leading to a further appeal, this time by welfare rights advocates. Similarly, when other district courts held that state rules requiring coerced maternal cooperation rulings were illegal, the U.S. Department of Health, Education, and Welfare declined to acquiesce in the judges' interpretation of federal law. This too stimulated appeals to the U.S. Supreme Court. But by the time the Court affirmed the lower courts' decisions, HEW's position had been endorsed by a new federal statute.

When HEW issued regulations restricting the newly enacted good cause exception pending the agency's formulation of final regulations, a U.S. District Court, in the remanded *Roe v. Norton* case, rejected HEW's regulations. But when welfare rights advocates sued HEW on the very same issue in a different U.S. District Court, that federal judge held against them. This led to yet another appeal to the U.S. Supreme Court, and to a second nondefinitive Supreme Court opinion.

In sum, in a regime of adversarial legalism, litigation bred more litigation, conflicting decisions, legal complexity,[10] and legal uncertainty. By creating a system in which the courts are open to challenges to governmental authority and public interest lawyers' creative arguments, adversarial legalism turns the judiciary into an arena of continuing political struggle. Because judges can and do make policy decisions, the competing political parties each strive to appoint judges who will be ideologically sympathetic. In split decisions by panels of the U.S. Court of Appeals, judges appointed by Republican presidents tend to vote differently from judges appointed by Democrats (Gottschall, 1986: 49–54). The same is true among U.S. District Court judges (Rowland and Carp, 1983). Thus outcomes often depend on which judge or appellate panel hears the case.

Legal conflict and uncertainty vitiate legal authority. As in the coerced maternal cooperation story, administrative agencies and state governments often are inclined to treat judicial decisions that reject their policies as just one more political obstacle to be overcome by tactical means—including the possibility of drawing a more sympathetic judge in the next round of litigation or of lobbying Congress to pass legislation overriding the judge's decision. Opponents of the federal courts' liberal rulings on AFDC repeatedly sought congressional legislation that would overturn them; for years, they won in the Senate but failed in the House of Representatives, but in the early 1980s, after President Reagan was elected, Congress enacted laws that reversed many earlier court rulings (Melnick, 1993: 120–130). Overall, between 1975 and 1990 Congress reversed or modified at least 300 lower court and 100 Supreme Court decisions (Eskridge, 1991).

The same perpetual struggle over the law recurs in other areas of social policy. The U.S. Social Security Administration (SSA), together with state agencies in charge of initial case processing, implements a federal statute that provides a pension to permanently disabled workers. Determining "permanent disability" under the SSDI program is difficult, however, for Congress has defined that term stringently, and medical evidence cannot fully determine whether a person is unable to work (Mashaw, 1983). To guide those difficult judgments, the SSA has struggled to craft rules that enhance consistency, and it also provides several levels of administrative review. Claimants denied coverage can ultimately appeal to the federal courts.

Repeatedly, however, the different regional U.S. Circuit Courts of Appeal have diverged in their interpretation of the governing statute. Within each circuit, three-judge panels dominated by Republican judges differ significantly from predominantly Democratic panels in their propensity to uphold the SSA's judgments (Haire and Lindquist, 1997: 230–236). The SSA, which is responsible for uniform national application of the law, often has refused to abide by adverse court decisions until the intercircuit conflict is resolved by the Supreme Court. But the Supreme Court, which decides fewer than 150 cases a year—fewer than 1 in 200 court of appeals decisions—cannot address all such legal conflicts, and those it does resolve are not resolved promptly (Strauss, 1987). Here too, by channeling policy disputes into a decentralized, politically staffed court system, adversarial legalism engenders a balkanized, uncertain, and continually contestable body of public law.

Finally, because benefit-dispensing agencies such as the SSA are subject to frequent judicial review,[11] the appellate process *within* agencies has tended to adopt the forms of adversarial legalism, creating a further source of legal uncertainty. In a typical year in the 1970s, Jerry Mashaw found that more than half of the 250,000 SSDI denials, even after administrative reconsideration, were appealed to administrative law judges (ALJs). While ALJs technically are SSA employees, they are substantially independent; in 1983 they brought a class action against the SSA in federal court, arguing that in attempting to monitor and sanction ALJs who deviate from agency policy, the SSA was improperly constraining their independent legal judgment. In 1979, in over half of the appeals, the ALJ reversed the administrative denial. Reversal rates by different ALJs ranged from 70 percent to 20 percent (Mashaw, 1983: 42; Kagan, 1984: 823).

The Limits of Adversarial Legalism

In the early, idealistic days of the national Legal Services Program, Geoffrey Hazard (1969) pointed out that while courts are often good at "civil justice"—remedying particular illegal actions by individuals or organizations—they have only limited powers to provide "social justice." After all, whom can they hold legally responsible for systemic inequalities in income? How can a court remedy those inequalities, short of massive redistributions of money and power that are well beyond the authority and competence of judges to order?

Hazard overstated his point a bit. In the late 1960s and early 1970s welfare rights lawyers used litigation to drive state and local governments toward higher standards of *procedural* justice. Yet some of the resulting court rulings had genuine substantive consequences. *King v. Smith,* in which the Supreme Court struck down Alabama's presumption that a "man in the house" demonstrated ineligibility for welfare benefits, made an estimated 500,000 children eligible for public assistance (Davis, 1993: 68). In 1972 the Court ruled against HEW's policy of allowing state AFDC eligibility policies to vary from federal standards *(Carleson v. Remillard).* That decision stimulated a flood of litigation in which the lower courts invalidated state rules on issues such as verification procedures, methods for determining applicants' income, and failure to register for welfare-to-work programs.[12] Those rulings also resulted in AFDC benefits for more needy families.

But as in the maternal cooperation cases, if welfare advocates could appeal to courts, state governments could respond by appealing to Congress, and Congress eventually amended the AFDC law to rein the courts in. By the mid-1980s the Supreme Court, with a majority of justices appointed by Republican presidents, routinely ordered the lower federal courts to defer to state and federal administrators' judgments, as in the days before the welfare rights lawyers' campaign (Melnick, 1993: 104–108; Melnick, 1996: 346–347). Congress also cut back funding for the Legal Services Corporation, especially for offices that specialized in welfare rights advocacy in the appellate courts.

In other ways too, victories in court often triggered political or administrative reactions that eroded or reversed the apparent gains. In the 1960s and 1970s courts expanded welfare recipients' procedural rights to ensure that legally eligible families were not denied coverage. But conservative politicians forcefully pressured welfare agencies to avoid the opposite error—payment of benefits to those who were really ineligible (Brodkin and Lipsky, 1983). *Goldberg v. Kelly,* by mandating a pretermination hearing, made it more difficult to cut off benefits to AFDC recipients whom officials believed to be ineligible. Politicians then pushed welfare administrators to adopt tougher evidentiary standards for *new* applicants. Caught between the threat of lawsuits by rights advocates and intensified accountability demands from conservative politicians, welfare officials sought refuge by mechanically following rules. Welfare offices soon were staffed with checklist-oriented clerks, displacing social workers and their discretionary assessments of clients' particular needs (Simon, 1983). As the administrative system was reshaped by adversarial legalism and political counterreaction, welfare clients increasingly felt lost in impenetrable legal mazes (Sarat, 1990; Briar, 1966; Abel-Smith and Titmuss, 1987: 238–244).

At bottom, therefore, adversarial legalism has been unable to nudge American welfare policy toward the levels of social provision provided by Western European welfare states. In even its most liberal era, the Supreme Court declined to read a right to subsistence or a socially guaranteed minimum standard of living into a U.S. Constitution that was drafted before the modern welfare state had been dreamed of (Kagan, 1982). American judges lack the power to tax; hence they have only limited authority to promulgate redistributive policies or compel legislatures to do so. In *Shapiro v. Thompson* (1969) the Supreme Court held that states that provided unusually generous AFDC payments could no longer impose a one-year residency requirement on migrants from low-AFDC states in the South. But the Court could not block the response of high-payment states, which was to reduce benefits to all AFDC recipients, hoping to weaken their attractiveness as "welfare magnets" (Peterson and Rom, 1990; Peterson, 1996). And in 1996, when Congress ended AFDC as a federal entitlement and required states to limit the duration of AFDC benefits and establish welfare-to-work programs, adversarial legalism did not enable liberal welfare advocates to erect significant constitutional or legal roadblocks.[13]

Adversarial legalism proved to be a limited weapon in other areas of social policy as well. The United States is unique in the extent to which liberalization of abortion laws came about through litigation, and unique in establishing an untrammeled judicially established right to first-trimester abortion (*Roe v. Wade*, 1973). But in contrast to most European governments, which include abortion services in their universal health care programs, adversarial legalism has not provided American women with a constitutional right to a government-funded abortion, and in many locations actual access to abortion services is very difficult (Glendon, 1987). Similarly, during the 1960s and 1970s crusading lawyers used the federal courts to expose the abominable conditions in underfunded state mental hospitals (Rothman and Rothman, 1984). Adversarial legalism has nonetheless proved to be a thoroughly ineffective mechanism for providing adequate halfway houses for the mentally ill, or mechanisms by which persons who formerly would have been involuntarily committed could be induced to move to shelters to take helpful medicines (Curtis, 1986).

Nor has American adversarial legalism been of much use in expanding governmental guarantees of health care, or child care, or subsidized housing, or effective job training and placement of the unemployed. After all the litigation, the American system of social provision for the unemployed and the needy, viewed in comparison with the welfare states of northwestern Europe, remains significantly less comprehensive, less generous, more suspicious of fraud and abuse, more demeaning and legalistic, and difficult for recipients to deal with.[14]

Adversarial legalism is not a *cause* of the grudging and incomplete character of the American social welfare system. It can more properly be viewed as a *consequence*—the response of politically liberal lawyers and judges to a political system that has not provided a nationally uniform, broad-based regime of social and health insurance, public housing, and generous employee benefits. Adversarial legalism has helped reduce the most blatant forms of discrimination and insensitivity in the *administration* of existing policies. But it has not proved capable of producing significant effects on levels of, or gaps in, benefits and services.

Understanding the Limits of Adversarial Legalism: The Example of Educational Inequality

Both the sources and the limits of adversarial legalism in shaping social provision spring from the distinctive political structure of the United States. Among economically advanced democracies, historian Kenneth Jackson (1996: E15) points out, "Only in America are schools, police and fire protection and other services financed largely by local taxes. . . . In Europe, Australia, and Japan, such [funding] functions are essentially the responsibility of national or at least regional governments."[15] Moreover, in many European nations *regional* governments control land use outside the city limits, constraining the sprawl of new suburbs into the surrounding farmlands. Compared to the United States, European central governments raise proportionally far more money through taxation,[16] provide far more public housing, and disperse it more widely (Weir, 1995). Largely because of these political differences, most large European cities remain vibrant and multiclass economic and cultural centers.

The United States, with its traditional emphasis on local democratic governance and local finance, represents a stark contrast. Local governments operate more on their own, desperately searching for sources of revenue to meet political demands for education, transportation, and public safety. For county governments, there are strong fiscal temptations to authorize developers to supplant farms and open spaces with revenue-generating housing developments, golf courses, shopping centers, and industrial parks. In the United States newly settled areas can incorporate as suburban municipalities with relative ease (Briffault, 1990); henceforth they operate as semiautonomous principalities, free to zone out low-income housing and reject public housing for the poor.

Meanwhile, to summarize a sad but familiar story, suburbanization has eroded the property tax base of older cities, which find it harder and harder to meet minimal public expectations, much less to provide schools and services and safety at the same level as wealthier suburbs. A cycle of social-class segregation ensues: middle-class and working-class families of all races and businesses move to the suburbs, which intensifies poverty and concentrations of minorities in the inner cities, which induces further flight to the suburbs. As the electorate increasingly has become dominated by suburban voters preoccupied with their own local schools, property taxes, and traffic problems, neither state nor national politicians have been eager to propose redistributive measures (Peterson, 1996; Weir, 1995: 226–229). Thus many American cities contain large areas characterized by levels of poverty, ethnic and racial isolation, physical deterioration, drug addiction, and violence that are quantitatively and qualitatively very different from the immigrant neighborhoods of Western European cities (Wacquant, 1995).

Adversarial legalism springs from this tension between American ideals of equal opportunity and a fragmented political structure ill-prepared to respond. Consider, for example, the enormous amount of litigation concerning public education. American political culture strongly supports the ideal of equal educational opportunity. At the same time, the tradition of local educational governance and finance has meant that schools (and students) in property-tax-rich suburbs generally enjoy more resources per student than those in declining older cities, even after state and federal aid to poorer districts. Many urban schools, moreover, often have predominantly minority students from poor, less educationally engaged families; vandalism and violence are far more common than in the suburbs, as is the proportion of students with behavioral or developmental problems. Compared to suburban schools, teacher turnover generally is higher in inner-city schools, student achievement and aspiration levels far lower.

Yet state and federal politicians, confronting an electorate dominated by families who moved to the suburbs to find better schools, have not been eager to establish metropolitan school systems, blending the resources and students of city and suburb. Activists committed to equal opportunity, therefore, have often turned to the courts, arguing that the federal or state constitution *compels* certain educational reforms. The results have been limited. The U.S. Constitution forbids racial discrimination but does not mandate economic or educational equality of outcomes. Courts have been understandably reluctant to overturn long-standing traditions of rule by local democracy in public education. When some judges nevertheless acted boldly, they bumped up against the limits of legal coercion, stimulating a political backlash. At bottom, courts alone could not abolish or overcome the structural fragmentation of government that sustains economic and racial segregation.

Beginning in the 1970s, for example, reformers brought lawsuits challenging suburban zoning laws that banned construction of multiple-unit apartment houses, trailer parks, and small-lot single-family homes. They argued that such laws were unconstitutional because they excluded low-income African-Americans from suburban towns and their schools. The U.S. Supreme Court held, however, that the Constitution is not offended absent explicit proof that a suburban municipality's single-family zoning rules had been adopted *in order to* exclude African-Americans rather than simply to maintain amenities and control growth (*Village of Arlington Heights,* 1977). The Court also rejected constitutional challenges to state laws requiring that community residents must be allowed to vote on (and reject) plans to build low-income housing projects in their town or neighborhood (*James v. Valtierra,* 1971).

The New Jersey Supreme Court acted more boldly to integrate the suburbs. In the 1975 *Mt. Laurel* case it held that suburbs were obligated by the state constitution to provide their "fair share" of low-income housing, and in 1983 the court authorized builders to file lawsuits to compel suburbs to adjust their zoning regulations accordingly. But in 1985 the state legislature, besieged by the suburbs, enacted a compromise law that blunted the impact of the *Mt. Laurel* cases.[17] The New Jersey Supreme Court, with the renomination of chief justice Robert Wilentz under political attack, upheld the compromise law. Partly because the law watered down suburbs' obligations to provide affordable housing, partly because of a slump in the housing market, very little low-income housing was built in New Jersey's wealthier suburbs (Kirp, Dwyer, and Rosenthal, 1995). Adversarial legalism's attack on exclusionary zoning was not meaningless. In several states it stimulated legislatures to enact laws that required suburbs to make provision for low-income units in approving housing developments. But for the vast majority of families in declining cities, the path to a suburban education for their child has been paved not by adversarial legalism but by earning and saving enough money to afford a single-family house in the suburbs.

Another equalizing strategy, at least for African-Americans, was to bring lawsuits charging that the racial imbalance between city and suburban schools amounted to unconstitutional racial discrimination. In *Milliken v. Bradley,* first filed in 1970, NAACP lawyers asked a U.S. District Court to order that black students from Detroit, where about 70 percent of public school students were black, should be bused to predominantly white suburban schools. Judge Stephen Roth held the Detroit school board and the state government guilty of de jure discrimination by maintaining optional attendance zones that enabled "white youngsters to escape identifiably 'black schools'" and by other measures apparently intended to retard "white flight" from the city schools. The judge then ordered that some 310,000 of the region's 780,000 pupils be bused from city to suburb or vice versa (Wilkerson, 1979).

In 1974 the U.S. Supreme Court reversed, holding in a five-four decision that the courts could not order metropolitan busing absent a finding of deliberate discrimination by the suburban school districts in question. Chief Justice Burger's opinion asserted that "no single tradition in public education is more deeply rooted than local [control]," adding that a judicial ruling that allowed a judge to become a "de facto legislative authority" and "school superintendent" for the whole area would be beyond the qualifications of judges and antithetical to democratic accountability. In Los Angeles, Wilmington, and Louisville, courts did order metropolitan busing; the results were mixed, leading to considerable additional "white flight" and a great deal of political opposition, even from some black parents and educational leaders.[18] But by and large, *Milliken* stanched the effort to bridge the city-suburb structural divide by means of court-ordered busing of students.

One other litigation strategy has been more successful, perhaps because it involves redistributing money rather than households or school children. In *San Antonio Independent School District v. Rodriguez (1973),* Rodriguez's lawyers showed that Alamo Heights, a wealthy suburb of San Antonio, spent $594 annually per pupil. But in the predominantly Mexican-American Edgewood School District on the west side of San Antonio where Rodriguez's children went to school, local property taxes (although they were set at the highest rate in the area) generated only $26 for each pupil, and even after aid from the state and the federal government, Edgewood spent only $356 per student (Irons, 1980).

In 1971 the California Supreme Court had held in *Serrano v. Priest* that the state's local property tax system for funding public schools, as then operated, violated the state constitution because it resulted in sharp disparities in educational expenditures. In *Rodriguez,* however, the U.S. Supreme Court held in a five-four decision that even substantially different per-pupil spending in property-tax-rich and property-tax-poor municipalities did *not* violate the U.S. Constitution. Justice Powell's majority opinion indicated that the

Court was reluctant to impose a constitutional restructuring on every state, which would shift funding, and hence control of the schools, from locally elected officials to the state capital and to federal judges.

Reformers continued to attack state property tax systems under state constitutions, however (Heise, 1995). In twenty of the thirty-six states in which the state supreme court decided the issue, the court held the school-funding system unconstitutional on grounds that it generated inequity among school districts or because it violated state constitutional clauses that authorized the state to provide an "adequate" or a "thorough and efficient" system of public education (Reed, 1998: 176; Heise, 1995: 1743).[19] Comparing five states in which reformers won in court with three in which they lost, Douglas Reed (1998: 182–201) found that court orders have generally reduced inter-district inequality and have also led to increased state funding for education overall. But big disparities in spending and educational quality persist in many states (Miller, 2000), for legislatures, filled with locally elected representatives, have resisted making changes in the structure of school finance and governance that are large enough to have a real impact on educational inequality (Heise, 1998: 312).[20] Moreover, litigation has been completely powerless to remedy the very large differences *between* states in per-pupil expenditures.

Thus the same fragmentation of governmental authority that generated the inequality impedes efforts to reduce it. In many states initial court victories have led to ongoing litigation, legislative-judicial power struggles, and judicial micromanagement of funding formulae. In the wake of the New Jersey Supreme Court's *Robinson v. Cahill* decision in 1973, the Education Law Center challenged the state's school finance plans in court almost every year, resulting in no fewer than ten subsequent state supreme court decisions, each more detailed than its predecessor. One court order closed the state's public schools entirely until the legislature agreed to enact a state income tax to supplement the local property tax system. Another court order compelled the governor to raise the income tax, which led to his defeat in the next election. The New Jersey Supreme Court's most recent decision criticized the state's funding model for not providing enough money for security guards in urban schools (Goodnough, 1997; Lehne, 1978). To Mark Yudof (1991), a leading legal authority in the area, school finance litigation often is like a Russian novel: "long, tedious, and everybody dies in the end." That is a bit too cynical, in light of Reed's previously mentioned research on the equalizing effects of positive court decisions, but Yudof is surely correct in emphasizing the limits of adversarial legalism.

In the United States privately initiated litigation over public provision arises and persists because it seemingly promises to narrow the gap between legal ideals and a fragmented, fiscally pinched governmental system. In the 1980s and 1990s public interest law firms filed lawsuit after lawsuit against the city of Washington, D.C.—one class action on behalf of poorly served children in foster care, others on behalf of food stamp recipients, prisoners in over-crowded city jails, recipients of governmental mental health services, house-holds awaiting public housing, detainees in appallingly bad mental institutions, and youths in juvenile detention facilities. In each case the judge, appalled by the gap between the promises of the welfare state and the performance of a poorly administered, poorly funded municipal government, imposed a reform program on the relevant department (Plotz, 1994).

Yet litigation cannot bridge the gap. Courts can issue orders against overt discrimination, but they cannot increase the tax base of central cities, eliminate economic disparities between the poor and suburban middle classes, create governmental programs, guarantee jobs, build subsidized housing, or operate halfway houses for the mentally ill. The same fragmentation and weakness of governmental authority that create the opening and the justification for adversarial legalism are likely to impede the realization of egalitarian social goals, even in the face of litigation and court orders.

That is not to say that litigation on behalf of the poor has done no good. When governments are unresponsive to social needs, adversarial legalism, even if not a panacea, often is far better than doing nothing. Litigation some-times helps mobilize groups for direct political action and helps change pub-lic perceptions of the issues (McCann, 1994). Moreover, one should not un-derestimate the value of the *procedural* reforms—the protections against official arbitrariness, discrimination, and invasion of privacy—that have flowed from litigation by American civil rights groups, "poverty lawyers," and advocates for particular disadvantaged groups. And sometimes, as in the arena of school finance reform, litigation has made a substantive difference, stimulating action by governors and legislatures.

Nevertheless, the fact remains that adversarial legalism has not significantly closed the gap between the American welfare state and those of Western Europe or turned the legal victories of the civil rights movement into victories over urban poverty and racial isolation. To make changes of that order would require not litigation but a sustained intellectual and political movement yielding sweeping legislative changes in American tax, labor, and educational policy and in traditions of local home rule. That does not seem very likely in view of the political culture of the United States, especially in an era in which the buoyant, entrepreneurial American economy has done a better job of raising family incomes than many European welfare states with their higher taxes, demanding labor laws, higher unemployment, and slower economic growth.

9

Adversarial Legalism and Regulatory Style

Protect us, O Government, from harm! Protect us, surrounded as we are by the side effects of capitalist production and modern technologies. For we dwell in fear that we and our children will ingest or inhale invisible chemical toxins. Agricultural chemicals, mechanized logging, industrial pollutants, and massive construction projects threaten our remaining forests, marshes, and streams. We are vulnerable to dangerous machines and products, deceitful promoters, and all kinds of human error. In the name of human decency, O Government, protect us from harm!

Versions of this fervent prayer are voiced every month in legislative hearing rooms, television programs, and the newsletters of environmental organizations. In democracies governments take those prayers seriously. They commission studies that analyze risks and they enact additional regulatory obligations into law. Governmental inspectors fan out across the community, a white-collar police force enforcing regulations concerned with workplace safety, air and water pollution, heating and wiring in low-income housing, the quality of care in nursing homes, cleanliness in food-processing plants, and the proper maintenance of airliners, elevators, school buses, trucks, and railroad tracks. Regulatory officials, ensconced in paper-cluttered offices, scrutinize permit applications for factory expansions, new construction projects, new pharmaceutical products, and new stock issues. All in all, the rules and enforcement agents of the regulatory state have come to bulk very large in contemporary legal systems.

In recent decades there has been much political rhetoric about "deregulation," and some actual dismantling of "economic regulation," that is, programs that limit competition and stabilize markets in banking, commercial air and rail traffic, trucking, telecommunications, and retail sales. But few politicians talk seriously about eliminating (as opposed to fine-tuning) *social regulation* of the kind mentioned in the preceding paragraph, for most such programs are widely regarded as essential correctives for problems that are inadequately controlled by market incentives and liability law. Social regulation nonetheless remains a focus of political conflict, partly because it never fully answers the prayer for protection, and partly because the precautions it requires often are extremely costly and cumbersome.

In the United States the political struggle has resulted in systems of social regulation that do not differ greatly from those of other economically advanced democracies in terms of the kinds of social problems addressed or the substantive thrust of regulatory standards. But in terms of *regulatory style,* the United States is different: American forms of regulatory law, processes for making regulatory policy, and methods of enforcing regulatory rules are more legalistic and more adversarial. Adversarial legalism does not necessarily make American regulation less effective than regulation in other economically advanced democracies—although it sometimes does. But adversarial legalism clearly makes American regulation more costly, more inefficient, and more inflexible. That inefficiency and inflexibility, moreover, tend to undermine the kind of government-business cooperation that is essential for fully answering the public's regulatory prayers.

Adversarial Legalism in Action: PREMCO's Regulatory Experience

Between 1995 and 1998 I directed a research program that conducted ten detailed case studies of multinational corporations that have similar business operations in the United States and in Europe, Canada, or Japan. Each company studied interacts repeatedly with different national regulatory regimes with respect to the same technologies and regulatory issues. By "holding the regulated entity constant" (or as close as one might expect to come to that condition), the research highlighted the differences in national legal regimes as they actually operate. For example, Kazumasu Aoki and John Cioffi, authors of one of the case studies, compared the Japanese and American regulatory regimes for industrial wastes by studying the experience of "PREMCO" (a pseudonym), a leading multinational manufacturer of precision metal parts. PREMCO operates similar factories in both countries, generating virtually identical manufacturing wastes—solvents, oily water, and contaminated metal particles (Aoki and Cioffi, 2000).

It appears that PREMCO is an environmentally responsible corporation. The company won EPA recognition for developing a method to phase out the use of chlorofluorocarbons and trichloroethylene two years before the deadline established by the Montreal Protocol (designed to protect the earth's ozone layer). PREMCO also has instituted an aggressive corporate environmental auditing and waste reduction program, certified under the International Standards Organization's important ISO 14000 series. Aoki and

Cioffi found that in both its U.S. and Japanese factories, PREMCO had instituted similar shopfloor controls on the collection and storage of wastes, as well as controls on their shipment and disposal. The two *regulatory regimes* differed sharply, however. According to Aoki and Cioffi (2000: 34):

> Viewed through the lenses of PREMCO's comparative experience, American environmental regulations are more detailed and prescriptive, and American enforcement processes, in contrast with Japan's, emphasize the legalistic interpretation of formal regulations and the imposition of sanctions to modify economic behavior. In contrast to Japanese waste management regulation, the complex American regulatory scheme poses more difficulties in compliance, imposes substantial additional economic costs on regulated entities, and engenders antagonism and defensiveness on the part of firm personnel.
>
> The Japanese mode of environmental regulation is far more cooperative and non-adversarial. "Administrative guidance" (gyōsei shidō) reduces the Japanese regulatory system's reliance on formal legal rules, sanction-based enforcement, and litigious relations.[1] In addition, the Japanese regulatory framework tends to emphasize (1) "performance standards," rather than specific, mandatory methods of waste control, and (2) informal regulatory initiatives formulated and implemented jointly by industry associations and government ministries and agencies. In comparison with the United States, corporate antagonism towards regulators in Japan is extremely low, as the system appears to facilitate corporate acceptance of regulatory norms. Shopfloor environmental practices in PREMCO's Japanese plant are equal or superior to those imposed on the U.S. factories by prescriptive American regulations.

To illustrate this contrast Aoki and Cioffi recount the experience of AMERCO—PREMCO's subsidiary in the United States—with the environmental regulatory agency in the American state in which three AMERCO factories are located. The federal Resource Conservation and Recovery Act (RCRA) authorized the U.S. Environmental Protection Agency (EPA) to turn over the administration of the mandated waste control program to state governments, so long as the state adopts each provision of RCRA, along with implementing regulations and procedures that are at least as stringent as the federal program. The federal statute and rules, moreover, are extraordinarily detailed and prescriptive, and the regional EPA office monitors state RCRA enforcement regarding the number of violations found and penalties imposed.

Comprehension as well as compliance is a primary challenge under RCRA. The facilities managers at two AMERCO plants estimated that they spend approximately 15 to 20 percent of their time on RCRA issues (Aoki and Cioffi, 2000).[2] One prescriptive provision, for example, is "the twelve-hour rule," which provides that hazardous wastes must be moved from shopfloor collection containers to a satellite or a main storage area once every shift or every twelve hours. The state agency has classified waste oil as a hazardous waste under RCRA, which brings most of AMERCO's production processes within the ambit of RCRA regulations, including the twelve-hour rule.[3]

In October 1992 state RCRA inspectors visited AMERCO Plant A, a facility that was scheduled to close two weeks later. The inspectors issued a citation to the plant manager for a number of violations, including failures to properly collect, label, and store waste oil under the twelve-hour rule and other state RCRA provisions. AMERCO's current management officials insisted to Aoki and Cioffi that these violations did not result in any environmental contamination, or even in any significant environmental risks, and none was alleged by the regulators.

In April 1993 state regulatory officials launched simultaneous inspections of AMERCO Plants B and C (located in different cities) and cited them for numerous violations similar to those found in the 1992 inspection at Plant A. Once again, according to company officials and AMERCO's outside counsel (a former state environmental agency attorney), the vast majority of these violations posed no significant risk to the environment and none had caused any environmental contamination.

At that time, each of the three AMERCO factories regarded itself as autonomous in production, management, and regulatory affairs. But to the regulators, the failure of Plants B and C to respond to the warning provided by the first inspection was symptomatic either of persistently disorganized, haphazard waste management practices or of outright defiance. Consequently, for each violation of the twelve-hour rule, regulators cited the company not merely for violating the rule but for violating labeling, sealing, and storage requirements for hazardous wastes. Thus a single violation immediately mushroomed into four or five violations; two-thirds of the approximately 150 citations issued following the 1993 inspections were derived from violations of the twelve-hour rule. Subsequently, AMERCO submitted two status reports and additional correspondence confirming rectification of all violations, and in March 1994 the agency issued a notice of compliance to both plants. Nevertheless, two months later the agency sent AMERCO a legal notice demanding $495,000 in fines for violations found during *both* inspections at *all three* plants.

The company and its attorneys, outraged by the punitive response to its efforts to remedy the violations, argued that the regulators had grossly inflated the environmental risk factor and thus the size of the fine. Aoki and Cioffi's review of the litigation file convinced them that the company managers' position was justified.[4] Negotiations between AMERCO and the government took six months and cost the company over $50,000 in attorneys' fees—far more than the cost of remedying the original violations themselves. The government ultimately settled for approximately $200,000—$100,000 in fines, a $10,000 donation to a local environmental group, and a credit of $92,500 in return for $185,000 in capital expenditures for new pollution controls, which addressed issues that had not constituted violations and required the company to undertake waste reduction measures not mandated by RCRA.

AMERCO also hired a new environmental manager with responsibility for coordinating environmental compliance across all plants. But the bitterness between AMERCO and the agency reportedly persists, and shopfloor supervisors regard any possible agency RCRA inspection with trepidation. Moreover, a statewide political backlash, Aoki and Cioffi note, led in the late 1990s to the total repeal of the regulation that classified machine-lubricating waste oil as a hazardous waste under RCRA, reducing the risk of overregulation but increasing the risk of underregulation.

PREMCO-JAPAN's regulatory experience could hardly be more different. Rather than employing detailed, prescriptive legal rules, Japanese environmental statutes articulate broad regulatory goals. They are implemented through informal "administrative guidance" and custom-tailored agreements between individual firms and the prefects or municipal governments that enforce the national laws (Wallace, 1995; Young, 1984). Regulators view extensive consultation with regulated industry trade associations and with individual facilities as the most important means of formulating and achieving policy goals. Japanese law and administrative guidance, rather than prescribing the *means* of achieving regulatory goals—such as the U.S. twelve-hour rule—simply require industries, in Aoki and Cioffi's paraphrased translation, "to employ any necessary measures to prevent [hazardous wastes and ordinary wastes] from scattering, flowing away, seeping into the ground, or emitting an offensive odor." The sole prescriptive rule requires factories to enclose waste storage areas, post signs identifying them as such, and store wastes in sealed containers to prevent evaporation or exposure to high temperatures.

When violations of these waste storage provisions are found, Japanese law requires regulators to issue an "improvement order" containing no financial penalties. Only if an improvement order is ignored or if harm to human health occurs are officials authorized to seek legal sanctions—in this case, criminal penalties. But resort to formal enforcement mechanisms is discouraged and extremely rare. Thus, in the municipality in which PREMCO's Japanese plant is located, regulators told Aoki and Cioffi that formal sanctions have never been imposed for violation of storage standards and, in contrast with AMERCO's experience, regulators inspecting the Japanese plant have never formally found a violation of waste management regulations. Japanese regulators instead focus on monitoring the firm's waste manifests and on waste reduction as their primary regulatory goal.

Japanese environmental law requires companies and individual facilities to appoint a senior plant official as the factory's "pollution control supervisor" and in addition to appoint a "pollution control manager." These officials are then legally responsible for compliance with, and violations of, environmental regulations and orders. Here too the emphasis is on institutionalizing responsibility for overall environmental outcomes rather than for complying with specific legal rules. According to Aoki and Cioffi (2000: 46):

> In contrast with AMERCO, PREMCO has taken advantage of the opportunities afforded by the performance-based character of the Japanese waste storage standards to diffuse environmental knowledge, training, and responsibility throughout the firm, including to shopfloor workers and supervisors. Performance-based regulation also allows greater flexibility in compliance efforts. Perhaps as a consequence, PREMCO's Japanese managers display none of the negative attitudes towards environmental regulation and regulators detected among AMERCO's managers.

The American Regulatory Style

The PREMCO case, like the other case studies in the research project from which it emerged, replicates the findings of a substantial body of comparative sociolegal studies, covering different regulatory programs, concerning the distinctiveness of the American style of social regulation. Of course, there are a great number of regulatory programs in the United States at all levels of government. While some regulatory statutes and implementing rule books are highly prescriptive, setting out regulatory obligations in excruciating detail, others grant implementing agencies considerable discretion to balance regulatory goals and economic considerations, depending on the particular circumstances. Some American regulatory agencies have employed a legalistic enforcement style, automatically imposing fines on all detected rule violations, even those that pose no significant risk of harm, but most agencies employ a more flexible enforcement style, and some a decidedly accommodative, cooperation-seeking style. Different regional or state offices charged with implementing the same law have been found to employ different enforcement styles (Shover et al., 1984; Scholz and Wei, 1986). Repeatedly, politicians and agency chiefs announce plans for making regulation more cooperative (Fiorino, 1996: Michael, 1996; Freeman, 1997).

Nevertheless, as in the Aoki and Cioffi study, whenever researchers have carefully compared specific regulatory regimes in the United States with their counterparts in other economically advanced democracies, the American regulatory regime has been found to entail a number of distinctive features. First, American regulatory law almost invariably is more legalistic—that is, more detailed, prescriptive, and complex (yet confusing and difficult to comply with). Second, American regulatory regimes more often enforce the law legalistically: they are more likely to issue formal legal sanctions when they encounter rule violations, and their legal penalties tend to be much more severe. Third, relationships between regulators and regulated entities in the United States are much more often *adversarial;* legal contestation of regulatory rules and decisions, in administrative appeal boards or in courts, is far more common, both by regulated entities and by citizen advocates of stricter regulation. Fourth, regulatory rules and methods in the United States usually are more often enmeshed in political controversy and conflict, as rival interests and politicians battle over regulatory appointments and strive to lock their policy preferences into law.

The Form of the Laws

Law professor Edward Rubin, aware that the U.S. Federal Reserve Board's authorizing statutes and regulations governing bank safety and soundness fill numerous three-inch-thick binders, was astonished to learn that Germany's comparable statute and the Bundesbank's implementing regulations are bound in a pamphlet that is less than 100 pages in length. Part of the explanation, Rubin learned, is that German bank regulatory officials are career employees, subjected to much more extensive training than their American counterparts, and are trusted to make programmatically sensible judgments without constraint by immensely detailed legal rules (Rubin, 1997).

German environmental regulations are implemented by state *(lander)* and municipal officials, and are perhaps the most detailed of any nation's save the United States. Still, they are much less prescriptive and constraining than American rules.[5] Moreover, the purpose of detail in German regulations is different, according to Daniel Kelemen (1998). The prescriptiveness of American statutes and regulations reflects politicians' and interest groups' desire to control regulatory agencies that they do not fully trust; the rules are designed to prevent the agency's "capture" by regulated entities or, on the other hand, by regulatory zealots, and to facilitate judicial review that will check unwarranted administrative decisions. In Germany, in contrast, the detail of federal environmental regulations is designed to provide guidance to the state and local officials who are responsible for implementing federal law, and to *shield* regulatory administrators from judicial interference. "When plaintiffs [in German courts] argue that an administrative action violated their individual rights," Kelemen says, "the administration can point to the detailed requirements of the implementing regulation and maintain that they simply followed the letter of the law." Conversely, the detailed German air pollution regulations have the legal character of "administrative guidance," not binding law; hence administrators can (and often do) lawfully depart from them in individual permitting decisions, based on their duty to adjust regulatory requirements to particular circumstances and economic conditions.

Comparisons of U.S. environmental statutes and regulations with those of Sweden (Lundqvist, 1980) and Great Britain (Vogel, 1986) have also noted the far greater complexity and prescriptiveness of the American laws. Unique to the United States, for example, is the frequency with which Congress has stipulated firm deadlines for the promulgation of particular implementing regulations and for the achievement of pollution reduction goals—deadlines that almost invariably have not been met, resulting in lawsuits by environmental groups demanding compliance (Melnick, 1992a). Prescriptive, deadline-laden statutes, moreover, lead to prescriptive, deadline-laden regulations, and at the level of individual regulated enterprises, to permits, remediation plans, checklists for inspectors, and reporting requirements that far exceed in specificity those imposed by other countries (Kagan, 2000).

The Regulatory Policymaking Process

Many governments seek to manage the political struggle over regulatory standards by entrusting regulatory decisions to technocratic bureaucracies, largely shielded from political and legal interference. Other governments create "corporatist" forums in which representatives of the regulated industry and of proregulation advocacy groups, along with relevant scientific and regulatory experts, bargain toward consensus in formulating regulatory standards. The United States, in contrast, strives to subject the political struggle over regulatory policy to the constraints of legal rationality, which gives both regulated businesses and proregulation advocacy groups yet another set of weapons to foil regulatory decisions that they may dislike.

The U.S. administrative process for making regulatory policy, accordingly, is distinctive in its legal formality, its openness to interest group participation, its adversarial quality, and its subjection to judicial review. American statutes and court decisions insist on publication of draft regulations, followed by open hearings in which advocacy groups, business organizations, and other interests may present their critiques and demands. Private consultation between regulators and regulated firms is legally proscribed in many circumstances and politically dangerous in many more. Administrative law compels regulatory policymakers to spell out the scientific, technological, and economic evidence they think will justify the standard chosen. Major regulations are regularly challenged in court, where judges scrutinize the fairness of the agency's rulemaking procedures, its interpretation of the relevant statutory language, and the quality of its response to arguments submitted by industry and advocacy organizations.

In Great Britain the regulatory policymaking process is far less formal and less open to legal contestation, as indicated by David Vogel's (1986) study of environmental policy. Regulatory officials issue administrative guidelines stating presumptive emission limits and control technologies after private discussions among staff members, selected technical representatives of affected companies and trade associations, and "responsible" environmental groups. Judicial review of agency decisions is infrequent. Lawyers, therefore, do not play a significant role in the rulemaking process. The same contrasts emerge from Rose-Ackerman's (1995) comparison of German and American environmental policymaking, from Badaracco's (1985) superb comparative account of occupational health regulation in the United States, France, Germany, England, and Japan, and from an excellent comparison by Brickman, Jasanoff, and Ilgen (1985) of how Germany, France, the United Kingdom, and the United States regulate potential chemical carcinogens in pesticides, food additives, and workplaces. American regulatory policymakers, Brickman et al. (id. at 304) observe,

> are confronted with demanding statutory mandates, which are often enacted without great attention to bureaucratic or economic reality. These must be implemented under the critical eye of other governmental institutions and . . . warring private interests, each advancing interpretations of law, science, and economics consistent with its narrower objectives. Unable to strike bargains in private, American regulatory agencies are forced to seek refuge in "objectivity," adopting formal methodologies for rationalizing every action. . . . [L]iberal standing rules, coupled with elaborate legal definitions of agency responsibilities, have generated a multitude of lawsuits that keep American administrators continually on the defensive. . . . [The courts'] searching review . . . has forced administrators toward greater formality and rigor in building the evidence to support their decisions.

In the European nations Brickman et al. (id. at 305) studied, "the absence of legislative-executive competition," together with the traditions of governance by professional, apolitical public agencies and by corporatist bodies, have reduced "pressure for rigorous procedural and judicial controls on the bureaucracy." In consequence, "A confidential process of consultation and accommodation permits government officials to mediate among conflicting private interests. As a result, regulators are able to make the necessary trade-offs and compromises without presenting reasoned public justifications or drawing open political fire."

As Vogel observes, rulemaking in the United States reflects a very different method of taking economic considerations into account. In Great Britain business participation in making and implementing policy "is both assumed and assured" (Vogel, 1986: 170). In the United States consultation between business executives and regulatory officials is politically suspect; participation by business "must constantly be asserted" and "the importance given to economic considerations is in large measure dependent upon the lobbying and litigation skills of business." Economic concerns are addressed through formalized cost-benefit analyses or technical feasibility studies, whose almost inevitable methodological flaws create grounds for appeal to the courts, either by regulated businesses who feel the regulation is too stringent or by pro-regulation advocacy organizations who think it is too lenient. The difference is reflected in the character of the dialogue between the interested parties. Badaracco (1985: 120–121) points out:

> In the United States, procedural formalities guided and constrained contacts among the parties. . . . In contrast, very few rules or procedures constrained the meetings of the European and Japanese working parties. . . .
>
> Compared with the other four countries, parties in the United States [including regulatory officials] had far fewer opportunities to communicate through discussion or visits to VC [vinyl chloride] and PVC [polyvinyl chloride] plants. . . .
>
> Finally, in Europe and Japan, another opportunity for direct communication was explicit, direct discussions of the costs and benefits of possible VC controls. Such discussions were an established part of the decision process and were based on a relatively informal, judgmental approach, not on complex, quantitative models frequently used by U.S. regulatory agencies, although [the Occupational Safety and Health Administration], at the time of the VC problem, strongly opposed the use of cost/benefit analysis.

Implementation and Enforcement

The large, punitive fine imposed on PREMCO for only moderately serious, quickly remedied regulatory violations is far from unusual (Adler, 1998: 40,

41), and it contrasts sharply with the regulatory enforcement styles of other economically advanced democracies (Kagan, 2000). On the other hand, it is not entirely representative of American regulatory enforcement. Some American agencies, as noted earlier, pursue a flexible or even an accommodative enforcement style, emphasizing remedial orders more than punishment (Kagan, 1993). Some American agencies are too lenient, or perhaps simply understaffed and overwhelmed: reports regularly surface concerning cases in which regulatory officials declined or failed to punish obvious and significant regulatory violations (Lifsher, 1998). Regulated industries sometimes beat back legalistic enforcement in the political arena: in the late 1990s the meat and poultry industry managed to ward off legislation calling for larger and automatically imposed fines for regulatory violations (Rogers, 1998: A5).

Nevertheless, American regulatory officials are constantly subject to political pressures to employ legalistic methods and to prosecute regulatory violations. In response, agencies often measure their progress in terms of prosecutions brought and fines recovered. As noted in the PREMCO case, the federal EPA systematically audits state environmental agencies' records with respect to failure to seek legal sanctions against violators; periodic EPA reports criticizing failures to prosecute are sure to make newspaper headlines (Fialka, 1998: 40; Adler, 1998: 40). When President Reagan appointed pro-business administrators to federal regulatory agencies in the early 1980s and the number of formal enforcement actions dropped, the political backlash was so intense that virtually every agency reversed course; within two or three years the number of enforcement actions in those agencies had bounced back and then surpassed levels during the preceding Democratic administration (Wood and Waterman, 1991; Wood, 1988).[6] These political pressures for legalistic regulation are manifested both in day-to-day enforcement practices by regulatory bureaucracies and in the comparative harshness of American legal sanctions for regulatory violations. Notwithstanding variation among American agencies, numerous cross-national studies in various fields of social regulation have found regulatory implementation in the United States to be far more legalistic and deterrence-oriented than in other economically advanced democracies, where enforcement officials who encounter shortcomings more consistently employ a problem-solving, cooperation-seeking style (Boden and Wegman, 1978: 43, 45; Kelman, 1981; Wilson, 1985).

When John Braithwaite and colleagues (1993) compared nursing home regulation in the United States, England, Japan, and Australia, they found that enforcement in the United States was more legalistic and punishment-oriented. For most violations American state nursing home regulators accept the filing of a satisfactory plan of correction, but formal legal enforcement—administrative fines, suspensions of new admissions, and license revocations

—is far from infrequent,[7] and far more common than in the other countries. Each journalistic report of substandard care triggers demands for harsher penalties. Thus nursing home regulation in the United States, Braithwaite concludes, is "tougher than nursing home regulation in the rest of the world, and much tougher than most other domains of business regulation" (id. at 25–27). Moreover, Braithwaite was struck by the "culture of distrust" generated by the legalistic approach to regulation. At least until 1990, Braithwaite notes, federal training of state inspectors "emphasized the need for inspectors to be in control during [end-of-inspection] exit conferences, not to be distracted by questions raised by nursing home staff, [and] to stick to the facts of the deficiencies that require a written plan of correction"—a posture that would be shocking to nursing home regulators in Australia or England (id. at 36). In consequence, Braithwaite points out (id. at 48):

> Inspectors in the United States spend most of their time alone in a room poring over resident charts, whereas English and Australian inspectors spend most of their time out in the nursing home observing care and talking to staff, residents, and visitors about care. The theory of the recent [1990 federal statutory] reforms was that the inspection process would become more resident-centered and less document-centered. But our research team's observation is of no significant change because the new element of resident interviews has been balanced by extra documents for inspectors to check and extra pieces of paper for them to fill out.

The greater impersonality of American regulatory implementation—its often formalistic, "by the book" character—is commented on by numerous sociolegal studies (Bardach and Kagan, 1982; Axelrad, 2000).

Perhaps the most striking feature of American regulatory enforcement is the severity of its legal sanctions, both "on the books" and in practice. No other nation authorizes or imposes such weighty criminal penalties for violations of regulatory laws. In 1988 Congress increased criminal fines for insider trading to $1,000,000 for individuals and $2,500,000 for entities, and doubled the maximum prison term for violations of any securities law provision from five to ten years (Pitt and Shapiro, 1990: 238). In the late 1980s and early 1990s Congress upgraded most criminal offenses in environmental laws from misdemeanors to felonies, thereby increasing the maximum potential prison sentences. Under both federal and California law, courts can impose a criminal fine of up to $1,000,000 on a corporation for violations of water pollution law that "knowingly endanger another person"; for such violations individuals can be fined up to $250,000 and sentenced to prison for up to fifteen years.[8] Congress also funded large increases in the number of EPA investigators assigned to the task of building criminal prosecutions against environmental offenders (Blabolil et al., 1997). In the 1995–1997 period, EPA sought criminal penalties against more than 250 offenders per year, as compared to an average of 40 per year a decade earlier (U.S. Environmental Protection Agency, 1998). Increasingly, prosecutions for environmental violations have been brought against individual corporate officers, rather than corporate entities, and more than a third of those convicted are sentenced to prison (Blabolil et al., 1997; Kagan and Lochner, 1998).

American law also provides for much heavier *civil* penalties for regulatory offenses than does the law of other countries. The federal Clean Air Act and the Toxic Substances Control Act authorize civil penalties of up to $25,000 per day for ongoing violations. The EPA can impose administrative penalties equal to the financial "benefit" the violator gained by not making the required abatement. Several federal environmental statutes require violators to pay for the damages to natural resources caused by unauthorized pollution, a provision that encourages enforcement officials to act like trial lawyers seeking the largest possible damage calculations (Privatera, 1992: 3–6). In 1989 the Exxon *Valdez* (with third mate Robert Kagan at the wheel) went aground in Prince William Sound, Alaska, spilling eleven million gallons of oil in the wildlife-rich waters (Davidson, 1990). Exxon Corporation, after spending $2 billion on cleanup efforts, pled guilty to criminal charges and was fined $125 million, based on damages to the environment. In addition, the state of Alaska and the federal government each brought civil actions against Exxon for natural resource damages, and Exxon settled those suits for almost $1 billion (*Washington Post*, 1991: A14; Verhovek, 1999). Exxon also was sued for damages by scores of plaintiffs' lawyers who signed up thousands of fishermen, Indian tribes, and other private parties allegedly injured by the spill, and a federal court jury handed down a $5 billion punitive damages award.

Exxon's simultaneous exposure to criminal prosecution, governmental civil penalties, and private lawsuits for damages for the same accident highlights another distinctive feature of American regulatory law: the unique extent to which it encourages *private* enforcement of *public* law. Congress repeatedly has provided incentives for entrepreneurial lawyers to act as "private attorneys general." Thus the federal antitrust law holds out the prospect of "treble damage" awards to plaintiffs who can prove a violation in court. The federal Truth-in-Lending Act gave debtors a cause of action against lenders who fall afoul of the statute's complex disclosure rules. To encourage suits Congress provided that prevailing plaintiffs would receive a $100 minimum award, regardless of actual losses, plus their attorneys' fees. The act further enabled enterprising attorneys to bundle thousands of bank customers together in a class action, "raising the specter of enormous damages suits for minor violations of the statute" (Rubin, 1991: 237). As is typical for such one-way fee-shifting statutes, plaintiffs who lose do not have to reimburse the prevailing defendant's lawyers' fees.

One-way fee-shifting, together with the remarkable volume of reports that American corporations must file (disclosing financial data, industrial emissions, product complaints, chemical inventories, bank lending patterns, and more), has made class actions by entrepreneurial lawyers a prominent means of enforcing American regulatory law in many spheres, from securities laws to the Clean Water Act. Neither the private class action nor special incentives for private enforcement actions are prominent features of regulatory law in other countries (Greve, 1989b).

The combination of criminal, civil, and private enforcement results in regulatory penalties in the United States that dwarf those in other countries. Karpoff, Lott, and Rankine (1998: 4), after studying legal responses to 283 environmental violations by publicly traded companies in the 1980–1991 period, wrote:

> We find that legal penalties frequently are substantial. The mean fine or damage award in our sample is $9.43 million (the median is $600,000), and the average forced compliance or remediation cost is $59.97 million (the median is $8 million). There is no robust evidence that the legal penalties are related to firm size, or, for that matter, the characteristics of the violation, the party bringing the action, or the type of action brought. These results are consistent with arguments that legal penalties are idiosyncratic and difficult to predict.

The adverse publicity that accompanies formal legal penalties adds another element to the deterrence equation. Karpoff and colleagues found that initial press announcements containing allegations of a violation are associated with losses in the defendant corporation's share value on the stock exchange (an average of 1.5 percent, and almost 2 percent if the announcement includes mention of a formal legal charge). Not surprisingly therefore, multinational corporations view American regulatory regimes as more unpredictable and more threatening than those of any other economically advanced democracy (Kagan, 2000).

The Consequences of Legalistic Regulation

With its detailed and demanding rules, its potential to impose very tough penalties for deviations, its often legalistic enforcement style, and its openness to prodding by citizen advocacy organizations, social regulation in the

United States is generally quite effective. U.S. securities regulation has helped make American financial markets more attractive for investors from around the world. American environmental regulation has been quite effective in reducing pollution from major industrial sources, municipal waste treatment plants, and motor vehicles.[9] Thanks in part to regulation, supplies of food, water, and pharmaceuticals in the United States are remarkably safe, its motor vehicles have state-of-the-art safety features, and its workplaces have reduced employee exposure to harmful chemicals. Major federal and state social regulatory agencies, tightly controlled by law, are generally regarded as honest and evenhanded; stories of corruption or of favoritism for some firms over others are rare.

But would these successes persist if American regulation were less adversarial and legalistic? Even if adversarial legalism does increase the deterrent power of American regulation, do its social benefits outweigh its social and economic costs, which, as we will see, include high levels of legal uncertainty, large expenditures on legal services and proof of compliance, delays in issuing new rules and making industrial changes, and a sometimes divisive relationship between government and regulated businesses? These are not easy questions to answer but seem well worth discussing.

Is Adversarial Legalism Necessary?

Lyle Scruggs (1998; 1999) used national reports to the Organization for Economic Cooperation and Development (OECD) to analyze *rates of progress* by seventeen economically advanced democracies in reducing pollution during the 1970s and 1980s. Notwithstanding the greater prescriptiveness and deterrent threat of American environmental regulation, Scruggs found that the United States ranked thirteenth of the seventeen nations in reducing air pollution (sulphur dioxide, nitrous oxide), solid wastes (measured by reductions in municipal wastes and proportion of paper and glass recycled), and water pollution (measured by percent of population served by waste water treatment plants, and by reduction in pesticide use per acre of arable land). In terms of rates of progress, the United States trailed Germany (which ranked first) and several countries with decidedly nonlegalistic enforcement styles—the Netherlands (second), Sweden (third), Japan (fourth), and the United Kingdom (eleventh) (id. at 70). The most important correlate of rapid environmental improvement, Scruggs found, was whether the nation had "neo-corporatist" institutions that fostered a more consensual mode of regulation—that is, whether well-organized, comprehensive industry associations were incorporated into the regulatory policymaking and enforcement process. "Pluralist" systems, in which political and economic power is more fragmented, ranked lower—and the United States is surely the most "hyper-pluralistic" of all the OECD countries.

Brickman, Jasanoff, and Ilgen (1985: 49) compared the U.S. rulemaking process with the corporatist, more closed and informal, methods used by Great Britain, Germany, and France in setting regulatory standards for carcinogenic substances (see also Jasanoff, 1986, 1999). They concluded:

> Germany has set the lowest [i.e., most stringent] standards for asbestos, nitrates, and benzene, and the United States the lowest for vinyl chloride. The United States has been the first to take significant restrictive action on many of the fourteen substances . . . but in several instances, particularly for pesticides, the Europeans have adopted final controls before the United States. After promulgation by an administrative agency, American regulations are more often amended, altered, or suspended than comparable policy measures in Europe. At least for carcinogens, then, the overall impression is of roughly comparable regulatory outputs among the four governments. Notwithstanding discrepancies in the handling of particular substances, no country appears notably more or less aggressive than another when regulatory records are compared over a period of years.

With respect to the effectiveness with which regulations are implemented, the social science evidence is limited. According to Allen (1989: 72), from the mid-1970s to the mid-1980s German chemical companies invested twice as much money as their American counterparts in complying with environmental protection measures. A comparative study found that Swiss, German, and French regulatory regimes reduced toxic effluents in the Rhine River more completely than did the comparable American regime for the Great Lakes (Verweij, 2001). Some useful insights are also provided by the previously mentioned case studies of multinational corporations (Kagan and Axelrad, 2000). Like the PREMCO study, they indicate that while the American regulatory processes entailed more adversarial legalism, regulatory *outcomes* in Germany, Japan, the Netherlands, and the United Kingdom, viewed in terms of the level of protection that the beneficiaries of regulation actually were accorded, were substantially similar to those achieved in the United States, at least when the targets of regulation are large corporations (Kagan, 2000; Wokutch, 1992).

Overall, then, the existing evidence suggests that American adversarial legalism does not necessarily yield better regulatory outcomes than are achieved by economically advanced democracies in which there are relatively strong political pressures for effective regulation. Yet that does not quite settle the issue. While some other countries achieve comparable regulatory outcomes with less legalistic, more cooperative regulatory methods, it might be argued that such methods would not work in the United States. American businesses, some observers have contended, are less deferential to governmental authority than are Japanese and European firms.[10] Perhaps, then, American regulation *must* be more adversarial, legalistic, and deterrence-oriented. There may be some merit to this argument, but it is worth noting that subsidiaries of American corporations in Japan or Western Europe do not have a reputation for being less compliant with those countries' regulations than are domestic companies.

Moreover, a regulation-disparaging American business culture may be just as much a *response* to the U.S. regulatory style as it is a cause of it. In a comparative study of innovation in reducing environmental harms, David Wallace (1995: xvii, xx) observed:

> firms are more comfortable innovating when risks are reduced, and risks are lower when environmental policy is stable and credible over the long term, and when regulatory processes are based on open, informed dialogue and executed by competent, knowledgeable regulators. . . .
>
> When policy-making has strong political independence from industry (e.g. due to the influence of environmental pressure groups), but dialogue is poor, environmental regulations are associated with high compliance costs. This can create a vicious circle, in which political polarization of environmental issues leads to less dialogue, resulting in poor and costly regulations and hence further polarization. However, political independence combined with good dialogue allows policy-makers to develop flexible regulatory mechanisms and schedules which accommodate innovation.

Wallace's prime example of poor industry-government dialogue and an inflexible regulatory structure is the United States.[11] Legalistic enforcement in the United States, with its implicit distrust of the business community, also sometimes stimulates a business subculture of legalistic resistance (Bardach and Kagan, 1982). A Swedish occupational safety inspector told Steven Kelman (1981: 608), "Anytime [I'm] forced to use orders or prohibitions to achieve compliance with the regulations . . . it implies I've failed. I'm supposed to try to persuade; if I come in with a hammer, it makes the employer negative." If PREMCO's American managers, as noted earlier, are more antagonistic toward government regulation and regulators than their counterparts in Japan, the primary reason has been their unhappy experience with U.S. regulatory officials who wielded a legalistic, adversarial, and punitive hammer. Overall, therefore, the existing research suggests that even if American adversarial legalism adds *something* to the deterrence equation, it is not clear quite how much it adds or whether that added deterrence outweighs adversarial legalism's substantial social costs.

The Social and Economic Costs of Legalistic Regulation

Comparative research indicates that, when contrasted with cooperative modes of regulation, American adversarial legalism generates much more legal uncertainty, much higher litigation and lawyering expenses, higher compliance and opportunity costs, and more defensiveness and alienation among regulated enterprises. These troublesome costs are borne by the society at large, not merely by regulated firms.

Unpredictability

In theory, a regulatory regime that emphasizes detailed, strictly enforced legal rules should be more stable and predictable than regimes that emphasize discretionary adjustment of policies to particular circumstances. Paradoxically, however, regulatory compliance officials in multinational enterprises characterize American regulation as more legally uncertain than regulation in Western Europe or Japan. The uncertainty stems from several features of American regulatory systems. Institutional fragmentation results in overlapping, imperfectly coordinated regulation by numerous local, state, and federal agencies, which may be dominated by different political parties with different regulatory policy preferences. Due to the political and legal openness of American government, business groups and advocacy organizations frequently battle for regulatory changes in agencies, courts, and legislatures, rendering American regulatory law particularly malleable. The ever-present prospect of legal and political challenge means that regulatory officials in the United States, compared to their counterparts in other countries, typically demand more scientific evidence to support permit applications, requests for variances, and new regulations, so that it is often unclear *when* a decision can be made and *whether* the studies and certifications provided will be regarded as legally sufficient.

"Q Corp." is a multinational electronic-parts maker with similar factories in California and Japan, subject to parallel water pollution regulations. Aoki, Kagan, and Axelrad (2000: 82) found that

> Q USA environmental managers spend much more time than their Q Japan counterparts striving to assimilate and reconcile regulatory requirements that are promulgated—separately and not always consistently—by federal agencies, state agencies, municipal agencies, and courts. Q USA officials spend much more time attending meetings,

communicating with regulatory enforcement officials, and going to private workshops aimed at clarifying the law and ascertaining how it applies to particular industrial operations. Q USA officials spend more time communicating with environmental lawyers retained by the company, from whom they seek a second opinion in an effort to reduce the legal uncertainty that they regularly experience.

Even so, legal uncertainty remains, because U.S. regulatory law is often in flux. To mention one example that affected Q USA, in 1987 Congress directed the states to adopt by 1990 numerical ambient water quality objectives for certain toxic pollutants. States were slow to do so, however, partly because of concern that their decisions would be challenged in the courts, either by industry or by environmentalists, for lack of an adequate scientific basis. In 1991 California promulgated the Inland Surface Water Plan (ISWP), but it omitted objectives for some bodies of water and some pollutants. The EPA then disapproved California's regulations as incomplete. Meanwhile, local California governments sued the state on the ground that the ISWP rules were too stringent and would compel them to build or renovate water treatment plants at great expense. A California court invalidated the ISWP rules for violating certain procedural requirements in the promulgation process. Back at the federal level, an environmental organization sued the EPA for failing to meet the 1987 law's deadline, and a federal court ordered EPA itself to issue regulations setting standards for the pollutants, which the agency did in 1992. The impact of the ongoing federal-state jousting on the local water treatment plant to which Q USA's effluents flow, and hence on Q USA's in-house treatment obligations, thus took years to figure out (Aoki et al., 2000: 94, note 51).

Lawyering Costs

Officials of PREMCO, the Japan-based metals manufacturing company mentioned earlier, assert that the corporation has spent more money on legal services for its U.S. subsidiary than for its corporate headquarters plus all its other manufacturing plants in Asia and Europe. A similar claim was made by several other multinational enterprises in the same research project. Their U.S. subsidiaries consult lawyers more often and longer on a wider range of matters, company officials say, because American law is generally more complex, changeable, and difficult to master; the legal sanctions for being wrong are generally much higher; litigation is more common; and litigation in the United States is vastly more expensive than in other economically advanced democracies (Nielsen, 1999; Ruhlin, 2000; Kagan, 2000).

Welles and Engel (2000) found that "Waste Corp.," a multinational builder and operator of waste disposal facilities, spent a staggering $15 million on legal services in the course of its efforts to obtain approval for a municipal solid waste landfill in California; for over ten years the company had approximately seven lawyers on retainer, busy addressing numerous regulatory agencies, two major administrative appeals, and three extended lawsuits. In Pennsylvania the same company retained seven lawyers (but only part-time) for the five years it took to get a landfill permit there, a process that entailed two administrative appeals but no lawsuits and "only" $1.45 million in lawyering costs. When Waste Corp. sought to develop a similar landfill in England, by contrast, the company retained two lawyers, part-time, for an eight-year process that also included at least one administrative appeal; its legal costs there were about $137,000. And in the Netherlands, despite having undergone two administrative appeals, the company did not have to retain lawyers at all (since lawyers are not required in administrative appeals) and spent "less than $50,000" on legal services.

Accountability Costs

Viewed in cross-national perspective, American regulatory regimes generally impose more extensive and specific requirements concerning reporting, record-keeping, testing, employee education, certifications, and so on. In addition to the costs of complying with substantive regulatory standards, therefore, regulated firms generally must spend more in the United States than they do overseas to prove that they are complying (Dwyer et al., 2000; Kagan, 2000). In the early 1990s "B Corp." notified regulatory authorities in the United States, England, and the Netherlands that it had discovered that solvents had leaked from deteriorating underground tanks and pipes in its factories in those countries. The American regulators, Lee Axelrad found, demanded far more comprehensive analysis, more voluminous documentation, and more costly reports than did the European authorities. The documents submitted to American regulators for contaminated sites, B Corp. regulatory compliance officials said, would fill a four-drawer filing cabinet, compared to the less than half of a single file drawer of documentation submitted to regulators in the other countries. And behind each additional ten pages of documentation lay scores of hours that company officers devoted to research, testing, measurement, analysis, and preparation and checking of draft reports.

All in all, B Corp. officials estimated that "extra" studies, submissions, and negotiations with U.S. regulators added $8 to $10 million to the costs of designing the cleanup plan for the two sites in the United States (out of total costs per site of an estimated $22 million), whereas the "extra" regulatory accountability costs for comparable site investigations and cleanup planning in the United Kingdom and the Netherlands were negligible (Axelrad, 2000). Moreover, as of the time Axelrad interviewed B Corp. officials, actual remediation efforts in England and the Netherlands were well under way, but at the American sites action remained on hold while the firm still waited to learn if officials considered the company's analysis sufficient. In this case, therefore, the additional demands of the U.S. regulatory regime confirmed the maxim that when pushed too far, *accountability* (proving one has done the right thing) can displace *responsibility* (doing the right thing) (Bardach and Kagan, 1982).

Opportunity Costs

Regulatory permitting systems are designed to slow the headlong rush of development and technological change, forcing business firms to look more carefully at potential adverse side effects before they leap. But prior regulatory review may also impose opportunity costs on society. Each month's further scrutiny of a new, perhaps more benign, pesticide means another month's delay in supplanting a more harmful pesticide. The European Union regulatory systems for prior review of genetically engineered products and new chemical substances are slower and impose longer delays on useful new products than the comparable U.S. regimes (Kraus, 2000; Johnson, Fujie, and Aalders, 2000). For most products and processes, however, American regulatory regimes impose *longer* delays and *larger* opportunity costs than comparable national regimes in Western Europe. American opponents of new projects generally have more opportunities to challenge regulatory approvals in court than their counterparts in other countries, and litigation, crawling at a deliberate pace, typically results in substantial opportunity costs. The greater prospect of judicial review, moreover, often seems to make American regulatory officials more cautious and legalistic in reviewing proposals than their counterparts abroad. When Ford applied for air pollution permits for its two German plants, the time from application to approval in Germany took five months and seventeen months, respectively; the same permit applications for Ford's plants in Minnesota and New Jersey took over four years (Dwyer et al., 2000).

Adversarial legalism's combination of higher lawyering costs, accountability costs, and opportunity costs probably reaches its apotheosis in the Superfund program, launched by Congress in 1980 to clean up nonoperative hazardous waste disposal sites and abandoned dumps. In contrast to parallel European regulatory programs (Church and Nakamura, 1994; Lohof, 1991; Kopp, Portney, and DeWitt, 1990), the Superfund program operates as if it were designed by a plaintiffs' personal injury lawyer. Thanks in part to expansive judicial rulings, it imposed absolute, joint and several, and retroactive liability for cleanup costs on any enterprise whose wastes found their way into the disposal site—regardless of the disposer's *share* of the wastes, regardless of whether it acted lawfully under the legal rules and containment practices prevailing at the time of disposal, and regardless of any demonstrated current harm to human health. EPA enforcement officials bring lawsuits against a few large corporate waste disposers, who then sue other "potentially responsible parties" (PRPs). As Landy and Hague (1992) describe the result, "the shovels often remain in the tool shed while the EPA pursues PRPs along the slow and tortuous path of litigation." According to research in the late 1980s, Superfund litigation, studies, and related transaction costs, governmental and private, added up to at least one-third of the funds actually expended on cleanup (Noah, 1993; Menell, 1991). Yet, by 1993 EPA had recovered only $829 million of the $4.3 billion in government expenditures that it had sought to collect from PRPs (*New York Times,* 1993). And "by mid-1990, . . . after 10 years of program operation, only sixty-three of the more than twelve hundred National Priorities List sites had been cleaned up" (Church and Nakamura, 1993: 129).

The opportunity costs engendered by adversarial and legalistic methods of regulation also impede the issuance and implementation of well-founded new regulations. Confronted with statutory demands for analytical perfection and with the prospect of lengthy appeals and judicial scrutiny of their decisions, OSHA and EPA officials delayed for years the promulgation of new regulations concerning workplace health hazards and toxic air pollutants while they struggled to find the money and the time to commission more research and conduct legally defensible cost-benefit analyses (Mendeloff, 1987; Dwyer, 1990). And as described by Mashaw and Harfst (1991), the National Traffic Safety Agency's motor vehicle safety rules were so often appealed to the courts and subjected to further demands for new tests and justifications that the agency partially retreated from issuing design standards altogether.

Divisiveness

One of adversarial legalism's more intangible costs is its corrosive effect on personal and institutional relationships. When a regulatory inspector and a regulated enterprise become locked in an adversarial posture, exchange of information and cooperation, so essential to effective regulation, are often reduced (Bardach and Kagan, 1982). Comparing U.S., British, and Australian nursing home regulation, Braithwaite (1993: 17) observed, "American nursing homes have higher fire safety standards than Australian nursing homes, better food and nutrition standards than English nursing homes, . . . better care planning, and more varied activities." But overall, Braithwaite (id. at 15–16) concluded, quality of care in the United States is worse, primarily because the highly prescriptive and legalistic American enforcement system elicits a defensive, legalistic approach to compliance rather than a fully cooperative response. Most disturbingly, he writes:

> Ask the complaints coordinator in an Australian state to tell you the worst abuse case they have known in the past year and most tell a story of a nasty shoving or bruising incident. To the follow-up question, "Haven't you had a worse case than that? What about someone punching or slapping a resident?" some answer, "No we haven't had a complaint like that since I started in the job." Ask the same question of people in a comparable position in the United States, and they often tell a story of the murder of a nursing home resident by a staff member. . . . They will tell a story of rape of an elderly woman or of stuffing a washcloth with feces on it in the mouth of a ninety year old woman. . . . In the United States, 197 individuals were convicted criminally in 1989 for abuse of nursing home residents; there have been no such criminal cases in Australia during the five years of our study.

More routinely, Braithwaite and colleagues found, legalistic and potentially punitive American nursing home regulation has encouraged a "ritualistic" bureaucratized attitude toward compliance, oriented to meeting the letter of the law rather than its ultimate purposes. After sitting in on meetings that included a facility director of nursing, a dietician, and a quality assurance coordinator (a position required by law), Braithwaite (1993: 41) observed, "The question that holds center stage during quality assurance meetings is not, 'What is the best way to design this program to deliver maximum improvement in quality of care?' It is, 'What is it that they [the regulators] want of us here? What is the minimum we have to do to satisfy the requirement of having a quality assurance program?'" Defensiveness is also manifested in a disturbingly high incidence of falsification of medical and other records in order to avoid violations (ibid.). Finally, Braithwaite (id. at 37–38) noted that legalistically enforced prescriptive regulations, which often govern "inputs" (facility design, staffing, programmed routines, and documentation) rather than goals, tend to discourage innovation:

> [I]f an Australian nursing home achieves good outcomes for residents with staffing levels that are below the industry average, or with professionally unqualified staff, regulators might applaud this as cost-efficient accomplishment of the outcomes. Notwithstanding the rhetoric of out-

come-orientation, regulatory practice in the United States will punish nursing homes that skimp on staffing inputs or that fail to use staff with mandated professional qualifications, regardless of resident outcomes.

Similar observations pervade comparative studies of other regulatory programs. Comparing "Q Corp.'s" environmental compliance programs at its factories in the United States and Japan, Aoki, Kagan, and Axelrad (2000) say, "One can think of [environmental managers in the U.S. plant] as playing legal defense instead of playing environmental offense. Q Japan officials have more time to do the latter." They go on (id. at 83):

> Whereas Q Japan environmental officials express dismay that Q USA has actually violated the law on occasion, Q USA officials, while clearly committed to the goals of environmental protection, seem to regard occasional violations of particular regulatory rules as something close to inevitable and as something less than shameful. In the U.S., where legal penalties often are imposed for unintentional violations that do not entail serious harm, the social stigma attached to a regulatory "violation" seems less severe than in Japan, where sanctions are reserved for serious violations.

> In Japan, we conclude, the regulatory regime appears to have gathered greater "normative gravity," partly because Q Japan officials view it as comprehensible, reasonable and predictable. This appears to facilitate the internalization of regulatory norms by operating managers and workers. The fluctuating, polycentric character of the American regime, in contrast, seems to *impair* the law's normative gravity (although not its threat) and to make it more difficult for regulatory norms and the idea of perfect compliance to permeate the corporate culture and the planning process.

The defensiveness stimulated by adversarial legalism also impedes U.S. administrators' efforts to institutionalize more cooperative modes of regulation. One of the most heralded of such programs is EPA's "Project XL," announced in a 1995 Clinton administration document, *Reinventing Environmental Regulation*. It authorizes state regulatory agencies to conclude agreements with regulated businesses under which, in return for relief from highly prescriptive regulatory requirements, the enterprise institutes performance-oriented pollution reduction methods that promise "superior" environmental benefits. The enterprise also must make public detailed records of its actual environmental performance and update goals in light of experience.[12] But progress in reaching Project XL agreements has been painfully slow. Although EPA set an initial goal of fifty projects, by the end of 1997 only seven had been finally approved, with twelve under development. The reason is that they take place in the shadow of adversarial legalism. Regulators must guard against the charge that they are casting aside the law to accommodate a polluter. Each of the scores of legal waivers for particular prescriptive regulations must be arduously negotiated. A negotiation between EPA and 3M Corporation broke down in part because "EPA could not provide 3M with satisfactory assurances that compliance with XL would immunize the company from civil liability for technical violations of existing statutes" (Dorf and Sabel, 1998: 384–385). Opposition from environmental advocacy groups, which often are reluctant to give up the power they gain from prescriptive rules and rights to litigate, almost scuttled EPA's showcase Project XL agreement with Intel (Skryzcki, 1997; Freeman, 1997: 61–66, 73).

Similarly, several American states have encouraged regulated companies to adopt programs of self-audits for compliance with environmental regulations by granting them immunity from prosecution if self-detected violations are promptly disclosed and corrected. But EPA has objected that such laws should not exempt the company from fines or *federal* prosecution in certain cases, and surveys suggest that prospects of criminal liability and private lawsuits have inhibited the expansion of corporate self-audit and disclosure programs (Adler, 1998: 40, 45–46). Large American companies thus have lagged well behind their counterparts in Europe and Japan in seeking certification of corporate environmental programs under the International Standards Organization's ISO 14000 program, which commits companies to certifiable environmental management and pollution reduction programs. The lag is at least partly due to the much more legalistic and threatening regulatory environment firms must deal with in the United States (Delmas, 2000; Aoki et al., 2000).[13]

This is not to say that all efforts to institute more cooperative modes of regulation in the United States founder, for many successful examples do exist (Rees, 1988; Weber, 1998). Rather, the point is that a regulatory system structured by adversarial legalism makes it particularly difficult to institutionalize more informal cooperative methods, and that the defensiveness it engenders often keeps American regulation from reaching the gains that would flow from cooperation (Brickman et al., 1985: 27; Wallace, 1995: 111).

Compared to other economically advanced democracies, the United States has been remarkably successful in fostering vibrant financial markets, promoting innovation and entrepreneurial activity, facilitating industrial restructuring, and creating new jobs. However costly American social regulation may be, the country's economic record suggests that adversarial legalism's negative economic effects have not been so large as to squelch investment in the United States or to undermine the competitiveness of American business as a whole. It may even have some positive economic effects. Compared to the closed-door decisionmaking methods of many other nations, American adversarial legalism provides both domestic and foreign companies greater assurance that they are competing on a relatively level regulatory playing field and that they have legal recourse against official arbitrariness or favoritism. In a nation that distrusts both government and corporate power, some observers argue, adversarial legalism helps legitimate the regulatory process because it emphasizes legal accountability, transparency, and rights of public participation.

Nor should we overglamorize the regulatory systems of other countries. It would not be difficult for those knowledgeable about particular regulatory problems to point to instances or entire regulatory arenas in which American regulation is considerably more effective and efficient, or in which other countries' regulatory regimes are poorly enforced. That said, it does not follow that adversarial and legalistic regulation is optimal for the United States. Even in a successful economy, wasteful legally imposed expenditures and regulatory uncertainties are troublesome. The United States benefits from the enormous market it offers both American and foreign businesses; they cannot afford to abandon the United States even if its regulatory system is especially costly. But those "extra" costs, even if they do not sink a dynamic economy, are often very significant for particular firms and generally wealth-depleting for the society as a whole. Regulatory waste and inefficiency are just as undesirable in the economic realm as governmental waste and inefficiency are in military procurement or highway building.

Even more significant, perhaps, are the social and political costs of adversarial regulation. Legalistic enforcement may be necessary for some firms and for some departments in larger firms, but there is little hard evidence that American businesses, overall, are less cooperative than businesses in other economically advanced democracies. Indeed, lack of cooperation between regulators and regulated enterprises often appears to be a *consequence* of adversarial legalism. In its prescriptiveness, punitiveness, and formalization of business-government relationships, American adversarial legalism induces mutual resentment, defensiveness, and mistrust. It thereby discourages the kind of cooperation that is essential to the full achievement of regulatory goals, and it gives regulation a bad name, making it more difficult to adopt justifiable new regulatory programs and rules. That is its most serious consequence.

10

Economic Development, Environmental Protection, and Adversarial Legalism

During the eighteenth century agricultural production in England and France lagged behind growing populations. Concerned about maintaining political stability, the central governments in both countries strove to increase food supplies. One obvious strategy was to increase agricultural efficiency by privatizing communally held lands. Another was to extend the amount of land under cultivation by draining and reclaiming low-lying areas (and in France by building irrigation projects as well). In England, as described in Jean-Laurent Rosenthal's *The Fruits of Revolution,* these programs moved ahead rapidly. The plans of the French monarchy, however, were almost completely stymied by an eighteenth-century version of adversarial legalism (Rosenthal, 1992).[1]

In France local opponents of irrigation and reclamation projects repeatedly brought lawsuits against the developers who had been chartered by the royal government. Litigation over each project typically lasted for years. Judges had to slog through a confusing legal tangle of ill-defined feudal property rights, local privileges, and easements. Project opponents who lost in one court often appealed to another, extending the litigation until the developer simply gave up (id. at 44–47, 86–87, 132). When the royal government in Paris sought to replace the lengthy judicial proceedings with a streamlined administrative process, a fragmented welter of politically entrenched local courts, church authorities, nobles, and local governments managed to block the reforms (id. at 138, 167, 177).

In England, conversely, property rights were relatively clear, as were legal rules for compensating the dispossessed. The Kings' Bench—judges trained in the Inns of Court in London and paid by the Crown—applied the law relatively consistently. Agricultural development projects moved ahead in France only after the French Revolution established the legal and political primacy of the National Assembly and of a strong, hierarchically organized, central bureaucracy. Sweeping aside feudal rules, the revolutionary government systematized the law of property. Proposals for draining communally held lands were subjected to an up-or-down vote by village councils (id. at 32). Disputes were channeled into administrative offices. The central government took over the finance and supervision of the judiciary, which henceforth emphasized legal predictability and tended to defer to the national legislature and the central bureaucracy on matters of policy.[2]

While the French Revolution was centralizing political authority and diminishing the centrifugal influence of locally responsive courts, the American Revolution was expressing an entirely different spirit. The American revolutionaries wanted to *limit* the power of a distant central government. The federal and the state constitutions established a large measure of autonomy for democratically elected local governments. They guaranteed individual and property rights against governmental abridgment, and to enforce those rights the Americans *fortified* judicial power. By insisting on trial by jury and on local selection of judges, they also made the courts responsive to community values and interests.

The centrifugal impulses of the American Revolution help account for some surprising analogies between eighteenth-century France and the contemporary United States. Here too, local and philosophical opponents of change often institute sequential lawsuits against ostensibly valuable development projects—efforts to build highways, drill oilfields, implement forestry plans, open waste disposal facilities, and construct new factories. As in eighteenth-century France, litigation drags on—and projects are delayed, abandoned, or made more costly—because adjudicatory processes are both slow and legally unpredictable. Like the French judiciary of the eighteenth century, American judges enjoy a large measure of independence from the central government, as well as from state government, and are willing to challenge decisions of governmental planners. In the contemporary United States adversarial legalism likewise arises from the fragmentation of governmental authority.

New construction projects, of course, are not always unmitigated boons. Infrastructural improvements, however beneficial for the collectivity, can disrupt neighborhoods, harm local ecosystems, and desecrate places of beauty. By the end of the twentieth century, swamp drainage and reclamation, even for agricultural uses, has come to be viewed by many as heedless destruction of rapidly vanishing, environmentally essential wetlands. As in eighteenth-century France, local communities often oppose development projects, crying NIMBY—"not in my back yard." In democracies, government officials, concerned about reelection, structure decisionmaking to accommodate those concerns. In the early 1990s, according to a comparative study by Jeffery Sellers (1995), local opponents of development projects filed legal appeals in Germany and in France (albeit in specialized administrative courts) about as often as they did in the United States.

The United States, however, remains unique in the *extent* to which adversarial legalism shapes the struggle between continuity and change, between environmental protection and economic growth. American developers, Sellers noted, are far more likely than their French or German counterparts to be accompanied by lawyers at every step of the planning process. American businesses, public interest advocacy groups, and municipal governments are far more likely than their French (or German or Japanese) counterparts to haul the central government into court. Armed with the weapons of adversarial legalism, proponents of the status quo can insist on the rational justification of governmental permits for still more highways and dams, ski slopes, shopping centers, and beachfront resorts. Because adversarial legalism can subject new projects and policies to sober second thought, they often are changed for the better.

But not always. Adversarial legalism, as emphasized throughout this book, has two faces. It also can make planning *less* rational. As in the Oakland Harbor dredging saga described in Chapter 2, adversarial legalism means that decisions sometimes are shaped less by rational analysis than by a panicky scramble to avoid the risks, delays, and costs of extended, legally unpredictable litigation. When threatened with litigation, project developers often feel compelled to make expensive side-payments demanded by local or ideological opponents. Some of these side-payments are justifiable "mitigations" of environmental or social harms caused by the project, but some are "exactions" that simply dip into the perceived deep pockets of the developer for public goods that the community has not been willing to pay for itself. Faced with the prospect of litigation, governmental planners often retreat into legal defensiveness, postponing desirable public initiatives. Trying to ensure governmental accountability through adversarial legalism is an inherently clumsy method of striking a sensible balance between environmental and economic development concerns, for it often results in outcomes that are shaped less by rational dialogue than by agonizing, lengthy wars of legal attrition. This chapter explores that phenomenon and discusses why it is so deeply entrenched in the American way of governance.

Adversarial Legalism in Action: The Los Angeles Century Freeway

The Century Freeway was designed to link Los Angeles Airport in West Los Angeles with communities and freeways to the east. After receiving federal funding for the Century Freeway in 1968, the state highway department (Caltrans) moved rapidly to acquire property along the seventeen-mile right-of-way, relocate displaced families, seek construction bids, and negotiate agreements with the several municipalities through which the roadway would pass. (Each municipality's consent is legally necessary when highways, as is often the case, require local street closures.) In early 1972, however, the Center for Law in the Public Interest filed a federal class action against state and federal transportation agencies—Caltrans and the U.S. Department of Transportation (DOT)—on behalf of people who lived along the freeway path. The Center's legal complaint was joined by other parties: the city of Hawthorne, which had a politically active neighborhood group that was upset about the thought of a highway carving up its area; the Sierra Club and the Environmental Defense Fund, which argued that the highway was environmentally unsound; and the NAACP, which argued that the choice of route denied minority communities and families the equal protection of the law (Hebert, 1972; Detlefsen, 1995: 20; 1994).

In terms of prior precedent, none of the plaintiffs' legal arguments were very strong. The Center for Law in the Public Interest argued that Caltrans and the DOT had not circulated an environmental impact statement (EIS) evaluating the project, as required by the National Environmental Policy Act (NEPA). Caltrans and DOT responded that NEPA had been enacted in 1969, *after* the Century Freeway project had been approved, and their lawyers had determined that its requirements were not applicable to the Century Freeway project. In any case, Caltrans and DOT argued, their environmental analysis had in fact been adequate.[3] Because the equal protection and other constitutional claims seemed rather far-fetched, Caltrans lawyers felt sure they would prevail on the merits. Nevertheless, U.S. District Court Judge Harry Pregerson issued a preliminary injunction against further property acquisition and ordered Caltrans to prepare an EIS.

The preparation and circulation of the EIS took from 1972 to 1978. During that time, work on the Century Freeway remained on hold. By the time of the 1972 injunction, 60 percent of the parcels had been acquired, and relocation funds had been paid to displaced residents. One-third of the right-of-way had been cleared, leaving large deserted areas that during the pendency of the litigation became sites for crime and illegal trash disposal. Local, state, and federal officials urged Caltrans to get the project completed. However, California's liberal governor Jerry Brown, elected in 1974, appointed a Caltrans director who was generally opposed to any further highway construction in Los Angeles (Detlefsen, 1994). Hence in 1979 Caltrans (over the objections of its senior engineers and planners) settled the litigation via a consent decree that made major concessions to the plaintiffs.

Two lanes of the planned highway were to be reserved for buses and multipassenger vans. Caltrans and the federal government would finance construction of 4,200 new housing units in the communities through which the freeway would pass, at an estimated cost of $300 million—even though most displaced residents presumably had already found new housing. (The originally budgeted cost of the freeway had been $500 million.)[4] In addition, the consent decree, as formulated under Judge Pregerson's auspices, provided for an elaborate affirmative action plan and an employment center, supervised by a plaintiff-dominated committee and paid for by Caltrans, using state and federal highway funds. The decree splintered the highway construction project into eighty-four contracts and subcontracts, which presumably would make it more feasible to hire companies owned by women and minorities (Hebert, 1986: 4). Minority hiring goals, based on the proportion of minorities in the freeway corridor, were fixed for each construction trade on all freeway and housing construction projects, bolstered by an apprenticeship program to be funded by Caltrans. Detailed rules were established to help plaintiffs' counsel hold Caltrans to the agreed-upon goals.

A decade of often acrimonious judicial hearings ensued, revolving around the implementation, interpretation, and amendment of the consent decree. Despite the judicial mandate commanding cooperation among the parties, an adversarial spirit prevailed. Although hardly anyone, including the communities along the route, thought that the Century Freeway should *not* be built, the freeway was not completed until 1993, more than twenty years after Judge Pregerson's injunction. One can scarcely imagine the intervening financial, environmental, and emotional harm engendered by thousands of pollution-spewing traffic jams.[5] Pursuant to demands made by plaintiffs in implementing the consent decree, one of the planned high occupancy vehicle lanes was converted to provide for a light rail system, although transportation planners doubted it would prove to be cost-effective. Between 1972 and 1986 the Center for Law in the Public Interest collected more than $2 million in legal fees.

The overall cost of the project ballooned to approximately $2.2 billion (Reinhold, 1993). Construction and administrative costs for the housing program were grossly inflated (Trombley and Hebert, 1987a, 1987b). Caltrans funds ultimately provided not only job training programs for minorities but tutoring and scholarships for poor children and housing for AIDS patients in West Hollywood, ten miles from the freeway (Reinhold, 1993). All in all, actual highway construction accounted for only 54 percent of the project's total cost. Even without those "extras," construction costs for the highway itself, burdened by the scores of separate contracts and subcontracts demanded by the affirmative action portions of the consent decree, reached over $100 million a mile, "more per mile than any other road in American history" (ibid.).[6] The Century Freeway consent decree drained Caltrans's budget, curtailing projects elsewhere in the state. California sank to last place among the fifty states in new highway construction.

The Century Freeway is not the only highway to be reshaped by litigation, and hence even the threat of a lawsuit sometimes suffices. After years of planning, for example, transportation officials in Boston obtained federal and state funding to build a third tunnel across Boston Harbor to ameliorate an infamously congested traffic pattern, together with a new, depressed highway through the city, replacing unsightly and outmoded elevated roadways. The officials' environmental analysis showed that the new tunnel/artery, by reducing congestion, would significantly improve air quality. However, the Conservation Law Foundation (CLF) opposed the project, contending that the new freeway ultimately would worsen pollution by drawing more cars onto the roads (Stipp, 1991). Backed by a number of transportation and environmental groups, CLF threatened to sue unless the Federal Highway Administration compelled project planners to institute a very costly set of traffic-cutting measures. To ward off such litigation, which threatened to unravel the delicately balanced web of political commitments supporting the plan, the Massachusetts Environmental Affairs Secretary conditioned his 1990 certificate of approval on a series of "environmental mitigation" projects demanded by CLF, including improvements to Boston's rapid transit rail system. Research showed that these measures not only would add some $3.6 billion to the project's original $5 billion cost but would be extremely inefficient ways to reduce pollution (Palmer, 1994). Other municipalities, environmental agencies, and neighborhood groups followed CLF's example, using the threat of litigation to extract an additional $2.8 billion for "mitigation projects," many of them rather far removed from any direct impacts of the tunnel/artery project.[7] As in the Century Freeway saga, adversarial legalism served primarily as a mechanism through which particular interests could extort public funds, while delaying widely demanded public works and injecting less, not more, rationality into the search for a sensible balance between economic development and environmental protection.

Why Adversarial Legalism Pervades Economic Development

Not every American development project or plan, of course, is held up and distorted by litigation. Sometimes politically skillful governmental officials invoke the specter of costly adversarial legalism to bring project proponents and opponents together and forge an acceptable compromise (Busch, Kirp, and Schoenholz, 1999; Kagan, 1997b: 872). Sometimes adversarial legalism remains dormant because potential opponents lack the knowledge, organization, or resources to bring lawsuits, even against very questionable projects (Foster, 1998). Sometimes the threat or the mere possibility of a lawsuit leads directly to project changes that are clearly desirable, both economically and socially.

Yet the Century Freeway saga, like the Oakland Harbor dredging story in Chapter 2, is far from unique. Scores of proposed waste disposal projects, from municipal landfills (Welles and Engel, 2000) to badly needed sites for both low-level (Gunnison, 1993) and high-level nuclear wastes (Topol, 1991; Deese, 1982), have been halted or delayed and subjected to large side-payments as a result of lawsuits filed by neighborhood groups and advocacy organizations. Litigation by an unrepresentative local group, while ultimately rejected by the appellate courts, halted funding for the Bronx Community Paper Company's innovative recycling plant, a project backed by both the National Resources Defense Council and a popular grassroots organization that was eager for the jobs the plant would bring to a depressed area (Harris, 1995: 32–40). It would be years before the project, then scaled back, could be refinanced. In the 1980s and 1990s a seemingly endless series of adversarial regulatory hearings, appeals, and lawsuits kept Chevron from shipping petroleum from a giant oil well and a recovery station at Point Arguello on the California coast—notwithstanding support from the U.S. Department of Energy and Chevron's expenditure of more than $2 billion on the project, including $100 million in additional environmental safeguards and mitigation projects demanded by local governments (Lee, 1990: D1; Lucas, 1990; Benedict, 1993).

During the 1980s virtually every Forest Service plan for particular forests was held up by legal challenge and appellate review, either in administrative forums or in the courts or both (*The Economist*, 1990). Lawyers for environmental advocacy groups used a blizzard of lawsuits in the early 1990s to bring logging to a virtual halt on extensive forest lands managed by the U.S. Forest Service and the Bureau of Land Management in the Pacific Northwest, arguing that timber harvesting would destroy habitats essential to the northern spotted owl.[8] Timber production and employment declined precipitously. The timber industry appealed to Congress for bills that allowed them back into the forests, which stimulated new lawsuits that blocked logging once again (Sher, 1993; Axline, 1996). In the 1970s and 1980s the construction of nuclear power plants in the United States was slowed to a crawl, then abandoned, but not because elected governments or even the public decided to reject nuclear power; American voters generally *rejected* ballot measures designed to block nuclear power plants (Boyle, 1998: 153). Like eighteenth-century France's marsh drainage program, American efforts to license nuclear plants were so often tied up in lengthy litigation by opponents that project sponsors, burdened by endless legal and financial uncertainty, often simply gave up.[9] Conversely, business firms have often turned to adversarial legalism to obstruct environmental measures that seek to change business practices—as when corporate sugar growers used litigation to block a federal government plan to restore the Florida Everglades by flooding huge sugar plantations built on former wetlands (McKinley, 1999).

In sum, the threat of adversarial legalism of the kind exemplified by the Century Freeway story is always present in the United States. It persists, despite outraged protests by elected officials who find their laboriously assembled plans stymied in court, because it reflects three distinctive features of American law and governance: reliance on (or at least provision for) *litigation to ensure governmental accountability;* court-enforceable *statutory demands for comprehensive environmental analysis* as a precondition to developmental action; and *high levels of legal uncertainty.* Those three features, in turn, arise from the confluence of the two basic factors referred to repeatedly in this book: *the distrust and consequent fragmentation of governmental authority* in the United States, combined with *powerful political demands for governmental action* to solve social problems.

Accountability through Lawsuits

In all economically advanced democracies, highway planning officials are expected to consider the interests of affected local communities, to analyze the impacts of various alternatives, to mitigate environmental disruption, to pay compensation and provide relocation assistance to displaced property owners along the right-of-way, and to act honestly and fairly in awarding construction contracts. In most democratic countries officials are held accountable to those standards primarily by administrative supervision and political oversight. Opposition political parties and the news media play an additional watchdog role. Thus in the Century Freeway and the Boston Tunnel cases, highway planners had to prepare detailed cost-benefit and environmental analyses. They had to defend their choices to superiors in the state capital and to the DOT in Washington, to legislative appropriations committees, and, in mandatory public meetings, to the community and the press. But far more than other democracies, the United States employs an additional accountability mechanism: litigation (and the threat of litigation).

Because of the unusually broad American rules concerning "standing to sue," virtually any interested party—including the world's widest array of public interest lawyers, acting as self-appointed "private attorneys general"—can bring lawsuits against alleged violations of public law. Thus in the Century Freeway case, the motive force was The Center for Law in the Public Interest, not particular clients. In the Boston Tunnel Project story, the Conservation Law Foundation, with hardly a mention of who its client might be, threatened to sue the agencies that financed the project. In its efforts to protect Northwest forests from logging, the Sierra Club Legal Defense Fund, adopting the spotted owl as its client, waged a sustained litigation campaign against many federal agencies, and ultimately was awarded some $1.2 million in attorneys' fees pursuant to the Equal Access to Justice Act. Conversely, far more than in other countries, *proponents* of development projects in the United States also use the courts, invoking federal law or constitutional provisions to challenge regulatory restrictions by governmental units. Timber companies, for example, petitioned the courts to overturn the Fish and Wildlife Service's decision to treat diminution of the spotted owl's habitat as a "taking" under the Endangered Species Act. The Port of Oakland sued a local water district for raising what a court ultimately ruled were legally unfounded objections to a dredged-material disposal plan.

Accountability through litigation both reflects and reinforces the extraordinary power of American courts. The United States is distinctive, Mirjan Damaska (1990: 424–425) emphasizes, in granting politically selected lower court judges the power to overturn decisions made by high officials of the central government, and in perpetuating a legal culture in which even lower court judges do not "shy away from deciding matters of great political importance . . . ; being people in their second career, relatively unconcerned about promotions, they make use of these powers in a comparatively bold manner." In the Oakland Harbor case, a state court judge halted dredging disposal operations that had been authorized by the U.S. Army Corps of Engineers, the EPA, various state agencies, and a federal court. A federal trial court judge, rejecting the environmental analyses of Forest Service experts, banned logging in thousands of acres of federal lands in the Pacific Northwest. In sum, when decentralized litigation becomes a primary method of ensuring governmental accountability, individual judges, for good or ill, can foil the plans of democratically elected governments.

The Slow-Motion Search for Comprehensive Rationality

Under the Marine Protection, Research, and Sanctuaries Act the EPA has authority to designate an ocean disposal site for dredged material, but the agency must first make official findings concerning:

(A) The need for the proposed dumping; (B) The effect of such dumping on human health and welfare, including economic, esthetic and recreational values; (C) The effect of such dumping on fisheries resources, plankton, fish, shellfish, wildlife, shore lines and beaches; (D) The effect of such dumping on marine ecosystems, particularly with respect to (i) the transfer, concentration and dispersion of such material and its byproducts through biological, physical and chemical processes, (ii) potential changes in marine ecosystem diversity, productivity, and stability, and (iii) species and community population dynamics; (E) The persistence and permanence of the effects of the dumping; (F) The effect of dumping particular volumes and concentrations of such materials; (G) Appropriate locations and methods of disposal or recycling . . . ; (H) The effect on alternate uses of oceans, such as scientific study, fishing, and other living resource exploitation, and nonliving resource exploitation.

The U.S. Army Corps of Engineers may issue a dredging permit when it would meet "the public interest," but federal regulations say the Corps must first consider and weigh

[a]ll factors which may be relevant . . . including the cumulative effects thereof: among these are conservation, economics, aesthetics, general environmental concerns, wetlands, historic properties, fish and wildlife values, food hazards, land use, navigation, shore erosion and accretion, recreation, water supply and conservation, water quality, energy needs, safety, food and fiber production, mineral needs, considerations of property ownership and, in general, the needs and welfare of the people.[10]

These legal demands for careful study and evaluation before public action reflect the ideal of *comprehensive rationality*. Who would not want government to look before it leaps? Shouldn't we expect project planners to attend to all the values and interests at stake and gather all the relevant facts? Well, perhaps not *all* the facts. As decision theorists such as Herbert Simon and Charles Lindblom have explained, *fully* complying with the demands of comprehensive rationality typically entails intolerable costs, both in money and delay (Simon, 1957; Braybrooke and Lindblom, 1963).

In the Oakland Harbor case, described in Chapter 2, for example, the EPA could not make the "findings" required by the statute quoted above until Congress appropriated the millions of dollars needed to do the requisite research—funds for which other socially useful programs also were clamoring. Even after the funds are authorized, research is usually painstakingly slow and costly.[11] By 1991, after four years of environmental impact analysis, expenditures by the Port of Oakland and the Corps of Engineers on sediment sampling and testing had reached almost $4 million, the equivalent of $8 a cubic yard for Phase I of the dredging project—more than the physical act of Phase I dredging ultimately cost. And since relevant research methodologies are adversarially scrutinized, scientific controversy erupted at every step, further delaying the regulatory and legal decision processes.

American laws demand comprehensive analysis but they also display an abiding distrust of the analysts. Thus the Corps of Engineers, before granting a harbor dredging permit, must submit its analyses to and "consult with" a variety of other agencies—the U.S. Fish and Wildlife Service (statutory guardian for migratory birds, fisheries, and threatened and endangered species), the National Marine Fisheries Service, the relevant *state* Department of Fish and Game, both federal and state environmental protection and water pollution control agencies, and the state Coastal Zone Management Agency. Each of those agencies, in turn, is legally bound to file evaluations of the project in terms of the agency's own particular governing statute, and to object to the Corps of Engineers' analysis if they find it wanting. In addition, relevant studies and plans often must be made available for public review and public hearings. Objections from other agencies and advocacy groups must be recorded and given a formal, reasoned response.[12]

In practice, the ideal of comprehensively rational analysis rarely can be fully achieved. Perfect research is too expensive. There is no methodology by which agencies can rationally find the "correct" balance among the multiplicity of factors they are legally supposed to take into account. Administrative decisionmakers, therefore, often just muddle through. They make a rough "guestimate" based on the information obtainable within a reasonable period of time (Braybrooke and Lindblom, 1963; March and Simon, 1958). They try to strike reasonable compromises among conflicting values. But when the law demands comprehensive rationality, including the filing of specific scientific findings, guestimates and compromises may not be good enough. Any private advocacy organization, any affected local government, any competing agency that objects to a particular compromise decision can challenge it in court. Adversarial legal procedures ensure embarrassing exposure of the inevitable gaps in the project planners' analysis or of their incompletely rationalized "satisficing" judgments.

Quixotic, judicially enforceable statutory demands for analytic perfection thus provide sturdy footholds for project opponents and delaying lawsuits. The Conservation Law Foundation's threatened lawsuit against the Boston Artery and Tunnel project was based on a challenge to the highway department's analysis concluding that reductions in congestion would reduce air pollution (Stipp, 1991). Environmental organizations and allied scientists pointed out defects in the environmental analyses and spotted owl protection plans formulated by the U.S. Forest Service, inducing judges to enjoin logging until more and presumably better analyses were adopted.

Aware of such stories, agency officials and project planners view litigation as an ever-present threat. Perhaps it won't materialize, but if it does, it could delay the start of the project by at least another year, perhaps more. In consequence, agencies expend a great deal of time and resources on "defensive science," striving to make their decisions judicially bulletproof. Transportation agencies trying to build a toll road near San Diego (the first new highway to be constructed in the increasingly traffic-jammed county in decades) produced more than 100 volumes of environmental impact reports, hoping to repel the legal challenges that environmental groups eventually filed in both state and federal courts and with the U.S. Fish and Wildlife Service (which was asked to block the road-building by declaring the California gnatcatcher an endangered species). Outside the courthouse, opponents of the San Diego toll road announced to supporters and the press that their goal was to stop the planned freeway (as well as any alternative routes) entirely. But their lawyers' arguments in the courthouse focused not on the basic policy debates concerning transportation or enhancement of air quality but on claimed defects in the environmental analyses (Fulton, 1992).

Legal Unpredictability

The threat of litigation is not terribly problematic when the law is clear and the adjudicative process is expeditious and predictable. When confronted with a legally meritorious claim, a rational defendant would leap to comply. If the defendant asserts a legally sustainable defense, the rational plaintiff would save his time and money. But in the American legal system, as we have seen, legal certainty is elusive. In the Century Freeway case, Caltrans officials and their lawyers felt sure that they had complied with the applicable laws and that the constitutional claims advanced by the NAACP and women's advocacy groups, viewed in light of existing legal precedents, were rather farfetched. But Judge Pregerson issued a preliminary injunction, pending trial. Caltrans officials still felt they would prevail after a full trial. The trial never occurred, for Caltrans came under intense political pressure to settle, and the Caltrans officials could not really be sure that they would have won in court.

Legal uncertainty abounds in the United States because surprising judicial decisions abound. In the Bronx Community Paper Company case, the National Resources Defense Council was assured by three law firms that the project was legally solid, only to lose in court. (An appellate court eventually reversed that decision, but by then project sponsors had withdrawn funding promises.) In the Pacific Northwest forest controversy, there were conflicting views of what the law required among district court judges, between district courts and the Ninth Circuit Court of Appeals, among judges on the Ninth Circuit, and between the Supreme Court and the lower courts.

The legal disagreement and uncertainty arose partly because American law governing land use and environmental protection, viewed in cross-national comparison, is both extraordinarily complex and extraordinarily vague (or as legal scholars often put it, "indeterminate"). The *complexity* of American law reflects the characteristic fragmentation of governmental authority in the United States: to secure permission to transport petroleum from Point Arguello, Chevron had to obtain approvals from no less than forty-four federal, state, regional, and local governmental bodies—each applying its own statutes, regulations, and ordinances. The *indeterminacy* of U.S. environmental law arises in large measure from the method of lawmaking in American legislative bodies, which tend to be more politically permeable than legislatures in parliamentary systems and to operate on a more ad hoc basis. American environmental laws are drafted by fractious legislative committees, responding to particular crises and to crosscutting political pressures. Lobbyists corner committee members to push for last-minute amendments. A motor vehicle manufacturing company official, reflecting on his experience with Congress when it was enacting standards for hydrocarbon emissions, complained: "You'll never tell me . . . this process of running around the hall in and out of a conference committee at 11 o'clock at night . . . is a rational process. The people bartering on what the emission levels should be on automobiles wouldn't know a hydrocarbon if they tripped over it. . . . But there they are, [saying] 'I'll give you this, if you give me that.' It's almost like you're out in Nevada." (Dimento, 1986: 118–119).

Legislators seeking to build a winning coalition offer specific protections, exceptions, or rights to particular constituencies, and the legislation that emerges therefore often lacks coherence. Despite their mind-numbing detail, politically cobbled-together environmental statutes often leave undefined the most crucial issues—such as what counts as an "endangered" species, or whether habitat diminution amounts to a "taking" of an endangered species. And this too, as we have seen, means that policy disputes end up in court, where a diverse array of judges decide the issues, albeit with little finality.

Legal unpredictability is exacerbated by the politically selected American judiciary. In most other democracies the professionally selected and evaluated judiciary treats legal consistency as a preeminent ideal. In the United States many judges do value consistency, but to many others achieving justice in the particular case (or acquiring a reputation for being a compassionate or creative judge) is even more important. Individual judges who feel strongly about a policy issue, such as Judge Pregerson in the Century Freeway case, do not hesitate to turn their feelings into law.

Legal variability and malleability encourage continued adversarial struggle. As in the Oakland Harbor case and the Northwest logging disputes, interests that lose a policy battle in one agency or court may try another, or run to the legislature to seek ad hoc "corrective" legislation, for there is almost always a chance that a different decisionmaker will be more responsive. Thus to the participants in these controversies, "the law" often appears to be simply an arena for ongoing political struggle, not the authoritative normative anchor that it represents in most other democratic nations.

Fragmented Government and Adversarial Legalism

Many American politicians and scholars have been troubled by the role of adversarial legalism in American economic and environmental governance. The U.S. Advisory Commission on Intergovernmental Relations (1992) reported that badly needed "new highways, airports, . . . wastewater treatment plants, and solid waste facilities" have frequently been subjected to immensely costly delays because "federal rules and procedures governing decisionmaking for protecting the environment often are complex, conflicting, difficult to apply, adversarial, costly, inflexible, and uncertain." Yet the same politicians who are disturbed when their programs are bogged down by litigation rarely take a public stand against legal rights to challenge national bureaucracies in court. President Clinton sought to lift the economically devastating judicial injunctions against logging in the Pacific Northwest by proposing a grand political compromise, but neither he nor a Republican Congress curtailed private rights to sue the government under the Endangered Species Act or curtailed judges' authority to rewrite U.S. Forest Service plans.

Underlying this pattern, as emphasized throughout this book, are the tensions generated by a political culture that demands "total justice"—active governmental protection from harm, injustice, and environmental degradation—but remains highly mistrustful of governmental authority. Responding to electoral pressures, politicians of both parties repeatedly endorse ambitious regulatory goals, but they also insist, again in response to political traditions and pressures, that governmental regulatory authority be structurally fragmented, procedurally checked, scientifically grounded, and legally constrained. Policies intended to control hazardous technologies and other sources of harm are therefore forced through the complex gates of detailed legal prescriptions, legalistic enforcement, adversarial litigation, demanding scientific and economic analyses, and judicial oversight.

The reasons for the persistence of American adversarial legalism are highlighted by comparing the United States with its neighbor to the north. Like the United States, Canada is geographically huge, environmentally diverse, and politically decentralized, with strong provincial governments. Canada has large and active environmental advocacy groups, and its environmental policies address the same issues as those covered by U.S. law (Hoberg, 1991: 107–131; Harrison and Hoberg, 1991: 3–28).[13] As in the United States, Canadian communities have often resisted plans for expanding ports and constructing waste disposal facilities, yet Canada has not experienced high levels of adversarial legalism (Hoberg, 1993; Nemetz et al., 1986). Canadian environmental activist organizations generally refrain from litigating; instead, they concentrate on lobbying and public education (Roman and Pikkov, 1990). Canadian law does not favor class actions by "private attorneys general." In 1972 and 1973 the Canadian national government established an environmental impact analysis requirement akin to that established by the 1969 U.S. National Environmental Protection Act (NEPA), but Canadian courts usually have declined to halt ongoing projects pending the completion of an environmental analysis, and Canadian judges do not emulate American judges' willingness to reexamine the adequacy of administrative bodies' policy responses to arguments against their proposed plans or regulations (Lucas, 1993: 170; Howlett, 1994). In contrast to the adversarial legalism that has accompanied the U.S. Endangered Species Act, Canadian species protection policies are governed by legal provisions that grant broad discretion to environmental agencies and their wildlife experts. The implementation process is based on cooperative decisionmaking by committees, which include provincial governmental officials and the leaders of major environmental organizations.

How can we account for these differences? *Political culture* undoubtedly plays a significant role. Unlike their American cousins, Canadians didn't revolt against the British crown. In comparative opinion polls Canadians tend to be more respectful of authority and more communal in their attitudes, Americans more individualistic, antistatist, and rights-oriented (Lipset, 1991). James Q. Wilson (1989: 304) points out, "Americans always entertain the suspicion that the government is doing something mischievous behind their backs and greet with outrage any indication that important decisions were made in a way that excluded any affected interest, no matter how marginal."

In addition to political culture, however, differences in *political structure* help explain the American emphasis on adversarial legalism. In a study of environmental regulation in federal governments, Daniel Kelemen (1998) observed that compared to the central governments of *parliamentary* federal systems such as Canada, Australia, and Germany, political authority in the United States is unusually fragmented. Not only is power divided between Congress and the presidency, which often have been dominated by competing political parties, but American political parties exert less control over individual legislators than do parties in parliamentary regimes. Frequent elections mean frequent shifts in power and influence. The president, various congressional committees, and competing interest groups all engage in a nonstop battle for control of regulatory personnel and policies, whose funding and enforcement priorities shift from administration to administration, congressional session to congressional session (Wood and Waterman, 1991). Worried that their political adversaries will gain control in the future, contending interests fight for detailed statutory provisions, mandated analytic requirements, formal participatory procedures, or bureaucratic arrangements that will enable them to reshape unfavorable administrative decisions, by appeals to court if necessary (Moe, 1989). Richard Lazarus (1991: 311) writes: "Amendments to the Clean Air Act and Clean Water Act in 1977, to the Clean Water Act, CERCLA, FIFRA, RCRA, the Safe Drinking Water Act, and TSCA during the 1980s, and to the Clean Air Act in 1990, all exhibit the same trend. Each eliminated substantial EPA discretion, imposed more deadlines, and included more prescription."[14]

Accountability by detailed law and litigation provides a means of continuing the struggle to constrain power and influence policy. Administrators find themselves without the capacity to set priorities and implement them flexibly. With reference to the EPA, Lazarus (id.) continues:

Congress has repeatedly demanded that the agency perform impossible tasks under unrealistic deadlines. Courts have rejected many of the agency's efforts to provide itself with more leeway in their implementation, while the White House, OMB [the Office of Management and Budget], and congressional appropriation committees have simultaneously resisted subsequent agency efforts to comply with judicial mandates. The agency spends much of its limited resources defending its decisions in court, negotiating with OMB and the White House, and justifying its decisions to Congressional committees. A virtual state of siege and a crisis mentality have persisted at the agency for much of its existence as Congress has responded to each EPA failure by passing even more restrictive deadline legislation that the agency again fails to meet.

In Canada's parliamentary central government (and in its parliamentary provincial governments as well) bureaucracies are less politicized, and they are subject to unified political control by governments that are dominated by a single, cohesive political party for four or five years on end. The dominant party does not need courts to control administrative decisions. As a senior Canadian official put it: "Canadian regulatory officials are directly subject to the authority of Parliament's leadership in Cabinet. Thus it is unnecessary for Parliament to spell out legislative intent in great detail . . . this is in contrast to the American context where social regulation was written with the explicit objective of denying discretion and flexibility to the regulators."[15] In parliamentary systems, such as Canada's, the government in power can quickly amend the law to reverse administrative or judicial decisions that displease it. Hence it does not feel the need to write such detailed rules or encourage citizen suits to monitor the bureaucracy. Tight legal controls are not necessary because political controls suffice. Relations among regulators and the regulated are therefore less likely to be abraded by legal conflicts about the applicability of highly prescriptive regulations.

Another structural feature of American government—the strength of its political traditions of local government—is also of great importance. With respect to environmental protection, for example, the regulation of land use, waste disposal, and drinking water supply have remained primarily the province of locally elected, locally financed municipal or (for unincorporated areas) county governments. For the most part, local officials, not state and federal governments, control the location of new housing developments, shopping centers, and industrial parks. To a larger degree than most economically advanced democracies, local governments in the United States rely heavily on local taxes, particularly property taxes, to finance basic governmental services, including education, public safety, infrastructure maintenance, and so on. Compared to most economically advanced democracies, therefore, the national government in the United States has fewer financial levers with which to control state and local governments. Policy clashes between separately elected city and state governments, and between state and federal regulatory officials, are common. For environmental advocacy groups—such as the Center for Law in the Public Interest and the NAACP in the Los Angeles Century Freeway case—adversarial legalism provides a vital handhold for pushing state and local governments to adhere to national policy norms.

In contrast, in Great Britain, the Netherlands, Germany, and Japan, much land use planning authority is vested in provincial governments. Cities are confined to tight borders. Suburbs are not created at will. Municipalities and provincial governments get large proportions of their budgets from the national government, and hence tend to be responsive to their political paymaster's concerns. Since towns are less dependent on local revenues than in the United States, business firms are less inclined to base location decisions on variations in local property tax rates. In America, conversely, revenue-hungry (or job-hungry) local governments face stronger incentives to favor economic development over environmental protection (Peterson, 1995; Kagan, 1999a). In short, decentralized governance makes environmental protection more difficult in the United States than in more hierarchically ordered polities.

From the perspective of American environmentalists, the logical remedy would be to mimic European land use regulation, shifting authority over local land use decisions to a higher level of government at which environmental values might weigh more heavily than local concerns about maximizing property tax revenues or speeding the flow of traffic. But in the United States the powerful political forces maintaining local control generally have blocked that route. The next best strategy, from the environmental standpoint, has been to construct a more complex set of institutional and legal checks on local decisions that threaten environmental values. That strategy has led to national or state laws that require local project proponents—those who wish to build paper factories, dredge ports, or drill for oil—to obtain permits not only from local governments but also from a network of federal, state, or regional agencies responsible for protecting specific environmental values—for example, water, air, endangered species, wetlands, beaches, and so on. Secondly, the environmental regulatory strategy has been to empower neighborhood groups and environmental advocacy groups to file lawsuits that challenge local land use decisions or development projects pushed by the state or federal government (such as new highways), alleging that they fail to meet legally mandated environmental assessment criteria embodied in law. Thus the patterns of costly litigation evidenced in the Century Freeway story, the Oakland dredging project, and so on arise from laws and procedures that were designed to implement national environmental policies in a highly decentralized governmental structure. Sometimes they do so. But just as often, what Richard Stewart, a former Assistant Attorney General for Environment and Natural Resources (1990: 346), has called a "self-contradictory attempt at central planning through litigation" tends to misfire.

Skewed Consequences

It should be restated that adversarial legalism sometimes results in *improvements* in public policy. Lawsuits have often exposed governmental failures to analyze environmental impacts adequately, compelled the formulation of better designs, and forced the abandonment or relocation of projects that would be better forgotten about or put elsewhere. But often the projects should not be abandoned. The Century Freeway and Oakland Harbor cases illustrate how accountability through litigation can readily generate two unfortunate outcomes: the use of the legal process to extort particularistic benefits, and political responsiveness skewed in favor of intense political factions.

Litigation-Based Delay and Extortion

When public law is constantly subject to judicial reinterpretation and legislative intervention, those who oppose governmental programs and projects are encouraged to try their hand at litigation. The National Research Council panel (1986: 89–90) that studied the port expansion decision process observed: "Objectors do not necessarily have to win in the courts to win their point. If the courts provide a vehicle for substantial delay and that delay is costly to the proposers of the project, the threat of going to court becomes a powerful negotiating tool in the hands of objectors. . . . [I]t is an essential reality for all of the participants in regulatory decision-making." Thus even the *threat* of litigation, as in the Boston Tunnel case, may be enough to win challengers not only a seat at the bargaining table but also enough leverage to demand and obtain their preferred "environmental mitigation" measures. As I wrote (1990b: 125) in an earlier analysis of the Oakland Harbor case:

> The Port of Oakland was willing to pay for expensive upland disposal . . . so long as it could retain large container lines as customers. Jack Benny's hesitation notwithstanding, most people, when forced at gunpoint to choose between their money and their life, willingly surrender their money. The ports and shipping companies are willing to pay because their economic life is on the line. The issue is whether the legal arrangements that compel them to do so [lead to expenditures] that are socially beneficial.

Sometimes they are, but there is no guarantee.

When Caltrans, hoping to avoid further litigation in the Century Freeway case, agreed to construct costly mass transit facilities and to build a large housing project, that decision was not backed by a careful cost-benefit analysis. Nor did that decision flow from a legislative debate or a carefully prepared state or national transportation plan. It was an ad hoc decision, made in private, often hectic negotiations in the shadow of the courthouse. The decision was shaped primarily by the wish list of a particular public interest law firm—whose views evidently had not managed to gain approval through democratic and administrative political processes. Even less can be said in favor of a plan that Chevron agreed to in order to break free of the regulatory appeals and lawsuits that had blocked a proposed pipeline from Point Arguello to Los Angeles refineries: it agreed to pipe the oil two hundred miles north to San Francisco and then ship it by ocean tanker to Los Angeles, tripling the risk of oil spills from tankering operations.

The Asymmetrical Responsiveness of Judicial Governance

While public law litigation is designed to make public policymaking more responsive to neglected interests and values, it often ends up *privileging* special interests and values over the general interest. That is not merely an occasional misfire of a basically sound system; it arises from the basic nature of policymaking and policy implementation via adversarial litigation and judicial governance.

Adversarial legalism was injected into the planning and implementation of American development projects because governmental and corporate project planners are not infrequently insensitive to local and environmental concerns. Once built, superhighways cannot be dismantled or moved; the communities and neighborhoods they disrupt cannot be reassembled. Tree farms do not recreate the ecosystems or the beauty of mature forests leveled by clear-cutting. Public interest lawyers and courts, it was hoped, would make public policy responsive to *all* relevant voices in the affected community, not just the powerful proponents of development. Again, valuable redesigns of development projects have been achieved because the mechanisms of adversarial legalism lent strength to the politically weak.

The powerful tools of adversarial legalism, however, are costly to invoke and clumsy and difficult to calibrate. In the declining industrial town of Chester, Pennsylvania, 65 percent African-American and very poor, the mechanisms of adversarial legalism lay dormant in the 1980s and 1990s as government officials, local and state, issued permit after permit to waste processing companies of various kinds. According to a *New York Times* reporter who visited Chester in 1996, the air was "thick with acrid smells and, often, smoke. Dump trucks rumble through throughout the day" and "the first thing you notice is the smell" (Janovsky, 1996). Property values in Chester plummeted. There is significant evidence that cancer rates are much higher than might be expected (Foster, 1998). In the mid-1990s, when a Philadelphia public interest lawyer contested a permit for yet another waste processing facility in Chester, and then appealed it to the courts, a victory in one court was overturned by another. Only direct political action, both in the streets and the election of a new city government, started to turn the tide. Across the nation, minority neighborhood victories in "environmental justice" lawsuits have been few and far between.

At the same time, the mechanisms of adversarial legalism, intended to give all interests a voice, can make the government *disproportionately* responsive to those who *do* wield them. Consider, for example, the Century Freeway case. Once the Center for Law in the Public Interest, the Sierra Club, and the NAACP obtained a preliminary injunction, they were guaranteed not only a voice throughout the subsequent negotiations and the administration of the consent decree, but the dominant voice; they could demand particular benefits for particular groups in return for agreeing to let the project proceed. Once Judge Pregerson incorporated the settlement in a judicial decree, the Center for Law in the Public Interest and the other advocacy groups retained a virtual veto over any subsequent proposals to change the plan. The judge and a committee dominated by the plaintiffs' lawyers became a special, undemocratic government for the highway project—impervious to the views of the elected government of Los Angeles or of two subsequently elected Republican governors (who did not share the antihighway attitudes of the Democratic administration that embraced the settlement years earlier).

A similar skewing of political responsiveness characterized the Oakland Harbor story. For years, as a sequence of regulatory bodies and courts slowly processed repeated challenges to proposed disposal sites for dredged sediment, local elected political leaders—the mayor of Oakland, state and federal legislative representatives—were powerless to respond to the resulting loss of port business, municipal revenues, and jobs. As in eighteenth-century France, adversarial legalism paralyzed political leadership, enabling particularized interests to trump the general interest.

Of course, as Ronald Dworkin (1977) has emphasized, legal rights are *intended* to operate as political trump cards. Legal rights intentionally privilege certain principles—often those that protect political minorities or fragile values—regardless of general preferences. Thus law often *mandates* a "skewed responsiveness." This seems entirely justifiable when one is thinking of rights that are morally compelling and relatively unambiguous—such as the right to a fair trial, freedom of political speech or of religion, immunity from racial discrimination, or relief from inhumane prison conditions.

In contemporary American public law, however, the number of trump cards has multiplied so rapidly as to permeate the entire game, and it takes months or years of costly litigation to see if they were properly put into play. When too many cards are legal trumps, the compromise so essential to effective governance in a pluralistic society is more elusive. When the scope and applicability of the legal rights are uncertain and malleable, the conflict can be resolved only by lengthy administrative and judicial procedures, followed by lengthy appeals. Under those circumstances, the mere threat of playing a trump card—not its validity or appropriateness under the particular circumstances—holds up public projects in ways that may *unjustifiably* deplete the aggregate social and economic welfare. The sensitive balance between change and preservation is often decided, therefore, not by rational analysis or political compromise but by the compulsion to escape the stultifying miasma of extended, repetitive litigation.

Once in place, fragmentation of regulatory power is difficult to reverse. In eighteenth-century France, it took a violent revolution. In American democracy, organized political and economic interests, concerned that the government will be dominated after the next election by political leaders who are unfriendly to their vision of the public interest, seek to preserve legal rights and statutory protections that may help block policy changes they dislike. Thus municipal governments resist centralization of land use decisionmaking by metropolitan, regional, or state government. State governments argue that they, not the federal government, should be responsible for implementation of federal environmental laws, while environmentalists, worried that the state regulators will be too accommodating to industry, insist that federal laws and agencies should closely control state decisions. Both proregulation advocacy groups and regulated businesses resist legal reforms that would grant regulatory officials broad discretion and curtail the right to challenge their decisions in court. Business interests, suspicious of the EPA, battle to ensure that the Army Corps of Engineers retains jurisdiction over fill permits for wetlands, while environmentalists battle for EPA jurisdiction; in consequence, control over wetlands is fragmented among both agencies, plus state and local agencies. Because governmental authority remains fragmented and constrained by detailed laws, complex procedural requirements, and broad rights to judicial review, adversarial legalism persists in American regulation.

Conclusion:
Can the United States Tame
Adversarial Legalism?

In the United States adversarial legalism accelerated and persisted in the last third of the twentieth century because Americans (and the interest groups they form) wanted their governments to wield power. They wanted that power to be used to control risk, protect the environment, provide security, combat crime and discrimination, and remedy injustice. But in the same era, as government grew, so did popular mistrust of governmental power. Americans of conflicting political persuasions seemed to worry that government, when granted more funds and more power to do good, would be arbitrary, wasteful, or incompetent or would be captured by their ideological opponents. Politicians and interest groups insisted, therefore, that as governmental authority was enhanced, it should also be fragmented and constrained by legal rules. Big government and big business alike should be made politically responsive through legal processes. Legislatures and courts translated these sentiments into detailed legal mandates, procedures, rights, and penalties. Citizens and groups were empowered to pursue their financial interests and political goals through litigation. To negotiate the ensuing set of legal risks and opportunities, individuals, business firms, political interests, schools, and government agencies all felt compelled to arm themselves with lawyers and legal claims, and their critics have done the same.

History, however, may not be destiny. Conceivably, the cycle of mistrust and litigation can be broken. Conceivably, adversarial legalism, having risen, will also decline. In the 1980s and 1990s a conservative U.S. Supreme Court, in contrast to the Warren Court, created few doctrines that encouraged new waves of litigation, and many Rehnquist Court rulings consciously sought to dampen adversarial legalism. The Court struck down federal laws that enabled citizens to sue state governments. The justices gave law enforcement officers more leeway in obtaining evidence through searches and interrogations, cautioned federal courts to defer to regulatory agencies' rulemaking judgments (*Chevron U.S.A. v. NRDC*, 1984), limited broad "standing to sue" rules for "private attorneys general" (*Lujan v. Defenders of Wildlife*,

1992), denounced lawsuits based on "junk science" (*Daubert v. Merrell Dow Pharmaceuticals*, 1993), and held that "excessive" punitive damages are unconstitutional (*BMW of North America v. Gore*, 1996).[1]

American legislatures have also tried to dampen adversarial legalism. In the 1980s and 1990s many states enacted statutes aimed at curtailing tort litigation. Congress enacted laws that constrained extortive class actions based on securities law, limited lawsuits against small-aircraft manufacturers, discouraged repetitive appeals to the federal courts in death penalty cases, restricted litigation in immigrants' rights and deportation cases, and provided a limited shield against lawsuits for "Y2K" computer problems. The Environmental Protection Agency and many state environmental agencies repeatedly reaffirmed their desire to encourage more cooperative rather than adversarial and legalistic modes of regulation. The movement to substitute alternative dispute resolution of various kinds for adversarial litigation in the courts continues to grow in some types of cases. In Franklin County, Ohio, with a population of over one million (including Ohio's capital city, Columbus), product liability and medical malpractice cases declined through the 1990s to hardly a trickle each year, defendants won most jury verdicts in such cases, and when plaintiffs won, the amounts awarded declined (Merritt and Barry, 1999).

Are these signs that American adversarial legalism is now on the road to decline? In a global economy that is increasingly intolerant of inefficient institutions, will the American way of law gradually become less adversarial, less legalistic? Any sweeping change in that direction seems unlikely. For reasons already discussed, adversarial legalism is deeply rooted in the American system of government and in American political culture. Yet law, like the political struggles from which it springs, is never fixed. Adversarial legalism's most inefficient, inequitable, and otherwise disturbing characteristics will constantly be under attack. Although most of American adversarial legalism's fundamental features will almost certainly endure and even thrive, incremental reforms will be advocated repeatedly, and surely some will be adopted. This chapter, however, will concentrate on the kind of big changes that would *substantially* curtail adversarial legalism and review the obstacles to those changes that spring from American politics.

Incremental Changes, Big Changes

Not long after the Port of Oakland finally emerged from the swamp of adversarial legalism and received approval to dredge its harbor to a depth of forty-two feet, it began planning to deepen the ship channels to fifty feet in order to accommodate still larger transpacific containerships. Where would the millions of cubic yards of dredged sediments be deposited? This time, the

Port, after consulting with a multiagency, broadly consultative committee organized by the Corps of Engineers, proposed dumping some of the mud in a shallow area near the edge of San Francisco Bay. There it would be planted with marsh grasses, restoring the shoreline wildlife habitat. Environmental groups, instead of threatening to litigate, embraced the plan. The Bay Conservation and Development Commission, usually opposed to any plans to "fill" the bay, gave its approval. A new federal law, passed in the wake of the first deadlock over dredging the harbor, authorized the Corps of Engineers to accept (and fund) environmentally constructive dredging disposal plans even if they are not the least expensive alternative. In other port areas as well, interagency teams and inclusive local planning groups now work at formulating dredging plans consensually (Busch, Kirp, and Schoenholz, 1999: 247).

As David Kirp and his colleagues have suggested, this latest chapter of the Oakland Harbor story shows that politicians, agencies, and interest groups can learn from past fiascoes, adopting methods of negotiation that tame adversarial legalism and produce creative compromises (ibid.). That happens, virtually every day, in many parts of the United States. Public servants of good will prod contending interests to compromise and avoid litigation. Finding ways to avoid litigation is the stock in trade of many practicing lawyers.

Yet adversarial legalism has not really been tamed. It may be pushed out of the clearing on particular issues, but it always lurks in the bushes, ready to spring into action. It *can* do so because the legal structures of adversarial legalism are always in place, ready for use. It *will* do so whenever one of the contending interests rejects the proposed compromise and decides to seek vindication in the courts—or determines that inflicting the delays and costs of a lawsuit on the other parties will enhance its bargaining power. In 1995 the Secretary of the U.S. Department of Transportation lamented that dredging projects remain "submerged in conflicting missions and mandates . . . and a pyramid of federal rules and regulations, plus state and local laws which make it a miracle every time a port dredging project is brought to fruition" (Busch, Kirp, and Schoenholz at 247). In October 1997 a West Oakland citizens' organization brought a suit against the consensually negotiated harbor dredging plan, demanding that federal funds be withheld until planners examine measures to reduce air pollution from the increase in traffic that will flow from larger containerships (DelVecchio, 1997). They also threatened a suit arguing that the port expansion would violate "environmental justice" regulations by disproportionately polluting the minority neighborhood adjacent to the port.[2]

Adversarial legalism, as noted earlier, has two dimensions. First, it entails *legal structures and rules* that foster an adversarial and legalistic style of policy implementation and dispute resolution. Second, it entails the actual day-to-day, dispute-by-dispute *practice of legal contestation*. The incidence of adversarial legalism as day-to-day practice varies, sometimes intensifying in particular policy areas, sometimes subsiding when it seems too costly to bear. But the structures of adversarial legalism are more enduring. As we have seen, those basic structures include the fragmentation of governmental and regulatory authority among levels of government and many agencies; a dense web of highly prescriptive, analytically and procedurally demanding statutes; and ready access by affected interests to a politically selected, self-confident, and rather unpredictable judiciary. These structural features empower those who object to new government regulations or new development projects to block or delay them through litigation and make it harder to bestow legal finality on negotiated compromise plans (Kagan, 1999b: 129–130). Thus adversarial legalism shapes outcomes even if it continues to lurk in the bushes.

Similarly, state legislatures have enacted many statutes designed to reduce adversarial legalism by making it a bit harder for aggrieved plaintiffs to win tort cases or making tort cases less attractive to contingency fee lawyers. These statutes establish caps on punitive damages, require efforts at mediation before a lawsuit can proceed in court, reduce the exposure of parties who are only secondary causes of accidents, and so on. Some of these changes seem to affect the *rate* and severity of tort claims (Danzon, 1986; Glaberson, 1999), but they are only incremental changes. After years of debate about "tort reform," the basic legal structures of the American system for compensating personal injuries and judging wrongdoing remain strikingly different from those of other economically advanced democracies. Still in place are the American tort system's basic engines of adversarial legalism—trial by jury; lawyer-dominated (not judge-dominated) litigation; a politically selected, legally creative judiciary; indeterminate and potentially very large money damages; entrepreneurial, contingency fee driven lawyering; and the American rule on counsel fees, in which losers do not have to pay the winners' fees.

Because litigation in a regime of adversarial legalism is so costly, divisive, and troublesome, there are always pressures to avoid it and to adopt legal reforms that strive to reduce its incidence. But the everyday practice of adversarial legalism in the United States will decline *significantly* only in the event of structural changes or large, nonincremental changes in legal rules. Taming adversarial legalism will require basic changes in the American way of law.

Imagining Significant Reductions in Adversarial Legalism

Adversarial legalism is a legally formal mode of policy implementation and dispute resolution that involves relatively high levels of influence and control by conflicting interests, parties, and lawyers rather than strong hierarchical authority and control.[3] Sharp reductions in adversarial legalism, it follows, would require concentrating governmental authority and shifting power from parties and lawyers to governmental officials and programs—and in the litigative process, to judges. This section presents a series of scenarios that provide examples of that kind of radical change. Warning! They may appear shocking to readers steeped in the traditions of American adversarial legalism, although some of them reflect reform ideas that have circulated in the legal literature.

I describe the changes very briefly, for I do not offer them as reform proposals. That would require a lengthy discussion of the risks as well as the benefits of each idea; more hierarchical approaches that work well in Western Europe, for example, may not work so well in the American political context, and there is more to be learned about the weaknesses of Western European models. My purpose in this section, therefore, is first of all to indicate that plausible ways of sharply constraining adversarial legalism do exist—plausible in the sense that they resemble institutional practices employed by other economically advanced democracies and at least ostensibly would improve the quality of justice in some important respects. But as the succeeding section of this chapter will discuss, these reform scenarios are not *politically* plausible in the United States at this time. Thus a second reason for outlining large, disjunctive scenarios is that they will help illuminate the attitudes that entrench adversarial legalism in American life and make it difficult to tame.

Criminal Justice

Adversarial legalism in the criminal justice systems of the United States, as we saw in Chapter 4, is in large part a response to the highly decentralized and weakly coordinated character of American police departments, prosecutors' offices, and judiciaries. In principle, therefore, the need for intensely adversarial legal challenges would decline (at least to some degree) if the United States emulated the more centralized judiciaries and prosecutorial organizations of European countries, with their more professionalized methods of recruitment and promotion and their elaborate mechanisms for ensuring a higher level of legal uniformity. In the United States such an organizational change would require much stronger controls by *state* governments over the recruitment, training, coordination, and discipline of police, prosecutors, and judges.

At the adjudication stage the length, cost, and adversariness of criminal trials would decline if American states were constitutionally permitted to emulate the British practice, whereby a much larger range of criminal prosecutions are referred to lower criminal courts for less formal nonjury trials (and sharply limited penal sanctions). Cheaper, simpler trials for routine cases would give far more American defendants a real opportunity to have their say in court rather than exchanging a guilty plea for a lesser charge and penalty.

In jury trials for serious charges, adversarial legalism would diminish if American judges were vested with greater authority (like British judges) to preclude lengthy questioning, legal wrangling, and peremptory challenges concerning the composition of the jury; to assume a larger role in questioning witnesses, constraining demeaning and obfuscatory questioning by lawyers, and in summing up the evidence; and to comment on the defendant's failure to testify on his own behalf (which, of course, would give him a strong incentive to testify).

The incentive for criminal defendants and lawyers to mobilize the full armory of adversarial legalism almost surely would decline if American criminal penalties (including—or especially—the penalties for murder and for narcotics possession) were reduced to levels closer to those employed by Western European nations. Of course, there are also philosophical and practical reasons to reduce penalties, aside from their impact on adversarial legalism.

Finally, much costly and sometimes justice-defeating legal jousting stems from the oppositional suspect-state relationship that is encouraged by the breadth of the privilege against self-incrimination, as applied in the United States. Adversarial legalism would almost surely decline if the federal and state constitutions were amended to abolish the privilege whenever defendants in legal proceedings are granted strong *institutional* protections against coercion, abuse, harassment, or trickery.[4] For example, criminal defendants (like other citizens who have relevant knowledge) could be legally obligated to testify at trial, as long as a competent defense lawyer is present to object to misleading or bullying questions.[5]

Civil Justice

Historically, debt collection cases have been the most common—and in some eras the most politically controversial—type of civil case on the dockets of American courts (Kagan et al., 1977). But in the last thirty years, even as the amount of outstanding debt and the numbers of delinquent debtors have mushroomed, contested litigation concerning home mortgages and commercial loans has *declined,* and contested litigation concerning the exploding numbers of overdue consumer loans has hardly increased (Kagan, 1984).

One reason, highlighted by a comparison of credit card debt collection in Germany and the United States (Ruhlin, 2000), is that creditors in the United States often find litigation too costly for smallish debts if the debtor gives any signs of putting up a legal defense. However, debt litigation has also declined because the United States has developed a series of public and private insurance regimes—social security, unemployment insurance, crop insurance, mortgage insurance, health insurance, liability insurance, government-supplied disaster insurance, Federal Housing Administration and Veterans Administration loan guarantees, deposit insurance, and so on—all of which enable debtors who are afflicted with sudden losses to survive financially and pay at least part of their debts. At the same time, governmental regulation of banks, insurance companies, and pension funds has sharply reduced the incidence of failure among these major debtors (Kagan, 1984).

EXTENDING COMPENSATION THROUGH SOCIAL INSURANCE
Debt litigation's decline teaches that insurance and regulatory programs can reduce the incidence of adversarial legalism by providing less costly, less conflictual, and more reliable alternatives to litigation. Thus, as discussed in Chapter 7, in countries that make collectively financed health insurance and generous disability insurance available to the victims of accidents and environmentally caused illnesses, tort litigation is far less common; all victims (not just those who can get a lawyer and prove the defendant was at fault) obtain at least a reasonable amount of needed funds more certainly, equitably, and quickly than in the United States. Suppose, then, that American governments provided legal rights to adequate health insurance and medical care to all Americans, and revised state tort laws to relieve defendants from having to compensate plaintiffs for medical costs that are covered by employer- or government-provided health or disability insurance. Thenceforth, injured people in the United States would have much lower incentives to turn to the inefficient and unreliable tort system to obtain compensation for losses flowing from personal injuries.

There are other approaches as well. For injuries from motor vehicle accidents, tort claims could be foreclosed either by enacting serious no-fault (mandatory self-insurance) programs in all states,[6] or by providing automatic (moderate) compensation without fault via a publicly funded motor vehicle accident commission, similar to a workers' compensation agency (Sugarman, 1993b). Alternatively, as in countries such as Switzerland, American governments could compel employer-financed workers' compensation insurance plans to cover accidents sustained on the way to and from work (without regard to fault). As in Sweden, American states could also create automatic, collectively funded, administratively implemented systems that provide compensation (without regard to fault) for injuries caused by "medical accidents" or by pharmaceuticals that have unanticipated adverse side effects (Weiler, 1991).

Would eliminating or drastically reducing tort suits in these areas destroy an important safeguard against negligence? It is hard to say. As we saw in Chapter 7, the regulatory or accident-preventing functions of tort law seem spotty. But if, as seems likely, tort law's regulatory effects would be missed in some respects, governments could increase expenditures for direct safety regulation of dangerous activities, or create other incentives for responsible behavior.

ABOLISHING OR CHIPPING AWAY AT THE CIVIL JURY Lawyer-dominated trial by jury, as discussed in Chapter 6, is slow and costly. With its unexplained verdicts by nonprofessional "one-time" decisionmakers, it is a source of inconsistency and unpredictability. Suppose, then, that the United States (like Great Britain and most Canadian provinces) were to abandon lawyer-dominated jury trials in the realm of civil litigation. Trial by jury could be replaced by trials before a panel of judges or, as in Germany, before a mixed panel of judges and democratically selected lay persons; in contrast to American jury trials, each trial court could be expected to explain its decisions in writing and could be subjected to searching appellate (hierarchical) review. Increased predictability would dampen litigation, and outcomes would be less influenced by inequality in the contending parties' financial resources and in the abilities of the contending lawyers.

An alternative approach to reducing adversarial legalism would be to divert particular types of civil litigation from civil court juries to specialized administrative tribunals or agencies that use less formal, less costly procedures. The workers' compensation system provides one model. Small claims courts provide another model, as does private arbitration of commercial disputes. England, the Netherlands, Germany, and Japan provide a wide range of inexpensive alternative forums to deal with "personal plight cases" (Kritzer, 1996: 125). In England, for example, where informal industrial tribunals handle claims for compensation for unfair dismissal, workplace discrimination, and unequal pay, a majority of claimants do not use lawyers (Blankenburg and Rogowski, 1986). Dutch employers must process planned dismissals through a local labor-exchange bureau, which resolves potential disputes over unjust dismissal and employee entitlements beforehand, sharply reducing the incidence of (and avoiding the costs of) postdismissal litigation (Blankenburg, 1994: 802–803). In Germany individual disputes over coverage of health care services and payments to providers regularly are heard by a network of *Sozialgerichte,* or social courts. Cases are heard by panels of one professional judge and two lay judges—one from the insurance industry and one who represents insureds, or one representing doctors in disputes over cost control or utilization issues (Jost, 1998: 658). In the Netherlands and Japan governments and trade associations provide respected free legal advice bureaus and mediation services, often specialized by type of dispute.

The broader point is that where governments, industry associations, and bar associations are committed to providing cheaper, less adversarial, and less legalistic alternatives to full-scale litigation, they can find ways of doing so. An impressive body of research by social psychologist Tom Tyler (1990) and his colleagues indicates that people regard governmental decisionmaking as just when they perceive that the decisionmaker is not biased against them, and when they feel that the decisionmaker listens carefully, treating them (and their arguments) with respect. In many ways, informal administrative tribunals are better designed to meet Tyler's norms of "procedural justice" than are formal courts shaped by adversarial legalism. Informal tribunals, much like American small claims courts, allow the disputants to speak for themselves—not merely through lawyers. And because informal administrative hearings are inexpensive and rapid, the disputant *does* get her day in court, as compared with costly U.S.-style litigation, in which trials are so expensive and frightening that 90 percent of cases are resolved by pretrial bargaining between lawyers and settlements are deeply influenced by who can best bear the costs of litigation.

In the Dutch, German, and British informal tribunals, legitimacy and the feeling of neutrality are enhanced by a combination of hierarchy, representation, and expertise. The tribunals are not mediators, as in many American alternative dispute resolution procedures. They are hierarchical decisionmakers whose decisions have a high degree of finality. The panels of adjudicators are somewhat representative in that they include lay people. The panels are specialized by subject matter, which makes them more expert. The adjudicators also take the initiative to draw out the facts and explain their decisions—unlike American judges, who sit passively while competing lawyers attempt to discredit opposing litigants and reshape the truth, and unlike American juries, which do not interact with the disputants and do not explain their decisions.

One effect of a more "proactive" method of adjudication is revealed by a comparative study of workers' compensation adjudication in American states. When injured workers suffer "permanent partial disability," the determination in most states of the extent of permanent disability is plagued by adversarial battles between physicians chosen as separate expert witnesses, one by lawyers for the claimant and another by the employer or the employer's insurance company. A 1988 study by the Workers Compensation Research Institute found that in permanent partial disability claims in New Jersey, dueling attorneys were involved in 100 percent of the cases and dueling doctors in 79 percent; the total "friction costs" expended on those professionals were equal to 46 percent of total payments to the injured workers. Wisconsin provided an amazing contrast. In Wisconsin cases involving only claimed loss of earning capacity, the friction costs were comparable to New Jersey's. But for another, larger category of "functional impairment" claims in Wisconsin, friction costs had been reduced to merely 14 percent of compensation payments; attorneys were involved in only 32 percent of the cases and dueling physicians in only 6 percent (WCRI, 1988).

How did Wisconsin cut adversarial litigation costs so sharply in functional impairment cases? The state employed four techniques, each of which reduced adversarial control and increased hierarchical control over processes and outcomes. First, administratively prescribed "mandatory minimum ratings" guaranteed the claimant a certain level of compensation for common events, such as back surgery. Second, the Wisconsin workers' compensation bureaucracy assumed an active role: it used reports from the treating physician to compute presumptive benefits, informed the defendant of the amount presumptively due, and imposed penalties if the defendant failed to pay or contest the award promptly. Eighty percent of claims are resolved in this way, without lawyers or adversary experts—compared to 0–1 percent in New Jersey and 12 percent in Wisconsin cases not subject to this proactive regime. Third, the Wisconsin program placed heavy emphasis on the disability assessment of the *treating* physician, who usually is chosen by the worker. But when the defendant chooses to contest that assessment and obtain one from a "defendants' physician," the Wisconsin compensation judges employ "final offer adjudication": they must choose either the treating physician's or the company physician's assessment rather than an intermediate point. In consequence, experience shows, physicians who offer extreme ratings (high or low) have been stigmatized and screened out of the system, claimants choose more neutral physicians, and defendants only infrequently contest the initial assessment (WCRI, 1988).

The same principles would reduce adversarial friction costs (and hence distortion of settlements by asymmetrical incentives to avoid those costs) in other kinds of civil litigation as well. In tort cases the unpredictability of outcomes and litigation costs could be drastically reduced if states would legislate presumptive rules for the calculation of "noneconomic" (e.g., "pain and suffering") damages for common types of personal injuries (Blumstein et al., 1990), as is done by legislatures in most other economically advanced democracies.[7]

The Wisconsin strategy of increasing staff involvement in the adjudicatory process suggests that adversarial conflict in high-stakes civil litigation would decrease if judges called on government-paid, neutral expert witnesses, rather than the current practice, in which competing experts are chosen and coached by conflicting lawyers and paid not for establishing the just result but for advancing the interests of one party or another. Court appointment of experts is the practice in most continental European judicial systems.

COUNSEL FEES Adversarial legalism in civil justice (and in the private enforcement of public law) would decline if the United States abandoned the "American rule," according to which opposing litigants pay their own lawyers. The replacement would be some version of the "loser pays" rule, which is the norm in most other countries. Because litigation in the United States is so costly and legally uncertain, adversarial litigation is often used as a coercive instrument. Many plaintiffs and defendants feel compelled to abandon just claims and just defenses when they are confronted by a legal adversary who can afford to inflict the high costs and delays of litigation on his opponent. Under the loser-pays rule, plaintiffs with legally questionable cases are more reluctant to sue. Defendants with weak defenses have strong incentives to settle quickly, before discovery and other costs mount. Of course, there is a significant drawback to the loser-pays rule: risk-averse people with claims that are probably but not conclusively meritorious will be reluctant to risk the possibility of losing and hence will not sue. But against those injustices, one must weigh the injustices of the current system, which harm parties with *clearly* meritorious claims and defenses. A number of proposed variations in the loser-pays rule seek the best of both worlds, such as applying it only when parties reject reasonable early settlement offers (Horowitz, 1995).

Public Law

Notwithstanding the global growth of judicial power (Tate and Vallinder, 1995), American judges remain the world's superstars of judicial politics. American courts, federal and state, more often reshape important policies concerning land use, environmental regulation, social welfare programs, educational policy, and institutional priorities. To multinational corporations, regulation in the United States entails more adversarial legalism, more defensive lawyering, more fearsome legal penalties, and more legal uncertainty (Kagan, 2000). In no other country do interest groups, advocacy organizations, and "public interest" law firms, serving as "private attorneys general," so often and so successfully pursue their policy objectives through litigation. What kinds of legal changes might substantially reduce adversarial legalism in American public law without losing adversarial legalism's positive contributions to corporate and governmental accountability? This is a huge question, not amenable to facile answers, but some interesting possibilities are provided by comparative analysis.

REGULATION One scenario for reducing adversarial legalism in American public law is illustrated by Joseph Badaracco's (1985) comparison of how the United States, Great Britain, Germany, France, and Japan went about reducing employee exposures to cancer-causing polyvinyl chloride. American regulatory officials were buffeted by conflicting pressures from legislatures, executive branch politicians, regulated business corporations, labor unions, advocacy organizations, and court decisions. Every agency decision had to be fortified by "objective" scientific evidence, compliance with formal procedures, and legal justifications, which slowed the process down, sometimes delaying protections. The European and Japanese policymaking and implementation processes were far less legalistic, far more cooperative—and equally effective. The "secret" lay in three factors:

Legal discretion. In balancing economic and regulatory concerns, government officials in the other nations were far less closely constrained by prescriptive statutory provisions concerning substantive standards, mandatory procedures, deadlines, and analytic requirements.

Administrative finality. Partly because statutes in the other countries were far less prescriptive, the lead government agency had final authority to *balance* competing considerations and make a definitive decision. Its decision was not reversible by courts, absent gross violation of the law. In other words, policymaking and policy-implementing agencies in the other countries had more hierarchical authority than their American counterparts, and were less subject to adversarially exercised legal challenge. *Political accountability,* that is, public criticism by competing political parties, or appeals to higher political officials, substituted for the *legal accountability* and judicial review that characterizes the U.S. system.

Regularized participation. In the other countries, affected interests (industry, labor, environmentalists) participated in policy formulation but not through litigation or the threat of appeal. A stable cadre of technically qualified interest group representatives consulted regularly with government officials and served on influential policy-recommending committees.

In Germany, France, Japan, and the United Kingdom, as Badaracco tells the story, legal discretion, final administrative authority, and regularized participation combined to foster cooperation. In the United States dissatisfied interests could abandon negotiations and run to court. But in the more hierarchical systems, refusal to compromise was risky. Because governmental decisionmaking authority was concentrated and final, interest group participants on agency-assembled panels were compelled to reach agreement or else risk an unappealable hierarchical decision over which they had no influence. Through regularized informal interaction on committees, mutual trust and accommodation based on expertise became more likely to prevail. The adversarial position-taking, defensive science, threats to litigate, and defensive rule-following characteristic of the American regulatory process were neither necessary nor profitable. In the other countries, because the agencies enjoyed more final authority, they could proceed more incrementally and nonlegalistically than their American counterparts, issuing temporary "guidelines" that they could gradually tighten based on experience rather than formally binding (and appealable) legal regulations.

To reduce adversarial legalism in American regulatory policymaking, therefore, the first requirement would be extensive statutory reform. Regulatory laws and regulations would have to be redrafted so as to grant officials more discretion, according their decisions a higher degree of finality. If legal or judicial accountability were to be relaxed, however, how could the political legitimacy of regulatory decisions be preserved or bolstered? In the Western European model, regulatory agencies acquire reputations for making decisions that are both grounded in expert judgment and attentive to conflicting values and interests. Regulatory officials generally are regarded as responsible professionals, not as "mindless bureaucrats" or as ideologically motivated political appointees. To emulate that model, American governments would have to staff agencies with well-trained professionals, granting them adequate authority, resources, and remuneration to make those jobs coveted ones. To emulate the European model, representatives of various values and interests, instead of seeking to reshape policy through post hoc appeals to court, would be incorporated directly into the decisionmaking process—by appointment to panels or to committees that have significant influence on policy development and policy formulation.

Adversarial legalism has also made American regulatory *enforcement* uniquely legalistic and punitive. The result has been more legal conflict in the United States than in comparable regulatory programs in other economically advanced democracies, plus higher legal costs, accountability costs, and opportunity costs, (Kagan, 2000). American regulation also engenders a more defensive, less cooperative form of business-government interaction. Even efforts to create more cooperative programs, such as EPA's Project Excel or collaborative ecosystem management plans, all too often are inhibited by the threat of private lawsuits and other potential legal liabilities. Here too, experience abroad suggests that the key to reducing adversarial and legalistic relationships is to grant frontline regulatory bureaucrats more legal discretion and to back that up with extensive training, so that they can exercise that discretion with confidence. As Ayres and Braithwaite's *Responsive Regulation* (1992) demonstrates, regulatory officials must have a graduated range of readily imposed and meaningful sanctions at their disposal, but if they do, official discretion to tailor remedies to particular contexts is likely to yield better results than mechanistic enforcement of detailed regulations (Bardach and Kagan, 1982).

SOCIAL WELFARE AND CIVIL RIGHTS   In no sphere of public policy has adversarial legalism enjoyed so many important successes than in the struggle for civil rights for marginalized groups and in the attempt to bring a greater measure of procedural justice to social welfare systems. Adversarial legalism has opened up alternative channels of political action on behalf of the politically weak, such as prison inmates, unwed mothers, handicapped persons, and racial, religious, and ethnic minorities. Adversarial legalism has called attention to social problems that political elites had declined to recognize, such as sexual harassment in the workplace, prison crowding, or the inequity (for children in tax-poor municipalities) of funding public education primarily through local property taxes. Adversarial legalism is useful for challenging bureaucratic indifference or callousness or cultural bias, and for bringing procedural regularity to a wide range of governmental decisions, from the punishment of school children to the administration of immigration services. Since the roots of political and bureaucratic unresponsiveness are difficult to extirpate, adversarial legalism in this realm, it might be argued, should not be squelched but should be encouraged to flourish.

It should be noted, however, that adversarial legalism has only a mixed record in solving the problems of civil rights and mass justice. Civil rights litigation has had only limited success, at best, in integrating the suburbs and improving inner-city housing, schools, and mental health services. Substantively, the United States lags well behind the welfare states of Western Europe in providing for the basic needs of the poor and of single mothers. The racial isolation and social pathologies endured by poorer African-Americans in many American cities are worse than that suffered by minorities in the cities of Western Europe and Canada (Wacquant, 1995). From the standpoint of poor clients, welfare administration remains a complex and often unresponsive legal maze. Both in principle and in practice, the most potent method of reducing social inequality is not to provide the socially marginalized with lawyers and rights to litigate but to provide more generous governmental funding for high quality education, job training, and social welfare programs and for well-staffed bureaucracies to administer them. As in countries such as Denmark, France, Germany, the Netherlands, and Sweden, that kind of social provision in the United States probably would dampen reformers' incentives to turn to adversarial legalism, both to influence policy and to challenge individual decisions.

Obstacles to Change

To reduce adversarial legalism *significantly*, the previous section indicates, the United States would have to *strengthen* the role and authority of government—substituting social insurance programs for tort litigation, shifting control from juries and lawyers to judges or other adjudicators, shielding governmental agencies from challenge in court, and limiting criminal suspects' rights to refuse to cooperate with the state. Doing so responsibly would require governmental appropriations adequate to ensure that governmental bureaucracies, police departments, and courts are well funded, well staffed, and well respected. Similarly, to persuade people to surrender their right to sue in exchange for better social insurance or regulation, those programs must be well funded, well staffed, and well respected.

As many readers will already have noted, the political obstacles to such changes in the United States are formidable, to say the least. Merely to list the changes reminds us of the powerful forces that bolster the current regime of adversarial legalism. They include a professional legal culture that is wedded to the institutions of adversarial legalism; a political structure in which determined interest groups rely on adversarial legalism to manage political uncertainty and protect their values; and a political culture that is mistrustful of, and often hostile to, hierarchical authority and expanded government. We have considered all three factors earlier, but it may be useful at this point to touch on them again.

Legal Culture

In 1995 Eric Leonard, a twenty-two-year-old man accused of serial murders, was sitting in a Sacramento, California, courtroom while his lawyers were arguing for a change of venue for his trial. According to a reporter (Coronado, 1995) attending the hearing,

> the defendant raised his hand, waving it ever so slightly. "I am guilty," Leonard said. Immediately, . . . the courtroom fell silent. . . . When it appeared that Leonard was about to repeat his statement, . . . Assistant Public Defender Caroline Lange swung her arm around Leonard and whispered frantically in his right ear. His other attorney . . . spoke into the left ear. Before anything else could happen, Judge Thomas M. Cecil —noticeably jarred—said "Lets take a break and go off the record." He quickly left the bench, and proceedings were adjourned for the day. Neither Cecil, Deputy District Attorney John O'Mara nor the defense attorneys would comment on Leonard's unsolicited remark.

In this remarkable scenario lawyers and a judge did not treat a serial killer's voluntary courtroom confession as a welcome discovery of the truth or of the defendant's capacity for remorse. They treated it as a disturbing interruption. Their response shows how deeply the American legal profession is wedded to the ideology of adversarial legalism. And it suggests how staunchly the legal profession would resist efforts to reduce adversarial legalism by such measures as eliminating criminal defendants' right of silence and shifting control of the case from lawyers to judges.

From one perspective, the Sacramento defense attorneys were simply responding rationally to the incentives created by the institutions of American adversarial legalism. This was, after all, a prosecution for several murders. In California, as in many other American states, the defendant's life was at stake. If a defendant is going to confess, the lawyers take it as their obligation to see that the confession is withheld until it can be traded for a plea bargain ensuring that the penalty will be imprisonment, not execution. Until then, their job, as they see it, is to use adversarial techniques—such as ensuring the defendant's silence, making motions to exclude evidence, trying to obtain the most favorable jury they can, arguing that the trial should be moved to a distant county—in order to increase the prosecution's costs and increase its willingness to agree to a plea bargain. I suspect, however, that the defense lawyers' desperate efforts to stop their murderous but perhaps now contrite client from saying more was dictated not so much by instrumental calculations but by a professionally induced adversarial instinct.

Put another way, the defense lawyers' adversarial stance was rooted in the ethos of American "legal culture." American lawyers—unlike British barristers and European lawyers—are trained to believe that their primary responsibility is not to uncover the truth and produce the "correct" legal disposition but to get the best possible result for their clients. They also can be counted on to mount intense political resistance to any proposed legal changes that would sharply diminish their abilities to do so.

Consider too the *judge*'s behavior in the Sacramento hearing. Why did he not follow up on the defendant's statement? Was he not interested in determining the truth? Underlying his passivity, I suspect, is a set of beliefs shaped by adversarial legalism: the lawyers for both sides, not the judges, are responsible for bringing out the relevant evidence. It also is risky for a judge to depart from the adversarial script, for an appellate court might find that he has transgressed the defendant's constitutional rights. Finally, in the system's list of goals, following the adversarial procedures properly ranks somewhat higher than determining the truth. The power of this ethic is underscored by the *prosecutor*'s failure to follow up on the defendant's confession.

Significantly curtailing adversarial legalism in the criminal justice systems of the United States, therefore, would conflict with the ethos of the legal profession and the American judiciary. Both could be counted on to fight like wildcats against significant changes in basic legal rules and the structure of legal institutions. In other spheres of law, policy, and governance, reducing adversarial legalism significantly would similarly shift control and influence from lawyers to judges and governmental agencies. The American legal profession would denounce those changes as contrary to American legal traditions (which they are) and as an enormous threat to the pursuit of justice (which is more debatable).

Moreover, American lawyers can be an extraordinarily potent political force when their interests and ideology are challenged. Plaintiffs' lawyers, bolstered by their capacity to raise and deploy huge amounts of money for political campaign contributions, have successfully watered down most political efforts to adopt no-fault systems for motor vehicle accidents, limit money damages in tort cases, restrict the fearsomeness of product liability law and class actions, and substitute government-funded compensation plans for lawsuits by individuals harmed by asbestos, tobacco, and other dangerous products. Bankruptcy lawyers and judges have organized politically to block plans to shift consumer bankruptcy cases to administrative agencies (Barnes, 1997). Any proposal to abandon or restrict jury trials for civil cases, amend the privilege against self-incrimination, and indeed to adopt virtually any of the sweeping changes discussed in the preceding section, would immediately trigger much more intense, well-publicized, and outraged opposition from the bar and the judiciary.

Politics

If adversarial legalism benefits American lawyers (who surely are not the most popular occupational group in the United States) while burdening the rest of the population with a costly, unpredictable, and often unjust method of governance and adjudication, why should we expect the lawyers' preferences to prevail? One truism in American politics is that it is difficult to enact and implement policy changes that might benefit the public at large if the changes impose "concentrated costs" on well-organized, intensely engaged groups—in this case, the lawyers. Reducing adversarial legalism might benefit many Americans, but those benefits would be widely diffused. Hence it is difficult to imagine building broad political coalitions to support the political changes discussed in the previous section.

Consider, for example, the idea of substituting collectively funded, administratively implemented compensation plans for tort suits concerning highway, medical, and product-based injuries. Traditionally, the Democratic Party is ideologically disposed toward government programs that provide universal coverage for individual catastrophes. But in recent decades Democratic Party leaders have generally *opposed* tort reform proposals pushed by Republicans (which seek only to make recovery by injured persons more difficult), and Democrats have rarely sponsored new social-insurance-based compensation programs that would displace tort litigation. In the 1990s President

Clinton's health care initiatives sought, if anything, to *expand* the role of medical malpractice litigation in assuring quality control, and the Democratic White House did not push efforts to establish an administrative compensation system for the thousands of asbestos victims who await an uncertain fate in litigation.

In explaining Democrats' diffidence about, or hostility to, serious tort reform, political commentators have pointed to the large campaign contributions marshaled by plaintiffs' lawyers, especially those whose coffers have been filled by enormous fees derived from asbestos, tobacco, and securities class action litigation (Gigot, 1999). But just as important, the Democratic Party, while more the "party of government" than the Republicans, also incorporates a strong populist strain, suspicious of hierarchically exercised governmental power and solicitous of individual citizens' rights to challenge government and business corporations in court. The close relationship between American trial lawyers and the Democratic Party thus is ideological as well as instrumental. Hence the Democratic Party is likely to oppose any proposals that would transfer authority from citizen juries to judges or to administrative agencies, or curtail citizens' rights to sue business corporations, or limit rights to appeal bureaucratic decisions to courts, or curtail defendants' right to silence or the role of defense lawyers in criminal procedure.

Political conservatives and the Republican Party, one might imagine, would be philosophically more attuned to reforms that strengthen hierarchies against populist legal challenge. On the other hand, creating effective hierarchical *substitutes* for adversarial legalism would require more active government bureaucracies and larger government expenditures—both of which offend the Republican Party's populist-cum-individualist strain. Thus important Republican constituencies are likely to oppose litigation-reducing reforms that would also increase taxes to finance compensation plans for the injured or increases in the size and professionalism of regulatory offices or direct governmental cleanup of toxic waste sites (rather than the Superfund litigation). Republicans can also be expected to oppose state-level recruitment and supervision of police and prosecutors (even if that would reduce the need for control via adversarial legalism) or reforms that would substitute narcotics addiction treatment programs for punitive, litigation-producing criminal enforcement.

Business organizations are unhappy about legalistic enforcement and about adversarial legalism in the regulatory process more generally, but they also mistrust regulatory discretion and have been reluctant to forswear the protection of detailed laws and judicial review as safeguards against regulatory unreasonableness. Indeed, most of the regulatory reform proposals advocated by the Republican Congress in the mid-to-late 1990s called for protections that would have *increased* adversarial legalism. Similarly, the Republican Party, pushed by certain business groups—liability insurance companies, large manufacturers of consumer products, health care professionals, and high-tech firms troubled by extortive class actions—has supported legislation designed to curtail product liability suits, medical malpractice suits, and securities class actions. But the Republican reform advocates have not proposed any meaningful alternatives, such as reliable, administratively operated compensation plans, which would satisfy the public's and the Democratic Party's concern about adequate care and income replacement for accident victims.

In sum, resistance to measures that would sharply curtail adversarial legalism would not be confined to American lawyers and judges, and it would be based on more than adherence to American legal tradition. The Democratic Party would strongly oppose some proposals, the Republicans others, and many such proposals would be opposed by both.

Political Culture and Mistrust of Government

Compared to the United States, Western European democracies have not relied as much on legal accountability because their political leaders, business communities, and electorates seem to have a greater faith in the professionalism, competence, and neutrality of regulatory agencies, police departments, prosecutoriates, judiciaries, and local governmental units. The lack of that faith is the most fundamental obstacle to significant reductions in adversarial legalism in the United States. Nor is that lack of faith completely divorced from reality. Americans' mistrust of governmental professionalism, competence, and neutrality—and their corresponding reluctance to abandon adversarial legalism as a tool of accountability—is based on hard experience. It is not merely the residue of earlier generations, when government was more corrupt, racist, and incompetent than it is today. The lack of faith is based on current experience as well.

In Manhattan Family Court, 220,000 cases are filed each year. They involve claims for acknowledgment of paternity, child support, child custody, protective orders against abusive spouses, and protection of abused or neglected children. The Family Court is not built around the ideals of adversarial legalism. Instead, it reflects a Progressive Era faith in compassionate expert investigation and paternalistic intervention. There are no jury trials. In most cases the crucial finding of facts and presentation of evidence are dominated not by competing lawyers but by state-supported social workers who actively investigate the circumstances of the troubled family. The Family Court judges enjoy a good deal of what we have called hierarchical authority.

New York City's Family Court, however, leaves much to be desired. According to a detailed 1997 report by the *New York Times,* it is staffed by forty-three judges, but each is confronted with up to fifty cases a day and an ongoing caseload of as many as 800 active cases (Sexton, 1997). Consequently, according to a Legal Aid lawyer who works in the Manhattan Family Court, "the judges make precipitous decisions based on what they see in the five seconds they look up." A prosecutor specializing in sex crimes told a reporter, "The victims who come through Family Court often feel revictimized. They appear, but their cases do not get called. The judges, with so many cases, lose sensitivity" (ibid.). The Family Court judges, in turn, complain that the Child Welfare Department caseworkers, whose reports they rely on in custody and child abuse cases, are overburdened, fail to complete investigations and reports on time, or fail to do them adequately. Meanwhile, mothers seeking return of their children cry in the hallways, having been told that the investigation has not been done and the case must be postponed once again (ibid.).

However sad, there is something distressingly familiar about that portrait of the Manhattan Family Court—ill-supported, short of the required professional expertise, organizationally incapable of treating its troubled clientele with the dignity they deserve. Americans regularly encounter accounts of similarly understaffed, overburdened, and hence unjust institutions, from juvenile courts (Butterfield, 1997) and welfare bureaus to public defenders' offices and local regulatory agencies. A hierarchical decisionmaking system that relies not on adversarial lawyering but on expert judgment and governmental fact-finding would require adequate, indeed generous, public funding. In Germany and France hierarchical, proactive judicial systems work expeditiously and enjoy reasonable levels of legitimacy because courts are well funded and well staffed. But American voters, suspicious of governmental waste and incompetence, are reluctant to pay higher taxes to support their public agencies and courts at the levels of staffing and training that German and French electorates routinely approve. Consequently, in the United States one might expect much political resistance to many reforms that would significantly reduce adversarial legalism, such as accident compensation commissions for highway injuries; reliance on government-supplied physicians and other experts (rather than dueling experts hired by adversarial lawyers) to assess the causes and degree of injuries; granting regulatory officials and welfare agencies more discretion and final authority; and shifting a broad range of less serious criminal offenses to magistrate's courts that do not provide jury trials.

In the United States, opponents will argue, specialized courts and administrative agencies sooner or later would end up like the Manhattan Family

Court—starved for funds by conservative, tax-cutting governments, short on required expertise, and overburdened, demoralized, and unresponsive. When the Equal Employment Opportunity Commission and its state counterparts are so understaffed that backlogs of uninvestigated complaints run into the tens of thousands, it could be argued that it would be foolish to surrender the right to bring lawsuits directly against discriminatory employers. If the history of workers' compensation in many states is any guide, today's statutorily prescribed benefits for injured persons may be capped at stingy levels by tomorrow's legislature or gradually eroded by inflation. In a country in which judicial appointments are often based not on professional merit but on past loyalty to political party leaders, it seems risky to transfer authority from lawyers and juries to an unevenly competent judiciary. In sum, opponents would say, hierarchical authority and expertise may sound good in principle, but given the hard realities of the American political system, justice will quickly slip away without the prod of adversarially invoked rights and aggressive lawyering.

Mistrust of such reforms goes beyond the concern that government bodies will be underfunded to the fear that they will be politically biased—a concern that derives from the distinctive political structures of American government. As discussed earlier, in most economically advanced parliamentary democracies, governmental bureaucracies are respected for their professionalism and political neutrality. Elected governments and cabinet ministers come and go, but the ministries remain. A new government does not, as in the United States, result in a wholesale changing of the entire leadership stratum, each new administration intent on bending the bureaucracy to its particular political agenda. Members of parliaments, in contrast to American members of Congress or state legislatures, do not pressure agency officials through oversight hearings or repeated telephone calls to give particular and sympathetic attention to valued constituents.

In the United States, however, there is an ongoing struggle for influence on government bureaucracies. That struggle generates political uncertainty and risk both for governmental officials and for the citizens, organizations, and businesses that must deal with them. Environmentalists worry that after the next election, the Environmental Protection Agency may have new top administrators who are unsympathetic to their values, and regulated businesses feel exactly the same way. Following any election, the National Labor Relations Board, state workers' compensation commissions, county prosecutors' offices, and municipal police forces can and do change policy direction, and the new administration may be unresponsive to constituencies and values favored by the outgoing agency heads.

Political uncertainty breeds the desire for predictability. For interest groups who think that an electorally changeable government cannot be trusted, adversarial legalism provides something of an insurance policy. Proposals to reduce adversarial legalism by granting agencies more discretionary authority threaten to cancel that insurance. Proposals to reduce adversarial legalism, therefore, are likely to encounter strong opposition from a wide range of interest groups, from the American Civil Liberties Union to the American Petroleum Institute.

If administrative agencies were granted more discretion and made less vulnerable to judicial reversal, one method of ensuring their responsiveness and legitimacy, it was suggested earlier, would be to restructure them, incorporating representatives of relevant social and economic groups into the agencies' decisionmaking structure. But American political traditions and social realities generally resist such neocorporatist structures. In a country in which neither industry nor labor is tightly organized and in which a wide variety of environmental, civil rights, and other advocacy organizations are even less organized, who can authoritatively "represent" any particular sector or interest? In the Oakland Harbor story, channel-dredging was brought to a halt when the Half Moon Bay Fishermens' Association went to court, complaining that their interests had not properly been represented when the EPA, the Corps of Engineers, the Pacific Coast Federation of Fishermens' Associations, and two environmental groups agreed on a particular ocean site for disposal of the dredged sediments.

Such "underrepresented" social and political groups would provide powerful political support for the objection that corporatist agencies are insufficiently accountable, vulnerable to capture by particular interests, or, on contentious issues, prone to breakdown, deadlock, and inaction. If administrative discretion and behind-closed-doors negotiations supplant formal hearings, legal procedures, and judicial review, Americans would ask how can we be sure discretion will not be abused, that the politically weak will not be overwhelmed by the "politically correct" or the economically powerful, or that the Corps of Engineers will not revert to environmental insensitivity? In short, the key to the diminution of adversarial legalism would seem to be a bit of magic—in a disbelieving age, to restore faith in the competence and public-spirited nature of governmental authority.

Knowledge and Legal Change

To recapitulate, in order to reduce the incidence of adversarial legalism significantly, American courts and legislatures would have to effect major changes in legal institutions as well as in specific legal rules. Each proposed change would evoke intense political and intellectual opposition, and few of those changes seem likely to enjoy powerful and dedicated political support. But the logical conclusion—that adversarial legalism is *not* likely to decline significantly in the United States—may not be the end of the story.

All too often, social scientists have resembled nearsighted detectives, stooped over to search for clues that might explain existing patterns of activity, oblivious to the waves of change looming up behind their backs. Surprising things can and do happen. Forty years ago a majority of American adults smoked cigarettes and did so virtually anywhere they wanted. Today, in many cities office workers who want a smoking break are compelled by law to huddle outside in doorways (Kagan and Skolnick, 1993). Notwithstanding the political power of giant tobacco companies and notwithstanding the addictive qualities of cigarettes, both law and behavior have changed. They changed largely because of what we now *know*—in this case, about the carcinogenic and other adverse effects of tobacco smoke. The moral is that knowledge can change politics and hence can change legal rules and institutional practices. Knowledge usually cannot trump determined political opposition, but it can affect both public sentiment and the goals of activists, politicians, and judges.

In terms of effective major changes in American adversarial legalism, there may be an analogue to the spread of knowledge about cigarette's toxic effects: enhanced consciousness of the costs and limits of many current legal institutions and practices. The primary barrier to that consciousness is the "legal parochialism" of the American legal profession, political leaders, and journalists—by which I mean their relative ignorance of alternative ways of dealing with the problems of criminal, civil, and social justice, and their complacent belief that for all its shortcomings, the American legal system and its basic approach are the best in the world.

In some ways, complacency about the American legal system is understandable. The system seethes with activity and change. It is marked by abundant self-examination, recurrent reform measures, and trust in legal solutions to social and governmental problems. Moreover, the United States is the world's paramount economic power. American capitalism, like American science and technology, is extraordinarily creative and dynamic. Foreign investment flows into the United States like a river of gold. Thus if there are problems with the legal system, many Americans might think, those problems must be rather insignificant in the larger scheme of things. Consequently, there is little inclination to look abroad for ideas for improvements.

That complacency, however, may be a mistake. To be sure, American adversarial legalism is far from the worst of all methods of law and governance. In some respects, and at some moments, it is the best. By dispersing power and emphasizing judicial independence, adversarial legalism may provide stronger barriers against the tyranny of ideologically extreme governments, either of the Left or of the Right, than those erected by hierarchically organized legal institutions. But as Martin Krygier (2001) has written, explicating a point repeatedly made by Philip Selznick, measures designed primarily to reduce our fears often are ill-suited to help us attain our hopes. As a system for meeting the day-to-day challenge of providing justice in contemporary democratic societies, adversarial legalism has serious deficiencies.

The simple truth that might lead to significant change in America's legal consciousness, therefore, is that adversarial legalism is not the only way, and often not the best way, of achieving justice. In certain respects and selective areas, the quality of justice could be improved by investing in administrative and judicial institutions and devising legal and governmental practices that simultaneously reduce adversarial legalism and achieve higher levels of efficiency and reliability.

Between the radical changes discussed earlier and the status quo lie many intermediate positions. Significant change often occurs in increments over time rather than in big leaps. Within the next twenty-five years, legal reforms that move in the direction of the institutional changes discussed earlier may well become politically possible. Even now, American regulatory agencies constantly seek to avoid the delays of litigation by trying new, less conflictual ways of formulating and implementing regulatory goals and standards. In any given month, an all-seeing satellite focused on the United States would observe dozens of legislative committees, governors' task forces, lawyers' committees, and academic analysts discussing or proposing nonadversarial, nonlegalistic solutions to particular problems. Thus while adversarial legalism will not be wholly tamed—and it should not be *wholly* tamed—pieces of it can and almost surely will be dismantled or improved.

Notes

References

Index

Notes

1. The Concept of Adversarial Legalism

1. Feldman (2000) describes an exception. He shows that in the United States, Japan, and France alike, contaminated blood products infected thousands of hemophiliacs with HIV. Litigation ensued in all three countries, but the legal sanctions levied against respondent companies and government officials in Japan and France were harsher than in the United States, and the litigation in those countries became more of a political cause celebre. It does appear, however, that the behavior by Japanese and French government officials and companies was more clearly egregious, since "both Japan and France delayed the licensing of a U.S. blood test and continued using unheated blood products months after they had been abandoned in the United States" (id. at 694).

2. Sellers (1995) is a partial exception, since he found that appeals to courts of local land use decisions in the 1980s and 1990s were as common and just as likely to be successful in France and Germany as in the United States. The French and German appeals were to special administrative courts rather than to courts of general jurisdiction, as in the United States.

3. The typology in Table 2 reflects the distinction between hierarchical and party-influenced modes of legal decisionmaking and adjudication developed by Thibaut and Walker (1978) and Damaska (1986), as well as the typology of bureaucratic decision modes in Mashaw (1983), from which I derive the additional category "expert judgment."

4. For the broader use of the term "legalism" to refer to rule-oriented governance or decisionmaking, see Shklar (1964); Wilson (1968); Levin (1972: 193). For use of the term to refer to the "extreme" form of that mode of decisionmaking—rigid adherence to rules, without regard to their purpose or to the fairness of the outcome—see Nonet and Selznick (1978); Kagan (1978: 6, 92–93).

5. See, for example, Nielsen (2000), showing that a majority of Americans who condemn racist and sexually harassing public speech think that it generally should not be subject to legal prosecution.

6. Cross-national and historical data on national litigation rates—for example, focusing on civil litigation per 100,000 population—are very spotty and probably misleading. Litigation rates are very sensitive to differences in the various kinds of civil courts: those dealing with smaller versus larger claims, courts of general jurisdiction versus those that specialize in certain types of cases. Those jurisdictional

boundaries are not the same across nations and change over time, making it difficult for researchers to be sure they are comparing like with like. Review articles dealing with such studies indicate that the American litigation rate, while higher than that of most countries, is not extraordinarily higher. Galanter (1983); Clark (1990); Markesinis (1990); Kritzer (1991).

2. The Two Faces of Adversarial Legalism

1. National Prison Project (1990); Bureau of Justice Statistics (1991). In California during the 1980s, thirty-five of the state's fifty-eight county jail systems had been sued and were operating under court orders (Welsh, 1992: 601). Ultimately, there was a political backlash against the extent of judicial management of prisons. In late 1996 Congress enacted a statute making it easier to terminate judicial decrees governing penal institutions—an invitation that was accepted by many states, cities, and county governments (Sullivan, 2000).

2. For a more critical view of judicial reform orders in prisons, arguing that they may have adverse consequences for internal authority and inmate security, see DiIulio (1990).

3. There is little doubt that deepening Oakland's harbor would be economically desirable, both for the region, where port activity is a vital source of economic sustenance, and for the national economy as a whole. If, moreover, Oakland should become incapable of handling the most modern vessels, the only major ports on the entire West Coast would be in Los Angeles and in Puget Sound, hundreds of miles away from Oakland's valuable rail and highway links to California's Central Valley and to the East.

4. A search in 1989 revealed 123 reported court cases, in federal courts alone, concerning dredging and disposal plans (McCreary, 1989: 43). See also National Research Council (1985: 89–90); Wessel and Hershman (1988: 253–286); Kagan (1991b: 327); Strum (1993a, 1993b, 1993c).

3. The Political Construction of Adversarial Legalism

1. On the incidence of lawsuits by injured people, see Hensler et al. (1991); Sloan and Hsieh (1995). On disparaging those who do litigate, see Engel (1984: 551), Greenhouse (1986), and Sanders (1987: 601–616).

2. In a corporatist political economy, private actors are represented by a limited number of large, relatively stable, interest associations. Business firms are represented by federations of sectorial employers' organizations, employees by federations of labor unions. Their negotiations over policy take place under the watchful eye of a government ministry (Schmitter, 1979:13).

3. The "general expectation of compensation" that Friedman discerns does not mean that most Americans expect to be compensated for all harms, regardless of fault. Surveys show that at least for injuries arising in contexts other than motor vehicle accidents, most citizens do not automatically blame others or initiate lawsuits (Hensler et al., 1991). Jurors are skeptical about exaggerated claims or those in which the claimant seemed at least partially at fault (Hans and Lofquist, 1992).

Still, there is little doubt that citizens, on balance, now expect and even demand governmental or legal remedies for kinds of harms or losses (from natural disasters to bank failures to discrimination) that their grandparents would have accepted fatalistically.

4. See comparative studies, Table 1, Chapter 1.

5. Some scholars have argued that Hartz and others have neglected the extent to which profoundly illiberal political ideas, such as nativism, sexism, and racism, have contended with liberalism in American political culture and law. See, for example, Smith (1993). Still, viewed comparatively, liberalism is what best distinguishes the American political culture from that of most other economically advanced democracies.

6. Sheldon Goldman (1967) found that four-fifths of federal appellate court judges had been "political activists" at some point in their careers. See also Kagan et al. (1984).

7. Adversarial legalism is not necessarily either effective or efficient. For years, southern politicians evaded the thrust of the Supreme Court's decision by intimidating potential litigants (Peltason, 1961: 58). Significant progress toward desegregation occurred only in the latter half of the 1960s, after activism in the streets and the decline of intransigent southern Democrats finally produced a potent federal Civil Rights Act, which enabled federal bureaucrats to employ "hierarchical" levers, such as withdrawing federal funds from the recalcitrant school districts. Still, because the Supreme Court had transformed desegregation into an issue that hinged on interpretation of constitutional rights, controversial policy questions (such as the desirability of crosstown busing for racial balance) constantly ended up in the courts. Yet the courts were powerless to offset "white flight" to the suburbs.

8. According to some studies in the 1970s, pretrial hearings on motions to suppress evidence occurred in almost one in ten criminal prosecutions and in almost 40 percent of prosecutions relying on evidence obtained by search warrant (Nardulli, 1983: 585; Davies, 1983: 611).

9. Among these major enactments were the Civil Rights Act (1964), the National Traffic and Motor Safety Act (1966), the National Environmental Protection Act (1969), the Clean Air Act (1970), the Occupational Safety and Health Act (1970), the Clean Water Act (1972), the Equal Employment Opportunity Act (1972), the Employees Retirement Income Security Act (1974), and the Surface Mining and Reclamation Act (1977). See Vogel (1989: chs. 3–4); Sunstein (1990). In addition, congressional regulation of state and local government bodies reached new heights, sometimes through direct regulations, such as the Voting Rights Act, sometimes by means of conditions attached to federal laws providing funding for housing and welfare programs, mass transit, and so on (Mayhew, 1991; Conlan, 1985).

10. Moreover, in 1986, after the Supreme Court had recently ruled that plaintiffs who prevailed in court in EAHCA cases could not collect attorneys' fees from the school district, Congress unanimously passed legislation providing for such fee payments in administrative as well as judicial proceedings (Melnick, 1995: 44; Kirp, 1982).

11. See Schuck (1983); Taylor (1984) (implied rights to sue for enforcement of the National Environmental Protection Act); Rabkin (1989) (implied private rights to sue Office of Civil Rights concerning enforcement priorities).

12. Elsewhere Vogel writes, "The most characteristic, distinctive, and persistent belief of American corporate executives is an underlying suspicion and mistrust of government. It distinguishes the American business community . . . from every other bourgeousie." Vogel (1996: 3).

13. Scholars measure labor union centralization in terms of the level at which bargaining is conducted (national, regional, the local plant); the degree of control central federations exert over local union strike activities and finances; and the absolute number of union organizations. Merging various studies, Joel Rogers (1990) found that, on a scale of 0 (least centralized) to 7 (most centralized), Austria in the 1980s scored 7, the Netherlands 5.7, Germany 1.3, and the United States 0. See also Wilensky (1976: 21–25, 48–50; 1983: 53–54, 71–72).

14. See pages 24–25.

15. The Comprehensive Environmental Response, Compensation and Liability Act (CERCLA) imposes absolute, joint and several, and retroactive liability for cleanup costs on any enterprise whose wastes found their way into the disposal site—regardless of the disposer's *share* of the wastes, regardless of whether it acted perfectly lawfully under the legal rules and containment practices prevailing at the time of disposal, regardless of any demonstrated current harm to human health. The "responsible parties" so designated then are entitled to sue other parties who had sent wastes to the same site in order to compel them to bear their fair share of the cleanup costs. The result is virtually endless litigation and negotiation before the sites are contained (Landy and Hague, 1992; Church and Nakamura, 1993).

4. Adversarial Legalism and American Criminal Justice

1. McCleskey's lawyers argued that the conviction was flawed, inter alia, because (1) Georgia's death penalty was applied in a discriminatory manner; (2) the lineup at which McCleskey was identified was improperly conducted; (3) McCleskey's inculpatory pretrial statements were improperly admitted into evidence, because they had not been given voluntarily; and (4) McCleskey's prior criminal record had been improperly admitted into evidence (*McCleskey v. State*, 1980).

2. The prosecution's expert witness challenged the implication that this data proved racial bias. He argued that "black on white" homicides tended to be different from intraracial homicides in that they entailed more aggravated circumstances (e.g., the killing occurred in the course of an armed robbery or the victim was a police officer, as in McCleskey's case). He also argued that there were so few "white on black" homicides that no pattern could be ascertained, and that they tended to involve more statutorily prescribed mitigating circumstances (Rothman and Powers, 1984: 3, 10–11). Subsequent studies in Florida, North Carolina, Mississippi, and Illinois, however, found similar race-of-victim effects in capital cases (Butterfield, 1998a; Weisburd, 1999).

3. In the decade 1900–1909 there were at least 885 lynchings in southern states, and 621 between 1910 and 1919 (Paternoster, 1991).

4. Juries impose death sentences on convicted murderers in about 20 percent of the cases presented to them (Paternoster, 1991: 168–69; Baldus et al., 1990: 88–89).

5. In 1980, 6 percent of all criminal charges in France involved "victimless" or "consensual" crimes; in the United States, "comparable offenses accounted for over 30% of all arrests, notifications, or citations for nontraffic violations" (Frase, 1990: 569–570).

6. A comparative study found that approximately 40 percent of robberies reported to the police in the United States involve firearms, compared to 12 percent in Germany and 9 percent in England (Lynch, 1988: 196–197; Zimring and Hawkins, 1997: 115). According to Handgun Control, an advocacy group, in 1996 handguns were used to murder 15 people in Japan, 30 in Great Britain, 106 in Canada, and 9,390 in the United States (Herbert, 2001).

7. Moreover, the cost of legal defense in capital cases adds to delay, as states postpone adequate appropriations for death penalty appeals (Verhovek, 1995).

8. Between 1977 and March 1990, only thirteen states actually executed anyone, and only six (Alabama, Florida, Georgia, Louisiana, Texas, and Virginia) executed more than five persons (*The Economist*, 1990: 26).

9. In Texas, where ninety-two executions occurred between 1976 and 1994, thirty-seven arose from crimes prosecuted in the Houston area, whereas only five stemmed from convictions in Dallas, whose population is two-thirds the size of Houston's (Lewin, 1995).

10. See *Harris v. Alabama* (1995), which upheld an Alabama law granting judges broad discretion to disregard jury decisions on sentencing. Justice Stevens, in dissent, noted that Alabama judges had overridden five jury recommendations of death sentences under that statute, while sentencing to death forty-seven defendants for whom the jury had recommended life sentences.

11. On inadequate funding of defense counsel in capital cases, see Coyle et al. (1990: 30–44); Redick, Jr. (1993: 22); Margolick (1994); Bright (1994). On funding of defense counsel and the low level of adversarial activity in general, see McConville and Mirsky (1986–1987); Stuntz (1997).

12. In May 1986 Justice Blackmun told a group of federal judges that during the preceding term "the excruciating agony" of last-minute death penalty decisions had "haunted and debilitated the Court" (White, 1987; Noonan, Jr., 1993; Dubber, 1997).

13. Anti-Terrorism and Effective Death Penalty Act of 1996, enacted April 1996. The Supreme Court quickly upheld its constitutionality in *Felker v. Turpin* (1996).

14. Redelet, Bedau, and Putnam (1992); *Herrera v. Collins* (1993); Terry (1993: A8); Applebome (1993: 2); Lewis (1995: A23) ("In the last 20 years, 54 Americans under sentence of death have been released from prison because of evidence of their innocence"); Connors et al. (1996). For an argument that instances of wrongful conviction and execution have been exaggerated in recent years, see Cassell (2000).

15. In a 1994 poll 85 percent of Americans surveyed said that courts in their area did not deal with criminals "harshly enough" (Bureau of Justice Statistics, 2000: 130–131).

16. Between 1955 and 1971, according to a careful study by Richard Berk and his associates, the number of groups that lobbied the California legislature on crime policy issues expanded, and the "elite or professional model of legislation faded" (Berk, Brackman, and Lesser, 1977: 86). In Great Britain, in contrast, a later study showed that civil servants reasserted influence on British crime policy, after initially having been ignored by the Thatcher administration (Reiner and Cross, 1991: 4–7).

17. According to a former counsel to the House Judiciary Subcommittee on Crime, no separate hearings were held on the crack penalty provision. It was written into the comprehensive bill with only about three and a half hours of discussion. "The 100-to-1 ratio [between penalties for crack and powder cocaine] was originally a 50-to-1 ratio in the subcommittee's bill, and was arbitrarily doubled to symbolize redoubled congressional seriousness." In retrospect, "It was more like the floor of the Stock Exchange when there is a rush to sell or buy a particular commodity. Everyone felt that the spotlight for solving the drug crisis was on them. And if it wasn't, they wanted it to be" (Manley, 1994).

18. In 1995, 88.4 percent of those convicted in federal courts for selling crack cocaine were black; 4.5 percent were white. In large part due to the preponderance of black crack dealers, the average sentence served by black inmates in federal prisons (seventy-one months) far exceeded the average served by white inmates (fifty months). In the early 1980s, before the crack law, the average time in federal prisons served by blacks was comparable to that of whites (Skolnick, 1998: 90, 94; Tonry, 1995).

19. In Germany, a federal polity, police and prosecutorial offices are organized at the level of the states (lander). But the German Penal Code and Code of Criminal Procedure are federal laws, operating nationwide. And, as Damaska (1975: 488) observes, "a striving for [national] uniformity is nevertheless obvious."

20. The federal government in the United States does operate many specialized police forces with narrow mandates, such as the FBI, the Drug Enforcement Administration, the Border Patrol, and the Immigration and Nationalization Service, together with the small criminal branches of regulatory agencies such as the Environmental Protection Agency, the Food and Drug Administration, and the Securities and Exchange Commission.

21. Researchers in the Capital Jury Project also found that jurors who voted for the death penalty frequently did not follow or understand their instructions (Mansnerus, 1995). After probing interviews with juries in cases he had chronicled, Adler (1994) described them as "lots of sincere, serious people who . . . were missing key points, focusing on irrelevant issues, succumbing to barely recognized prejudices, failing to see through the cheapest appeals to sympathy or hate, and generally botching the job" (id. at xiv).

22. In Germany lawyers have the right to cross-examine witnesses but generally prefer to ask the judge to pursue any additional line of questioning that the lawyer thinks would be helpful (Frase and Weigend, 1995: 367).

23. In its 1972 decision in *Papachristou v. Jacksonville*, the Supreme Court invalidated laws that criminalized vagrancy, reasoning that their inherent vagueness violated the right to due process of law and invited discriminatory application. Many cities

responded by establishing noncriminal "detoxification centers" to which the police could commit (for a short time) incapacitated chronic public inebriates (Aarmson et al., 1978).

24. State and local expenditures on defense lawyering in criminal cases increased from $46 million nationally in 1970 to $315 million in 1978 (Stuntz, 1997: 5, 50).

25. Mandatory arrest policies were also spurred by a Minneapolis study indicating that arresting abusive men reduced recidivism in domestic violence cases, although subsequent research has questioned the benefits of mandatory (as opposed to discretionary) arrest in such cases (Sherman, 1992).

26. Fisher (2000) points out that England enforces the obligation to disclose exculpatory evidence in criminal cases quite effectively by means of a hierarchical system that prescribes and regulates police recording and communication of all evidence. In the decentralized American system, in contrast, each police department is essentially self-regulating in this regard.

27. Studies have shown that in some localities arrests of African-Americans for drug offenses are highly disproportionate to the percentage of African-Americans who are drug users (Human Rights Watch, 1996). Similarly, state highway patrols have been found to stop and question African-American drivers much more often than white motorists. Studies of several California cities revealed that the rate of arrests subsequently determined to be unfounded for African-Americans is at least four times as high as for whites, and in some places seven or twelve times as high (Bass, 1997: 8–10).

28. Craig Bradley found that in the 1980–1984 period, the U.S. Supreme Court decided thirty-five cases involving the interpretation of the Fourth Amendment's restrictions on searches and seizures. Few were decided unanimously. Seven had no majority opinion at all, as the justices disagreed about what restrictions the Constitution should be read to require (Bradley, 1993: 49). After examining 223 state appellate decisions on search and seizure issues, Bradley concluded that in at least a third of the cases, either the trial court judge or the state appellate judges had misunderstood Supreme Court precedents (id. at 47–48). Between 1985 and 1990 an increasingly conservative Supreme Court decided forty-three Fourth Amendment cases, reversing the court below in 85 percent of the cases that had been decided in the government's favor (Bookspan, 1991). Two legal scholars asked 547 police officers about the legal propriety of searches undertaken in six fact situations described in cases that had been decided by the Supreme Court. Taking the Court decision as the correct answer, the police officers' mean score was 3.4 out of 6—only slightly better than the 3.0 one would expect from random guessing. A group of lawyers scored 4.4 on the same test (Heffernan and Lovely, 1991: 537).

5. Deciding Criminal Cases

1. Excluding jury deliberation time, which averaged about three hours (National Center for State Courts, 1988: 19), the median trial took slightly more than eleven hours.

2. A study of nine urban trial courts in 1986–1987 indicated that "trial days" av-

eraged less than three and a half hours (National Center for State Courts, 1988: 79).

3. In one California trial of a man charged with murdering two police officers, the defense alone cost the state nearly $1 million, including $255,000 on forensic and legal experts, $100,000 for private investigators, $50,000 for paralegals, and the rest for attorneys' fees (Verhovek, 1995: A1, A13).

4. On the other hand, Hughes (1984: 588) reports that in England the average Crown Court jury trial in 1980 took 8.5 hours—not all that much shorter than the eleven-hour median trial in a sample of American criminal courts. See National Center for State Courts (1988: 9).

5. In Los Angeles County 48 percent of jurors who received jury duty notice in 1995 did not respond. In Dallas, Texas, the response rate ranges between 22 and 37 percent. In Baltimore an estimated 100 jurors don't report each day (Gerlin, 1995: B1).

6. American "crime commissions' in the 1920s complained of extensive reliance on guilty pleas. Plea bargaining has been documented in Great Britain, although it clearly is less pervasive and not officially legitimated, as in the United States (Baldwin and McConville, 1979).

7. A former prosecutor and defense lawyer, describing his experience, writes: "The simple fact was that the evidence against most defendants was overwhelming. . . . Defendants who had little hope of winning at trial . . . correctly guessed that judges would usually reward of plea of guilty (even one entered without a bargain) with a greatly reduced sentence" (Lynch, 1994: 118). In Alaska, after plea bargaining was forbidden by statute (which appears to have been complied with) guilty pleas remained very prevalent, largely because, as one judge put it, "Human nature doesn't want to engage in a fruitless act" (Rubinstein and White, 1979: 81).

8. But see Ramseyer and Rasmusen (1998).

9. As pointed out by William Pizzi (1999: 54), a leading American treatise on defense of criminal cases asserts that either before or after arrest, a client should always be advised to "say nothing at all to the police, tell them nothing under any circumstances." See Amsterdam (1988, vol. 5: 120).

10. Lynch (1994: 120) provides a vivid example.

11. Prior to California's 1994 enactment of a statewide "three-strikes" law mandating life imprisonment for a third felony conviction, about 90 percent of felony cases were resolved by guilty pleas, according to the state Legislative Analysts' Office; after the effective date of the three-strikes law, a majority of defendants in third-strike cases insisted on a jury trial (Butterfield, 1995: A1, A9; Bandow, 1995: A17). The prosecutor in Santa Clara County, California, refused to engage in plea bargaining. In consequence, 60 to 70 percent of felony cases went to trial, and it became almost impossible to get a civil trial heard in the county courthouse. In other California counties, prosecutors disregarded the clear words of the statute and engaged in plea bargaining, which cut the trial rate for three-strikes cases to a third of the Santa Clara County level (Eisenberg, 1995: 50–58).

12. In jurisdictions where state prosecutors have this discretion to manipulate the applicability of statutory sentence enhancements, such as California and Arizona,

the percentage of felony cases resolved by guilty plea is unusually high (Lowenthal, 1993: 78–85). In Arizona, Lowenthal discovered, prosecutors dismissed repetitive offender allegations in 76 percent of all cases in which such charges had been initially made, and dismissed "dangerous felony" enhancement charges 77 percent of the time, indicating those charges often are used as plea bargaining chips (id. at 82–83).

13. Overcharging by prosecutors, Alschuler (1983: 939) notes, means that when defendants on occasion refuse to yield and insist on trial, the trials themselves become more complex and longer.

14. On the role of prosecutorial hierarchies in coordinating charging policies in France and the Netherlands, see Frase (1990: 560–563, 616) and Downes (1988: 15).

15. After a careful comparison of the available evidence, Richard Frase (1990: 639) concludes, "'Cooperation bargaining' has a relatively modest effect on sentencing in France." Compared to the United States, it entails modest concessions by prosecutors for modest degrees of cooperation.

16. Thomas Weigend (1980: 409) notes that French commentators (who tend "to be anything but uncritical") deplore the arbitrariness that can occur in the process of *correctionalisation,* whereby prosecutors reduce charges *before* filing and send the case to a lower court, in which maximum penalties are lower and trial procedures simpler. But "none of them charges that the *procureur* systematically uses that device to induce or reward confessions." In Germany many criminal cases referred by the police are disposed of via the *Strafbefehl* (penal order) by which the defendant can accept without trial a judgment of guilt, but the penalty is limited to a monetary fine. Unlike American plea bargaining, however, Weigend says (id. at 414), "neither side views the procedure as an exchange of trial rights for a sentence discount" and "the German defendant is not punished for demanding trial." The German practice of "conditional dismissal" offers a dismissal and a monetary fine to defendants in minor cases who decline trial, but unlike an American guilty plea, there is no criminal conviction (id. at 417–418).

17. German defendants who decline to contest "penal orders" are given lesser sentences, and those who confess at trial tend to be given lighter sentences; informing defendants of these options in advance might be considered a form of "implicit" plea bargaining. Langbein (1979b) forcefully distinguishes the "implicit plea bargaining" in the penal order cases from the outright bargaining and reductions in the legal charges that characterize American plea bargaining. Although German plea bargaining may be conducted in a more constrained manner than in the American version, by one estimate it affects about 20–30 percent of all trials in Germany (Hermann, 1992: 756; Frase and Weigend, 1995: 344–345).

18. A 1978 study of more than 400 lower court criminal trials in Lower Saxony indicated that the average trial length, when the defendant confessed (in whole or in part), was fifty minutes, and about seventy minutes when there was no confession (Weigend, 1980: 411).

19. Lay judges in Germany are elected by the local community and serve a term of four years, during which they must be available for a certain number of trial days per year. Hence they acquire some experience (Pizzi, 1999: 98). While they are

clearly subordinate to the professional judges, surveys indicate that the German lay judges think the professionals are generally fair to them as well as to the defendants (Machura, 2000).

20. According to a study of nine urban trial courts in 1986–1987, jury selection averaged about one-third of total trial time. In Oakland, California, jury selection in the average robbery and aggravated assault case consumed more than eight hours. In the fastest criminal court, in Elizabeth, New Jersey, jury selection averaged 20 percent of total trial time, or somewhat more than one hour (National Center for State Courts, 1988: 30, 40, 112).

21. But see Friedman (1998).

22. In France the defendant who wishes to remain silent "must at least stand mute while the presiding judge poses questions suggesting the defendant's guilt. Moreover, French law does not forbid drawing adverse inferences from the defendant's silence" (Frase, 1990: 679). In Germany the court is precluded by law from drawing such a negative inference (Frase and Weigand, 1995: 343). American defendants have an absolute right not to take the witness stand, and "the exercise of this right [at least since the Supreme Court's 1965 decision in *Griffin v. California*)] may not be the basis for adverse comment [to the jury] by the court or the prosecution" (Frase, 1990: 679).

23. The ability of lay judges in Germany to question witnesses, even though they often decline to do so (Machura, 2000), stands in marked distinction to the role of lay jurors in the United States, who are forced to sit mutely during the trial as well as during the legal instructions they belatedly receive from the judge. Any teacher knows that if the students don't ask questions, one can never be sure they understand the material. Little wonder that studies show that jurors in capital punishment cases often misunderstand the judge's instructions (*San Francisco Chronicle*, 1995; Mansnerus, 1995; Garvey et al., 2000).

24. Similarly, Frase notes (1990: 673) of French trials, "Judicial control of the taking of proof, combined with the practice of calling the defendant as first witness, allows the proof of guilt to focus only on the contested issues, thus improving the speed and quality of the guilt determination process." See also Peters (1992: 259, 285, 288).

25. For an account of the Dutch system, see also Pizzi (1999: 94–97).

26. Ibid. Peters (1992: 285, 288) offers a fascinating and detailed analysis of several similar criminal cases in the Netherlands and Japan, focusing on the extent to which Dutch and Japanese investigations and trials are open to the subjective understandings of the accused. He notes that in Holland, as contrasted with the more authoritarian and bureaucratic Japanese system, in the reconstruction of the events and motives surrounding the crime, "defense counsel played a major role . . . suggesting an additional, alternative reconstruction from the perspective of his client" in addition to offering legal defenses.

27. A Magistrate's court cannot impose prison sentences exceeding six months; if it decides a long sentence is appropriate, it may send the case to Crown Court for a trial by jury (Pizzi, 1999: 116).

28. In the New Haven, Connecticut, lower criminal court studied by Feeley, any defendant who might initially have thought about demanding a trial to prove his in-

nocence soon came to realize that it would take money and time—money for a bail bondsman and for an attorney (if the defendant was not indigent); several days away from work to confer with his lawyer and to appear in court; time rounding up defense witnesses. In Feeley's (1979: 9) sample of 1,640 cases, not a single defendant invoked his right to trial by jury. Instead, defendants chose a quick, lawyer-negotiated plea bargain; the usual sentence was a fine (usually less than a bail bond, a tenth the typical defense lawyer's fee) or a few days in jail, suspended because of the time already served between arrest and arraignment. For most defendants, the costs of the adversarial legal process would only exacerbate the punishment (id at 241).

29. British criminal defendants and lawyers, surveys have indicated, regard magistrate's courts as more "pro-police" than Crown Courts (McConville, 1994). On the other hand, there is an acquittal rate of 22–24 percent (similar to that of U.S. juries), even though many cases involve "strict liability" minor offenses, and penalties are mild. Moreover, there is little evidence that defendants who insist on a magistrate's trial and are convicted are punished more harshly than those who plead guilty (Darbyshire, 1997a, 1997b). Darbyshire (1997b) does note, however, that in an increasingly racially diverse country, British magistrates are overwhelmingly white, disproportionately members of the Conservative Party, and rather old. In nonmetropolitan areas magistrates often are laymen and may not even have a law-trained clerk.

30. For a comparative description of American versus British recruitment of judges, see Atiyah and Summers (1987: ch. 12).

31. Some defense lawyers use the voir dire to eliminate alert, well-informed jurors and select the least capable and fair-minded ones in the pool. For a play-by-play description, see Adler (1994). In Dallas a prospective woman juror declined to answer some questions on a thirteen-page questionnaire handed her by the court—concerning her religion, income, political views, and memberships—on grounds that they were irrelevant to her ability to be an impartial juror. The judge held her in contempt, then sentenced her to three days in jail and a $200 fine; the sentence was upheld on appeal (Minow and Cate, 1994: A6).

32. "Constant objections stemming from a desire to overlook nothing are . . . not a feature of English procedure" (Hughes, 1984: 589–590).

33. To be sure, American appellate courts frequently employ a "harmless error rule" to avoid reversal for procedural error, but the large difference in trial practice, wherein American defense lawyers strive to "build a record" of procedural challenge rulings that may support an appeal, suggests there remain major differences in the two appellate processes.

34. British barristers, James Q. Wilson (1995) points out, can and often do represent the prosecution in a case one week and the defense the next. Nor to they have the same incentives as an ambitious American defense lawyer to seek lucrative, high profile cases by building a reputation for superaggressive advocacy.

35. In early 1999 a team of *Chicago Tribune* reporters published a remarkable series of articles that detailed deception and other misbehavior by American prosecutors, who often went unpunished (Armstrong and Possley, 1999a); Possley and Armstrong, 1999). According to Armstrong and Possley (1999a: 1C), "Since a

1963 Supreme Court decision designed to curb misconduct by prosecutors, at least 381 defendants nationally have had a homicide conviction thrown out because prosecutors concealed evidence suggesting innocence or presented evidence they knew to be false."

36. Police in England are instructed to warn suspects before they are questioned, "You do not have to say anything. But it may harm your defence if you do not mention something now which you later rely on in court."

37. In a carefully constructed sample survey, a majority of police officials, lawyers, and community leaders, as well as a majority of the public at large, chose "a rich person usually gets treated better than a poor person in the American court system" rather than "almost every citizen can expect an equally fair trial" (McClosky and Brill, 1983: 150–151).

38. In 1992 almost 80 percent of state felony defendants were classified as "indigent" for purposes of state-provided defense counsel (Stuntz, 1997: 7). With respect to race and criminal punishment, see Cassia Spohn et al. (1981–1982: 821–877), whose study found no relationship between race and overall sentence severity, after controlling for seriousness of charge and prior criminal record; she found, however, that black males were sentenced to prison 5 percent more often than white males. A study of federal court sentencing found that controlling for offense and criminal history, black offenders received sentences that are six months (13 percent) longer than those for white offenders, partly because judges were more likely to give longer sentences to offenders with less education (Mustard, 1997).

39. A past president of the Los Angeles Criminal Bar Association estimated in 1994 that the fee for a "celebrity" defense lawyer in a capital murder case can start at $500,000. O. J. Simpson's criminal defense team, by some estimates, would command total fees of up to $5 million. In contrast, in the average murder case, according to a private criminal justice research group, court-appointed defense lawyers put in an average of 500 to 750 hours per case, at an average reimbursement rate, nationally, of $50 per hour (which would yield total defense costs of $25,000 to $37,500) (Mydans, 1994: 8). In Houston, Texas, for court-appointed lawyers for indigent defendants charged with murder, "the pay ranges from less than $10,000 for a quick capital trial to as much as $40,000 for one that lasts several months" (Barrett, 1994).

40. Long before the O. J. Simpson case verdict, Langbein wrote (1995: 32–33), "Money is the defining element of our modern American criminal justice system. If Simpson walks, as most lawyers think he will, what will have decided the outcome is not that O. J. is black, but that he is rich. He can afford to buy what F. Lee Bailey, Alan Dershowitz, Johnnie Cochran and the others have to sell: the consultants on jury packing, the obliging experts who will contradict the state's overpowering DNA and related evidence, and the defense lawyer's bag of tricks for sowing doubts, casting aspersions and coaching witnesses." See also Stephen Adler (1994) for an excellent and detailed journalistic account of the successful defense of Imelda Marcos.

41. See Citron (1991); Bright (1994) ("Poor people accused of capital crimes are of-

ten defended by lawyers who lack the skills, resources, and commitment to handle such serious matters").

42. For a vivid example, see Thomas (1986: 1, 12).

6. Adversarial Legalism and Civil Justice

1. Continental European legal systems, Langbein (1994: 2043) notes, also avert will litigation because substantive law statutes commonly guarantee children at least a minimum fraction of the parent's estate. And "in the English and Commonwealth systems, the so-called 'family provision' statutes empower the court of equity to make discretionary provision for children (and others) if the court determines that the testator disinherited them unfairly." The United States, in contrast, emphasizes testamentary freedom, including the parent's right to disinherit children. But ironically, an experienced trial lawyer wrote, "the average jury . . . is visited with a strong temptation to rewrite [the will] in accordance with the jury's idea of what is fair and right" (ibid.).

2. See, for example, *Watson v. Dingler*, 831 S.W.2d 834 (Tex. App., Houston 14th District 1992); *In re Estate of Lamberson*, 407 So. 2d 358 (Fla. App., 5th Dist. 1981); *Newman v. Smith*, 82 So. 236 (Fla. 1918); 79 Am. Jur. §§390–391 (New York: Lawyer Cooperative Publications, 1996 ed.).

3. The report of the Council on California Competitiveness (1992) displays a graph showing 281 lawyers per 100,000 population in the United States, 111 in Germany, and 82 in England and Wales. In 1970 the United States provided 63 judges for every million citizens, compared to 81 in France, 93 in Sweden, 103 in Italy, and 213 in West Germany (Johnson and Drew, 1978: 8). In 1985 the United States had 94 judges per million population, and West Germany then had 279 (Curran, 1986: 3; Clark, 1988: 1807).

4. German litigants are empowered to challenge the court's choice of a neutral expert witness for good cause. They also can comment on the court-appointed expert's report (to which the expert is asked to reply), and if they make an adequate argument, can ask the court to seek a second opinion from another expert (Langbein, 1985: 839–840).

5. In Los Angeles Superior Court the median jury trial in 1984 took thirty hours; the median nonjury civil case trial took ten hours (Kakalik et al., 1990, table D.6). In courts in nine urban counties in Northern California, Colorado, and New Jersey in 1986, the median jury trial (excluding day-of-trial pretrial motions) took 13.5 hours, and the median nonjury trial 5 hours. One might wonder if the nonjury trials were intrinsically less complex. The data do not say. But the Los Angeles data exclude very simple "short-cause" nonjury trials (those estimated before trial to require no more than one trial day), which suggests that the nonjury trial cases analyzed were not particularly simple. Indeed, the average Los Angeles nonjury trial took twenty-five hours (compared to thirty-six hours for the average jury trial), which suggests that nonjury trials often involved very complex cases (ibid.). The vast majority of civil trials in the United States are jury trials, as opposed to judge-only trials. (Daniels and Martin, 1995: 66).

6. In the late 1980s the average trial in the U.S. District Court in San Francisco took five days, but each year five to seven trials exceeded one month (Bilocki, 1989: 43–47). The mean length for a civil jury trial in Cook County, Illinois, in the period 1959–1979 was 3.8 days (Priest, 1993: 103, 115).

7. A study based on 1992 data from forty-five populous counties produced similar results: median time to jury verdict was 2.5 years, but 5.5 years in Chicago, 4.5 years in Alameda County, California, and over 4 years in Fairfield County, Connecticut (Heise, 2000: 835, 837).

8. The German social courts (Sozialgerichte) of first instance, for example, sit in panels designed to increase specialization. There usually are three judges, one professional and two lay judges. According to Timothy Jost (1998: 657–658), "In disputes regarding insurance coverage, one of the lay judges represents insureds, and the other represents employers. In matters concerning the relationship between health insurance companies and insurance doctors, one of the lay judges represents the insurance companies, the other the doctors."

9. There are some specialized trial courts in the United States, including bankruptcy tribunals, family courts, juvenile courts, and small claims courts. Large cities may have special housing courts. And there are specialized administrative tribunals that deal with workers' compensation cases, labor representation and unfair labor practice cases (the National Labor Relations Board), federal tax cases, and patent appeals.

10. In France the new judge first takes a special two-year course in a national judge-training school (Meador, 1983: 20).

11. According to Langbein (1985: 850), "evaluations by senior judges pay particular regard to (1) a judge's effectiveness in conducting legal proceedings, including fact-gathering, and his treatment of witnesses and litigants; and (2) the quality of his opinions—his success in mastering and applying the law." The judge also receives an "efficiency rating" based on factors such as case disposition and reversal rates.

12. A survey of judges on the U.S. Court of Appeals in the 1960s found that four-fifths had been "political activists" at some point in their careers (Goldman, 1967). About three-quarters of the state supreme court judges during the 1900–1970 period reached the bench after having held another public office or after "a career *closely* involved with politics." Almost half joined the high court without having had any prior experience as a lower court judge (Kagan et al., 1984: 376, 378).

13. See also MacCoun (1993: 137–180); Lempert (1993: 181–247); Vidmar, (1993: 293); Vidmar and Rice (1993: 896).

14. More recent experimental studies also suggest modest differences between decisionmaking by judges and juries (MacCoun, 1993: 165–167; Sentell, 1991: 98–99). Defenders of the civil jury argue that the 20 percent judge-jury disagreement rate in the Kalven and Zeisel study is comparable to the rate of disagreement among experts of various kinds (e.g., scientists engaged in peer review) and comparable to the rate at which appeals courts reverse trial judges (Diamond, 1983; Clermont and Eisenberg, 1992). Nonetheless, an analysis of a large database of decisions by judges and juries (in different cases) found, after controlling for nu-

merous variables likely to affect case outcomes, that juries make significantly larger money damage awards to injured plaintiffs than judges do, and juries are significantly more likely to find for plaintiffs in medical malpractice and product liability cases (Helland and Tabarrok, 2000). The authors also found that juries drawn from counties with higher poverty rates gave larger damage awards, controlling for other case factors, than juries in less poor counties or judges in poor counties.

15. In Texas and in Pennsylvania judges impaneled separate juries to hear evidence on several defendants' liability in asbestos cases, then separated the juries to hear evidence on damages for separate plaintiffs. Even though the juries heard the same evidence, in the same courtroom, at the same time, on the same issue (the defendants' liability), several juries arrived at different verdicts on liability (Hensler, 1985: 65).

16. American trial and appellate court judges can and do set aside or reduce jury awards that strike them as unreasonably high, but they don't always do so and rarely do they raise "unreasonably low" verdicts. There are few legal standards to guide judges' decisions to reduce "unreasonably high" verdicts, and American judges, unlike their continental European counterparts, are not legally required to justify particular verdicts.

17. Daniels and Martin (1995: 75–77, table 3.2) combed through jury verdict reporters for eighty-two sites, covering 100 counties in sixteen states for the years 1988–1990. Seventeen of the eighty-two sites—including the entire states of Alaska and Idaho—had fewer than fifty jury verdicts during the three-year period. Fewer than half of the sites—thirty-nine of eighty-two—had more than ten medical malpractice verdicts between 1988 and 1990, and only eleven reported fifty or more verdicts (id. at 126). There were no products liability verdicts in eleven sites, and only twenty-two of eighty-two sites reported ten or more such verdicts. Of these twenty-two sites, twelve recorded more than twenty and only five had more than fifty verdicts (id. at 171, table 5.2). Because these aggregate data fail to distinguish among different types of medical malpractice and products liability cases, the data tend to overstate the number of useful jury verdicts available to lawyers seeking to evaluate their client's claims. Daniels and Martin, who attack the comparison of the tort system with a "lottery," thus concede that "[j]ury verdicts, as a general proposition, are not predictable and uniform in the aggregate, if for no other reason than the lack of fungibility among the cases going to trial" (id. at 60).

18. In Evan Osborne's (1999: 193, 195) analysis, the overall correlation between attorneys' expectations and individual awards was .54 (and, in a regression analysis, R^2 = .41). That led Osborne to conclude that jury decisions are not "random events" (id. at 197) (as if any serious observer had ever argued that they were). Yet the statistics also indicate that attorney expectations explain only about half the variance in outcomes, which suggests a relatively high level of legal unpredictability, even for practitioners, in all types of civil cases.

19. Two other flagmakers, neither of which had sold the flag, settled for $14,000 and $1,500 respectively (Van de Putte, 1995: A14).

20. Molot (1998: 992) notes that liberal American pleading rules, in which a lawyer

need only state a claim and search for evidence later via pretrial discovery, also encourage the tactic of making and retaining weak legal claims, as does judicial reluctance to strike weak claims and defenses through early motions for partial summary judgment. The infamous Paula Jones civil lawsuit against President Bill Clinton provided a striking example of this phenomenon. The trial judge eventually (and belatedly) held that Jones's lawsuit was unfounded since she offered no evidence that she had suffered any legally cognizable damages. But before that occurred, Jones's lawyers were able to probe the president's private sex life in a wide-ranging pretrial discovery process, which led to untruthful statements under oath by the president, which led to an investigation by an Independent Counsel, multiple appeals to the courts by the White House, and then to impeachment by the House of Representatives.

21. Most national legal systems have declined to follow the American lead, although some Canadian provinces and some Australian states have authorized class actions in mass tort cases (Flemming, 1994: 519–523).

22. A study of all federal class actions in the Northern District of California from 1979 to 1984 found that in most cases plaintiffs' substantive justice claims were transformed into narrow procedural issues about notice and rights to be heard, providing few significant results for anyone except the lawyers (Garth, 1992: 237, 257).

23. In settlement of an action on behalf of 700,000 owners of Ford Broncos who claimed the vehicle was prone to deadly rollovers, plaintiffs ended up with free inspections and better safety warnings, while two plaintiffs' lawyers got $4 million in fees and expenses (Geyelin, 1994: B1). At a 1996 meeting of dozens of corporate attorneys who specialize in defending product liability class actions, a law school professor asked how many had "bought off" plaintiffs' counsel by offering to boost their fees in return for a settlement. "Roughly half the audience members raised their hands," a journalist reports (Boot, 1996: A18).

24. In December 1995 a Republican Congress, overriding a presidential veto that had been sought by the securities class action lawyers (who contribute lavishly to Democratic political campaigns), sought to curb such abuses by requiring plaintiffs to plead specific facts in order to pursue a securities fraud class action and by providing certain defenses to defendants (Taylor, 1995b).

25. As a reviewer of Schuck's book wrote, "the $180 million figure bore no intelligible relationship to the probability of success in the litigation, let alone to any rational estimate of economic or intangible loss actually suffered by the claimants" (Rabin, 1989: 819). Two of the defendant chemical companies subsequently sued the government in an effort to recover the amounts they paid in the settlement, but the Court of Appeals for the D.C. Circuit concluded that had the companies actually litigated the Agent Orange suit, rather than settling, they would have prevailed, and hence they were not entitled to indemnification (Barrett, 1996: B7; *Hercules, Inc. v. United States*, 1994). On the other hand, some years later a committee of the governmentally funded Institute of Medicine (IOM) issued a report that found it plausible to link extensive Agent Orange exposure to soft tissue sarcoma, chloracne, lymphoma, and other diseases. A 1996 IOM re-

port said there is "limited or suggestive" evidence of an association between exposure and spina bifida in the veterans' offspring (National Institute of Medicine, 1996).

26. The term "blackmail settlement" was used by U.S. Court of Appeals judge Richard Posner, *In the Matter of Rhone-Poulenc Rorer*, 51 F.3d 1293, 1298 (7th Cir. 1995), rejecting certification in a class action claim on behalf of hemophiliacs who contracted AIDS from HIV-infected blood early in the epidemic. See Feldman and Boyer (1999).

27. Galanter and Kahill (1999: 1374).

28. In the Netherlands, until the late 1990s almost 60 percent of private households were entitled to legal aid assistance and court fee waivers (Blankenburg, 1994); reforms then reduced coverage to approximately 47 percent. Even in the aftermath of Thatcher-era cutbacks in legal aid, in 1990 about 37 percent of the British population was eligible for subsidized assistance from solicitors (Kritzer, 1996: 141). In the United States government-funded civil legal assistance is available to individuals below the poverty level and those with incomes between 100 and 125 percent of the poverty level; in 2000, 17 or 18 percent of households were covered. Letter from Legal Services Corporation, November 2000.

29. In 1996 the federal government budget for the Legal Services Corporation was reduced from $400 million to $278 million (*New York Times*, 1996b: A14; Gottlieb, 1996: A8; Pear, 1995: A1, A9).

30. In September 1997 the securities industry discontinued mandatory arbitration of disputes with employees. Critics had charged that the pool of arbitrators was too closely linked with employers (Bales, 1998: 526).

7. The Tort Law System

1. Because the average mesothelioma victim dies one year after the disease has become manifest, the actual amounts paid to asbestos victims in the Netherlands are far less than the average tort recovery in the United States (Vinke and Wilthagen, 1992: 18).

2. Johns-Manville, the largest asbestos manufacturer, was compelled to jettison entire divisions, slashing its workforce by one-third, or about 9,000 employees. As of 1988 it had paid $100 million in legal fees alone (Brown, 1988).

3. As of 1984, asbestos claimants in the aggregate had received somewhat more than $235 million in damages. Their lawyers had earned $164 million. And the defendants had incurred more than $600 million in expenses (Kakalik et al., 1983: p. 39).

4. Moreover, Sugarman (1989) points out, whereas workers whose disease stems from asbestos can sue the manufacturer in tort—with its prospect, however uncertain, of obtaining large "pain and suffering" damages—other workers with equally severe illnesses or injuries that stem from other causes are restricted to more limited workers' compensation recoveries.

5. Thus "a disabled victim of [noncancerous] asbestosis will receive $50,000 under the Johns-Manville settlement but only between $5800 and $7500 [under the

so-called *Georgine* class settlement with another coalition of manufacturers]" (Coffee, 1995: 1396). An appellate court later abrogated the *Georgine* settlement.

6. In New York City tort cases increased from less than 1 percent of all civil cases in 1870 to 3.6 percent in 1890, and then to almost 12 percent in 1910 (Bergstrom, 1992: ch. 2, pp. 31–57). Bergstrom found that the increase in New York City tort suits reflected neither radical changes in the kinds of hazards that gave rise to the injuries in question nor changes in the law. The critical development, he concludes, was a shift in the attitudes of claimants and jurors—toward a greater willingness to perceive and impose responsibility for injury on others, particularly on the organizations that managed enterprises and technologies (id. at ch. 7). For a similar increase in tort suits in Boston, see Robert Silverman (1981), and in St. Louis, Wayne McIntosh (1980–1981: 832, 836). Tort cases swelled from 5.7 percent of state supreme court cases in 1870–1880 to 16.4 percent in 1905–1935 (Kagan, Cartwright, Friedman, and Wheeler, 1977: 142).

7. In Sweden, for example, specialized no-fault plans for motor vehicle accidents, industrial injuries, medical malpractice, and adverse reactions to pharmaceuticals are said to have reduced the incidence of arguments between accident victims and insurance companies over who caused the injury, standardized the amounts awarded, and diverted most disputes to a special board, whose informal but expeditious, expertise-based judgments rarely are appealed to the courts or to formal arbitration (Hellner, 1986; Oldertz, 1986).

8. In addition to medical expenses and lost earnings, the New Zealand scheme originally allowed limited recoveries (up to about $18,000 U.S.) for intangibles such as pain and suffering and loss of function, but in 1992 recoveries for pain and suffering were eliminated to reduce overall costs. Injured persons were, however, authorized to bring tort actions for damages not covered under the compensation scheme. The accident compensation system is funded by levies on employers and employees, a gasoline tax, and general revenues (Bell and O'Connell, 1997). If the Accident Commission determines that a negligent or inappropriate action occurred at the hands of a health care professional, it is supposed to communicate that information to the appropriate professional disciplinary body.

9. The Accident Commission rejects only a tiny proportion of the approximately 150,000 claims filed and judicial review proceedings are rare (Gellhorn, 1988: 194).

10. In 1990 California's statutory benefit levels for workers' compensation—which tend to reflect the lobbying strength of organized labor—were comparatively low, ranking thirty-fourth among the fifty states. But in terms of average cost per worker (forty-seven cents for every dollar of payroll), California ranked about third (*The Economist*, 1992: 29). A major reason was a high litigation rate, reaching nearly 36 percent of claims (CWCI, 1991b). Direct litigation costs—fees for both sides' attorneys, forensic physicians, and so on—averaged over $7,000 per case in 1990; the average award for successful applicants was $11,879. See also CWCI (1991a); Frammolino (1988: 3).

11. Almost half of persons injured in motor vehicle accidents attempt to collect compensation from another party to the accident, pursuant to tort law. Yet only three

of 100 nonmotor vehicle accidents lead to liability claims (Hensler et al., 1991). See also the Wisconsin Civil Litigation Project, which surveyed households in five states. For every 1,000 potential tort cases, mostly involving personal injuries, 857 persons with grievances said they made claims against the alleged tortfeasor or an insurance company (about the same rate for most other kinds of legally cognizable grievances). Moreover, 57.9 percent of respondents with personal injury grievances saw a lawyer (much higher than the rate for most other kinds of grievances). But only 201 "disputes" emerged from the 857 grievances, and only 38 resulted in a lawsuit (Miller and Sarat, 1981: 544).

12. Health insurance or workers' compensation insurers can claim reimbursement for amounts paid to an injured person who subsequently obtains damages for the same expenses from the tortfeasor or her insurance company. In many cases, however, that leads to an additional adversarial, legalistic struggle.

13. See National Center for State Courts (1986); U.S. General Accounting Office (1988)

14. Annual TV advertising expenditures by lawyers, the Television Bureau of Advertising reports, grew from about $17 million in 1983 to over $100 million in 1991 (Geyelin, 1992).

15. According to the *New York Times*, 813 lawsuits were brought against tobacco companies in the period between 1954 and 1994. Of those suits, only twenty-three went to trial and the industry lost only twice; both losses were overturned on appeal (Collins, 1995).

16. Ramseyer and Nakazato found that 80–95 percent of victims' families in fatal traffic accident cases file claims, and that in the ensuing settlements they "recover, on average, about 80–110 percent of the amount they would earn if they sued and won against a fully insured defendant" (Ramseyer and Nakazato, 1989: 280).

17. Daniel Foote (1995) provides an excellent account. The Tokyo traffic court judges, who led the movement, sought to create damage schedules that minimized the need for case-by-case examination (except for lost earnings) and sought to provide payments that did not vary according to the wealth or status of injured claimants, such as fixed sums for pain and suffering, per month of hospitalization, and so on. They also worked out rules of thumb for assessing comparative fault in common accident scenarios. The judge-devised standards were disseminated, Foote points out, in a special 161-page issue of a mass circulation newspaper in 1975. Judges meet to reconcile divergent practices in courts in different cities. See also Ramseyer and Nakazato (1989: 269).

18. See Ramsmeyer and Nakazato (1989: 270): "[I]n a world of asymmetric information and 'bounded rationality,' parties are far more likely to make similar estimates of the litigated outcome under the relatively clear and unified Japanese system than under the plastic and fragmented American one." This lack of predictability leads to more litigation. Atiyah and Summers (1987: 176) make a similar point: "[T]he findings and awards of American juries are much less predictable than those of English judges, and unpredictability leads to uncertainty which naturally encourages more litigation and more appeals."

19. A California Department of Motor Vehicles official estimated in 1991 that of eighteen million registered drivers, four to six million lower-income Califor-

nians—at least a quarter of all motorists—were driving without insurance (Wiebel, 1991).

20. See also Munch (1977: 38–39).

21. Appellate courts often reduce very large jury awards for pain and suffering and punitive damages (Broder, 1986; Shanley and Peterson, 1983: ix–x), but even that process seems unguided by law: judges rarely compare the appealed award to awards in similar cases (Geistfeld, 1995: 783).

22. The Harvard medical injury study, based on a careful review of hospital records in New York, discovered that fewer than one in three serious injuries apparently stemming from negligence led to a malpractice suit. See Harvard Medical Practice Study (1990).

23. According to an expert panel's review of over 1,000 claims against anesthesiologists, among plaintiffs who received *inadequate* care, one in five did not receive any compensation (Cheney et al., 1989).

24. In the same intensive review of claims against anesthesiologists cited in note 23, the expert panel concluded that 46 percent of the claimants had *not* received inadequate care. But of those, 42 percent received compensation—although not as much as those with comparable injuries for whom the care was found to be inadequate (Cheney et al., 1989: 1601–1602; Metzloff, 1993: 1181). A study of medical malpractice claims in Hawaii found that in 24 percent of the claims for which a screening panel deemed "no liability," the claimant nevertheless filed suit. Of the fifty-one closed cases in that category, plaintiffs received some compensation in thirty cases (or 60 percent), and in ten cases, more than $100,000 (Metzloff, 1988: 209). See also Farber and White (1991: 203–204) (expert panel review of 252 cases from one hospital found that of 95 cases found to involve *appropriate* care, 24 percent received some payment). See also Sloan and Van Wert (1991: 131–168).

25. See Bovbjerg et al. (1991: 15–16) (1980 malpractice verdicts were 6.5 times higher than reported auto accident verdicts; in a 1985 study, eleven times higher). See also Hammit et al. (1985: 754–755) (finding that "medical malpractice awards against doctors are almost 2.5 times as great as awards against other individuals in average case types, and awards against hospitals are 85% larger").

26. But see Vidmar (1993).

27. For other studies questioning tort law's effectiveness as a deterrent, see Schwartz (1994: 381–382); Laitin (1994); Abel (1990); Elliot (1989); Grady (1988: 305–306); Bruce (1984); Flemming (1984); O'Connell (1979); Dunlop (1975).

28. After reviewing a number of studies, Gary Schwartz (1994: 402) concluded that American malpractice law probably leads to "a substantial measure" of both the desirable and the excessive kinds of "defensive medicine." See also Mendelson and Rubin (1993). In a study of a large urban hospital in Indiana, 34.5 percent of physicians responded that the threat of malpractice liability was a significant influence on the ordering of tests and procedures, and 29.3 percent said it was a major influence (McIntosh and Murray, 1994: 26). The researchers estimated that legal liability added $450 in costs per patient admitted, of which "defensive medicine," whereby doctors order unnecessary tests and procedures in order to avoid legal liability, contributed $327, or 3.9 percent of the of total medical costs per patient. See also Weiler (1991).

29. Compare Danzon (1991: 203) ("informed observers believe that the elimination of liability [in New Zealand] has led to laxer standards of medical care") with Gellhorn (1988: 200) ("No study has shown that, as a consequence [of New Zealand's 1974 reform] the quality of medical service has suffered"). See also Brown (1985: 1002).

30. Although all liability suits against manufacturers alleged that design or manufacturing defects led to the crashes, neither Federal Aviation Administration nor National Transport Safety Board investigations of 203 Beechcraft accidents that led to liability claims or lawsuits in the 1980s found that any were due to such defects. Pilot error was the predominant cause (Martin, 1991: 485). At best, Craig (1991: 457) finds that "some evidence suggests that liability litigation has improved the dissemination of information about flight safety, and that, arguably, has encouraged pilots to fly their planes more safely."

31. A spokesman for Cessna, once the leading American manufacturer of small aircraft, stated that the company had spent an average of $20 to $25 million annually on defending product liability suits—the same amount the company previously had spent on research and development of small aircraft (Weintraub, 1994a: D1). After the bill was passed, Cessna returned to the business of building small airplanes and announced plans to build 2,000 planes a year in the future (Bryant, 1995).

32. In October 1997 a South Carolina jury handed down a $250 million punitive damages award against Chrysler Motors; the case involved serious injuries to a child in 1990, when he was thrown from a 1985 Plymouth minivan after an accident. The jury found Chrysler at fault for failure to put a stronger latch on the rear door. But Chrysler, under pressure from the National Highway Traffic Safety Agency, had strengthened the latches beginning in the 1995 model year, two years before the verdict, and had recalled earlier models for repairs (Geyelin, 1997).

33. See also Huber (1985); Kitch (1985); Lunzer (1985: 256). Ultimately, Congress enacted a vaccine injury compensation program. It removed vaccine cases from the tort-jury trial system and instead established an enterprise liability/limited compensation scheme, administered through the Federal Claims Court, funded through a tax on vaccines. Manufacturers again started making and marketing new vaccines (Burke: 2001).

34. The risky clients, of course, go on to hire less prominent and perhaps more compliant accountants, presumably increasing the risk of fraud to the public.

35. A National Research Council report concluded that U.S. liability law has generally deterred pharmaceutical companies from investing in research on new methods of contraception (Mastroianni et al., 1990). Wyeth was facing hundreds of lawsuits concerning its product Norplant, a different kind of contraceptive encased in silicone and implanted in the upper arm. Many of these suits were brought by a network of lawyers who specialized in silicone breast implant litigation. Meanwhile, the United States has the developed world's highest rate of out-of-wedlock births by teenage females (and the highest rate of children in poverty), largely because sexually active American girls less often use contraceptives.

36. Finally, after some companies were sued for not warning subsequent employers about a former employee's violent tendencies, a number of states passed laws pro-

viding employers with varying degrees of protection against defamation suits. Similarly, high school guidance counselors and college admissions offices complain that fear of litigation by parents has made high schools much more cautious about saying anything negative about students in letters of recommendation (Bronner, 1998).

37. Galanter (1998) emphasizes that McDonald's coffee was hotter than the standard in the trade; that the company had experienced some 700 prior claims, some of which it had settled; that McDonald's had rejected subsequent settlement proposals by the plaintiff's lawyer and by a court-appointed mediator that called for a $225,000 payment; and that the parties eventually settled for approximately $600,000. From this "system blame" perspective, McDonald's is apparently to be faulted for not settling all cases regardless of the plaintiff's negligence.

38. The California State Automobile Association's guide on what to do in an accident unequivocally states, "Do not discuss the accident with anyone, sign anything (except a traffic ticket), accept blame, or blame anyone until you contact your insurance company" (CSAA, 1997: 12). See generally Wagatsuma and Rossett (1986). At an "Accident and Injury" seminar held for the public by lawyers and chiropractors in California, a lawyer told the audience that after an accident, "If you say you feel OK, I guarantee that little statement will come back to haunt you" (Rubinstein, 1997: C1).

39. Peter Pringle (1998), a British journalist, argues that in Britain the tobacco companies have been more forthcoming than in the United States because until very recently they were not threatened by lawsuits there.

40. In 1986 Congress enacted an "enterprise liability" law that enabled parents of children who suffered side effects from vaccines to recover substantial but not unlimited damages from the manufacturer without proving fault. However, Congress granted victims the option to bring a tort suit instead (Burke, 2001). In 1987 the state of Virginia adopted a no-fault law that guarantees compensation for babies born with defects or who suffer injuries during or immediately after birth—even if the doctors, nurses, or hospitals have not been negligent (Sugarman, 1989: 109). Florida enacted a similar "bad baby law," but it allows for tort cases as well. The Florida compensation program has cut transactions costs compared to tort claims, but lawyers seem to have worked to restrict the program's visibility and use (Bovbjerg, Sloan, and Rankin, 1997).

41. Lipsen (1991: 248–249) wrote that forty-one states adopted tort law changes generally favorable to defendants. "The most popular changes include: revising the doctrine of joint and several liability (thirty-one states); modifying the collateral source rule (twenty states); altering common law treatment of punitive damages (twenty-five states); and establishing defenses for compliance with the 'state of the art' (eleven states), and government standards (nine states). Additionally, seventeen states have limited 'pain and suffering' damages."

42. From 1986 to 1993 the number of tort cases filed in twenty-two selected states stopped rising, remaining steady at about 390,000 per year. Bureau of Justice Statistics (1995).

43. Among other things, the law curbed suits in federal courts by providing a "safe harbor" from liability for statements concerning a stock's future performance, by

limiting attorneys' fees, by granting judges the authority to punish attorneys who brought "frivolous" claims, and by restricting accountants' liability for failing to detect fraud (Taylor, 1995a; Dewar, 1995).

44. Through the first nine months of the Clinton-Gore reelection campaign in 1995–1996, lawyers and law firms contributed $2.5 million, more than twice that of retired persons' organizations (the next largest contributor) and five times that of "business services" (the third largest contributor category) (Peltz, 1995; Schmitt, 1996). These large contributions are comprehensible in light of a *Forbes* magazine study listing sixty-three plaintiffs' lawyers who made more than $2 million each in 1987 and 1988, with at least fifteen others likely to belong in that category, and another fifty in the $1–$2 million range (Bell and O'Connell, 1997: 182).

45. One survey revealed that almost two-thirds of those who had filed a personal injury lawsuit considered the legal process they experienced unfair. Hensler et al. (1991: 139–140).

8. Adversarial Legalism and the Welfare State

1. Constitution of Chile, 1925, article 10, no. 14. The Chilean Constitution also committed the state to apportion "sufficient" money for a national health care system (Couso, 1997).

2. In 1997 Congress also added a guaranteed health insurance program for uninsured children, such as those whose parents had lost Medicaid benefits after obtaining employment. But the program is administered by state governments, many of which by the end of 1999 had not aggressively publicized this entitlement; consequently, many eligible children had not been enrolled (Pear, 1999: 1).

3. In the early 1990s the lowest-paid decile (10 percent) of male employees in Western European countries earned almost 70 percent of the *median* wage in their countries; the lowest paid decile in the United States earned only 38 percent of the median wage. Richard Freeman (1994: 13) wrote, "I estimate that among men in the bottom decile, Americans earn roughly 45 percent of what Germans earn, 54 percent as much as Norwegians, half as much as Italians, and so on." These disparities reflect not only the higher minimum wage laws in Europe but also the fact that a much larger proportion of European workers are covered by collective bargaining agreements than American workers—which in turn stems in large measure from differences in American labor law (Freeman, 1994; Kagan, 1990a).

4. In recent years, facing persistent high unemployment, some European welfare states have curtailed some benefits. Nevertheless, a recent analysis by the Center on Budget and Policy Priorities indicates that a single parent of three in France, unemployed for several years, would receive $1,166 monthly in cash benefits from the government, whereas her counterpart in the United States would receive $767 in AFDC and food stamps (Whitney, 1998: A1).

5. OECD figures indicate that the United States spends a smaller proportion of gross domestic product on public pensions than any of the sixteen rich democracies studied except for Ireland and Australia. American public pensions (social se-

curity) are also less generous than most, replacing only 30 percent of the average wage, compared to over 50 percent in Sweden, France, Japan, New Zealand, and Belgium, and 39 percent or more in Italy, Germany, Austria, Denmark, and the Netherlands. Great Britain, like the United States, has a large privately provided pension system and a correspondingly less generous public system (*The Economist*, 1996b: 105).

6. In recent years some European welfare states, such as France, have cut back family allowances based on the recipient family's income, and introduced means testing to programs such as child care allowances.

7. Similarly, when U.S. officials suspect American physicians, hospitals, or HMOs of seeking excessive reimbursement, they often bring civil or criminal actions in general courts. In Germany those disputes are decided by special arbitration committees, staffed by representatives of the health care plans and the doctor's union, and its decisions are appealable to the social courts (Jost, 1998). In the United States legislatures and judges (rather than specialists as in Germany) end up trying to draw fine distinctions between justifiable and nonjustifiable medical services and between fraud and excusable error by providers, and then embed those distinctions in penal laws. Medical malpractice litigation has likewise become an important mechanism for regulating the efforts of "managed care plans" to constrain physicians' decisions about costly individual services for patients; hence American judges and juries make many decisions about which restrictions on provision are justifiable (Sage, 1999).

8. See Sugarman (1985a). This section draws extensively on Sugarman's account and analysis.

9. Illinois, California, New York, and Oregon, like Connecticut, had enacted rules curtailing benefits for AFDC mothers who declined to cooperate in identifying their children's fathers. Lower federal courts had ruled, in separate cases, that these states had violated federal law. In 1973 the Nixon administration's Department of Health, Education and Welfare, refusing to acquiesce in those courts' interpretation of the federal law, issued regulations stating that benefits *could* be withheld. In a new case a U.S. District Court held that those HEW regulations conflicted with the federal statute. In March 1975 the Supreme Court affirmed that decision (Sugarman, 1985a: 405–406).

10. As one indicator of the system's legal complexity, recall that not once but twice, after Connecticut lost in a lower court, its appeals were rejected not on the merits but because of procedural legal errors by the state's lawyers. One could speculate that these errors occurred not because of legal complexity but because Connecticut lawyers were incompetent or overworked. But any legal system that cannot be properly activated except by extremely competent, well-staffed legal offices is justifiably classified, I would argue, as highly complex.

11. In a typical year in the 1970s, according to Mashaw (1983: 18), approximately 10,000 decisions by the SSA Appeals Council led to filings for judicial review in the federal courts.

12. For an excellent overall account of the role of the courts in expanding welfare rights, see R. Shep Melnick (1993).

13. In *Saenz v. Roe* (1999) welfare activists did successfully challenge California's at-

tempt to limit welfare payments to recent arrivals from states with less generous welfare policies. The Supreme Court, adopting a new interpretation of the Fourteenth Amendment, held that California's law, which limited welfare payments for the first year of California residency to the levels the applicant had been entitled to in the state from which she moved, violated the right to travel, which was a constitutionally protected "privilege and immunity" of citizens of the United States.

14. For a striking comparison of poor urban neighborhoods in the United States and France, see Loic Wacquant (1995: 543–570). See also McLanahan and Garfinkel (1995) for an analysis indicating that the American welfare system has tended to promote greater dependency than France's and Sweden's more generous systems because it generally has failed to cover poor fathers and has provided fewer incentives for AFDC recipients to seek and stay employed—partly because the United States doesn't provide guarantees of health care and other universal benefits for all families, employed or not, and partly because American governments have not provided generously subsidized child care.

15. See generally Jackson (1985). This is not so in France, where local taxes on corporations contribute some 50 percent of municipal tax receipts, and local governments compete—as in the United States—to attract businesses (Levy, 1999: ch. 4).

16. OECD figures indicate that in the early 1990s total tax revenues in the United States amounted to about 30 percent of gross domestic product, compared to an average of 41 percent in the countries of the European Union and 39 percent for all OECD countries (*The Economist*, 1994: 112).

17. The New Jersey legislation empowered suburbs to discharge their "fair share" obligation by subsidizing construction of low-income housing in older cities, and replaced lawsuits with a state administrative system for determining each municipality's housing obligations.

18. On Louisville, see Wilkerson (1979: ch. 9). In Los Angeles a court order pursuant to the state constitution compelled a massive busing plan, blending students from widely different communities in a huge county-wide school district. When the program was first instituted in 1978 for grades four through eight, one-way rides averaged almost fifty minutes. Massive numbers of students were withdrawn from the public schools. After busing was extended to other grades, "white flight" increased further, so that racial and ethnic integration did not really increase. Moreover, California voters in 1979 overwhelmingly voted for a ballot initiative prohibiting court-ordered busing except as a remedy for explicit violations of the federal constitution (Kagan, 1982).

19. In another article Heise (1998) observes, "it does not appear that . . . state education clauses in Wyoming's Constitution or state constitutions elsewhere *require* judicially-mandated school finance reform. . . . [E]ven where different states share similar education clauses, no consistent pattern of judicial results has emerged."

20. There is considerable debate about how much spending differences matter in terms of educational performance. Spending in the United States in rich and poor districts alike is high in cross-national terms. In 1991 annual per-pupil expenditure for elementary and secondary schools in the United States averaged $5,780,

compared to $1,768 in Belgium, $1,982 in Ireland, $2,450 in Spain, $3,559 in the United Kingdom, and $3,785 in France (Heise, 1995: 1743). On the correlation, or lack of it, between per-pupil expenditures and educational quality and achievement, see Hanushek (1989, 1994); Odden and Picus (1992: 277–281).

9. Adversarial Legalism and Regulatory Style

1. This distinctive characteristic of Japanese regulation has been analyzed by scholars in the United States and Japan. See, for example, Upham (1987); Haley (1986); Young (1984); Yamanouchi (1974).
2. One U.S. Court of Appeals opinion described the effort to comprehend RCRA a "mind-numbing journey" (*American Mining Congress v. EPA*, 1987).
3. Because RCRA creates a very strict regulatory system for "hazardous wastes" and a minimal one for "nonhazardous wastes," there has been a great deal of litigation over whether or not particular wastes are "hazardous" (Fortuna and Lennett, 1987: 25).
4. Aoki and Cioffi (2000) note that the agency's chief of environmental enforcement later apologized in private to company officials for what he conceded was unfairly harsh treatment.
5. For example, John Dwyer and colleagues compared Ford Motor Company's experience with air pollution controls at its German and American assembly plants. German and American regulations, they noted, prescribed similar emissions levels for the pollutants produced during the vehicle painting process, and both required use of the best available control technology. The EPA's regulations, however, prescribed specific emission levels for each of three different coating processes, while the German regulations called for a single overall emission limit for the plant, which gives manufacturers more flexibility in adjusting production runs and processes, and reduces monitoring and reporting requirements (Dwyer, Brooks, and Marco, 2000). See also Rose-Ackerman (1995).
6. Similarly, when the Reagan administration sought to replace legalistic regulation of nursing homes with a more consultative approach and a larger measure of government-supervised industry self-regulation, intense political opposition from consumer groups, the courts, and members of Congress who supported the consumer groups forced a rapid return to the legalistic implementation policy (Braithwaite, 1993: 26–27).
7. In 1989, Braithwaite (1993: 23–24) reports, California and Texas imposed 1,800 and 1,700 administrative penalties respectively, although most states imposed fewer than 100. New Jersey suspended admissions on more than 130 occasions, Texas 218 times. In 1989, 53 nursing homes in the United States had their licences revoked, and 130 were decertified for purposes of receiving vital Medicaid benefits.
8. 33 U.S.C. §1319(c)(d); Cal. Water Code §§13385–13386.
9. As summarized in a 1999 article by Greg Easterbrook (pp. 19, 22), "Twenty five years ago, only one-third of America's lakes and rivers were safe for fishing and swimming; today two-thirds are, and the proportion continues to rise. . . . Since 1970, smog has declined by about a third, even as the number of cars has in-

creased by half; acid rain has fallen by 40 percent; airborne soot particles are down 69 percent . . . airborne lead, a poison, is down 98 percent. . . . Toxic emissions by industry declined 46 percent from 1988 to 1996."

10. For a discussion of American business culture in this context, see Vogel (1986). According to Daniel Okimoto (1989: 158), government-business relations in Japan are "informal, close, cooperative, flexible, reciprocal, non-litigious, and long-term in orientation," while in the United States most business-government relations "can be characterized as formal, distant, rigid, suspicious, legalistic, narrow, and short-term oriented."

11. In the United States, Wallace (1995: xvii) found, "an adversarial approach to public policy has exacerbated the tensions which accompany environmental issues. Political toughness has found expression through poor relations between policy-makers and industry, leading to an inflexible and costly regulatory structure."

12. On Project XL and other initiatives in cooperative regulation, see Weber (1998).

13. For an example, see Aoki, Kagan, and Axelrad (2000). On the promise of regulatory programs that encourage corporate self-regulation, environmental management programs, and ISO 14000, see Gunningham and Grabosky (1998).

10. Economic Development, Environmental Protection, and Adversarial Legalism

1. I would like to thank Earl Finbar Murphy of the College of Law, Ohio State University, for calling Rosenthal's impressive book to my attention.

2. A 1790 French law states that the "judicial functions are and will remain forever separate from the administrative functions. The judges will not be allowed . . . to disturb in any manner whatsoever, the activities of the administrative corps, nor to summon before them administrators, concerning their functions" (Abraham, 1980: 272). On the decline of project-blocking litigation after the legal reforms of the French Revolution, see Rosenthal (1992: 52–53, 95–96, 119, 137, 179).

3. A legal analysis prepared by the Center for Law in the Public Interest, analyzing federal cases concerning the adequacy of environmental impact statements, concluded that there was very little encouraging precedent available (Detlefsen, 1994: 16).

4. Most occupants of dwellings in the right-of-way had long since found new housing with the aid of federal relocation grants. The argument, however, was that the freeway project had demolished 6,000 dwellings, that the housing stock of the communities had thereby been depleted, and that Caltrans was obligated to "mitigate" its adverse impact on the human environment.

5. An *Economist* article (1996a) pointed out that not only do cars in traffic jams cause three times the pollution of free-flowing traffic but that "Hell is not other people, as [Jean Paul Sartre] claimed, it is other people in other cars in front of you, holding you up in a traffic jam."

6. Soundwalls alone, erected at the behest of municipalities along the route, cost $500,000 per mile (Trombley and Hebert, 1987a, 1987b).

7. Of the 113 "mitigation projects" listed by the Central Artery Environmental Oversight Committee, fewer than fifty are directly related to the project. The oth-

ers include a study of the feasibility of water transportation to North Shore suburbs; improvements to the Lynn, Massachusetts, Central Square bus terminal and parking facilities; $150 million for the city of Cambridge; $80 million for a new park along the Charles River; a $5 million rat control program; and $5 million for restoring a long-graveled-over marsh in Revere, Massachusetts (Palmer, 1994).

8. Environmentalists identified the northern spotted owl, whose range extends from northern California to Canada, as an "indicator species" for the health of old-growth forests. In fact, considerable uncertainty prevailed concerning how much owl populations have declined, what their habitat needs actually are, and many related issues in forest biology. Hence the U.S. Fish and Wildlife Service (FWS) declined to "list" the spotted owl. A federal district court judge disagreed. While the FWS was preparing a response, in early 1989 the Sierra Club Legal Defense Fund and other environmental groups sued the U.S. Forest Service under the National Forest Management Act, challenging the legal adequacy of the Forest Service's new plan for protecting the spotted owl habitat in Washington and Oregon national forests. In March U.S. District Court judge William Dwyer issued a sweeping preliminary injunction, stopping 140 proposed timber sales pending trial in June. Congress responded by passing an appropriations bill rider that stipulated that "management of areas according [to existing Forest Service plans] . . . is adequate for purposes of meeting the statutory requirements that are the basis for the [spotted owl] cases" in Judge Dwyer's court. Judge Dwyer dissolved the preliminary injunction, but when the Sierra Club Legal Defense Fund appealed, the Ninth Circuit Court of Appeals held the congressional rider unconstitutional. The timber industry then appealed; the Supreme Court eventually (in 1992) reversed the court of appeals. Meanwhile, in May 1991, pursuant to still another Sierra Club suit based on different legal grounds, Judge Dwyer enjoined all timber sales that may affect the spotted owl, finding that the owl "is now threatened with extinction" (a highly contestable claim) and minimizing concerns about the economic effects of an injunction. The Ninth Circuit affirmed, leaving the injunction in effect in national forests throughout the owl's entire range.

9. In the 1976–1982 period, an average of fifty-six court cases were filed against the Nuclear Regulatory Commission *each year,* mostly alleging failure to follow procedural requirements concerning safety and siting (Delmas and Heiman, 2001). See generally Boyle (1998); Joppke (1993); Barkenbus (1984); Weingast (1980). The actuality or threat of litigation resulted in mounting delays in licensing processes for nuclear plants—from an average of twelve months for plants completed in 1960, thirty-three months for those completed in 1973, and fifty-six months for 1981 plants (Chubb, 1989: 85). Chubb noted that in France, as in other countries, power plants "equivalent to American reactors in quality and safety . . . [were] built in much less time and at far lower cost" (id. at 75). Beginning in the early 1980s German courts issued rulings that sharply curtailed the role of courts in antinuclear litigation (Greve, 1989b: 212–213). The American courts did not.

10. 33 C.F.R. §320.4(a)(1).

11. Dredged material must be tested according to a number of different protocols to determine its likely effect on marine organisms and water quality. The protocols may differ according to the mode of dredging and disposal, and according to the

different disposal sites under consideration. In addition, analyses must be performed on the area to be dredged, to assess the effects on water flow, bottom-dwelling organisms, and fisheries. If a new alternative disposal site is proposed, it can take months or even years to analyze and compare it to others. For one relatively small dredging project in Boston Harbor in which no major controversy or litigation occurred, the cost of consulting contracts for environmental testing and report writing represented approximately 25 percent of the cost of the actual dredging and disposal (Kagan, 1990b: 112).

12. In principle, legal commands concerning interagency consultation will encourage true interagency collaboration and problem-solving. Sometimes that does occur, but more often busy bureaucrats simply communicate through memoranda forged within, not across, agencies. On the obstacles to interagency collaboration in an institutionally and legally fragmented system (and on ways in which those obstacles can be and sometimes have been surmounted), see Bardach (1998).

13. On some topics, however, Canadian and U.S. policy responses diverge. See Hoberg (1990).

14. The acronyms in the text have the following referents: CERCLA—Comprehensive Environmental Response, Compensation, and Liability Act of 1980; FIFRA—Federal Insecticide, Fungicide, and Rodenticide Act; RCRA—Resource Conservation and Recovery Act; TSCA—Toxic Substances Control Act.

15. Cited in Schrecker (1992: 95–96).

Conclusion

1. Many of the Supreme Court decisions that seem to constrain adversarial legalism, it should be noted, are far from definitive, thereby inviting further testing and revision in the courts or investing significant discretion in the lower courts. Hence they may not actually reduce litigation very much, if at all. I am grateful to Peter Schuck for pointing this out.

2. To avoid further delay, the Port settled the cases by agreeing to spend considerable sums on refitting port equipment to reduce air pollution, although its analyses indicated that the resulting contribution to cleaner air in the vicinity would be minimal.

3. See Table 2, Chapter 1.

4. In addition to prevention of coercion and abuse of criminal suspects, the privilege against self-incrimination has been defended on grounds that no person, on philosophical principle, should be forced to cooperate with a government that he might find intolerable or to be made the instrument of his own undoing. Yet there are many situations—in employment relationships, in civil trials, and more—in which that radical individualism is rejected. A sweeping right to silence in criminal cases, as opposed to a limited one that can be overcome by a showing of probable cause, has been rejected by many serious legal scholars (Greenawalt, 1981; Dripps, 1991; Amar and Lettow, 1995; Alschuler, 1996). For a defense of the privilege, see Schulhofer (1991).

5. Even more radically, suppose that criminal suspects, if arrested on probable cause, were legally obliged to answer police or prosecutors' questions in a formal setting

in which the questioning is videotaped by a court official and a defense lawyer is present to object to misleading or deceptive questioning (but not to prevent questioning). Conversely, information obtained from the suspect in other settings (e.g., in the back of the squad car or in the station house before the videotaped questioning) would not be admissible in evidence in court. Police would face reduced incentives to pressure suspects to confess before a lawyer gets to them. And the additional cost to the state of providing well-trained and compensated defense lawyers for all pretrial questioning would undoubtedly be far outweighed by the savings in expenses for trials and pretrial jousting.

6. By "serious no-fault" I mean those programs that would preclude lawsuits for all personal injury claims (as in New Zealand and Quebec) or, as in Michigan, for all injuries that do not result in serious disfigurement, permanent impairment, or six months' total disability.

7. Establishing democratically legislated rules for the calculation of damages would also justify shifting such decisions from juries to judges. Judicial decisions that depart from the rules could then be subjected to judicial review and the further elaboration of a more predictable law of damages. Adversarial legalism could be further reduced by requiring plaintiffs who demand monetary settlements much higher than the guidelines suggest (or defendants who offer much skimpier settlements) to pay their opponents' legal bills if the case goes to trial and the jury or judge adheres to the statutory presumption.

References

Aarmson, David, C. Thomas Dienes, and Michael Musheno. (1978) "Changing the Public Drunkenness Laws: The Impact of Decriminalization." *Law & Society Rev.* 12: 405.

Abel, Richard. (1987) "The Real Tort Crisis: Too Few Claims." *Ohio State L.J.* 48: 443.

——— (1990) "A Critique of Torts." *UCLA L. Rev.* 37: 785.

Abel-Smith, Brian, and Kay Titmuss, eds. (1987) *The Philosophy of Welfare: Selected Writings of Richard M. Titmuss.* London: Allen & Unwin.

Abraham, Henry. (1980) *The Judicial Process.* New York: Oxford University Press.

Abraham, Katherine, and Susan Houseman. (1993) *Job Security in America: Lessons from Germany.* Washington: Brookings Institution.

Abraham, Kenneth S., and Lance Liebman. (1993) "Private Insurance, Social Insurance, and Tort Reform: Toward a New Vision of Compensation for Illness and Injury." 93 *Columbia L. Rev.* 93: 75.

Ackerman, Bruce, and William Hassler. (1981) *Clean Coal/Dirty Air.* New Haven: Yale University Press.

Adler, Jonathan. (1998) "Bean Counting for a Better Earth: Environmental Enforcement at the EPA." *Regulation* (Spring), pp. 40–43.

——— (1994) *The Jury.* New York: Doubleday.

Aggerholm, David A. (1989) "Sediment Regulation in Puget Sound," in Western Dredging Association, ed., *Dredging,* pp. 100–109. Proceedings of the XIIth World Dredging Congress, Orlando, Fla. Fairfax, Va.: Western Dredging Association.

Aks, Judy, Anne Bloom, Michael McCann, and William Halton. (2000) "Hegemonic Tales and Subversive Statistics: A Twenty-Year Study of News Reporting about Civil Litigation." Paper presented at annual meeting of Law and Society Association, Miami Beach, Fla., May 26–29.

Alexander, Janet Cooper. (1991) "Do the Merits Really Matter? A Study of Settlements in Securities Class Actions." *Stanford L. Rev.* 43: 497.

Allen, Christopher. (1989) "Political Consequences of Change: The Chemical Industry," in Peter Katzenstein, ed., *Industry and Politics in West Germany.* Ithaca, N.Y.: Cornell University Press.

Alschuler, Albert N. (1983) "Implementing the Criminal Defendant's Right to Trial: Alternatives to the Plea Bargain System." *U. Chicago L. Rev.* 50: 931.

—— (1986) "Mediation with a Mugger: The Shortage of Adjudicative Services and the Need for a Two-Tier System in Civil Cases." *Harvard L. Rev.* 99: 1808.

—— (1990) "The Vanishing Civil Jury." *U. Chicago L. Forum* 1990: 1.

—— (1996) "A Peculiar Privilege in Historical Perspective: The Right to Remain Silent." *Mich. L. Rev.* 94: 2625.

—— (1998) "Explaining the Public Wariness of Juries." *DePaul L. Rev.* 48: 407.

Amar, Akhil, and Renee Lettow. (1995) "Fifth Amendment First Principles: The Self-Incrimination Clause." *Mich. L. Rev.* 93: 857.

American Law Institute. (1991) *Reporters' Study: Enterprise Responsibility for Personal Injury,* vol. 1. Philadelphia: American Law Institute.

American Mining Congress v. EPA. (1987) 824 F.2d 1177, 1189 (D.C. Cir.).

Amsterdam, Anthony. (1988) *Trial Manual for the Defense of Criminal Cases,* 5th ed. Philadelphia: American Law Institute-American Bar Association.

Anderson, Eugene, Irene Warshauer, and Adrienne Coffin. (1983) "The Asbestos Health Hazards Compensation Act: A Legislative Solution to a Litigation Crisis." *J. Legislation* 10: 25.

Angell, Marcia. (1996) *Science on Trial: The Clash of Medical Evidence and the Law in the Breast Implant Cases.* New York: Norton.

Aoki, Kazumasu, and John Cioffi. (2000) "Poles Apart: Industrial Waste Management Regulation and Enforcement in the United States and Japan," in Robert A. Kagan and Lee Axelrad, eds., *Regulatory Encounters: Multinational Corporations and American Adversarial Legalism.* Berkeley: University of California Press.

Aoki, Kazumasu, Robert A. Kagan, and Lee Axelrad. (2000) "Industrial Effluent Control in the United States and Japan," in Kagan and Axelrad, eds., *Regulatory Encounters: Multinational Corporations and American Adversarial Legalism.* Berkeley: University of California Press.

Applebome, Peter. (1991) "Georgia Inmate Is Executed after 'Chaotic Legal Move.'" *New York Times,* September 26, p. A18.

—— (1993) "On the Fast Track from the Courtroom to Death Row." *New York Times,* March 7, sec. 4, p. 2.

Argersinger v. Hamlin. (1972) 407 U.S. 25.

Armstrong, Ken, and Maurice Possley. (1999a) "The Verdict: Dishonor." *Chicago Tribune,* January 10, p. 1C.

—— (1999b) "Break Rules: Be Promoted." *Chicago Tribune,* January 14, p. 1N.

Atiyah, P. S., and Robert S. Summers. (1987) *Form and Substance in Anglo-American Law: A Comparative Study of Legal Reasoning, Legal Theory, and Legal Institutions.* Oxford: Clarendon Press.

Axelrad, Lee. (2000) "Investigation and Remediation of Contaminated Manufacturing Sites in the United States, the United Kingdom, and the Netherlands," in Robert A. Kagan and L. Axelrad, eds., *Regulatory Encounters: Multinational Corporations and Adversarial Legalism.* Berkeley: University of California Press.

Axline, Michael. (1996) "Forest Health and the Politics of Expediency." *Environmental Law* 26: 613.

Ayres, Ian, and John Braithwaite. (1992) *Responsive Regulation*. New York: Oxford University Press.

Badaracco, Joseph L. (1985) *Loading the Dice: A Five Country Study of Vinyl Chloride Regulation*. Boston: Harvard Business School Press.

Bailis, Daniel, and Robert MacCoun. (1996) "Estimating Liability Risks with the Media as Your Guide: A Content Analysis of Media Coverage of Tort Litigation." *Law & Human Behavior* 20: 419.

Baldus, David, et al. (1983) "Comparative Review of Death Sentences." *J. Criminal Law & Criminology* 74: 661.

Baldus, David, George Woodworth, and Charles Pulaski, Jr. (1990) *Equal Justice and the Death Penalty: A Legal and Empirical Analysis*. Boston: Northeastern University Press.

Baldwin, John, and Michael McConville. (1979) "Plea Bargaining and Plea Negotiation in England." *Law & Society Rev.* 13: 287.

Bales, Richard. (1998) "Creating and Challenging Compulsory Arbitration Agreements." *Labor Law* 13: 511.

Bandow, Doug. (1995) "California's Three Strikes Law Strikes Out." *Wall Street J.*, April 19, p. A17.

——— (1998) "Many Torts Later, the Case against Implants Collapses." *Wall Street J.*, November 30, p. A23.

Bardach, Eugene. (1982) "Self-Regulation and Regulatory Paperwork," in E. Bardach and Robert A. Kagan, eds., *Social Regulation: Strategies for Reform*. San Francisco: Institute for Contemporary Studies.

——— (1998) *Getting Agencies to Work Together: The Practice and Theory of Managerial Craftsmanship*. Washington, D.C.: Brookings Institution Press.

Bardach, Eugene, and Robert A. Kagan. (1982) *Going by the Book: The Problem of Regulatory Unreasonableness*. Philadelphia: Temple University Press.

Barkenbus, J. N. (1984) "Nuclear Power and Government Structure: The Divergent Paths of the United States and France." *Social Science Quarterly* 65: 37.

Barnes, Jeb. (1997) "Bankrupt Bargain? Bankruptcy Reform and the Politics of Adversarial Legalism." *J. Law & Politics* 13: 893.

Barnett, Randy E. (1994) "Bad Trip: Drug Prohibition and the Weakness of Public Policy." *Yale L.J.* 103: 2593.

Baron, Roger M., and Ronald J. Baron. (1986) "The Penzoil-Texaco Dispute: An Independent Analysis." *Baylor L. Rev.* 38: 253.

Barrett, Paul. (1994) "On the Defense: Lawyer's Fast Work on Death Cases Raises Doubts about System." *Wall Street J.*, September 7, pp. A1, 5.

——— (1996) "High Court Says U.S. Need Not Pay Hercules for Agent Orange Liability." *Wall Street J.*. March 5, p. B7.

Bass, Jack. (1993) *Taming the Storm: The Life and Times of Judge Frank M. Johnson, Jr.* New York: Doubleday.

Bass, Sandra. (1997) "Blacks, Browns, and the Blues: Police and Minorities in California." *Public Affairs Report* 38: 1. Institute of Governmental Studies, University of California, Berkeley.

Bates v. State Bar. (1977) 433 U.S. 350.

Bayley, David. (1976) *Forces of Order: Police Behavior in Japan and the United States.* Berkeley: University of California Press.

———— (1979) "Police Function, Structure, and Control in Western Europe and North America: Comparative and Historical Studies." *Crime & Justice* 1: 109.

Bell, Peter, and Jeffrey O'Connell. (1997) *Accidental Justice: The Dilemmas of Tort Law.* New Haven: Yale University Press.

Bellows, Randy. (1988) "Notes of a Public Defender," in Philip B. Heyman and Lance Liebman, eds., *The Social Responsibilities of Lawyers.* Westbury, N.Y.: Foundation Press.

Benedict, Roger. (1993) "Chevron: Political Risks for New Oil Ventures in U.S. Exceed Those in Former Soviet Union." *The Oil Daily,* April 12, p. 3.

Bergstrom, Randolph E. (1992) *Courting Danger: Injury and Law in New York City, 1870–1910.* Ithaca, N.Y.: Cornell University Press.

Berk, Richard, Harold Brackman, and Selma Lesser. (1977) *A Measure of Justice: An Empirical Study of Changes in the California Penal Code.* New York: Academic Press.

Berkowitz, Peggy. (1986) "In Canada, Different Legal and Popular Views Prevail." *Wall Street J.,* April 4, p. 21.

Bernstein, David. (1999) "The Breast Implant Fiasco." *Cal. L. Rev.* 87: 457.

Bernstein, Herbert. (1988) "Whose Advantage After All?: A Comment on the Comparison of Civil Justice Systems." *U.C. Davis L. Rev.* 21: 587.

Berton, Lee. (1995) "Big Accounting Firms Weed Out Risky Clients." *Wall Street J.,* June 26, p. B1.

Berton, Lee, and Joann Lublin. (1992) "Seeking Shelter: Partnership Structure Is Called in Question as Liability Risk Rises." *Wall Street J.,* June 10, p. A1.

Bilocki, Dennis. (1989) "A More Efficient Method of Jury Selection for Lengthy Trials." *Judicature* 73: 43.

Blabolil, Sandee, et al. (1997) "Environmental Crimes." *American Criminal L. Rev.* 34: 493.

Blackmon, Glenn, and Richard Zeckhauser. (1991) "State Tort Reform Legislation: Assessing Our Control of Risks," in Peter Schuck, ed., *Tort Law and the Public Interest.* New York: W. W. Norton.

Blake, Francis. (1990) "The Politics of the Environment: Does Washington Know Best?" *American Enterprise* (March/April), pp. 6–7.

Blankenburg, Erhard. (1994) "The Infrastructure for Avoiding Civil Litigation: Comparing Cultures of Legal Behavior in the Netherlands and West Germany." *Law & Society Rev.* 28: 789.

Blankenburg, Erhard, and Freek Bruinsma. (1991) *Dutch Legal Culture.* Deventer, Netherlands: Kluwer.

Blankenburg, Erhard, and Ralf Rogowski. (1986) "German Labor Courts and the British Industrial Tribunal System: A Socio-Legal Comparison of Degrees of Judicialisation." *J. Law & Society* 13: 67.

Blumstein, James, Randall Bovbjerg, and Frank Sloan. (1990) "Beyond Tort Reform: Developing Better Tools for Assessing Damages for Personal Injury." *Yale J. on Regulation* 8: 171.

BMW of North America v. Gore. (1996) 517 U.S. 559.

Boden, Les, and David Wegman. (1978) "Increasing OSHA's Clout: Sixty Million New Inspectors." *Working Papers for a New Society* (May/June).

Bok, Derek. (1971) "Reflections on the Distinctive Character of American Labor Laws." *Harvard L. Rev.* 84: 1461.

——— (1983) "A Flawed System of Law Practice and Training." *Harvard Magazine* (May/June), pp. 38–45.

Boland, Barbara, et al. (1990) "The Prosecution of Felony Arrests, 1987." Washington, D.C.: U.S. Department of Justice, pp. 91–97.

Bombaugh, Robert. (1971) "The Department of Transportation's Auto Insurance Study and Auto Accident Compensation Reform." *Columbia L. Rev.* 71: 207.

Bookspan, Phyllis. (1991) "Reworking the Warrant Requirement." *Vanderbilt L. Rev.* 44: 473.

Boot, Max. (1996) "Stop Appeasing the Class Action Monster." *Wall Street J.,* May 8, p. A18.

Bork, Diana Culp. (1996) "A Florida Judge Lets Junk Science into Her Courtroom." *Wall Street J.,* June 26, p. A15.

Bovbjerg, Randall, Frank Sloan, and James Blumstein. (1989) "Valuing Life and Limb in Tort: Scheduling Pain and Suffering." *Northwestern L. Rev.* 83: 980.

Bovbjerg, Randall, Frank Sloan, Avi Dor, and Chee Ruey Hsieh. (1991) "Juries and Justice: Are Malpractice and Other Personal Injuries Created Equal?" *Law & Contemporary Problems* 54: 15.

Bovbjerg, Randall, Frank Sloan, and Peter Rankin. (1997) "Administrative Performance of 'No Fault' Compensation for Medical Injury." *Law & Contemporary Problems* 60: 71.

Bowman, Robert. (1990) "Federal Officials Downplay Government's Role in Dredging, Port Projects." *Pacific Shipper,* March 19, pp. 7–8.

Boyle, Elizabeth Heger. (1998) "Political Frames and Legal Activity: The Case of Nuclear Power in Four Countries." *Law & Society Rev.* 32: 141.

Bradley, Craig. (1993) *The Failure of the Criminal Procedure Revolution.* Philadelphia: Pennsylvania University Press.

Braithwaite, John. (1985) *To Punish or Persuade: Enforcement of Coal Mine Safety.* Albany, N.Y.: SUNY Press.

——— (1993) "The Nursing Home Industry," in Michael Tonry and Albert J. Reiss, Jr., eds., *Beyond the Law: Crime in Complex Organizations.* Chicago: University of Chicago Press.

Braithwaite, John, John Walker, and Peter Grabosky. (1987) "An Enforcement Taxonomy of Regulatory Agencies." *Law & Policy* 9: 323–350.

Braybrooke, David, and Charles E. Lindblom. (1963) *A Strategy of Decision.* New York: Free Press.

Brazil, Wayne. (1980a) "'Views from the Front Lines' Observations by Chicago Lawyers about the System of Civil Discovery." *American Bar Foundation Research J.* 1980: 219.

——— (1980b) "Civil Discovery: Lawyers' Views of Its Effectiveness, Its Principal Problems and Abuses." *American Bar Foundation Research J.* 1980: 787.

———— (1990) "A Close Look at Three Court-Sponsored ADR Programs: Why They Exist, How They Operate, What They Deliver, and Whether They Threaten Important Values." *U. Chicago Legal Forum* 1990: 303.

Brereton, David, and Jonathan D. Casper. (1981) "Does It Pay to Plead Guilty? Differential Sentencing and the Functioning of Criminal Courts." *Law & Society Rev.* 16: 45.

Briar, Scott. (1966) "Welfare from Below: Recipients' Views of the Welfare System," in Jacobus ten Broek, ed., *The Law of the Poor.* San Francisco: Chandler Publishing.

Brickman, Lester. (1992) "The Asbestos Litigation Crisis: Is There a Need for an Administrative Alternative?" *Cardozo L. Rev.* 13: 1819.

Brickman, Lester, Michael Horowitz, and Jeffrey O'Connell. (1994) *Rethinking Contingency Fees.* New York: The Manhattan Institute.

Brickman, Ronald, Sheila Jasanoff, and Thomas Ilgen. (1985) *Controlling Chemicals: The Politics of Regulation in Europe and the United States.* Ithaca, N.Y.: Cornell University Press.

Briffault, Richard. (1990) "Our Localism, Part I: The Structure of Local Government Law." *Columbia L. Rev.* 90: 1.

Bright, Stephen B. (1994) "Counsel for the Poor: The Death Sentence Not for the Worst Crime but for the Worst Lawyer." *Yale L.J.* 103: 1835.

Brill, Stephen. (1989) "*U.S. v. Int'l Brotherhood of Teamsters and SEC v. Drexel Lambert:* When the Government Goes Judge-Shopping," in Stephen Brill, ed., *Trial by Jury.* New York: American Lawyer Press/Touchstone.

Broder, Ivy. (1986) "Characteristics of Million Dollar Awards: Jury Verdicts and Final Disbursements." *Justice System J.* 11: 349.

Brodkin, Evelyn, and Michael Lipsky. (1983) "Quality Control in AFDC as an Administrative Strategy." *Social Services Rev.* 57: 1.

Bronner, Ethan. (1998) "High Schools Fear Telling Colleges All about Johnny." *New York Times,* March 11, p. A1.

Brookings Institution. (1989) *Justice for All: Reducing Costs and Delay in Civil Litigation—Report of a Task Force.* Washington, D.C.: Brookings Institution.

Brown v. Board of Education of Topeka. (1954) 347 U.S. 483.

Brown, Craig. (1985) "Deterrence in Tort and No-Fault: The New Zealand Experience." *Cal. L. Rev.* 73: 976.

Brown, Warren. (1988) "Surviving 'Creative Bankruptcy': As a Business Strategy Firms Find That It Exacts a Heavy Price." *Washington Post,* November 6, pp. H1, H7.

Bruce, Christopher J. (1984) "The Deterrence Effects of Automobile Insurance and Tort Law: A Survey of the Empirical Literature." *Law & Policy* 6: 67.

Bryant, Adam. (1995) "Small Planes Are Coming Back." *New York Times,* March 19, p. F11(L).

Bureau of Justice Statistics. (1991) *Jail Inmates, 1990.* Washington, D.C.: U.S. Department of Justice.

———— (1995) *Tort Cases in Large Counties.* Washington, D.C.: U.S. Department of Justice.

———— (2000) *Sourcebook of Criminal Justice Statistics*. Washington, D.C.: U.S. Department of Justice.

Burke, Tom. (2001) *Litigation and Its Discontents*. Berkeley: University of California Press.

Busch, Christopher, David Kirp, and Daniel Schoenholz. (1999) "Taming Adversarial Legalism." *NYU J. Legislation & Policy* 2: 179.

Butterfield, Fox. (1995) "California Courts Clogging under Its 'Three Strikes' Law." *New York Times,* March 23, pp. A1, A9.

———— (1997) "Few Options or Safeguards in a City's Juvenile Courts." *New York Times,* July 22, p. A1.

———— (1998a) "New Study Adds Evidence of Bias in Death Sentences." *New York Times,* June 7, pp. 1, 22.

————(1998b) "Southern Curse: Why America's Murder Rate Is So High." *New York Times,* July 26, sec. IV, pp. 1, 16.

———— (2000a) "Racial Disparities Seen as Pervasive in Juvenile Justice." *New York Times,* April 26, p. A1.

———— (2000b) "Death Sentences Overturned in 2 of 3 Appeals." *New York Times,* June 12, p. A1.

California State Automobile Association (1997) *VIA* (the magazine of the CSAA) (November/December), p. 12.

Carleson v. Remillard. (1972) 406 U.S. 598.

Carroll, Stephen, Allan Abrahamse, and Mary Vaiana. (1995) *The Costs of Excess Medical Claims for Automobile Personal Injuries*. Santa Monica, Calif.: RAND Institute for Civil Justice.

Carson, Iain. (1996) "Survey: Living with the Car." *The Economist,* June 22, p. 13.

Casper, Gerhard, and Richard Posner. (1976) *The Workload of the Supreme Court*. Chicago: American Bar Foundation.

Casper, Gerhard, and Hans Zeisel. (1972) "Lay Judges in the German Criminal Courts." *J. Legal Studies* 1: 135.

Casper, Jonathan. (1972) *American Criminal Justice: The Defendant's Perspective*. Englewood Cliffs, N.J.: Prentice Hall.

Cassell, Paul. (2000) "We're Not Executing the Innocent." *Wall Street J.,* June 16, p. A14.

Charkham, Johnathan P. (1994) *Keeping Good Company: A Study of Corporate Governance in Five Countries*. Oxford: Clarendon Press.

Charles, Sara. (1985) "Sued and Nonsued Physicians' Self-Reported Reaction to Malpractice Litigation." *American J. Psychology* 142: 437.

Charles, Sara, et al. (1988) "Physicians on Trial—Self-reported Reaction to Malpractice Trials." *Western J. Medicine* 148: 358.

Chase, Oscar. (1995) "Helping Jurors Determine Pain and Suffering Awards." *Hofstra L. Rev.* 23: 763.

Cheney, Frederick W., et al. (1989) "Standard of Care and Anesthesia Liability." *JAMA (Journal of the American Medical Association)* 261: 1599.

Chevron U.S.A. v. National Resources Defense Council. (1984) 467 U.S. 837.

Chiang, Harriet. (1996a) "Dearth of Lawyers in Death Row Cases." *San Francisco Chronicle,* January 23, p. A1.

——— (1996b) "Lucas's Legacy—Order in the Court." *San Francisco Chronicle,* April 29, pp. A1, A9.

Chin, Audrey, and Mark Peterson. (1985) *Deep Pockets, Empty Pockets: Who Wins in Cook County Jury Trials?* Santa Monica: RAND Institute for Civil Justice.

Chinloy, Peter. (1989) *The Cost of Doing Business: Legal and Regulatory Issues in the United States and Abroad.* New York: Praeger.

Chubb, John E. (1989) "U.S. Energy Policy," in J. E. Chubb and Paul Peterson, eds., *Can the Government Govern?* Washington, D.C.: Brookings Institution.

Church, Thomas W., and Robert Nakamura. (1993) *Cleaning Up the Mess: Implementation Strategies in Superfund.* Washington, D.C.: Brookings Institution.

——— (1994) "Beyond Superfund: Hazardous Waste Cleanup in Europe and the United States." *Georgetown International Environmental L. Rev.* 7: 56.

Citron, Roger. (1991) "(Un)*Luckey v. Miller:* The Case for a Structural Injunction to Improve Indigent Defense Services." *Yale L.J.* 101: 481.

Clark, David. (1988) "The Selection and Accountability of Judges in West Germany: Implementation of a Rechtstaat." *S. Cal. L. Rev.* 61: 1795.

——— (1990) "Civil Litigation Trends in Europe and Latin America since 1945." *Law & Society Rev.* 24: 549.

Clermont, Kevin, and Theodore Eisenberg. (1992) "Trial by Jury or Judge: Transcending Empiricism." *Cornell L. Rev.* 77: 1124–1177.

Coffee, Jr., John C. (1995) "Class Wars: The Dilemma of the Mass Tort Class Action." *Columbia L. Rev.* 95: 1343.

Coglianese, Cary. (1997) "Assessing Consensus: The Promise and Performance of Negotiated Rulemaking." *Duke L. J.* 46: 1255, 1296–1301, 1316, 1343–1349.

Cole, Susan K. (1989) "Oakland Wins Certification for Dredging Disposal Plan, but Obstacles Remain." *Pacific Shipper,* July 24, 1989, pp. 6–7.

Collins, Glenn. (1995) "A Tobacco Case's Legal Buccaneers." *New York Times,* March 6, p. D3.

Condlin, Robert (1985) "'Cases on Both Sides': Patterns of Argument in Legal Dispute-Negotiation." *Md. L. Rev.* 44: 65.

Congressional Quarterly. (1995) "Business PACs Pick Their Cause." 53(18): 1234.

Conlan, Timothy. (1985) *New Federalism; Intergovernmental Reform from Nixon to Reagan.* Washington, D.C.: Brookings Institution.

Conley, John M., and William M. O'Barr. (1987) "Fundamentals of Jurisprudence: An Ethnography of Judicial Decision Making in Informal Courts." *North Carolina L. Rev.* 66: 467.

Connors, Edward, et al. (1996) *Convicted by Juries, Exonerated by Science: Case Studies for the Use of DNA Evidence to Establish Innocence after Trial.* Washington, D.C.: National Institute of Justice.

Cooney, Mark. (1994) "Evidence as Partisanship." *Law & Society Rev.* 28: 833.

Cooter, Robert, and Tom Ginsburg. (1996) "Comparative Judicial Discretion: An Empirical Test of Economic Models." *International Rev. Law & Economics* 16: 295.

Coppock, Rob. (1985) "Interactions between Scientists and Public Officials: A Comparison of the Use of Science in Regulatory Programs in the United States and West Germany." *Policy Sciences* 18: 371.

Coronado, Ramon. (1995) "'Thrill Killer' Suspect Stuns Courtroom: 'I am guilty.'" *Sacramento Bee,* September 14, p. 1.

Council on California Competitiveness. (1992) *California's Jobs and Future.* Sacramento: Council on California Competitiveness.

Couso, Javier. (1997) "Entrenching Economic Rights: The 'Economic' Constitution of Chile." Paper delivered at International Conference on Institutions, Markets, and Economic Performance, Utrecht University, December 11–12.

Coyle, Mercia, et al. (1990) "Fatal Defense: Trial and Error in the Nation's Death Belt." *National L.J.,* June 11, pp. 30–44.

Craig, Andrew. (1991) "Product Liability and Safety in General Aviation," in Peter Huber and Robert Litan, eds., *The Liability Maze.* Washington, D.C.: Brookings Institution.

Cross, Frank, and Emerson Tiller. (1998) "Judicial Partisanship and Obedience to Legal Doctrine: Whistleblowing on the Federal Courts of Appeals." *Yale L.J.* 107: 2155.

Curran, Barbara A.. (1986) *Supplement to the Lawyer Statistical Report: The U.S. Legal Profession in 1985.* Chicago: American Bar Foundation.

Curran, Barbara A., and Clara N. Carson. (1994). *The Lawyer Statistical Report: The U.S. Legal Profession in the 1990s.* Chicago: American Bar Foundation.

Currie, David. (1990) "*Lochner* Abroad: Substantive Due Process and Equal Protection in the Federal Republic of Germany." *Supreme Court Rev.* 1989: 333.

Curtis, W. Robert. (1986) "The Deinstitutionalization Story." *The Public Interest* (Fall), p. 34.

CWCI. (1991a) "Research Notes: Workers' Compensation Litigation Costs, 1990." San Francisco: California Workers' Compensation Institute, September.

———. (1991b) "1991 Litigation Incidence." San Francisco: California Workers' Compensation Institute.

Damaska, Mirjan. (1975) "Structures of Authority and Comparative Criminal Procedure." *Yale L.J.* 84: 480.

——— (1986) *The Faces of Justice and State Authority: A Comparative Approach to the Legal Process.* New Haven: Yale University Press.

——— (1990) "Reflections on American Constitutionalism." *American J. Comparative Law* 38: 421.

——— (1997a) "The Uncertain Fate of Evidentiary Transplants: Anglo-American and Continental Experiments." *American J. Comparative Law* 45: 839.

——— (1997b) *Evidence Law Adrift.* New Haven: Yale University Press.

Daniels, Stephen, and Joanne Martin. (1995) *Civil Juries and the Politics of Reform.* Chicago, Ill.: American Bar Foundation, Northwestern University Press.

Danzon, Patricia. (1984) "The Frequency and Severity of Medical Malpractice Claims." *J. Law & Economics* 27: 115.

——— (1985) *Medical Malpractice: Theory, Evidence, and Public Policy.* Cambridge: Harvard University Press.

——— (1986) "The Frequency and Severity of Medical Malpractice Claims: New Evidence." *Law & Contemporary Problems* 49: 57.

———— (1990) "The 'Crisis' in Medical Malpractice: A Comparison of Trends in the United States, Canada, the United Kingdom and Australia." *Law, Medicine & Health Care* 18: 48.

———— (1991) "Malpractice Liability: Is the Grass on the Other Side Greener?" in Peter Schuck, ed., *Tort Law and the Public Interest*. New York: W. W. Norton.

Darbyshire, Penny. (1997a) "An Essay on the Importance and Neglect of the Magistracy." *Criminal L. Rev.* 1997: 627.

———— (1997b) "For the New Lord Chancellor—Some Causes for Concern about Magistrates." *Criminal L. Rev.* 1997: 861.

Daubert v. Merrell Dow Pharmaceuticals. (1993) 509 U.S. 579.

Davidson, Al. (1990) *In the Wake of the Exxon Valdez.* San Francisco: Sierra Club Books.

Davidson, Roger. (1981) "Subcommittee Government: New Channels for Policy Making," in Thomas Mann and Norman Ornstein, eds., *The New Congress*. Washington, D.C.: American Enterprise Institute.

Davies, Thomas Y. (1983) "A Hard Look at What We Know (and Still Need to Learn) about the 'Costs' of the Exclusionary Rule." *American Bar Foundation Research J.* 1983: 611.

Davis, Bob, and Peter Gumbel. (1995) "Red Tape Traumas: To All U.S. Managers Upset by Regulations—Try Germany or Japan." *Wall Street J.,* December 14, p. A1.

Davis, Martha F. (1993) *Brutal Need: Lawyers and the Welfare Rights Movement*. New Haven: Yale University Press.

Day, Patricia, and Rudolf Klein. (1987) "The Regulation of Nursing Homes: A Comparative Perspective." *Milbank Quarterly* 65: 303–334.

de Tocqueville, Alexis. (1835) *Democracy in America,* vol. I. New York: Vintage Books, 1945.

Deese, David A. (1982) "A Cross-National Perspective on the Politics of Nuclear Waste," in E. William Colglazier, ed., *The Politics of Nuclear Waste*. New York: Pergamon Press.

Delmas, Magali. (2000) "Globalization of Environmental Management Standards: Barriers and Incentives in Europe and the United States." Working Paper 2.70, Center for German and European Studies, University of California, Berkeley.

Delmas, Magali, and Bruce Heiman. (2001) "Government Credible Commitment in the French and American Nuclear Power Industries." *J. Policy Analysis & Management,* vol. 20, no. 3.

DelVecchio, Rick (1997) "West Oakland Group Sues to Block Port Project." *San Francisco Chronicle,* October 7, p. A19.

Department of Transportation. (1985) *Export Transportation and Intergovernmental Public Policy.* Washington, D.C.: U.S. Department of Transportation.

Dertouzos, James, Elaine Holland, and Patricia Ebener. (1988) *The Legal and Economic Consequences of Wrongful Termination.* Santa Monica: RAND Institute for Civil Justice.

Detlefsen, Robert. (1994) "The Role of Interest Groups in the Fashioning of Government Consent Decrees." Paper delivered at 1994 annual meeting of Western Political Science Association, Albuquerque, March.

——— (1995) "Government Consent Decrees and the Paradox of 'Consent': A Critical Case Study." *Justice System J.* 18: 13.

Dewar, Helen. (1995) "Congress Overrides Securities Bill Veto." *Washington Post,* December 23, pp. A1, C1.

——— (1996) "2 Senate Democrats Join Business Critics of Clinton on Product-Liability Bill." *Washington Post,* March 19, p. A4.

Dewees, Donald, and Michael Trebilcock. (1992) "The Efficacy of the Tort System and Its Alternatives: A Review of Empirical Evidence." *Osgoode Hall L.J.,* vol. 56.

Dewees, Donald, Michael Trebilcock, and Peter Coyte. (1991) "The Medical Malpractice Crisis: A Comparative Empirical Perspective." *Law & Contemporary Problems* 54: 217–251.

Diamond, Shari. (1983) "Order in the Court: Consistency in Criminal Court Decisions," in C. James Scheirer and Barbara L. Hammonds, eds., *The Master Lecturers Series: Psychology and the Law,* vol. 2, pp. 123–146. Washington, D.C.: American Psychological Association.

DiIulio, John J., Jr. (1987) "Prison Discipline and Prison Reform." *The Public Interest* (No. 89, Fall), p. 71.

——— (1990) *Courts, Corrections and the Constitution.* New York: Oxford University Press.

Diller, Matthew. (1995) "Poverty Lawyering in the Golden Age." *Mich. L. Rev.* 93: 1401.

Dimento, Joseph. (1986) *Environmental Law and American Business: Dilemmas of Compliance.* New York: Plenum Press.

Doe v. Harder. (1970) 301 F. Supp. 302 (N.D. Conn.), appeal dismissed, 397 U.S. 902.

Doe v. Shapiro. (1969) 302 F. Supp. 761 (D. Conn.), appeal dismissed, 396 U.S. 488 (1970).

Dorf, Michael, and Charles Sabel. (1998) "A Constitution of Democratic Experimentalism." *Columbia L. Rev.* 98: 267.

Douthwaite, Graham. (1988) *Jury Instructions on Damages in Tort Actions,* 2d ed. Charlotesville, Va.: Michie Co.

Downes, David M. (1988) *Contrasts in Tolerance: Post War Penal Policy in the Netherlands and England and Wales.* Oxford: Clarendon Press.

Dripps, Donald. (1991) "Self Incrimination and Self Preservation: A Skeptical View." *U. Ill. L. Rev.* 1991: 329.

Dubber, Markus. (1997) "American Plea Bargaining, German Lay Judges, and the Crisis of Criminal Procedure." *Stanford L. Rev.* 49: 547.

Dudziak, Mary. (1988) "Desegregation as a Cold War Imperative." *Stanford L. Rev.* 41: 61.

Duffy, Tom, and Rolph Landis. (1988) "Workers Compensation in Switzerland." *NCCI Digest* 3: 31. New York: National Council on Compensation Insurance.

Dunlop, Bruce. (1975) "No-Fault Automobile Insurance and the Negligent Action: An Expensive Anomaly." *Osgoode Hall L. J.* 13: 439.

Dunworth, Terence, and Joel Rogers. (1996) "Corporations in Court: Big Business Litigation in U.S. Federal Courts." *Law & Social Inquiry* 21: 497.

Dworkin, Ronald. (1977) *Taking Rights Seriously.* London: Duckworth.

Dwyer, John. (1990) "The Pathology of Symbolic Legislation." *Ecology Law Quarterly* 17: 233.

Dwyer, John, Richard Brooks, and Alan Marco. (2000) "The Air Pollution Permit Process for U.S. and German Automobile Assembly Plants," in Robert A. Kagan and Lee Axelrad, eds., *Regulatory Encounters: Multinational Corporations and American Adversarial Legalism.* Berkeley: University of California Press.

Eads, George, and Peter Reuter. (1984) "Designing Safer Products: Corporate Responses to Product Liability Law and Regulation." *J. Product Liability* 7: 263.

Easterbrook, Greg. (1999) "America the O.K." *The New Republic,* January 4–11, pp. 19, 22.

The Economist. (1990) "The Forest Service: Time for a Little Perestroika." March 10, p. 28.

———— (1992) "Twitching Millionaires." October 3, p. 29.

———— (1994) "Taxation." September 24, p. 112.

———— (1995) "Fighting Crime: The Case for Emptier Prisons." December 9, p. 25.

———— (1996a) "Crime in America." June 8, pp. 23–25.

———— (1996b) "Pensions." November 30, p. 105.

———— (1997) "Thwack the Law." January 25, p. 46.

———— (1998) "Maternity Leave." February 28, p. 110.

Edelman, Lauren. et al. (1992) "Professional Construction of Law: The Inflated Threat of Wrongful Discharge." *Law & Society Rev.* 26: 47.

Edelman, Peter. (1988) "Japanese Product Standards as Non-Tariff Trade Barriers: When Regulatory Policy Becomes a Trade Issue." *Standard J. International Law* 24: 292.

Eisenberg, Ira. (1995) "Blind Justice." *San Francisco Focus* (September), pp. 50–58.

Eisenberg, Theodore, and James Henderson, Jr. (1992) "Inside the Quiet Revolution in Products Liability." *UCLA L. Rev.* 39: 731.

Eisenberg, Theodore, et al. (1995) "Litigation Outcomes in State and Federal Court: A Statistical Portrait." Paper presented at annual meeting of the Law and Society Association, Toronto, June 2.

———— (1997) "The Predictability of Punitive Damages." *J. Legal Studies* 26: 623.

Eisenstein, James, Roy B. Flemming, and Peter F. Nardulli. (1988) *The Contours of Justice: Communities and Their Courts.* Boston: Little, Brown.

Ellickson, Robert. (1990) "The Homelessness Muddle." *The Public Interest* 99: 45.

Elliot, Donald. (1989) "Why Punitive Damages Don't Deter Corporate Misconduct Effectively." *Ala. L. Rev.* 40: 1053.

Ellman, Ira Mark. (1991) "Inventing Family Law." *Davis L. Rev.* 32: 855.

Engel, David. (1984) "The Oven Bird's Song: Insiders, Outsiders, and Personal Injuries in an American Community." *Law & Society Rev.* 18: 551.

Environmental Law Institute. (1985) *Statutory Deadlines in Environmental Legislation.* Washington, D.C.: ELI.

Epp, Charles R. (1998) "Litigation Stories: Official Perceptions of Lawsuits against Local Governments." Paper presented at annual meeting of the Law and Society Association, Aspen, Colo., June 4–7.

Epstein, Lee. (1985) *Conservatives in Court.* Knoxville: University of Tennessee Press.

Epstein, Richard. (1982) "Manville: The Bankruptcy of Product Liability Law." *Regulation* (March/April), pp. 15–19, 43–46.

Erlanger, Howard, Elizabeth Chambliss, and Marygold Melli. (1987) "Participation and Flexibility in Informal Processes: Cautions from the Divorce Context." *Law & Society Rev.* 21: 585.

Eskridge, William, Jr. (1991) "Overriding Supreme Court Statutory Interpretation Decisions." *Yale L.J.* 100: 331.

Esping-Anderson, Gosta. (1990) *The Three Worlds of Welfare Capitalism.* Princeton, N.J.: Princeton University Press.

Farber, Henry, and Michelle White. (1991) "Medical Malpractice: An Empirical Examination of the Litigation Process." *RAND J. Economics* 22: 199.

Feeley, Malcolm M. (1979) *The Process Is the Punishment: Handling Cases in a Lower Criminal Court.* New York: Russell Sage Foundation.

Feeley, Malcolm M., and Edward Rubin. (1998) *Judicial Policy Making and the Modern State: How the Courts Reformed America's Prisons.* New York: Cambridge University Press.

Feldman, Eric. (2000) "Blood Justice: Courts, Conflict, and Compensation in Japan, France, and the United States." *Law & Society Rev.* 34: 561.

Feldman, Eric, and Ronald Boyer, eds. (1999) *Blood Feuds: AIDS, Blood, and the Politics of Medical Disaster.* New York: Oxford University Press.

Felker v. Turpin. (1996) 518 U.S. 651.

Fialka, John. (1998) "EPA Probers Find Big Flaws in Major Clean Air Effort." *Wall Street J.,* December 28, p. A16.

Fiorina, Morris. (1991) "Divided Government in the States." *PS: Political Science and Politics* (December), p. 646.

——— (1996) *Divided Government,* 2d ed. Boston: Allyn and Bacon.

Fiorino, Daniel. (1996) "Toward a New System of Environmental Regulation: The Case for an Industry Sector Approach." *Environmental Law* 26: 457.

Fisher, Stanley. (2000) "The Prosecutor's Ethical Duty to Seek Exculpatory Evidence in Police Hands: Lessons from England." *Fordham L. Rev.* 68: 101.

Fiss, Owen. (1984) "Against Settlement." *Yale L.J.* 93: 1073.

Flanagan, Robert J. (1987) *Labor Relations and the Litigation Explosion.* Washington, D.C.: Brookings Institution.

Flanagan, Robert J., David Soskice, and Lloyd Ulman. (1983) *Unionism, Economic Stabilization, and Incomes Policies: European Experience.* Washington, D.C.: Brookings Institution.

Flemming, John. (1984) "Is There a Future for Torts?" *La. L. Rev.* 44: 1193.

——— (1994) "Mass Torts." *American J. Comparative Law* 42: 507.

Fletcher, George P. (1994) "The Deliberators." *New York Times Book Rev.,* December 11, pp. 14–25 (review of Jeffrey Abramson, *We, the Jury*).

Foote, Caleb. (1956) "Vagrancy-Type Law and Its Administration." *U. Pa. L. Rev.* 104: 603.

Foote, Daniel. (1992) "The Benevolent Paternalism of Japanese Criminal Justice." *Cal. L. Rev.* 80: 317.

——— (1995) "Resolution of Traffic Accident Disputes and Judicial Activism in Japan." *Law in Japan* 25: 19.

Foppert, David. (1992) "Does No-Fault Stack Up?" in *Best's Review: Property—Casualty Insurance Edition*. Oldwick, N.J.: Best Company, Inc.

Fortuna, Richard, and David Lennett. (1987) *Hazardous Waste Regulation—the New Era*. New York: McGraw-Hill.

Foster, Sheila. (1998) "Justice from the Ground Up: Distributive Inequities, Grassroots Resistance, and the Transformative Politics of the Environmental Justice Movement." *Cal. L. Rev.* 86: 775.

Frammolino, Ralph. (1988) "Claims for Stress Devour Billions, Reformers Charge." *Los Angeles Times*, March 15, p. 3.

Frankel, Marvin. (1975) "The Search for Truth: An Umpireal View." *U. Pa. L. Rev.* 123: 1031.

Franklin, Marc. (1967) "Replacing the Negligence Lottery: Compensation and Selective Reimbursement." *U. Va. L. Rev.* 53: 774.

Frase, Richard S. (1990) "Comparative Criminal Justice as a Guide to American Law Reform: How Do the French Do It, How Can We Find Out, and Why Should We Care?" *Cal. L. Rev.* 78: 545.

Frase, Richard S., and Thomas Weigend. (1995) "German Criminal Justice." *Boston College International & Comparative L. Rev.* 18: 317.

Freeman, Jody. (1997) "Collaborative Governance in the Administrative State." *UCLA L. Rev.* 45: 1.

Freeman, Richard. (1994) "How Labor Fares in Advanced Economies," in R. Freeman, ed., *Working under Different Rules*. New York: Russell Sage Foundation.

Freeman, Richard, and Lawrence Katz. (1994) "How Labor Fares in Advanced Economies," in R. Freeman, ed., *Working under Different Rules*. New York: Russell Sage Foundation.

Frieden, Bernard J. (1979) "The New Regulation Comes to Suburbia." *The Public Interest* 55: 15.

Friedman, Lawrence M. (1973) *A History of American Law*. New York: Simon & Schuster.

——— (1978) "Civil Wrongs: Personal Injury Law in the Late 19th Century." *American Bar Foundation Research J.* 1978: 351.

——— (1979) "Plea Bargaining in Historical Perspective." *Law & Society Rev.* 13: 257.

——— (1985) *Total Justice*. New York: Russell Sage Foundation.

——— (1986) "A Search for Seizure." *Law & History Rev.* 4: 1.

——— (1993) *Crime and Punishment in American History*. New York: Basic Books.

Friedman, Lawrence M., Robert A. Kagan, Bliss Cartwright, and Stanton Wheeler. (1981) "State Supreme Courts: A Century of Style and Citation." *Stanford L. Rev.* 33: 773.

Friedman, Lawrence M., and Robert Percival. (1981) *The Roots of Justice: Crime and Punishment in Alameda County, California, 1870–1910*. Chapel Hill: University of North Carolina Press.

Friedman, Richard. (1998) "Anchors and Flotsam: Is Evidence Law 'Adrift'?" *Yale L. Rev.* 107: 1921.

Fulton, William. (1992) "The Gnatcatcher Follies." *California Lawyer* (May), p. 42.

Gaiter, Dorothy. (1996) "Eating Crow: How Shoney's, Belted by a Lawsuit, Found the Path to Diversity." *Wall Street J.*, April 16, pp. A1, A11.

Galanter, Marc. (1974) "Why 'the Haves' Come Out Ahead: Speculations on the Limits of Legal Change." *Law & Society Rev.* 9: 95.

——— (1983) "Reading the Landscape of Disputes: What We Know and Don't Know (and Think We Know) about Our Allegedly Contentious and Litigious Society." *UCLA L. Rev.* 31: 4.

——— (1988a) "The Life and Times of the Big Six; or, The Federal Courts since the Good Old Days." *Wis. L. Rev.* 1988: 921.

——— (1988b) "The Quality of Settlements." *J. Dispute Resolution* 1988: 55.

——— (1990) "The Civil Jury as Regulator of the Litigation Process." *U. Chicago Legal Forum* 1990: 201.

——— (1992) "Law Abounding: Legislation around the North Atlantic." *Modern L. Rev.* 55: 1.

——— (1993) "The Regulatory Function of the Civil Jury," in Robert Litan, ed., *Verdict: Assessing the Civil Jury System.* Washington, D.C.: Brookings Institution.

——— (1994) "Predators and Parasites: Lawyer-Bashing and Civil Justice." *Ga. L. Rev.* 28: 633.

——— (1998) "An Oil Strike in Hell: Contemporary Legends about the Justice System." *Ariz. L. Rev.* 40: 717.

Galanter, Marc, and Mia Kahill. (1999) "Most Cases Settle: Judicial Promotion and Regulation of Settlement." *Stanford L. Rev.* 46: 1374.

Galanter, Marc, and Joel Rogers. (1991) "A Transformation of American Business Disputing? Some Preliminary Observations." Working Paper DPRP 10-3, Institute for Legal Studies, University of Wisconsin, Madison.

Garth, Bryant. (1992) "Power and Legal Artifice: The Federal Class Action." *Law & Society Rev.* 26: 23.

——— (1993) "From Civil Litigation to Private Justice: Legal Practice at War with the Profession and Its Values." *Brooklyn L. Rev.* 59: 931.

Garvey, Stephen, Sheri Lynn Johnson, and Paul Marcus. (2000) "Correcting Deadly Confusion: Responding to Jury Inquiries in Capital Cases." *Cornell L. Rev.* 85: 627.

Gaylin, Willard. (1974) *Partial Justice: A Study in Bias in Sentencing.* New York: Knopf.

Geistfeld, Mark. (1995) "Placing a Price on Pain and Suffering: A Method for Helping Juries Determine Tort Damages for Nonmonetary Injuries." *Cal. L. Rev.* 83: 773.

Gelb, Joyce. (1989) *Feminism and Politics: A Comparative Perspective.* Berkeley: University of California Press.

Gellhorn, Walter. (1988) "Medical Malpractice Litigation (U.S.)—Medical Mishap Compensation (N.Z.)." *Cornell L. Rev.* 73: 170.

Gerlin, Andrea. (1994a) "Patent Lawyers Forgo Sure Fees on a Bet." *Wall Street J.,* June 24, p. B1.

——— (1994.) "A Matter of Degree: How a Jury Decided That a Coffee Spill Is Worth 2.9 Million." *Wall Street J.,* September 1, p. A1.

——— (1995) "Jury-Duty Scofflaws Try Patience of Courts." *Wall Street J.,* August 9, p. B1.

Geyelin, Milo. (1991) "Overhaul of Legal System Faces Hurdles." *Wall Street J.,* August 15, p. B2.

——— (1992) "Debate Intensifies over State Regulations That Restrict TV Advertising by Lawyers." *Wall Street J.*, August 31, p. B1.

——— (1994) "Critics Call Bronco II Settlement a Lemon." *Wall Street J.*, October 18, p. B1.

——— (1997) "Costly Verdict: Why One Jury Dealt a Big Blow to Chrysler in Minivan-Latch Case." *Wall Street J.*, November 19, pp. A1, A10.

Gibson, James. (1980) "Environmental Constraints on the Behavior of Judges: A Representational Model of Judicial Decision-Making." *Law & Society Rev.* 14: 343.

Gifford, Donald G. (1991) "The American Tort Liability System," in Werner Pfennigsdorf with D. G. Gifford, eds., *A Comparative Study of Liability Law and Compensation Schemes in Ten Countries and the United States.* Oak Brook, Ill.: Insurance Research Council.

Gigot, Paul. (1999) "Gore Slams Doerr on Silicon Valley." *Wall Street J.*, May 11, p. A12.

Gilson, Ronald, and Robert Mnookin. (1994) "Disputing through Agents: Cooperation and Conflict between Lawyers in Litigation." *Columbia L. Rev.* 94: 509.

Ginsberg, Benjamin, and Martin Shefter. (1990) *Politics by Other Means: The Declining Importance of Elections in America.* New York: Basic Books.

Givelber, Daniel J., et al. (1984) "*Tarasoff:* Myth and Reality—An Empirical Study." *Wis. L. Rev.* 1984: 443.

Glaberson, William. (1999) "Damage Control: Some Plaintiffs Losing Out in Texas' War on Lawsuits." *New York Times,* June 7, p. A1.

——— (2000) "Court Rulings Curb Efforts to Rein in Judicial Races." *New York Times,* October 7, p. A8.

Glendon, Mary Ann. (1987) *Abortion and Divorce in Western Law.* Cambridge: Harvard University Press.

——— (1991) *Rights Talk: The Impoverishment of Political Discourse.* New York: Free Press.

Goerdt, John. (1991) "Explaining the Pace of Civil Case Litigation: The Latest Evidence from 37 Large Urban Trial Courts." *Justice System J.* 14: 289.

Goldberg v. Kelly. (1970) 397 U.S. 254.

Goldman, Eric. (1977) *Rendezvous with Destiny* [1952], rev. ed. New York: Vintage Books.

Goldman, Sheldon. (1967) "Judicial Appointments to the U.S. Courts of Appeal." *Wis. L. Rev.* 1967: 186.

Goldsmith, Barbara. (1987) *Johnson v. Johnson.* New York: Alfred Knopf.

Goodnough, Abby. (1997) "Court Rejects New Jersey School Plan." *New York Times,* May 15, p. A18.

Goodwyn, Lawrence. (1978) *The Populist Moment: A Short History of the Agrarian Revolt in America.* New York: Oxford University Press.

Gornick, Janet, Marcia Meyers, and Katherine Ross. (1997) "Supporting the Employment of Mothers: Policy Variation across Fourteen Welfare States." *J. European Social Policy* 7: 126.

Gottlieb, Martin. (1996) "A Lawyer for the Poor Plans to Fight on His Own." *New York Times,* January 28, p. A8.

Gottschall, John. (1986) "Reagan's Appointments to the U.S. Courts of Appeals." *Judicature* (June/July), pp. 49–54.

Gould, William. (1984) *Japan's Reshaping of American Labor Law.* Cambridge: MIT Press.

Grady, Denise. (1996) "In One Country, Chronic Whiplash Is Uncompensated (and Unknown)." *New York Times,* May 7, p. B11.

Grady, Mark. (1988) "Why Are People Negligent? Technology, Nondurable Precautions and the Medical Malpractice Explosion." *Northwestern U. L. Rev.* 82: 293.

Graham, John D. (1991) "Product Liability and Motor Vehicle Safety," in Peter Huber and Robert Litan, eds., *The Liability Maze.* Washington, D.C.: Brookings Institution.

Green, M. (1989) "The Inability of Offensive Collateral Estoppel to Fulfill Its Promise: An Examination of Estoppel in Asbestos Litigation." *Iowa L. Rev.* 70: 141.

Greenawalt, R. Kent. (1981) "Silence as a Moral and Constitutional Right." *Wm. & Mary L. Rev.* 23: 15.

Greenhouse, Carol. (1986) *Praying for Justice: Faith, Order and Community in an American Town.* Ithaca: Cornell University Press.

Greenhouse, Linda. (1991) "Supreme Court Puts Sharp Curbs on Repeated Death Row Appeals." *New York Times,* April 17, p. A1.

Greve, Michael S. (1989a) "Environmentalism and Bounty Hunting." *The Public Interest* 97: 15.

——— (1989b) "The Non-Reformation of Administrative Law: Standing to Sue and Public Interest Litigation in West German Environmental Law." *Cornell International L.J.* 22: 197.

——— (1992) "Private Enforcement, Private Rewards: How Environmental Suits Became an Entitlement Program," in M. S. Greve and Fred Smith, Jr., eds., *Environmental Politics: Public Costs, Private Rewards.* New York: Greenwood.

Griffin v. California. (1965) 380 U.S. 609.

Griffin, Stephen. (1991) "Bringing the State into Constitutional Theory." *Law & Social Inquiry* 16: 659.

Griffiths, John. (1986) "What Do Dutch Lawyers Actually Do in Divorce Cases?" *Law & Society Rev.* 20: 135.

Gross, Samuel, and Kent Syverud. (1996) "Don't Try: Civil Jury Verdicts in a System Geared to Settlement." *UCLA L. Rev.* 44: 1.

Gunningham, Neil, and Peter Grabosky. (1998) *Smart Regulation.* Oxford: Clarendon Press.

Gunnison, Robert B. (1993) "Nuclear Dump Plans for Mojave Are Halted." *San Francisco Chronicle,* November 25, pp. A1, A21.

Haire, Susan, and Stefanie Lindquist. (1997) "Social Security Disability Cases in the U.S. Courts of Appeals." *Judicature* 80: 230.

Haley, John. (1986) "Administrative Guidance versus Formal Regulation: Resolving the Paradox of Industrial Policy," in Gary Saxonhouse and Kozo Yamamura, eds., *Law and Trade Issues of the Japanese Economy.* Seattle: University of Washington Press.

Hammit, James K., et al. (1985) "Tort Standards and Jury Decisions." *J. Legal Studies* 14: 751.

Hanf, Kenneth, and Cor Smits. (1991) "Maintenance Dredging in the Port of Rotterdam: Trading Off Environmental Quality and Economic Development." Paper presented at annual meeting, Law and Society Association, Amsterdam, June 26–29.

Hans, Valerie, and William Lofquist. (1992) "Jurors' Judgments of Business Liability in Tort Cases: Implications for the Litigation Explosion Debate." *Law & Society Rev.* 26: 85.

Hanson, Roger, et al. (1992) "Indigent Defenders Get the Job Done and Done Well." Williamsburg, Va.: National Center for State Courts.

Hanushek, Eric. (1989) "The Impact of Differential Expenditures on School Performance." *Education Researcher* 18: 45.

——— (1994) "Money Might Matter Somewhere: A Response to Hedges, Laine, and Greenwald." *Education Researcher* 23: 5.

Harris v. Alabama. (1995) 513 U.S. 504.

Harris, Lis. (1995) "Banana Kelly's Toughest Fight." *New Yorker,* July 24, pp. 32–40.

Harris, Lyle, and Mark Curriden. (1991) "McCleskey Is Executed for '78 Killing." *Atlanta Constitution,* September 25, pp. A1, A13.

Harrison, Kathryn, and George Hoberg. (1991) "Setting the Environmental Agenda in Canada and the United States: The Cases of Dioxin and Radon." *Canadian J. Political Science* 24: 3.

Hartz, Louis. (1955) *The Liberal Tradition in America: An Interpretation of American Political Thought since the Revolution.* New York: Harcourt, Brace & World.

Harvard Medical Practice Study. (1990) *Patients, Doctors and Lawyers: Medical Injury, Malpractice Litigation, and Patient Compensation in New York.* Cambridge: Harvard University Press.

Hawkins, Keith. (1984) *Environment and Enforcement: Regulation and the Social Definition of Deviance.* Oxford: Oxford University Press.

Hawley, Ellis. (1966) *The New Deal and the Problem of Monopoly.* Princeton, N.J.: Princeton University Press.

Hazard, Geoffrey. (1969) "Social Justice through Civil Justice." *U. Chicago L. Rev.* 36: 699.

Hazard, Geoffrey, and Michele Taruffo. (1993) *American Civil Procedure.* New Haven: Yale University Press.

Hebert, Ray. (1972) "Class Action Lawsuit Hits Century Freeway." *Los Angeles Times,* February 18, p. 1.

——— (1986) "Century Freeway—When It's Born, an Era Will Die." *Los Angeles Times,* June 22, p. 4.

Heffernan, Richard, and Richard Lovely. (1991) "Evaluating the Fourth Amendment Exclusionary Rule: The Problem of Police Compliance with the Law." *Michigan J. Law Reform* 24: 537.

Heilbroner, David. (1990) *Rough Justice: Days and Nights of a Young D.A.* New York: Pantheon Books.

Heise, Michael. (1995) "State Constitutional Litigation, Educational Finance, and Legal Impact: An Empirical Analysis." *U. Cincinnati L. Rev.* 631: 735.

——— (1998) "Schoolhouses, Courthouses, and Statehouses: Educational Finance, Constitutional Structure, and the Separation of Powers Doctrine." *Land & Water L. Rev.* 33: 282.

———— (2000) "Justice Delayed? An Empirical Analysis of Civil Case Disposition Time." *Case Western Reserve L. Rev.* 50:813.

Helland, Eric, and Alexander Tabarrok. (2000) "Runaway Judges? Selection Effects and the Jury." *J. Law, Economics & Organization* 16: 306–333.

Hellner, Jan. (1986) "Compensation for Personal Injury: The Swedish Alternative." *American J. Comparative Law* 34:613.

Hensler, Deborah R. (1985) *Asbestos in the Courts.* Santa Monica, Calif.: RAND Institute for Civil Justice.

———— (1990) "Court-Ordered Arbitration: An Alternative View." *U. Chicago Legal Forum* 1990: 399.

Hensler, Deborah R., et al. (1987) *Trends in Tort Litigation.* Santa Monica, Calif.: RAND Institute for Civil Justice.

———— (1991) *Compensation for Accidental Injuries in the United States.* Santa Monica, Calif.: RAND Institute for Civil Justice.

Herbert, Bob. (1998) "Fighting Citizen Abuse." *New York Times,* June 21, pp. 4, 15.

———— (2001) "Addicted to Guns." *New York Times,* January 1, p. A17.

Hercules, Inc. v. United States. (1994) 24 F.3d 188.

Hermann, Joachim. (1992) "Bargaining Justice—A Bargain for German Criminal Justice?" *U. Pittsburgh L. Rev.* 53: 755.

Hermann, Philip. (1962) "Predicting Verdicts in Personal Injury Cases." *Insurance L.J.* 475: 505.

Herrara v. Collins. (1993) 506 U.S. 390.

Heymann, Philip, and Lance Liebman. (1988) "No Fault, No Fee: The Legal Profession and Federal No-Fault Insurance Legislation," in P. Heymann and L. Liebman, eds., *The Social Responsibilities of Lawyers.* Westbury, N.Y.: Foundation Press.

Himmelfarb, Gertrude. (1994) "A De-Moralized Society: The British/American Experience." *The Public Interest* no. 117: 57.

Hoberg, George. (1990) "Risk, Science and Politics: Alachlor Regulation in Canada and the United States." *Canadian J. Political Science* 23: 257.

———— (1991) "Sleeping with an Elephant: The American Influence on Canadian Environmental Regulation." *J. Public Policy* 11: 107.

———— (1993) "Environmental Policy: Alternative Styles," in Michael Atkinson, ed., *Governing Canada: State Institutions and Public Policy.* Toronto: Harcourt-Brace-Jovanovich-Canada.

———— (1997) "Governing the Commons: Environmental Policy in Canada and the United States," in Keith Banting and G. Hoberg, eds., *Degrees of Freedom: Canada and the United States in a Changing World.* Montreal: McGill-Queens University Press.

Hoebel, E. Adamson. (1964) *The Law of Primitive Man.* Cambridge: Harvard University Press.

Holden, Benjamin, Laurie Cohen, and Eleena de Lisser. (1995) "Color Blinded? Race Seems to Play an Increasing Role in Many Jury Verdicts." *Wall Street J.,* October 4, p. A1.

Hollingworth, J. Rogers, Jerald Hage, and Robert Hanneman. (1990) *State Intervention in Medical Care: Consequences for Britain, France, Sweden, and the United States.* Ithaca, N.Y.: Cornell University Press.

Horowitz, Michael. (1995) "Making Ethics Real, Making Ethics Work: A Proposal for Contingency Fee Reform." *Emory L.J.* 44: 173.

Horwitz, Morton. (1977) *The Transformation of American Law, 1780–1860.* Cambridge: Harvard University Press.

Howlett, Michael. (1994) "The Judicialization of Canadian Environmental Policy, 1980–1990: Canada-U.S. Convergence?" *Canadian J. Political Science* 27: 99.

Huber, Evelyn, Charles Ragin, and John Stephens. (1994) "Social Democracy, Christian Democracy, Constitutional Structure, and the Welfare State." *American J. Sociology* 99: 711.

Huber, Peter W. (1985) "Safety and the Second Best: The Hazards of Public Risk Management in the Courts." *Columbia L. Rev.* 85: 277.

——— (1988) "Environmental Hazards and Liability Law," in Robert Litan and Clifford Winston, eds., *Liability: Perspectives and Policy.* Washington, D.C.: Brookings Institution.

——— (1990) "Junk Science and the Jury." *U. Chicago Legal Forum* 1990: 273.

——— (1997) "Easy Lawsuits Make Bad Medicine." *Forbes,* April 21, p. 166.

Huber, Peter W., and Robert Litan. (1991) "Overview," in P. W. Huber and R. Litan, eds., *The Liability Maze.* Washington, D.C.: Brookings Institution.

Hughes, Graham. (1984) "English Criminal Justice: Is It Better Than Ours?" *Ariz. L. Rev.* 26: 507.

Hulbert, Richard. (1997) "Comment on French Civil Procedure." *American J. Comparative Law* 45: 747.

Human Rights Watch. (1996) "Race and Drug Law Enforcement in the State of Georgia." *Human Rights Watch* 8: 1.

Huntington, Samuel. (1981) *American Politics: The Promise of Disharmony.* Cambridge, Mass.: Belknap Press.

Huppes, Gjalt, and Robert A. Kagan. (1989) "Market-Oriented Regulation of Environmental Problems in the Netherlands." *Law & Policy* 11: 215.

Hurst, J. Willard. (1956) *Law and the Conditions of Freedom in Nineteenth Century United States.* Madison: University of Wisconsin Press.

ICJ (Institute for Civil Justice). (1995a) "How Big Is the Price Tag for Excess Auto Injury Claims?" Research brief, p. 1. Santa Monica, Calif.: RAND Institute for Civil Justice.

——— (1995b) "Understanding Mass Personal Injury Litigation." Research brief. Santa Monica, Calif.: RAND Institute for Civil Justice.

Ikenberry, G. John. (1988) "Conclusion: An Institutional Approach to American Foreign Economic Policy." *International Organization* 42: 219.

In re "Agent Orange" Product Liability Litigation. (1984) 597 F. Supp. 740 (E.D.N.Y.), 611 F. Supp. 1223 (E.D.N.Y. 1985).

Irons, Peter. (1980) "Demetrio Rodriguez v. San Antonio," in P. Irons, ed., *The Courage of Their Convictions: Sixteen Americans Who Fought Their Way to the Supreme Court.* New York: Penguin Books.

Jackson, Kenneth T. (1985) *Crabgrass Empire: The Suburbanization of the United States.* New York: Oxford University Press.

——— (1996) "America's Rush to Suburbia." *New York Times,* June 9, p. E15.

Jacob, Herbert. (1984) *The Frustration of Policy: Responses to Crime by American Cities.* Boston: Little, Brown.

Jacob, Herbert, Erhard Blankenburg, Herbert Kritzer, Doris Marie Provine, and Joseph Sanders. (1996) *Courts, Law and Politics in Comparative Perspective.* New Haven: Yale University Press.

Jacobs, Margaret. (1994) "Arbitration Clauses Come under Scrutiny." *Wall Street J.,* December 22, p. B2.

——— (1997) "Prodding Unwed Dads to Admit Paternity." *Wall Street J.,* October 16, p. B1.

Jacobs, Margaret, and Michael Siconolfi. (1995) "Losing Battles: Investors Fare Poorly Fighting Wall Street—And May Do Worse." *Wall Street J.,* February 8, pp. A1, A9.

James v. Valtierra. (1971) 402 U.S. 137.

Janovsky, Michael. (1996) "Suit Says Racial Bias Led to Clustering of Solid Waste Sites," *New York Times,* May 29, p. A15.

Jasanoff, Sheila. (1986) *Risk Management and Political Culture.* New York: Russell Sage Foundation.

——— (1999) "Cross-National Differences in Policy Implementation," in Bridget Hutter, ed., *A Reader in Environmental Law.* Oxford: Oxford University Press.

Jenkins, Holman, Jr. (1996) "Let Tobacco CEOs Speak Candidly." *Wall Street J.,* February 13, p. A15.

——— (1999) "Now on Video: America's Scariest Special Interest." *Wall Street J.,* April 21, p. A23.

Johnson, David. (1998) "The Organization of Prosecution and the Possibility of Order." *Law & Society Rev.* 32: 247.

Johnson, Earl, Jr., and Ann Barthelmes Drew. (1978) "This Nation Has Money for Everything—Except Its Courts." *Judges J.* (Summer), p. 10.

Johnson, Lori, Tatsuya Fujie, and Marius Aalders. (2000) "New Chemical Notification Laws in Japan, the United States, and the European Union," in Robert A. Kagan and Lee Axelrad, eds., *Regulatory Encounters: Multinational Corporations and American Adversarial Legalism.* Berkeley: University of California Press.

Joppke, Christian. (1993) *Mobilizing against Nuclear Power: A Comparison of Germany and the United States.* Berkeley: University of California Press.

Jost, Timothy Stoltzfus. (1998) "Health Care Rationing in the Courts: A Comparative Study." *Hastings International & Comparative L. Rev.* 21: 639.

Kagan, Robert A. (1978) *Regulatory Justice: Implementing a Wage Price Freeze.* New York: Russell Sage Foundation.

——— (1982) "What If Abe Fortas Had Been More Discreet?" in Nelson W. Polsby, ed., *What If? Explorations in Social-Science Fiction.* Lexington, Mass.: Lewis Publishing.

——— (1984) "Inside Administrative Law." *Columbia L. Rev.* 84: 816.

——— (1987) "Constitutional Litigation in the United States," in Ralf Rogowski and Thomas Gawron, eds., *Constitutional Courts in Comparison.* Gummersbach, West Germany: Theodor Heuss Academie.

——— (1988) "What Makes Uncle Sammy Sue?" *Law & Society Rev.* 21: 718.

——— (1990a) "How Much Does Law Matter? Labor Law, Competition, and Waterfront Labor Relations in Rotterdam and U.S. Ports." *Law & Society Rev.* 24: 35.

——— (1990b) *Patterns of Port Development: Government, Intermodal Trans-*

poration, and Innovation in the United States, China and Hong Kong. Berkeley: Institute of Transportation Studies.

—— (1991a) "Adversarial Legalism and American Government." *J. Policy Analysis & Management* 10: 369.

—— (1991b) "The Dredging Dilemma: Economic Development and Environmental Protection in Oakland Harbor." *Coastal Management* 19: 313–341.

—— (1993) "Regulatory Enforcement," in David Rosenblum and Richard Schwartz, eds., *Handbook of Regulation and Administrative Law.* New York: Marcel Dekker.

—— (1994) "Do Lawyers Cause Adversarial Legalism?" *Law & Social Inquiry* 19: 1.

—— (1995) "What Socio-Legal Scholars Should Do When There Is Too Much Law to Study." *J. Law & Society* 22: 140.

—— (1997a) "Should Europe Worry about Adversarial Legalism?" *Oxford J. Legal Studies* 17: 165.

—— (1997b) "Political and Legal Obstacles to Ecosystem Planning." *Environmental Law Quarterly* 24: 871.

—— (1999a) "Trying to Have It Both Ways: Local Discretion, Central Control, and Adversarial Legalism in American Environmental Regulation." *Ecology Law Quarterly* 25: 718.

—— (1999b) "Adversarial Legalism: Tamed or Still Wild?" *NYU J. Legislation* 2: 101.

—— (2000) "The Consequences of Adversarial Legalism," in R. A. Kagan and Lee Axelrad, eds., *Regulatory Encounters: Multinational Corporations and American Adversarial Legalism.* Berkeley: University of California Press.

Kagan, Robert A., and Lee Axelrad. (1997) "Adversarial Legalism: An International Perspective," in Pietro Nivola, ed., *Comparative Disadvantages? Social Regulations and the Global Economy.* Washington, D.C.: Brookings Institution.

Kagan, Robert A., and Lee Axelrad, eds. (2000) *Regulatory Encounters: Multinational Corporations and American Adversarial Legalism.* Berkeley: University of California Press.

Kagan, Robert, Bliss Cartwright, Lawrence M. Friedman, and Stanton Wheeler. (1977) "The Business of State Supreme Courts, 1870–1970." *Stanford L. Rev.* 30: 121.

Kagan, Robert A., Robert Detlefsen, and Bobby Infelise. (1984) "American State Supreme Court Justices, 1900–1970." *American Bar Foundation Research J.* 1984: 371.

Kagan, Robert A., Lawrence M. Friedman, Bliss Cartwright, and Stanton Wheeler. (1977) "The Business of State Supreme Courts." *Stanford L. Rev.* 30: 12.

Kagan, Robert A., and Todd Lochner. (1998) "Criminal Prosecution for Regulatory Offenses in the United States: Trends and Patterns in the Federal System." Paper prepared for Conference on Criminal Prosecution for Regulatory Offenses, Centre for Socio-Legal Studies, Oxford, England.

Kagan, Robert A., and William Nelson. (2000) "The Politics of Tobacco Regulation in the United States," in Robert Rabin and Stephen Sugarman, eds., *Regulatory Tobacco.* New York: Oxford University Press.

Kagan, Robert A., and Robert Eli Rosen. (1985) "On the Social Significance of Large Law Firm Practice." *Stanford L. Rev.* 37: 399.

Kagan, Robert A., and Jerome Skolnick. (1993) "Banning Smoking: Compliance without Enforcement," in Robert Rabin and Stephen Sugarman, eds., *Smoking Policy: Law, Politics and Culture.* New York: Oxford University Press.

Kakalik, James S., et al. (1983) *Costs of Asbestos Litigation.* Santa Monica, Calif.: Institute for Civil Justice, RAND Corporation.

——— (1984) *Variation in Asbestos Litigation Compensation Expenses.* Santa Monica, Calif.: Institute for Civil Justice.

——— (1990) "A RAND Note: Strategies for Reducing Civil Delay in the Los Angeles Superior Court: Technical Appendixes." Santa Monica, Calif.: Institute for Civil Justice.

Kakalik, James S., and Nicholas M. Pace. (1986) *Costs and Compensation Paid in Tort Litigation.* Santa Monica, Calif.: Institute for Civil Justice, RAND Corporation.

Kalven, Harry. (1964) "The Dignity of the Civil Jury." *Va. L. Rev.* 50: 1055.

Kalven, Harry, and Hans Zeisel. (1966) *The American Jury.* Boston: Little, Brown.

Kamerman, Sheila B., and Alfred J. Kahn. (1988) "What Europe Does for Single-Parent Families." *The Public Interest* 93: 70–86.

Kamin, Samuel. (1999) "The Death Penalty and the California Supreme Court." Ph.D. dissertation, Jurisprudence and Social Policy, University of California, Berkeley.

Kaplan, David. (1991) "New Rules on Death Row." *Newsweek,* April 29, p. 68.

Karpoff, Jonathan, John Lott, Jr., and Graeme Rankine. (1998) "Environmental Violations, Legal Penalties, and Reputation Costs." Working paper, University of Washington, http://faculty.washington.edu/karpoff//

Katzenstein, Peter, ed. (1978) *Between Power and Plenty: Foreign Economic Policies of Advanced Industrial States.* Madison: University of Wisconsin Press.

Katzmann, Robert. (1995) "Making Sense of Congressional Intent: Statutory Interpretation and Welfare Policy." *Yale L.J.* 104: 2345.

Kelemen, R. Daniel. (1998) "Regulatory Federalism: The European Union in Comparative Perspective." Ph.D. dissertation, Stanford University.

Kelman, Steven. (1981) *Regulating America, Regulating Sweden: A Comparative Study of Occupational Safety and Health Policy.* Cambridge: MIT Press.

——— (1992) "Adversary and Cooperationist Institutions for Conflict Resolution in Public Policymaking." *J. Policy Analysis & Management* 11: 178–206.

Kennedy, Eugene. (1985) *Defendant: A Psychiatrist on Trial for Medical Malpractice.* New York: Free Press.

King v. Smith. (1968) 392 U.S. 309.

King, Anthony. (1997) *Running Scared: Why American Politicians Campaign Too Much and Govern Too Little.* New York: Martin Kessler Books.

King, Bernard. (1991) "The Continuing Explosion of ERISA Litigation." *Labor Law Developments, 1991.* New York: Matthew Bender.

Kirp, David L. (1979) *Doing Good by Doing Little: Race and Schooling in Britain.* Berkeley: University of California Press.

——— (1982) "Professionalization as a Policy Choice: British Special Education in Comparative Perspective." *World Politics* 34: 137.

Kirp, David L., John Dwyer, and Larry Rosenthal. (1995) *Our Town: Race, Housing and the Soul of Suburbia*. New Brunswick, N.J.: Rutgers University Press.

Kitch, Edward. (1985) "Vaccines and Product Liability: A Case of Contagious Litigation." *Regulation* (May/June), p. 11.

Klein, Richard, and Robert Spangenburg. (1993) *The Indigent Defense Crisis*. Washington, D.C.: American Bar Association.

Kluger, Richard. (1996) *Ashes to Ashes: America's Hundred Year Cigarette War, Public Health, and the Unabashed Triumph of Philip Morris*. New York: Alfred A. Knopf.

Kohler, Peter A., and Hans F. Zacher. (1982) *The Evolution of Social Insurance, 1881–1981: Studies of Germany, France, Great Britain, Austria and Switzerland*. New York: St. Martin's Press.

Kolata, Gina. (1995) "Will the Lawyers Kill Off Norplant?" *New York Times*, May 28, sec. 3, pp. 1, 5.

———— (1998) "Panel Can't Link Implants to Any Diseases." *New York Times*, December 2, p. A1.

Kopp, Thomas R., Paul Portney, and Deborah DeWitt. (1990) International Comparisons of Environmental Regulation. Washington, D.C.: Resources for the Future.

Krasner, Stephen. (1978) *Defending the National Interest*. Princeton, N.J.: Princeton University Press.

Kraus, Martine. (2000) "Licensing Biologics in Europe and the United States," in Robert A. Kagan and Lee Axelrad, eds., *Regulatory Encounters: Multinational Corporations and American Adversarial Legalism*. Berkeley: University of California Press.

Kritzer, Herbert. (1990) *The Justice Broker: Lawyers and Ordinary Litigation*. New York: Oxford University Press.

———— (1991) "Propensity to Sue in England and the United States of America: Blaming and Claiming in Tort Cases." *J. Law & Society* 18: 400.

———— (1993) "The Politics of Redress: Controlling Access to the Court System in England." Paper presented to the annual meeting of the Law and Society Association, Chicago, May 27–30.

———— (1996) "Courts, Justice, and Politics in England," in Herbert Jacob et al., eds., *Courts, Law and Politics in Comparative Perspective*. New Haven: Yale University Press.

Krygier, Martin. (2001) "Philip Selznick, Normative Theory and the Rule of Law," in M. Krygier, Robert A. Kagan, and Kenneth Winston, eds., *Legality and Community: On the Intellectual Legacy of Philip Selznick*. Berkeley: Institute of Governmental Studies Press.

Kukanza, Tina Knight. (1997) "*Varity Corp. v. Howe*: Will It Cause an Increase in Litigation against Employers Who Administer ERISA Plans?" *Mercer L. Rev.* 48: 974.

Laitin, Howard. (1994) "'Good' Warnings, Bad Products, and Cognitive Limitations." *UCLA L. Rev.* 41: 1193.

Lambert, Wade. (1995) "Costs of Settlements Reach Record in Suits against Directors, Officers." *Wall Street J.*, March 10, p. B6.

Lande, John. (1998) "Failing Faith in Litigation? A Survey of Business Lawyers' and Executives' Opinions." *Harvard J. Dispute Resolution* 3: 1.

Landes, William, and Richard Posner. (1975) "The Independent Judiciary in an Interest Group Perspective." *J. Law & Economics* 18: 875.

Landfried, Christine. (1995) "Germany," in C. Neal Tate and Torbjorn Vallinder, eds., *The Global Expansion of Judicial Power.* New York: New York University Press.

Landy, Marc, and Mary Hague. (1992) "The Coalition for Waste: Private Interests and the Superfund," in Michael Greve and Fred Smith, eds., *Environmental Politics: Public Costs, Private Rewards.* New York: Greenwood.

Landy, Marc, and Martin Levin. (1995) "The New Politics of Public Policy," in M. Landy and M. Levin, eds., *The New Politics of Public Policy.* Baltimore, Md.: Johns Hopkins Press.

Langan, Patricia, and Helen Grazadei. (1995) *Felony Sentences in State Courts, 1992.* Washington, D.C.: U.S. Department of Justice.

Langbein, John. (1979a) "Understanding the Short History of Plea Bargaining." *Law & Society Rev.* 13: 261.

———— (1979b) "Land without Plea Bargaining: How the Germans Do It." *Mich. L. Rev.* 78: 204.

———— (1985) "The German Advantage in Civil Procedure." *U. Chicago L. Rev.* 52: 823.

———— (1994) "Will Contests." *Yale L.J.* 103: 2039.

———— (1995) "Money Talks, Clients Walk." *Newsweek,* April 17, pp. 32–33.

Lawrence, Susan. (1990) *The Poor in Court: The Legal Service Program and Supreme Court Decision Making.* Princeton, N.J.: Princeton University Press.

Lazarus, Richard. (1991) "The Tragedy of Distrust in the Implementation of Federal Environmental Law." *Law & Contemporary Problems* 54: 311.

Lee, Louise. (1997) "Lots of Trouble: Courts Begin to Award Damages to Victims of Parking-Area Crime." *Wall Street J.,* April 23, p. A1.

Lee, Patrick. (1990) "Barrels of Losses at Point Arguello." *Los Angeles Times,* January 27, p. D1.

Leebron, David. (1989) "Final Moments: Damages for Pain and Suffering Prior to Death." *NYU L. Rev.* 64: 256.

Lehne, Richard. (1978) *The Quest for Justice: The Politics of School Finance Reform.* New York: Longman.

Lempert, Richard. (1993) "Civil Juries and Complex Cases," in Robert Litan, ed., *Verdict: Assessing the Civil Jury System.* Washington: Brookings Institution.

Leo, Richard. (1996) "*Miranda*'s Revenge: Police Interrogation as a Confidence Game." *Law & Society Rev.* 30: 259.

Lester, Charles. (1992) "The Search for Dialogue in the Administrative State: The Politics, Policy, and Law of Offshore Oil Development." Ph.D. dissertation, Jurisprudence and Social Policy Program, University of California, Berkeley.

Levin, Martin. (1972) "Urban Politics and Judicial Behavior." *J. Legal Studies* 1: 193.

Levine, James. (1983) "Jury Toughness: The Impact of Conservatism on Criminal Court Verdicts." *Crime & Delinquency* 29: 71.

———— (1992) *Juries and Politics.* Pacific Grove, Calif.: Brooks/Cole.

Levy, Jonah. (1997) "Globalization, Liberalization, and National Capitalisms." *Structural Change & Economic Dynamics* 8: 87.

———— (1999) *Tocqueville's Revenge.* Cambridge: Harvard University Press.

Levy, Jonah, Robert A. Kagan, and John Zysman. (1998) "The Twin Restorations: The Political Economy of the Reagan and Thatcher 'Revolutions,'" in Lee-Jay Cho and Yoon Hyung Kim, eds., *Ten Paradigms of Market Economies and Land Systems*. Anyang, Korea: Korea Research Institute for Human Settlements.

Lewin, Tamar. (1995) "Who Decides Who Will Die? Even within States, It Varies." *New York Times,* February 23, p. A1.

———— (1996) "U.S. Agency Wants the Pill Redefined." *New York Times,* July 1, pp. A1, A10.

Lewis, Anthony. (1995) "Is It a Zeal to Kill?" *New York Times,* December 8, p. A23.

Lewis, Neil. (1996) "A Compromise on Restricting Liability Suits." *New York Times,* March 14, p. B12.

Liang, Bryan. (1997) "Assessing Medical Malpractice Jury Verdicts: A Case Study of an Anesthesiology Department." *Cornell J. Law & Public Policy* 7: 121.

Lifsher, Mark. (1998) "EPA Urged to Move against Firm." *Wall Street J.,* June 17, pp. A1, A4.

Lipsen, Linda. (1991) "The Evolution of Products Liability as a Federal Policy Issue," in Peter Schuck, ed., *Tort Law and the Public Interest*. New York: Norton.

Lipset, Seymour Martin. (1991) *Continental Divide: The Values and Institutions of the United States and Canada*. New York: Routledge.

———— (1996) *American Exceptionalism: A Double-Edged Sword*. New York: W. W. Norton.

Litan, Robert, Peter Swire, and Clifford Winston. (1988) "The U.S. Liability System: Background and Trends," in R. Litan and C. Winston, eds., *Liability: Perspectives and Policy*. Washington, D.C.: Brookings Institution.

Litt, David, Jonathan Macey, Geoffrey Miller, and Edward Rubin. (1990) "Politics, Bureaucracies, and Financial Markets: Bank Entry into Commercial Paper Underwriting in the United States and Japan." *U. Pa. L. Rev.* 139: 369.

Lohof, Andrew. (1991) "The Cleanup of Inactive Hazardous Waste Sites in Selected Industrialized Countries." Washington, D.C.: American Petroleum Institute.

Lohr, Steve. (1995) "Vigorous Defense Stalls Injury Claims on Repetitive Strain." *New York Times,* May 28, p. 19.

Louis, Arthur. (1987) "The Reference Run-Around." *San Francisco Chronicle,* November 9, p. C1.

Lowenthal, Gary. (1993) "Mandatory Sentencing Laws: Undermining the Effectiveness of Determinate Sentencing Reform." *Cal. L. Rev.* 81: 61.

Lucas, A. R. (1993) "Judicial Review of Environmental Assessment: Has the Federal Process Been Judicialized?" in Steven A. Kennett, ed., *Law and Process in Environmental Management*. Calgary: Canadian Institute of Resources Law.

Lucas, Charlotte-Anne. (1990) "Chevron's Albatross: Point Arguello Project a Multi-Billion-Dollar Disaster." *San Francisco Examiner,* February 4, pp. D1, D16.

Lujan v. Defenders of Wildlife. (1992) 504 U.S. 555.

Lundqvist, Lennart J. (1980) *The Hare and the Tortoise: Clean Air Policies in the United States and Sweden*. Ann Arbor: University of Michigan Press.

Lunzer, Francesca. (1985) "Scared Shotless." *Forbes,* November 18, p. 256.

Lynch, David. (1994) "The Impropriety of Plea Agreements: A Tale of Two Counties." *Law & Social Inquiry* 19: 115.

Lynch, James. (1987) *Imprisonment in Four Countries* (Bureau of Justice Statistics Special Report). Washington, D.C.: U.S. Department of Justice.

——— (1988) "A Comparison of Prison Use in England, Canada, West Germany and the United States." *J. Criminal Law & Criminology* 79: 180–217.

Macaulay, Stewart. (1979) "Lawyers and Consumer Protection Laws." *Law & Society Rev.* 14: 115.

Machura, Stefan. (2000) "Justice Evaluations by German Lay Assessors." Paper presented at annual meeting of Law and Society Association, Miami Beach, Fla., May.

Mackay, Murray. (1991) "Liability, Safety, and Innovation in the Automotive Industry," in Peter Huber and Robert Litan, eds., *The Liability Maze*. Washington, D.C.: Brookings Institution.

MacCoun, Robert. (1993) "Decisionmaking by Civil Juries," in Robert Litan, ed., *Verdict: Assessing the Civil Jury System*. Washington, D.C.: Brookings Institution.

——— (1996) "Differential Treatment of Corporate Defendants by Juries: An Examination of the 'Deep Pockets' Hypothesis." *Law & Society Rev.* 30: 121.

Maltby, Lewis. (1994) "The Projected Impact of the Model Employment Termination Act." *Annals of the American Academy of Political & Social Science* 536: 103.

Manley, Howard. (1994) "Harsh Line Drawn on Crack Cocaine." *Columbus Dispatch*, July 24, pp. A1, A14.

Mann, Kenneth. (1985) *Defending White Collar Crime*. New Haven: Yale University Press.

Mansnerus, Laura. (1995) "Rewriting the Rules of the Jury System." *New York Times*, November 4, p. A7.

March, James, and Herbert Simon. (1958) *Organizations*. New York: John Wiley.

Margolick, David. (1993) *Undue Influence: The Epic Battle for the Johnson & Johnson Fortune*. New York: William Morrow & Co.

——— (1994) "In a Death Penalty Case, the Defense Lawyer Is on Trial Himself, Accused of Incompetence and Worse." *New York Times*, June 3, p. B8.

Markesinis, Basil. (1990) "Litigation-Mania in England, Germany, and the USA: Are We So Very Different?" *Cambridge L.J.* 49: 233.

Marshall, Ineke Haen. (1996) "How Exceptional Is the United States? Crime Trends in Europe and the U.S." *Europe Meets U.S. in Crime and Policy*, vol. 4, no. 2 of *European J. Criminal Policy & Research*. Amsterdam and New York: Kluger Publications.

Martin, Roger. (1991) "General Aviation Manufacturing: An Industry Under Siege," in Peter Huber and Robert Litan, eds., *The Liability Maze*. Washington, D.C.: Brookings Institution.

Mashaw, Terry L. (1971) "Welfare Reform and Local Administration of Aid to Families with Dependent Children in Virginia." *Va. L. Rev.* 57: 818.

——— (1983) *Bureaucratic Justice: Managing Social Security Disability Claims*. New Haven: Yale University Press.

Mashaw, Jerry L., and Daniel Harfst. (1987) "Regulation and Legal Culture: The Case of Motor Vehicle Safety." *Yale J. Regulation* 4: 257–316.

——— (1991) *The Struggle for Auto Safety*. Cambridge: Harvard University Press.

Mastroianni, L., et al., eds. (1990) *Developing New Contraceptives: Obstacles and Opportunities.* Washington, D.C.: National Academy Press.

Mather, Lynn. (1998) "Theorizing about Trial Courts: Lawyers, Policymaking, and Tobacco Litigation." *Law & Social Inquiry* 23: 897.

Maxeiner, James. (1991) "The Expert in U.S. and German Patent Litigation." *IIC* 22: 595.

Mayhew, David. (1991) *Divided We Govern: Party Control, Lawmaking, and Investigations, 1946–1990.* New Haven: Yale University Press.

McCann, Michael. (1986) *Taking Reform Seriously: Perspectives on Public Interest Liberalism.* Ithaca, N.Y.: Cornell University Press.

——— (1994) *Rights at Work: Law and the Politics of Pay Equity.* Chicago: University of Chicago Press.

——— (1999) "How the Supreme Court Matters in American Politics," in Howard Gilman and Cornell Clayton, eds., *The Supreme Court in American Politics: New Institutional Perspectives.* Lawrence, Kans.: University Press of Kansas.

McCleskey v. Kemp. (1987) 481 U.S. 279.

McCleskey v. State. (1980) 263 S.E.2d 146 (Ga.), cert. denied, 449 U.S. 891.

McCleskey v. Zant. (1991) 499 U.S. 467.

McClosky, Herbert, and Alida Brill. (1983) *Dimensions of Tolerance: What Americans Believe about Civil Liberties.* New York: Russell Sage Foundation.

McConville, Michael. (1994) "An Error of Judgment," in M. McConville and Lee Bridges, eds., *Criminal Justice in Crisis* (1994). Aldershot, England: E. Elgar.

McConville, Michael, and Chester Mirsky. (1986–1987) "Criminal Defense of the Poor in New York City." *NYU Rev. Law & Social Change* 15: 581.

McCreary, Scott. (1989) "Resolving Science-Intensive Public Policy Disputes: Lessons from the New York Bight Initiative." Ph.D. dissertation, Massachusetts Institute of Technology, Cambridge.

McFate, Katherine. (1995) "Trampolines, Safety Nets, or Free Fall? Labor Market Policies and Social Assistance in the 1980s," in K. McFate, Roger Lawson, and William Julius Wilson, eds., *Poverty, Inequality, and the Future of Social Policy: Western States in the New World Order.* New York: Russell Sage Foundation.

McFate, Katherine, Roger Lawson, and William Julius Wilson, eds. (1995) *Poverty, Inequality, and the Future of Social Policy: Western States in the New World Order.* New York: Russell Sage Foundation.

McIntosh, David, and David Murray. (1994) *Medical Malpractice Liability: An Agenda for Reform.* Indianapolis: Competitiveness Center of Hudson Institute.

McIntosh, Wayne. (1980–1981) "150 Years of Litigation and Dispute Settlement: A Court Tale." *Law & Society Rev.* 15: 823.

McIntyre, Linda. (1987) *The Public Defender.* Chicago: University of Chicago Press.

McKinley, James, Jr. (1999) "Sugar Industry's Pivotal Role in Everglades Effort." *New York Times,* April 16, pp. A1, A19.

McLanahan, Sara, and Irwin Garfinkel. (1995) "Single Mothers and Social Policy," in Katherine McFate, Roger Lawson, and William Julius Wilson, eds., *Poverty, Inequality, and the Future of Social Policy: Western States in the New World Order.* New York: Russell Sage Foundation.

McMahon v. Bunn-O-Matic Corp. (1998) 150 F.3d 651 (7th Cir.).

McManus, Susan. (1993) "The Impact of Litigation on Municipalities." *Syracuse L. Rev.* 44: 833.

Meador, Daniel. (1983) "German Appellate Judges: Career Patterns and American-English Comparisons." *Judicature* 67: 16.

Meier, Barry. (1997) "In Fine Print, Customers Lose Ability to Sue." *New York Times,* March 10, p. A1.

Melnick, R. Shep. (1983) *Regulation and the Courts: The Case of the Clean Air Act.* Washington, D.C.: Brookings Institution.

———— (1992a) "Pollution Deadlines and the Coalition for Failure," in Michael Greve and Fred Smith, eds., *Environmental Politics: Public Costs, Private Rewards.* New York: Greenwood.

———— (1992b) "Administrative Law and Bureaucratic Reality." *Administrative L. Rev.* 44: 245–259.

———— (1993) *Between the Lines: Interpreting Welfare Rights.* Washington, D.C.: Brookings Institution.

———— (1995) "Separation of Powers and the Strategy of Rights: The Expansion of Special Education," in Marc Landy and Martin Levin, eds., *The New Politics of Public Policy.* Baltimore: Johns Hopkins Press.

———— (1996) "Federalism and the New Rights." *Yale Law & Policy Rev.* 14: 325.

Meltsner, Michael. (1973) *Cruel and Unusual.* New York: Random House.

Mendeloff, John. (1987) *The Dilemma of Rulemaking for Toxic Substances.* Cambridge: MIT Press.

Mendelson, David, and Robert Rubin. (1993) *Estimating the Costs of Defensive Medicine.* Fairfax, Va.: Lewin-VH1.

Menell, Peter. (1991) "The Limitations of Legal Institutions for Addressing Environmental Risks." *J. Economic Perspectives* 5: 93.

Menkel-Meadow, Carrie. (1991) "Pursuing Settlement in an Adversary Culture: A Tale of Innovation Co-Opted for 'The Law of ADR.'" *Fla. State L. Rev.* 19: 1.

Merritt, Deborah, and Kathryn Barry. (1999) "Is the Tort System in Crisis? New Empirical Evidence." *Ohio State L.J.* 60: 315.

Metzloff, Thomas. (1988) "Researching Litigation: The Medical Malpractice Example." *Law & Contemporary Problems* 51: 199.

———— (1991) "Resolving Malpractice Disputes: Imaging the Jury's Shadow." *Law & Contemporary Problems* 54: 43.

———— (1993) "Understanding the Malpractice Wars." (Review of Paul C. Weiler, *Medical Malpractice on Trial.*) *Harvard L. Rev.* 106: 1169.

Michael, Douglas. (1996) "Cooperative Implementation of Federal Regulations." *Yale J. Regulation* 13: 535.

Miller, Matthew. (2000) "Tax Base." *The New Republic,* April 3, p. 6.

Miller, Richard, and Austin Sarat. (1981) "Grievances, Claims and Disputes: Assessing the Adversary Culture." *Law & Society Rev.* 15: 525.

Milliken v Bradley. (1974) 418 U.S. 717.

Minow, Newton, and Fred Cate. (1994) "Court Quiz Show: Grilling Jurors by Questionnaire." *Wall Street J.* October 12, p. A6.

Mnookin, Robert, and Robert Wilson. (1989) "Rational Bargaining and Market Efficiency: Understanding *Penzoil v. Texaco.*" *Va. L. Rev.* 75: 295.

Moe, Terry M. (1989) "The Politics of the Bureaucratic State," in John Chubb and Paul Peterson, eds., *Can the Government Govern?* Washington, D.C.: Brookings Institution.

Moller, Erik. (1996) *Trends in Jury Verdicts since 1985.* Santa Monica: RAND Institute for Civil Justice.

Molot, Johnathan. (1998) "How Changes in the Legal Profession Reflect Changes in Legal Procedure." *Va. L. Rev.* 84: 955.

Montgomery, Bill, and Mark Curriden. (1991) "Entire Process Barbaric: Lawyers Assail Execution." *Atlanta Constitution,* September 25, p. A6.

Moses, Jonathan. (1992) "Accord Enriching Only Lawyers Assailed." *Wall Street J.,* January 23, p. B8.

Mt. Laurel I: Southern Burlington County NAACP v. Township of Mt. Laurel. (1975) 67 N.J. 151, 33 A.2d 713.

Mt. Laurel II: Southern Burlington County NAACP v. Township of Mt. Laurel. (1983) 92 N.J. 158, 456 A.2d 390.

Mt. Laurel III: Hills Development Corp. v. Township of Bernards. (1986) 103 N.J. 1, 510 A.2d 621.

Muir, William K., Jr. (1973) *Law and Attitude Change.* Chicago: University of Chicago Press.

Munch, Patricia. (1977) *Costs and Benefits of the Torts System If Viewed as a Compensation System.* Santa Monica: RAND Institute for Civil Justice.

Mustard, David. (1997) "Racial, Ethnic and Gender Disparities in Sentencing: Evidence from the Federal Courts." Working Paper 97-458. University of Georgia, Department of Economics.

Mydans, Seth. (1994) "Meter's Ticking for Costly Simpson Defense." *New York Times.* July 31, p. 8.

Myhre, Jonas. (1968) "Conviction without Trial in the United States and Norway: A Comparison." *Houston L. Rev.* 5: 647.

Nardulli, Peter. (1983) "The Societal Cost of the Exclusionary Rule: An Empirical Assessment." *American Bar Foundation Research J.* 1983: 585.

National Academy of Science. (1977) *Decisionmaking at the U.S. Environmental Protection Agency.* Washington, D.C.: National Academy Press.

National Center for State Courts. (1986) "A Preliminary Examination of Available Civil and Criminal Trend Data in State Trial Courts for 1978, 1981 and 1984." Williamsburg, Va.

——— (1988) "On Trial: The Length of Civil and Criminal Trials." Williamsburg, Va.

——— (1991) "State Court Caseload Statistics in 1989." Williamsburg, Va.

National Institute of Medicine. (1996) *Veterans and Agent Orange: Update 1996.* Washington, D.C.: National Academy Press.

National Prison Project. (1990) "Status Report: State Prisons and the Courts." *National Prison Project J.* 22: 7.

National Research Council. (1985) *Dredging Coastal Ports: An Assessment of the Issues.* Washington, D.C.: National Academy Press.

Neal, David, and David L. Kirp. (1986) "The Allure of Legalization Reconsidered: The Case of Special Education," in D. L. Kirp and Donald Jensen, eds., *School*

Days, Rule Days: The Legalization and Regulation of Education. New York: Falmer Press.

Nelson, Steve. (1983) "Trial Lawyers Blaze Aggressive Trail." *Legal Times,* March 14, p. 1.

Nelson, William. (1990) "Contract Litigation and the Elite Bar in New York City, 1960–1980." *Emory L. Rev.* 39: 413.

Nemetz, Peter N., W. T. Stanbury, and Fred Thompson. (1986) "Social Regulation in Canada: An Overview and Comparison with the American Model." *Policy Studies* 14: 580.

New York Times. (1991) "Judge Accepts Pact, Ending Suits in Valdez Spill." October 9, p. A14.

——— (1993) "U.S. Writes Off Cleanup Costs of Toxic Sites." July 21, p. A16.

——— (1996a) "Maryland and Connecticut Join States Seeking Tobacco Money." May 2, p. A20(L).

——— (1996b) "Legal Services Survives, Barely." May 6, p. A14.

Nielsen, Laura Beth. (1999) "Paying Workers or Paying Lawyers: Employee Termination Practices in the United States and Canada." *Law & Policy* 21: 247.

——— (2000) "Situating Legal Consciousness: Experiences and Attitudes of Ordinary Citizens about Law and Street Harassment." *Law & Society Rev.* 34: 201.

Niemeijer, Bert. (1989) "Urban Land-Use and Building Control in the Netherlands: Flexible Decisions in a Rigid System." *Law & Policy* 11: 121–152.

Noah, Timothy. (1993) "Clinton, Facing Conflicting Advice on Superfund, May Attempt to Ease the Burden of Business." *Wall Street J.,* December 2, p. A16.

Noble, Kenneth. (1995) "Ecology War Brews in California Desert." *New York Times,* November 19, sec. 1, p. 12.

Nonet, Philippe. (1969) *Administrative Justice.* New York: Russell Sage Foundation.

Nonet, Philippe, and Philip Selznick. (1978) *Law and Society in Transition: Toward Responsive Law.* New York: Harper Colophon.

Noonan, John T., Jr. (1993) "Horses of the Night: *Harris v Vasquez.*" *Stanford L. Rev.* 45: 1011.

Northern Spotted Owl v. Hodel. (1988) 716 F. Supp. 479 (W.D. Wash.).

Nutter, Franklin, and Keith Bateman. (1988) "Product Liability in a Litigious Society." *Science* 240: 1589.

——— (1989) *The U.S. Tort System in the Era of the Global Economy.* Schaumberg, Ill.: Alliance of American Insurers.

O'Connell, Jeffrey. "Expanding No-Fault beyond Auto Insurance: Some Proposals." *Va. L. Rev.* 59: 749.

——— (1979) *The Lawsuit Lottery: Only the Lawyers Win.* New York: Free Press.

O'Connor, Karen, and Lee Epstein. (1985) "Bridging the Gap between Congress and the Supreme Court: Interest Groups and the Erosion of the American Rule Governing Awards of Attorneys' Fees." *Western Political Quarterly* 28: 238.

Odden, Allan, and Lawrence Picus. (1992) *School Finance: A Policy Perspective.* New York: McGraw Hill.

OECD. (1986) *OECD Economic Surveys: Netherlands.* Paris: Organization for Economic Cooperation and Development.

——— (1987) *OECD Economic Surveys: Netherlands.* Paris: Organization for Economic Cooperation and Development.

O'Hare, Michael, and Lawrence Bacow. (1983) *Facility Siting and Public Opposition.* New York: Van Nostrand.

Okimoto, Daniel. (1989) *Between MITI and the Market: Japanese Industrial Policy for High Technology.* Stanford, Calif.: Stanford University Press.

Oldertz, Carl. (1986) "Security Insurance, Patient Insurance and Pharmaceutical Insurance in Sweden." *American J. Comparative Law* 34: 635.

Olson, Walter. (1994) "The Jury Selection Ordeal." *Wall Street J.,* December 7, p. A19.

Opatrny, Dennis. (1995) "Little Danger of Sudden Wealth in Suing the SFPD." *San Francisco Chronicle,* June 4, p. C1.

Orfield, Myron, Jr. (1987) "The Exclusionary Rule and Deterrence: An Empirical Study of Chicago Narcotics Officers." *U. Chicago L. Rev.* 54: 1016.

Osborne, Evan. (1999) "Courts as Casinos? An Empirical Investigation of Randomness and Efficiency in Civil Litigation." *J. Legal Studies* 26: 187.

Osiel, Mark. (1990) "Lawyers as Monopolists and Entrepreneurs." (Review of *Lawyer in Society,*) ed. Richard Abel and Philip Lewis.) *Harvard L. Rev.* 103: 2009.

Ostrom, Brian, et al. (1993) "So the Verdict Is In: What Happens Next?" *Justice System J.* 16: 97.

——— (1996) "A Step above Anecdote: A Profile of the Civil Jury in the 1990s." *Judicature* 79: 233.

Paduano, Anthony, and Clive Stafford-Smith. (1987) "Deathly Errors: Juror Misperceptions Concerning Parole in the Imposition of the Death Penalty." *Columbia Human Rights L. Rev.* 18: 211.

Palmer, Thomas. (1994) "Commitments to Foes Raise Artery Price Tag." *Boston Globe,* September 14, pp. 1, 6.

Pantuliano, A. J. (1983) "A U.S. House Counsel's Comparative View of European and Japanese Patent Litigation," in Michael Meller, ed., *International Patent Litigation: A Country by Country Analysis.* Washington, D.C.: Bureau of National Affairs.

Papachristou v. City of Jacksonville. (1972) 405 U.S. 156.

Paris, Michael. (1998) "Legal Mobilization and the Rhetoric of Reform: School Finance Litigation in Kentucky, 1984–1990." Paper prepared for annual meeting of Law and Society Association, Aspen, Colo., June 3–7.

Parloff, Roger. (1993) "False Confessions." *American Lawyer* (May), pp. 58–62.

Paternoster, Raymond. (1991) *Capital Punishment in America.* New York: Lexington Books.

Pear, Robert. (1995) "As Welfare Overhaul Looms, Legal Aid for the Poor Diminishes." *New York Times,* September 5, pp. A1, A9.

——— (1999) "Clinton to Chide States for Failing to Cover Children." *New York Times,* August 8, pp. 1, 18.

Peltason, Jack. (1955) *Federal Courts in the Political Process.* New York: Random House.

——— (1961) *Fifty Eight Lonely Men: Southern Federal Judges and School Desegregation.* New York: Harcourt, Brace and World.

Peltz, James. (1995) "San Diego Trial Lawyer Played Key Role in Securities Fraud Bill." *Los Angeles Times,* December 23, p. D8.

Penner, Bernard. (1992) "The Prosecutor and *Ex Parte* Communications." *National Environmental Enforcement J.* (May), p. 3.

Peters, Antonie. (1992) "Some Comparative Observations on the Criminal Process in Holland and Japan." *J. Japan-Netherlands Institute* 4: 247.

Peterson, Mark. (1983) *Comparative Justice: Civil Jury Verdicts in San Francisco and Cook Counties, 1959–1980.* Santa Monica, Calif.: RAND Institute of Civil Justice.

———— (1987) *Civil Juries in the 1980s: Trends in Jury Trials and Verdicts in California and Cook County, Illinois.* Santa Monica, Calif.: RAND Institute of Civil Justice.

Peterson, Mark, and Molly Selvin. (1991) "Mass Justice: The Limited and Unlimited Power of Courts." *Law & Contemporary Problems* 54: 227.

Peterson, Paul. (1995) *The Price of Federalism.* Washington, D.C.: Brookings Institution.

———— (1996) "Devolution's Price." *Yale Law & Policy Rev.* 14: 111.

Peterson, Paul, and Mark Rom. (1990) *Welfare Magnets: A New Case for a National Standard.* Washington, D.C.: Brookings Institution.

Petzinger, Thomas. (1987) *Oil and Honor: The Texaco-Penzoil Wars.* New York: Putnam.

Pierce, Richard J., Jr. (1988) "Two Problems in Administrative Law: Political Polarity on the District of Columbia Circuit Court and Judicial Deterrence of Agency Rulemaking." *Duke L.J.* 1988: 300.

Pinello, Daniel. (1999) "Linking Party to Judicial Ideology in American Courts: A Meta-Analysis." *Justice System J.* 20: 219.

Pitt, Harvey, and Karen Shapiro. (1990) "Securities Regulation by Enforcement: A Look Ahead at the Next Decade." *Yale J. Regulation* 7: 149.

Pizzi, William. (1993) "Understanding Prosecutorial Discretion in the United States: The Limits of Comparative Criminal Procedure as an Instrument of Reform." *Ohio State L.J.* 54: 1325.

———— (1999) *Trials without Truth.* New York: New York University Press.

Plotz, David. (1994) "Guilty! Guilty! Guilty!" *Washington City Paper,* March 25, pp. 22–31.

Plyler v. Doe. (1982) 457 U.S. 202.

Polinsky, A. Mitchell. (1997) "Are Punitive Damages Really Insignificant, Predictable, and Rational?" *J. Legal Studies* 26: 663.

Polisar, Daniel, and Aaron Wildavsky. (1989) "From Individual to System Blame: A Cultural Analysis of Historical Change in the Law of Torts." *J. Policy History* 1: 129.

Pollock v. Farmers' Loan & Trust Co. (1895) 158 U.S. 601.

Polsby, Nelson. (1983) *The Consequences of Party Reform.* New York: Oxford University Press.

Possley, Maurice, and Ken Armstrong. (1999) "The Flip Side of a Fair Trial: Some Cook County Prosecutors Break the Rules to Win." *Chicago Tribune,* January 11, p. 1N.

Potter, Edward, and Ann Reesman. (1992) *Compensatory and Punitive Damages under Title VII—A Foreign Perspective*. Washington, D.C.: Employment Policy Foundation.

Priest, George L. (1985) "The Invention of Enterprise Liability: A Critical History of the Intellectual Foundations of Modern Tort Law." *J. Legal Studies* 14: 461.

——— (1990) "The Role of the Civil Jury in a System of Private Litigation." *U. Chicago Law Forum* 1990 : 161.

——— (1992) "Can Absolute Manufacturer Liability Be Defended?" *Yale J. Regulation* 9: 237.

——— (1993) "Justifying the Civil Jury," in Robert Litan, ed., *Verdict: Assessing the Civil Jury System*. Washington, D.C.: Brookings Institution.

Pringle, Peter. (1998) *Cornered: Big Tobacco at the Bar of Justice*. New York: Henry Holt.

Privatera, John. (1992) "Using CERCLA's Natural Resource Damage Provision to Focus and Organize a State Environmental Penalty Case." *National Environmental Enforcement J.* (March).

Provine, Doris Marie. (1998) "Courts in the Political Process in France," in Herbert Jacob et al., eds., *Courts, Law and Politics in Comparative Perspective*. New Haven: Yale University Press.

Quam, Lois, et al. (1987) "Medical Malpractice in Perspective." *British Medical J.* 294: 1529, 1597.

Rabe, Barry. (1994) *Beyond NIMBY: Hazardous Waste Siting in Canada and the United States*. Washington, D.C.: Brookings Institution.

Rabin, Robert. (1988) "Some Reflections on the Process of Tort Reform." *San Diego L. Rev.* 25: 13.

——— (1989) "Tort System on Trial: The Burden of Mass Toxics Litigation." 98 *Yale L. Rev.* 98: 813.

——— (1993) "Institutional and Historical Perspectives on Tobacco Tort Liability," in R. Rabin and Stephen Sugarman, eds., *Smoking Policy: Law, Politics, and Culture*. New York: Oxford University Press.

Rabkin, Jeremy. (1989) *Judicial Compulsions: How Public Law Distorts Public Policy*. New York: Basic Books.

Race, Margaret S. (1988) "Critique of Present Wetlands Mitigation Policies in the United States Based on Analysis of Past Restoration Projects in San Francisco Bay." *Environmental Management* 9: 71.

Ramseyer, J. Mark, and Minoru Nakazato. (1989) "The Rational Litigant: Settlement Amounts and Verdict Rates in Japan." *J. Legal Studies* 18: 263.

Ramseyer, J. Mark, and Eric Rasmussen. (1998) "Why Is the Japanese Conviction Rate So High?" Discussion paper, John M. Olin Center for Law, Economics, and Business, Harvard Law School.

RAND Institute for Civil Justice. (1995) "How Big Is the Price Tag for Excess Auto Injury Claims?" *RAND Institute for Civil Justice Research Brief* (May), p. 1.

Ranney, Austin. (1983) "The President and His Party," in Anthony King, ed., *Both Ends of the Avenue: The Presidency, the Executive Branch and Congress in the 1980s*. Washington, D.C.: American Enterprise Institute.

Redelet, Michael, Hugo Adam Bedau, and Constance Putnam. (1992) *In Spite of Innocence: Erroneous Convictions in Capital Cases*. Boston: Northeastern University Press.

Redick, William P., Jr. (1993) "The Crisis in Representation of Tennessee Capital Cases." *Tenn. Bar J.,* (March/April), p. 22.

Reed, Douglas. (1998) "Twenty Five Years after *Rodriguez:* School Finance Litigation and the Impact of the New Judicial Federalism." *Law & Society Rev.* 32: 175.

Rees, Joseph. (1988) *Reforming the Workplace: A Study of Self-Regulation in Occupational Safety.* Philadelphia: University of Pennsylvania Press.

Reiner, Robert, and Malcolm Cross, eds. (1991) *Beyond Law and Order: Criminal Justice Policy and Politics into the 1990s.* London: Macmillan Academic and Professional LTD.

Reinhold, Robert. (1993) "Final Freeway Opens, Ending California Era." *New York Times,* October 14, p. A1.

Reitz, John C. (1990) "Why We Probably Cannot Adopt the German Advantage in Civil Procedure." *Iowa L. Rev.* 75: 987.

Resnick, Judith. (1982) "Managerial Judges." *Harvard L. Rev.* 96: 376.

Rhode, Deborah. (1999) "A Bad Press on Bad Lawyers: The Media Sees Research, Research Sees the Media," in Patricia Ewick, Robert A. Kagan, and Austin Sarat, eds., *Social Science, Social Policy and the Law.* New York: Russell Sage Foundation.

Richards, Bill. (1992) "Elusive Threat: Electric Utilities Brace for Cancer Lawsuits Though Risk Is Unclear." *Wall Street J.,* February 5, p. A1.

Robbins, Jim. (1998) "A Broken Pact and a $97 Million Payday." *New York Times,* April 19, sec. 3, p. 1.

Robinson v. Cahill. (1973) 62 N.J. 473.

Roe v. Norton. (1973) 365 F. Supp. 65 (D. Conn.), remanded, 422 U.S. 391 (1975).

Roe v. Wade. (1973) 410 U.S. 113.

Roe, Mark. (1991) "A Political Theory of American Corporate Finance." *Columbia L. Rev.* 91: 10.

Rogers, David. (1993) "Entrenched Interests Prove Too Strong for Medical Malpractice Reform Plan." *Wall Street J.,* June 15, p. A16.

——— (1998) "Meat and Poultry Packers Defeat Move to Allow Civil Penalties in the Industry." *Wall Street J.,* June 17, p. A5.

Rogers, Joel. (1990) "Divide and Conquer: Further Reflections on the Distinctive Character of American Labor Laws." *Wis. L. Rev.* 1990: 1.

Roman, Andrew, and Mark Pikkov. (1990) "Public Interest Litigation in Canada," in Donna Tingley, ed., *Into the Future: Environmental Law and Policy for the 1990s.* Edmonton: Environmental Law Center.

Romano, Roberta. (1991) "The Shareholder Suit: Litigation without Foundation?" *J. Law, Economics & Organization* 7: 55.

Rosch, Joel. (1987) "Institutionalizing Mediation: The Evolution of the Civil Liberties Bureau in Japan." *Law & Society Rev.* 21: 243.

Rose-Ackerman, Susan. (1995) *Controlling Environmental Policy: The Limits of Public Law in Germany and the United States.* New Haven: Yale University Press.

Rosenberg, David. (1986) "The Dusting of America: A Story of Asbestos—Carnage, Cover-Up, and Litigation." (Review of Paul Brodeur, *Outrageous Misconduct: The Asbestos Industry on Trial.*) *Harvard L. Rev.* 99: 1693.

Rosenberg, Gerald. (1991) *The Hollow Hope: Can Courts Bring About Social Change?* Chicago: University of Chicago Press.

Rosenthal, Douglas. (1974) *Lawyer and Client: Who's in Charge?* New York: Russell Sage Foundation.

Rosenthal, Jean-Laurent. (1992) *The Fruits of Revolution.* Los Angeles: UCLA Press.

Ross, H. Laurence, and James Foley. (1987) "Judicial Disobedience of the Mandate to Imprison Drunk Drivers." *Law & Society Rev.* 21: 315.

Rothman, David J., and Sheila M. Rothman. (1984) *The Willowbrook Wars.* New York: Harper & Row.

Rothman, Stanley, and Stephen Powers. (1984) "Execution by Quota?" *The Public Interest* (Summer), p. 3.

Rowland, C. K., and Robert A. Carp. (1983) "The Relative Effects of Maturation, Period, and Appointing President on District Judges' Policy Choice: A Cohort Analysis." *Political Behavior* 5: 109.

Royko, Mike. (1985) "A Crash Course in How to Succeed Chicago Style." *San Jose Mercury News,* October 9, p. 7B.

Rubin, Edward L. (1991) "Legislative Methodology: Some Lessons from the Truth-in-Lending Act." *Georgetown L. Rev.* 80: 233.

———— (1997) "Discretion and Its Discontents." *Chicago-Kent L. Rev.* 72: 1299.

Rubinstein, Michael, and Teresa White. (1979) "Alaska's Ban on Plea Bargaining." *Law & Society Rev.* 13: 367.

Rubinstein, Steve. (1997) "Driver's Education Takes a Warped Turn during an Accident." *San Francisco Chronicle,* February 19, p. C1.

Ruhlin, Charles. (2000) "Credit Card Collection and the Law: Germany and the United States," in Robert A. Kagan and Lee Axelrad, eds., *Regulatory Encounters: Multinational Corporations and American Adversarial Legalism.* Berkeley: University of California Press.

Saenz v. Roe. (1999) 526 U.S. 489.

Sage, William. (1999) "Physicians as Advocates." *Houston L. Rev.* 35: 1529.

Saks, Michael J. (1992) "Do We Really Know Anything about the Behavior of the Tort Litigation System—And Why Not?" *Pa. L. Rev.* 140: 1147.

San Antonio Independent School District v. Rodriguez. (1973) 411 U.S. 1.

Sander, Richard, and E. Douglass Williams. (1989) "Why Are There So Many Lawyers? Perspectives on a Turbulent Market." *Law & Social Inquiry* 14: 431.

Sanders, Joseph. (1987) "The Meaning of the Law Explosion: On Friedman's *Total Justice.*" *American Bar Foundation Research J.* 1987: 601.

———— (1993) "From Science to Evidence: The Testimony on Causation in the Bendectin Cases." *Stanford L. Rev.* 42: 1.

———— (1996) "Courts and Law in Japan," in Herbert Jacob et al., eds., *Courts, Law and Politics in Comparative Perspective.* New Haven: Yale University Press.

———— (1998) "Scientifically Complex Cases, Trial by Jury, and the Erosion of Adversarial Processes." *DePaul L. Rev.* 48: 355.

Sanders, Joseph, and Craig Joyce. (1990) "'Off to the Races': The 1980s Tort Crisis and the Law Reform Process." *Houston L. Rev.* 27: 207.

San Francisco Chronicle. (1995) "Jurors Found Predisposed to Death Penalty." February 2.

Sarat, Austin. (1990) "'The Law Is All Over': Power, Resistance and the Legal Consciousness of the Welfare Poor." *Yale J. Law & Humanities* 2: 343.

Sarat, Austin, ed. (1997) *Race, Law and Culture: Reflections on Brown v. Board of Education.* New York: Oxford University Press.

Sarat, Austin, and William L. F. Felstiner. (1986) "Law and Strategy in the Divorce Lawyer's Office." *Law & Society Rev.* 20: 93.

Savelsberg, Joachim. (1994) "Knowledge, Domination, and Criminal Punishment." *American J. Sociology* 99: 911.

Sax, Joseph. (1997) "The Ecosystem Approach: Closing Remarks." *Environmental Law Quarterly* 24: 883.

Schkade, David, Cass Sunstein, and Daniel Kahneman. (2000) "Deliberating about Dollars: The Severity Shift." *Columbia L. Rev.* 2000: 1139–1175.

Schlesinger, Rudolph. (1977) "Comparative Criminal Procedure: A Plea for Utilizing Foreign Experience." *Buffalo L. Rev.* 26: 361.

Schlosser, Eric. (1994) "Reefer Madness." *The Atlantic Monthly* (August), pp. 45–63.

Schmidt, William. (1994) "Silence May Speak against the Accused in Britain." *New York Times,* November 11, p. A17.

Schmitt, Richard. (1996) "As Clinton Vows to Veto Products-Liability Bill, Some Ask if He's Too Beholden to Trial Lawyers." *Wall Street J.,* March 22, p. A14(W).

Schmitter, Philippe. (1979) "Still the Century of Corporatism?" in Philippe Schmitter and Gerhard Lembruch, eds., *Trends toward Corporatist Intermediation.* London: Sage.

Scholz, John T., and Feng Heng Wei. (1986) "Regulatory Enforcement in a Federalist System." *American Political Science Rev.* 80: 1249.

Schrecker, Ted. (1992) "Of Invisible Beasts and the Public Interest: Environmental Cases and the Judicial System," in Robert Boardman, ed., *Canadian Environmental Policy: Ecosystems, Politics, and Process.* Toronto: University of Oxford Press.

Schroeder, Elinor. (1986) "Legislative and Judicial Responses to the Inadequacy of Compensation for Occupational Disease." *Law & Contemporary Problems* 49: 151.

Schuck, Peter. (1983) *Suing Government: Citizen Remedies for Official Wrongs.* New Haven: Yale University Press.

——— (1986) *Agent Orange on Trial: Mass Toxic Disasters in the Courts.* Cambridge, Mass.: Belknap Press.

——— (1992a) "Legal Complexity: Some Causes, Consequences, and Cures." *Duke L.J.* 42: 1.

——— (1992b) "The Worst Should Go First: Deferral Registries in Asbestos Litigation." *Harvard L. Rev.* 15: 541.

——— (1993) "Mapping the Debate on Jury Reform," in Robert Litan, ed., *Verdict: Assessing the Civil Jury System.* Washington, D.C.: Brookings Institution.

——— (2000) *The Limits of the Law* (Boulder, Colo.: Westview Press).

Schulhofer, Stephen. (1984) "Is Plea Bargaining Inevitable?" *Harvard L. Rev.* 97: 1037.

——— (1991) "Some Kind Words for the Privilege against Self-Incrimination." *Valparaiso U. L. Rev.* 26: 311.

Schumpeter, Joseph. (1942) *Capitalism, Socialism and Democracy.* New York: Harper.

Schwartz, Gary. (1978) "Contributory and Comparative Negligence: A Reappraisal." *Yale L.J.* 87: 697.

———— (1991) "Product Liability and Medical Malpractice in Comparative Context," in Peter Huber and Robert Litan, eds., *The Liability Maze*. Washington, D.C.: Brookings Institution.

———— (1992) "The Beginning and the Possible End of the Rise of Modern American Tort Law." *Ga. L. Rev.* 26: 601.

———— (1994) "Reality in the Economic Analysis of Tort Law: Does Tort Law Really Deter?" *UCLA L. Rev.* 42: 263.

Schwartz, Richard D., and James Miller. (1964) "Legal Evolution and Social Complexity." *American J. Sociology* 70: 159.

Scruggs, Lyle A. (1998) "Sustaining Abundance: Environmental Performance in Advanced Societies." Ph.D. dissertation, Duke University, Durham, N.C.

———— (1999) "Institutions and Environmental Performance in Seventeen Western Democracies." *British J. Political Science* 29: 1–31.

Selke, William. (1991) "A Comparison of Punishment Systems in Denmark and the United States." *International J. Comparative & Applied Criminal Justice* 15: 227.

Sellers, Jeffery M. (1995) "Litigation as a Local Political Resource: Courts in Controversies over Land Use in France, Germany and the United States." *Law & Society Rev.* 29: 475.

Selvin, Molly, and Patricia A. Ebener. (1984) *Managing the Unmanageable: A History of Civil Delay in the Los Angeles Superior Court*. Santa Monica, Calif.: RAND Institute for Civil Justice.

Sentell, R. Perry. (1991) "The Georgia Jury and Negligence: The View from the Bench." *Ga. L. Rev.* 26: 85.

Serrano v. Priest. (1971) 487 P.2d 1241 (Cal.).

Sexton, Joe. (1997) "Opening the Doors on Family Court's Secrets." *New York Times,* September 13, pp. 1, 10.

Shanley, Michael, and Mark Peterson. (1983) *Comparative Justice: Civil Jury Verdicts in San Francisco and Cook Counties, 1959–1980*. Santa Monica, Calif.: RAND Institute for Civil Justice.

Shapiro v. Thompson. (1969) 394 U.S. 618.

Shapiro, Martin. (1988) *Who Guards the Guardians? Judicial Control of Administration*. Athens, Ga.: University of Georgia Press.

———— (1993) "The Globalization of Law." *Indiana J. Global Legal Studies* 1: 37.

Shefter, Martin. (1994) *Political Parties and the State: The American Historical Experience*. Princeton, N.J.: Princeton University Press.

Sher, Victor. (1993) "Travels with Strix: The Spotted Owl's Journey through the Federal Courts." *Public Land Rev.* 14: 41.

Sherman, Lawrence. (1992) "The Influence of Criminology on Criminal Law: Evaluating Arrests for Misdemeanor Domestic Violence." *J. Criminal Law & Criminology* 83: 1.

Shklar, Judith. (1964) *Legalism*. Cambridge: Harvard University Press.

Shover, Neil, et al. (1984) "Regional Variation in Regulatory Law Enforcement: The Surface Mining Control and Reclamation Act," in Keith Hawkins and John Thomas, eds., *Enforcing Regulation*. Boston: Kluwer-Nijhoff.

Silverman, Robert. (1981) *Law and Urban Growth: Civil Litigation in the Boston Trial Courts, 1880–1900*. Princeton, N.J.: Princeton University Press.

Simon, Herbert. (1957) *Administrative Behavior*, 2d ed. New York: Macmillan.

Simon, William H. (1983) "Legality, Bureaucracy, and Class in the Welfare System." *Yale L.J.* 92: 11.

Skolnick, Jerome. (1998) "The Color of the Law." *The American Prospect* (July/August).

Skolnick, Jerome, and James Fyfe. (1993) *Above the Law: Police and the Excessive Use of Force*. New York: The Free Press.

Skowronek, Stephen. (1982) *Building a New American State: The Expansion of National Administrative Capacities, 1877–1920*. New York: Cambridge University Press.

Skryzcki, Cindy. (1997) "The Regulators: The Perils of Reinventing; Critics See a Playground for Polluters in EPA's XL Plan." *Washington Post*, January 24, p. D1.

Sloan, Frank A., and Chen Ruey Hsieh. (1990) "Variability in Medical Malpractice Payments: Is the Compensation System Fair?" *Law & Society Rev.* 24: 997.

———— (1995) "Injury, Liability, and the Decision to File a Medical Malpractice Claim." *Law & Society Rev.* 29: 413.

Sloan, Frank A., and Stephen S. Van Wert. (1991) "Cost and Compensation of Injuries in Medical Malpractice." *Law & Contemporary Problems* 54: 131.

Sloane, Leonard. (1991) "Rising Fraud Worrying Car Insurers." *New York Times*, November 16, p. 15.

Smith, Rogers. (1993) "Beyond Tocqueville, Myrdal, and Hartz: The Multiple Traditions in America." *American Political Science Rev.* 87: 549.

Smith, Stephen. (1989) *Call to Order: Floor Politics in the House and Senate*. Washington, D.C.: Brookings Institution.

Somaya, Deepak. (2000) "Obtaining and Protecting Patents in the United States, Europe and Japan," in Robert Kagan and Lee Axelrad, eds., *Regulatory Encounters: Multinational Corporations and American Adversarial Legalism*. Berkeley: University of California Press.

Songer, Donald. (1988) "Tort Reform in South Carolina: The Effect of Empirical Research on Elite Perceptions Concerning Jury Verdicts." *S.C. L. Rev.* 39: 585.

Soular, Lawrence. (1986) "A Study of Large Product Liability Claims Closed in 1985." Schaumberg, Ill.: Alliance of American Insurors.

Spangenberg, Robert, and Marea Beeman. (1995) "Indigent Defense Systems in the United States." *Law & Contemporary Problems* (Winter), p. 31.

Speiser, Stuart. (1980) "How the Entrepreneurial Lawyer Changed the Rules of the Game." *National L.J.*, December 1.

Spitzer, Eliot. (1993) "Faster Justice in New York." *New York Times*, March 1, p. A15.

Spohn, Cassia, et al. (1981–1982) "The Effect of Race on Sentencing: A Re-Examination of an Unsettled Question." *Law & Society Rev.* 16: 71.

Steinmo, Sven. (1993) *Taxation and Democracy: Swedish, British and American Approaches to Financing the Modern State*. New Haven: Yale University Press.

Stewart, James B. (1983) *The Partners: Inside America's Most Powerful Law Firms*. New York: Simon & Schuster.

Stewart, Richard B. (1985) "The Discontents of Legalism: Interest Group Relations in Administrative Regulation." *Wis. L. Rev.* 1985: 655.

———— (1990) "Madison's Nightmare." *U. Chicago L. Rev.* 57: 335.

Stiefel, Ernst, and James Maxeiner. (1994) "Civil Justice Reform in the United States—Opportunity for Learning from 'Civilized' European Procedure Instead of Continued Isolation?" *American J. Comparative Law* 42: 147.

Stipp, David. (1991) "Interstate Highway Project in Boston May Face a Court Challenge with National Implications." *Wall Street J.,* June 25, p. A20.

———— (1993) "Dogma in Doubt: Extent of Lead's Risk to Kids, Need to Remove Paint." *Wall Street J.,* September 16, pp. A1, 12.

Stout, Hilary. (1990) "Codified Confusion: Tax Law Is Growing Ever More Complex, Outcry Ever Louder." *Wall Street J.,* April 12, pp. 1, 8.

Strauss, Peter. (1987) "One Hundred Fifty Cases per Year: Some Implications of the Supreme Court's Limited Resources for Judicial Review of Agency Action." *Columbia L. Rev.* 87: 1093.

Strum, Charles. (1993a) "U.S. Suspends Dredging Permit for Newark Bay." *New York Times,* January 27, p. B1.

———— (1993b) "U.S. Grants Permit for Dredging of Newark Bay Berths." *New York Times,* May 27, p. B7.

———— (1993c) "Judge Allows Dredging to Continue." *New York Times,* June 8, p. B5.

Stuntz, William. (1997) "The Uneasy Relationship between Criminal Procedure and Criminal Justice." *Yale L.J.* 107: 1.

Suchman, Mark, and Mia Cahill. (1996) "The Hired Gun as Facilitator: Lawyers and the Suppression of Business Disputes in Silicon Valley." *Law & Social Inquiry* 21: 679.

Sugarman, Stephen D. (1985a) "Roe v. Norton," in Robert Mnookin, ed., *In the Interest of Children: Advocacy, Law Reform, and Public Policy.* New York: W. H. Freeman.

———— (1985b) "Doing Away with Tort Law." *Cal. L. Rev.* 73: 559.

———— (1989) *Doing Away with Personal Injury Law: New Compensation Mechanisms for Victims, Consumers, and Business.* New York: Quorum Books.

———— (1993a) *Pay at the Pump: Auto Insurance.* Berkeley: Institute of Governmental Studies Press.

———— (1993b) "The California Vehicle Injury Plan (VIP): Better Compensation, Fairer Funding, and Greater Safety." Working Paper No. 21, Earl Warren Legal Institute, University of California, Berkeley.

Sullivan, John. (2000) "States and Cities Removing Prisons from Courts' Grip." *New York Times,* January 30, p. 1.

Summers, Robert, and Michele Taruffo. (1991) "Interpretation and Comparative Analysis," in D. Neal McCormick and R. Summers, eds., *Interpreting Statutes: A Comparative Study.* Aldershot: Dartmouth Publishing.

Sunstein, Cass. (1990) *After the Rights Revolution.* Cambridge: Harvard University Press.

Sunstein, Cass, Daniel Kahnemann, and David Schkade. (1999) "Assessing Punitive Damages." *Yale L.J.* 107: 2071.

Syverud, Kent. (1997) "ADR and the Decline of the American Civil Jury." *UCLA L. Rev.* 44: 1935.

Tanase, Takao. (1990) "The Management of Disputes: Automobile Accident Compensation in Japan." *Law & Society Rev.* 24: 651.

Taragin, Mark, et al. (1992) "The Influence of Standard of Care and Severity of Injury on the Resolution of Medical Malpractice Claims." *Annals of Internal Medicine* 117: 780.

Task Force on Medical Liability and Malpractice. (1987) Report. Washington, D.C.: Department of Health and Human Services.

Tate, C. Neal, and Torbjorn Vallinder. (1995) *The Global Expansion of Judicial Power.* New York: New York University Press.

Taylor, Jeffrey. (1995a) "House, Senate Set Package to Curtail Suits against Firms." *Wall Street J.,* November 29, p. A4.

——— (1995b) "Congress Sends Business a Christmas Gift." *Wall Street J.,* December 26, p. A2.

Taylor, Serge. (1984) *Making Bureaucracies Think: The Environmental Impact Strategy of Administrative Reform.* Stanford, Calif.: Stanford University Press.

Teff, Harvey. (1985) "Drug Approval in England and the United States." *American J. Comparative Law* 33: 567.

Terry, Don. (1993) "Despite New Evidence, a Prisoner Faces Death." *New York Times,* November 15, p. A8.

Thibaut, John, and Laurens Walker. (1978) "A Theory of Procedure." *Cal. L. Rev.* 66: 541.

Thomas, Jo. (1986) "Odds Heavily Favor Leniency for Drug Dealing in the City." *New York Times,* June 30, pp. 1, 12.

Thurber, James. (1991) "Representation, Accountability, and Efficiency in Divided Party Control of Government." *PS: Political Science & Government* (December), p. 653.

Thurow, Lester. (1992) "Communitarian vs. Individualistic Capitalism." *The Responsive Community* 2: 24.

Tonry, Michael. (1995) *Malign Neglect: Race, Crime and Punishment in America.* New York: Oxford University Press.

Topol, David. (1991) "Rethinking Who Is Left Holding the Nuclear Bag: The Legal and Policy Implications of *Nevada v. Watkins.*" *Utah L. Rev.* 4: 791.

Tort Policy Working Group. (1986) Report on the Causes, Extent, and Policy Implications of the Current Crisis in Insurance Availability and Affordability. Washington, D.C.: Government Printing Office.

Townsend v. Swank. (1971) 404 U.S. 282.

Trombley, William, and Ray Hebert. (1987a) "Litigation, Confusion: Road Paved with Good Intentions." *Los Angeles Times,* December 27, p. 1.

——— (1987b) "Bold Housing Program Develops Big Problems." *Los Angeles Times,* December 28, p. 1.

Trubek, David et al. (1983) "The Costs of Ordinary Litigation." *UCLA L. Rev.* 31: 72.

Tyack, David, and Aaron Benavot. (1985) "Courts and Public Schools: Education Litigation in Historical Perspective." *Law & Society Rev.* 19: 339.

Tyler, Tom. (1990) *Why People Obey the Law.* New Haven: Yale University Press.

Uhlman, Thomas M., and Darlene Walker. (1979) "'He Takes Some of My Time, I Take Some of His': An Analysis of Sentencing Patterns in Jury Cases." *Law & Society Rev.* 14: 323.

Upham, Frank. (1987) *Law and Social Change in Postwar Japan.* Cambridge: Harvard University Press.

Ursin, Edmund. (1981) "Judicial Creativity and Tort Law." *George Washington L. Rev.* 49: 229.

U.S. Advisory Commission on Intergovernmental Relations. (1992) *Intergovernmental Decisionmaking for Environmental Protection and Public Works.* Washington, D.C.: Government Printing Office.

U.S. Army Corps of Engineers. (1992a) *Appendix D: Finding of No Significant Impact and Environmental Assessment, Oakland Inner Harbor—38-Foot Separable Element of the Oakland Harbor Navigation Improvement Project.* San Francisco: U.S. Army Corps of Engineers.

———— (1992b) *Design Memorandum and Environmental Assessment, Final Oakland Inner Harbor—38-Foot Separable Element of the Oakland Harbor Navigation Improvement Project.* San Francisco: U.S. Army Corps of Engineers.

U.S. Department of Transportation. (1985) "Compensating Auto Accident Victims: A Follow-Up Report on No-Fault Auto Insurance Experiences." Washington, D.C.: DOT.

U.S. Environmental Protection Agency. (1998) *Enforcement and Compliance Assurance Accomplishments Report, FY 1997.* Washington, D.C.: EPA.

U.S. General Accounting Office. (1988) "Product Liability: Extent of 'Litigation Explosion' in Federal Courts Questioned." Washington, D.C.: GAO.

Utz, Pamela. (1978) *Settling the Facts: Discretion and Negotiation in Criminal Court.* Lexington, Mass.: Lexington Books.

Vallinder, Torbjorn. (1995) "When the Courts Go Marching In," in C. Neal Tate and T. Vallinder, eds., *The Global Expansion of Judicial Power.* New York: New York University Press.

Van de Putte, Pete. (1995) "A Red, White and Blue Mess." *Wall Street J.,* April 27, p. A14.

Van Kessel, Gordon. (1992) "Adversary Excesses in the American Criminal Trial." *Notre Dame L. Rev.* 67: 403.

Verhovek, Sam Howe. (1995) "Across the U.S., Executions Are Neither Swift nor Cheap." *New York Times,* February 22, pp. A1, A13.

———— (1999) "Across 10 Years, Exxon Valdez Casts a Shadow." *New York Times,* March 6, p. A1.

Verweij, Marco. (2001) "Why Is the River Rhine Cleaner than the Great Lakes (Despite Looser Regulation)?" *Law & Society Rev.,* vol. 34, no. 4.

Veterans and Agent Orange: Update 1996. Washington, D.C.: National Academy Press, 1996.

Village of Arlington Heights v. Metropolitan Housing Development Corp. (1977) 429 U.S. 252.

Vidmar, Neil. (1993) "Empirical Evidence on the Deep Pockets Hypothesis: Jury Awards for Pain and Suffering in Medical Malpractice Cases." *Duke L.J.* 43: 217.

Vidmar, Neil, Felicia Gross, and Mary Rose. (1998) "Jury Awards for Medical Malpractice and Post-Verdict Adjustments of Those Awards." *DePaul L. Rev.* 48: 265.

Vidmar, Neil, and Jeffrey Rice. (1993) "Assessments of Noneconomic Damage Awards in Medical Malpractice: A Comparison of Juries with Legal Professionals." *Iowa L. Rev.* 78: 883.

Vinke, Harriet, and Ton Wilthagen. (1992) "The Nonmobilization of Law by Asbestos Victims in the Netherlands: Social Insurance versus Tort-Based Compensation." Amsterdam: Hugo Sinzheimer Institute, University of Amsterdam.

Viscusi, Kip. (1990) "Do Smokers Underestimate Risks?" *J. Political Economy* 98: 125.

——— (1992) *Smoking: Making the Risky Decision.* New York: Oxford University Press.

——— (1997) "From Cash Crop to Cash Cow." *Regulation* (Summer), p. 27.

Vogel, David. (1986) *National Styles of Regulation: Environmental Policy in Great Britain and the United States.* Ithaca, N.Y.: Cornell University Press.

——— (1989) *Fluctuating Fortunes: The Political Power of Business in America.* New York: Basic Books.

——— (1990) "Consumer Protection and Protectionism in Japan." Paper presented at annual meeting of American Political Science Association, San Francisco.

——— (1995) *Trading Up: Consumer and Environmental Regulation in a Global Economy.* Cambridge: Harvard University Press.

——— (1996) *Kindred Strangers: The Uneasy Relationship between Politics and Business in America.* Princeton, N.J.: Princeton University Press.

Wacquant, Loic. (1995) "The Comparative Structure and Experience of Urban Exclusion: 'Race,' Class, and Space in Chicago and Paris," in Katherine McFate et al., eds., *Poverty, Inequality, and the Future of Social Policy.* New York: Russell Sage Foundation.

Wagatsuma, Hiroshi, and Arthur Rossett. (1986) "The Implications of Apology: Law and Culture in Japan and the U.S." *Law & Society Rev.* 20: 461.

Walker, Samuel. (1993) *Taming the System: The Control of Discretion in Criminal Justice, 1950–1990.* New York: Oxford University Press.

Wallace, David. (1995) *Environmental Policy and Industrial Innovation: Strategies in Europe, the U.S., and Japan.* London: Royal Institute of International Affairs, Earthscan Publications, Ltd.

Wall Street Journal. (1993) "Crass Action." April 1, p. A14.

Washington Post. (1991) "Judge Endorses $1 Billion Exxon Valdez Settlement." October 9, p. A4.

Weaver, Russell, and Geoffrey Bennett. (1993) "Is the *New York Times* 'Actual Malice' Standard Really Necessary? A Comparative Perspective." *La. L. Rev.* 53: 1153.

Weber, Edward. (1998) *Pluralism by the Rules: Conflict and Cooperation in Environmental Regulation.* Washington, D.C.: Georgetown University Press.

Weigend, Thomas. (1980) "Continental Cures for American Ailments: European Criminal Procedure as a Model for Law Reform." *Crime & Justice* 2: 381–428.

Weiler, Paul C. (1991) *Medical Malpractice on Trial.* Cambridge: Harvard University Press.

Weiler, Paul C., et al. (1993) *A Measure of Malpractice: Medical Injury, Malpractice Litigation, and Patient Compensation.* Cambridge: Harvard University Press.

Weingast, Barry. (1980) "Congress, Regulation, and the Decline of Nuclear Power." *Public Policy* 28: 232.

Weintraub, Richard. (1994a) "Waiting on the Fields of Flight." *Washington Post,* June 7, p. D1.

———— (1994b) "House Panel Backs Aircraft Liability Limits." *Washington Post,* June 22, p. F2.

Weir, Margaret. (1995) "The Politics of Racial Isolation in Europe and America," in Paul E. Peterson, ed., *Classifying by Race.* Princeton, N.J.: Princeton University Press.

Weir, Margaret, Ann Shola Orloff, and Theda Skocpol, eds. (1988) *The Politics of Social Policy in the United States.* Princeton, N.J.: Princeton University Press.

Weisburd, David. (1999) "Good for What Purpose? Social Science, Race, and Proportionality Review in New Jersey," in Patrick Ewick, Robert Kagan, and Austin Sarat, eds., *Social Science, Social Policy, and the Law.* New York: Russell Sage Foundation.

Welles, Holly, and Kirsten Engel. (2000) "A Comparative Study of Solid Waste Landfill Regulation: Case Studies from the United States, the United Kingdom, and the Netherlands," in Robert A. Kagan and Lee Axelrad, eds., *Regulatory Encounters: Multinational Corporations and American Adversarial Legalism.* Berkeley: University of California Press.

Welsh, Wayne. (1992) "The Dynamics of Jail Reform Litigation: A Comparative Analysis of Litigation in California Counties." *Law & Society Rev.* 26: 591.

Wessel, Ann E., and Marc J. Hershman. (1988) "Mitigation: Compensating the Environment for Unavoidable Harm," in M. J. Hershman, ed., *Urban Port and Harbor Management.* New York: Taylor & Francis.

Wheeler, Douglas. (1997) "The Ecosystem Approach: New Departures for Land and Water." *Environmental Law Quarterly* 24: 623.

White, Welsh S. (1987) "Patterns in Capital Punishment." *Cal. L. Rev.* 75: 2165.

———— (1993) "Capital Punishment's Future." *Mich. L. Rev.* 91: 1429.

Whitford, William C. (1979) "A Critique of the Consumer Credit Collection System." *Wis. L. Rev.* 1979: 1047.

Whitney, Craig. (1998) "French Jobless Find the World Is Harsher." *New York Times,* March 19, p. A1.

Wiebel, Tom. (1991) "Automobile Insurance: Identification of Issues and Possible Solutions." Sacramento: Department of Motor Vehicles (testimony).

Wildavsky, Aaron. (1990) "A World of Difference—The Public Philosophies and Political Behaviors of Rival American Cultures," in Anthony King, ed., *The New American Political System,* 2d ed. Washington, D.C.: AEI Press.

Wilensky, Harold. (1965) "Problems and Prospects of the Welfare State," in H. Wilensky and Charles Lebaux, eds., *Industrial Society and Social Welfare.* New York: Free Press.

———— (1975) *The Welfare State and Equality: Structural and Ideological Roots of Public Expenditures.* Berkeley: University of California Press.

———— (1976) *The "New Corporatism," Centralization, and the Welfare State.* Beverly Hills: Sage Publications.

——— (1983) *Political Legitimacy and Consensus: Missing Variables in the Assessment of Social Policy.* Berkeley: Institute of Industrial Relations.

Wiley, Jerry. (1981) "The Impact of Judicial Decisions on Professional Conduct: An Empirical Study." *S. Cal. L. Rev.* 55: 345.

Wilkerson, J. Harvie, III. (1979) *From Brown to Bakke: The Supreme Court and School Integration, 1954–1978.* New York: Oxford University Press.

Williams, C. Arthur. (1991) *An International Comparison of Workers Compensation.* Boston: Kluwer Academic Publishers.

Williams, Gerald. (1983) *Legal Negotiation and Settlement.* St. Paul, Minn.: West Publishing.

Wilson, Graham. (1985) *The Politics of Safety and Health.* Oxford: Clarendon Press.

Wilson, James Q. (1968) *Varieties of Police Behavior.* Cambridge: Harvard University Press.

——— (1980a) *American Government.* Lexington, Mass.: D. C. Heath.

——— (1980b) *The Politics of Regulation.* New York: Basic Books.

——— (1989) *Bureaucracy.* New York: Basic Books.

——— (1994) "What to Do about Crime?" *Commentary* (September), pp. 25–34.

——— (1995) "Reforming Criminal Trials." *Wall Street J.,* November 20, op-ed.

——— (1997) "Criminal Justice in England and America." *The Public Interest* (Winter), p. 3.

Wilson, William Julius. (1987) *The Truly Disadvantaged: The Inner City, the Underclass, and Public Policy.* Chicago: University of Chicago Press.

Winninghoff, Ellie. (1994) "In Arbitration, Pitfalls for Consumers." *New York Times,* October 22, p. 30.

Winter, Ralph K. (1992) "Forward: In Defense of Discovery Reform." *Brooklyn L. Rev.* 58: 263.

Wokutch, Richard E. (1992) *Worker Protection, Japanese Style: Occupational Safety and Health in the Auto Industry.* Ithaca, N.Y.: ILR Press.

Wolchover, David. (1989) "Should Judges Sum Up on the Facts?" *Criminal L. Rev.* 1989: 781.

Wold, Jon, and John Culver. (1987) "The Defeat of the California Justices." *Judicature* (April/May), p. 323.

Woo, Junda. (1993) "Legal Beat: Business Finds Suits on Security Hard to Defend." *Wall Street J.,* September 1, p. B1.

Wood, B. Dan. (1988) "Principals, Agents, and Responsiveness in Clean Air Enforcement." *American Political Science Rev.* 82: 213.

Wood, B. Dan, and Richard Waterman. (1991) "The Dynamics of Political Control of the Bureaucracy." *American Political Science Rev.* 85: 801.

Workers Compensation Research Institute. (1988) "Reducing Litigation." *WCRI Research Brief,* p. 4.

Yamanouchi, Kazuo. (1974) "Administrative Guidance and the Rule of Law." *Law in Japan* 7: 22.

Yeazell, Steven. (1994) "The Misunderstood Consequences of Modern Court Process." *Wis. L. Rev.* 1994: 631.

Young, Michael. (1984) "Judicial Review of Administrative Guidance: Governmentally Encouraged Consensual Dispute Resolution in Japan." *Columbia L. Rev.* 84: 923.

Yudof, Mark. (1991) "School Finance Reform in Texas: The Edgewood Saga." *Harvard J. Legislation* 28: 499.

Zehnder, Egon. (1987) "The Litigious Society: Is It Hampering Creativity, Innovation and Our Ability to Compete?" *Corporate Issue Monthly*, vol. 23.

Zimring, Frank, and Gordon Hawkins. (1986) *Capital Punishment and the American Agenda*. Cambridge: Cambridge University Press.

——— (1997) *Crime Is Not the Problem: Lethal Violence in America*. New York: Oxford University Press.

Index